WHAT IS VIENNA ACTION ISM?

Dr. Cantz'sche
Verlagsgesellschaft mbH & Co. KG

DCV

WIENER
AKTIONISMUS
MUSEUM

WAM

Edited by

WIENER AKTIONISMUS MUSEUM

EVA BADURA-TRISKA
JULIA MOEBUS-PUCK

Eva Badura-Triska/Julia Moebus-Puck

FOREWORD AND THANKS

All artistic avant-gardes of the twentieth century were initially met with a lack of comprehension and rejection. They challenged their audiences by crossing boundaries and leaving behind what was known and familiar, thereby often overstraining them. "Lagging behind", so to speak, it always took time to reflect, and accept the new in order to increasingly understand—at an appropriate interval of time—its significance and ultimately appreciate it. This applies in a particularly high degree to Vienna Actionism whose recognition is still not widespread. Undoubtedly, the reason for this lies in the high "shock potential" of this art, which directly confronts the viewer with the human body and its functions, without considering any taboos, thereby also addressing psychological layers of experience that are associated with fear and trauma in an equally ruthless manner.

Yet it is precisely in this unvarnished, uncompromising approach to the most elementary existential facts and experiences, which are all too often repressed, that the strength and significance of this art lie. Across time, it ranks among the most consistent and radical visual expressions, dedicated to dealing with the human condition and the tragic sides of life as well as with its affirmation and intensive perception. While realising these objectives, the Vienna Actionists also distinguished themselves by transcending panel painting in favour of working directly with substances, objects, and bodies in space and time, thus breaking through formal boundaries and paving new paths that positioned them at the forefront of the avant-garde developments of their time.

However, the decisive factor in all of this cannot be emphasised enough, which is the high aesthetic quality that characterises the artistic manifestations of Günter Brus, Otto Muehl, Hermann Nitsch, and Rudolf Schwarzkogler—the main representatives of this movement.

WHAT IS VIENNA ACTIONISM? is published on the occasion of the eponymous opening exhibition of the Wiener Aktionismus Museum (WAM, Vienna Actionism Museum) and is intended to serve as an easily accessible introduction to one of the internationally most important artistic manifestations of the twentieth century. It focuses on the 1960s and early 1970s, the core period of this movement, with brief glimpses into the period afterward, when Brus, Nitsch, and Muehl were no longer in such close contact and artistic exchange with each other and Schwarzkogler was already dead.

The book opens with a conversation with Philipp Konzett, the long-time collector and promoter of Vienna Actionism, who, together with five other collectors acquired the works of the former Friedrichshof collection which constitute the core holdings of the museum. He talks about the background and development of his enthusiasm for this art, as well as about the history of its reception and the intentions and future plans of the WAM. The first text then addresses a broad spectrum of aspects of this movement in the format of questions and answers, demonstrating its multifacetedness and complexity. Among other things, it deals with its position within the art world of its time, but also with its historical predecessors. Then the respective artistic developments of the four main representatives are traced, whereby it becomes clear that Brus, Muehl, Nitsch, and Schwarzkogler each had their own individual approaches and also followed their own paths despite their fundamentally common concerns. Another essay is devoted to the extremely complex role photography and film played in this art.

Finally, from the perspective of the twenty-first century, the significance of Vienna Actionism for the development and state of performance is explored.

We would like to thank everyone who was involved in the creation of this publication: Lisa Moravec for her text contribution and the translation of all texts into English; Mirjam Knapp and Martina Hackenberg for the German and Judith Köhler for the English editing; Studio Franz for the graphic design; Andrea R. Santoyo for her contributions as collection manager and finally the photographer Manuel Carreon-Lopez.

We would also like to thank everyone who provided us with information and materials or supported us by granting rights, in particular the representatives of the artists' estates of Günter Brus (Anna and Diana Brus and Udo Huber), Otto Muehl (Violaine Roussies and Archives Otto Muehl / MFGA Foundation), Hermann Nitsch (Rita Nitsch and the Nitsch Foundation), and Rudolf Schwarzkogler (Austrian Ludwig Foundation). We also thank the mumok, Vienna (Karola Kraus, Marie-Therese Hochwartner, Alexandra Pinter, Manuel Millautz) and the BRUSEUM Graz (Roman Grabner).

Finally, we would like to thank all those who have made the work of WAM–including this publication–possible through their idealistic and financial support, and who will continue to do so in the future. These include the founders of the WAM (Reza Akhavan, Jürgen Boden, Daniel Jelitzka, Philipp Konzett, Dirk Ströer and Christian Winkler), but especially also our founders, co-founders, donors and patrons: Christian Kirk, Herbert and Alexandra Schwabl, Bernd Kleboth and Birgit Blessing-Kleboth, Lukas Blaha, Lukas Schwarzer, Marchese Armando Fumanelli, Alexander Sporn, Peter and Sabine Nöthen and Walther Jungwirth. They make the significant contribution to the museum's challenging programme of exhibitions and events.

Eva Badura-Triska, Julia Moebus-Puck

Eva Badura-Triska/Julia Moebus-Puck

15 QUESTIONS FOR PHILIPP KONZETT

Mr. Konzett, the impetus for founding the WAM was the acquisition of the comprehensive holdings of Vienna Actionism from the Collection Friedrichshof. These were secured by you together with a group of collectors in 2022 to ensure that they remain together as a cultural heritage and are made accessible to the public.

Your long-standing interest, yes even enthusiasm, for Vienna Actionism was the driving force behind this. When did you first come in contact with this art?

I first came across works of Vienna Actionism in 1986, when I saw four *Aktionsskizzen* (Action Sketches) by Günter Brus in a gallery in Vienna. I was immediately drawn to these and decided to buy them.

How old were you at the time, and to what extent and in which form had you already engaged with art?

I was born in 1965, so I was 21 years old then. My involvement with art began at an early age. My parents worked as carpet dealers in Graz, focusing on high-quality kilims and other pieces of a special nature. That was the time when you could still find many old first-class pieces in their countries of origin, which has now become much more difficult. Of course, they wanted me to join their business and sent me to London to do an apprenticeship when I was 17. My enthusiasm for the carpet trade was, however, not particularly strong. Rather, it was in London that I developed an interest in tribal art. The city was a perfect place for this, with excellent museums and many traders specialising in this field. There I was able to increase my knowledge about it, learn the ropes and even managed to complete an internship at the British Museum. I could work on archiving pieces there. When I was still in London, I began dealing in such art myself, specialising in Borneo, an area that had previously received less attention than other regions. After my return to Austria in 1984, I began trading in this art in Graz as well and opened my own shop there in 1989.

When I then became interested in contemporary art in 1986, I saw Brus's drawings. They had a strong effect on me, not least because I felt the same primal power in them that thrilled me so much about tribal art: to me it seemed that this is really about existential questions, or existential experiences that are conveyed through physical sensations.

From then on, Vienna Actionism has never let go of me. I pursued this art, wanted to see and know more and more about it. I not only continually informed myself about it, but I also began to acquire it more and more.

Have you also sought contact with the artists?

No, in the beginning I was not aiming at that. Of course, I got to know them later, with the exception of Rudolf Schwarzkogler, who died in 1969. The representatives of Vienna Actionism are not of my generation and I first concentrated on their works. I also knew that they, like many artists, mainly wanted to speak about their current works and not about their predating ones, while I myself was—at least initially—more interested in what was already "historical" at the time.

So for you, the Vienna Actionists were more like, let's say, "older masters"?

Yes, you could put it that way. I was often asked why I collected these "old men" and not turned to more recent art as a young person. After all, painting by the Junge Wilde (Young Wild Ones) boomed in Austria in the 1980s and works by these artists were intensively purchased. In fact, when I acquired the first Action Sketches by Brus, a small picture by Herbert Brandl was up for discussion as an alternative. It would have cost the same. I really appreciate Brandl—and by the way, Brus's early informal paintings were an important reference point for his abstract paintings—but I decided on Actionism, specifically on the then older works. In the 1980s, Brus, Nitsch and Muehl were still very active as artists. I could also have bought their then recent pieces which can definitely be situated within the context of the return to the classic media of painting and drawing that defined the 1980s. In the meantime, however, I have also acquired some of their later works.

So, with the historic works of Vienna Actionism you collected "against the grain"?

You can certainly say that.

What was and is the current status of appreciation and acceptance of Vienna Actionism?

The path of Vienna Actionism to the recognition that it deserves was and still is a long and arduous one, and its goal has not yet been achieved. I firmly believe that this movement is of the same importance as the best international art of its time. It is also one of the most important manifestations of Austrian art. Undoubtedly, its quality is equal to Viennese art of the early twentieth-century, with its numerous figures that are of global significance, including the painters Gustav Klimt, Egon Schiele and Oskar Kokoschka. These were essential reference points for the Actionists to which they explicitly referred. The latter are now crowd pullers and people from all over the world are fascinated by the very special power of their creations. Everybody realises that basic existential questions are being raised here, in that both the body and the human psyche are addressed in a ruthless and taboo-free manner, to which internationally little can be compared. The exhibition *Körper, Psyche und Tabu* (Body, Psyche and Taboo) in the mumok in Vienna in 2016 (curated by Eva Badura-Triska) juxtaposed the Actionists with this early modern Austrian art and showed that in Viennese art after 1900 one can already find the first appearance of what is today referred to as Body Art. The conviction that the physical and the psychological dimensions of human experience are inseparably linked is to a large extent apparent in the work of Klimt, Schiele, Kokoschka, but also in that of Richard Gerstl, Max Oppenheimer and others. The same can be said about the Vienna Actionists as well as many other Austrian artists after World War II. Arnulf Rainer, Maria Lassnig, Franz West and Elke Krystufek are just a few of them. One can speak of a specific tradition in this country.

Who were the people who recognised the importance of this movement early on and supported it, and how did the field of supporters and collectors develop?

The artist and curator Peter Weibel, who was himself involved in this movement, created the first retrospective publication together with VALIE EXPORT in 1970 and continued to propagate this art, for example in video-talks that I heard as a young man in Graz. Among the personalities who were committed to Vienna Actionism from the 1970s onwards were the curator Harald Szeemann, who included Muehl and Nitsch in his exhibition Happening and Fluxus in Cologne in 1970 and invited Brus, Nitsch and Schwarzkogler to participate in documenta 5 in 1972; in Vienna and Innsbruck the dealers Julius Hummel, Kurt Kalb, Ursula Krinzinger and Heike Curtze; the art historians and museum directors Otto Breicha and Peter Weiermeier; in Italy the collectors and dealers Francesco Conz and Giuseppe Morra and in Germany the collector Hanns Sohm. In the 1980s, Hubert Klocker joined as an important theorist, curator and promoter, as did the museum directors and curators Konrad Oberhuber, Veit Loers and later Paul Schimmel and Peter Noever. A big step in 2002 was the purchase of large holdings for the mumok by Edelbert Koeb, who gave Vienna Actionism a great presence in his house and regularly exhibited it. These exhibitions were curated by Eva Badura-Triska and Hubert Klocker, who together also edited the most comprehensive survey on this artistic movement to date which was published by mumok in 2012. Furthermore, Hubert Klocker set up and ran an exhibition space as a forum for Vienna Actionism and its context at Friedrichshof, the former location of Otto Muehl's commune.

I have personally managed to initiate and contribute to the development of three significant and now extensive collections in Graz: the one of my former business partner Gerhard Sommer, as well as those of Theodor Poppmeier (THP Private Foundation) and of Reinhard Diethardt.

And where do you see yourself as a collector in all of this?

As I said, I only joined in the late 1980s without moving intensively in the relevant circles straight away. I just slowly grew into them. Over the years, I think, I managed to acquire a significant collection. What perhaps sets me apart from collectors, who were already active in Austria before, such as Julius Hummel or Kurt Kalb, is that right from the start I also bought things that are often referred to as documents, but in most cases have the status of "works" in Vienna Actionism, such as posters, invitations, folders, publications (often self-produced), but also manuscripts, notes, correspondences, newspaper reports and much more—and not to forget the numerous action photographs, negatives, as well as films and videos.

In addition, I also began to comprehensively collect the context of Vienna Actionism very early on, that is the many simultaneously happening international movements that expanded the concept of art. Like the Vienna Actionists, many artists in the 1960s transcended this by moving from painting, drawing and sculpture to the performative realm. My collection comprises many works of Gutai, Fluxus and No-Art, as well as extensive holdings of Joseph Beuys and Dieter Roth. There are also exemplary works by Yves Klein, Piero Manzoni, Andy Warhol and Bruce Nauman as well as by artists who acted in the wake of Vienna Actionism or in reaction to it, above all Franz West.

Do you make all of these holdings available to the WAM for its exhibitions?

Of course!

And what about the Friedrichshof collection, which actually forms the basis of the WAM?

The Friedrichshof was the place, which Muehl and the commune, he had founded on Praterstrasse in Vienna, acquired in 1972 and where they finally all lived as from 1975. In the 1980s, a remarkable collection on

Vienna Actionism was built up there–masterminded by the communard Theo Altenberg. A part of it was acquired by mumok in 2002 (under the direction and on the initiative of Edelbert Koeb) and forms an essential part of the museum's focus on Actionism. Also, the Leopold Museum later bought some works. The WAM has now acquired the remaining, still very numerous and important pieces. They form the considerable holdings from which we can draw. If required, works from my collection, as well as from those of the other collectors, can supplement this considerable fund.

What does the WAM plan to do with the Friedrichshof Collection in the long term? Should it be sold later?

No, definitely not. After all, that is one of the key reasons why we call ourselves a museum: we are committed to keeping these works together. We are not selling them, but are making them accessible to the public.

Who is "we"?

We, the six collectors Reza Akhavan, Jürgen Boden, Daniel Jelitzka, Dirk Ströer, Christian Winkler and myself, who acquired the Friedrichshof collection together. We have all been interested in Vienna Actionism for a long time and each of us has already collected in this field before we bought it together. In addition to these six owners and museum founders, there are other founders, people who make the museum's operations possible through their financial and other support.

The WAM is a private initiative, a private museum. What does this mean, what advantages and disadvantages does this have in comparison to publicly funded institutions?

As you say, there are pros and cons. The biggest advantage is of course that the institution lies completely in our hands. As long as we can finance the museum and its projects, we are accountable to no one for what we do, and how we do it. This also means that we can decide and implement things much more quickly and with fewer hurdles. In addition, we have no quota pressure. We can deal with challenging topics more easily than public houses, go into details and undertake in-depth considerations, even if they do not promise a large influx of audiences. Above all, we can concentrate on one field, in our case Vienna Actionism, without being accused of paying little or no attention to others. Ultimately, our concern is the permanent presentation of Vienna Actionism.

The disadvantage is also obvious: we have full financial responsibility and if we get in trouble, there is no safety net. The collectors then have to support the business with additional funds of their own.

And of course, like any young institution, we first have to build our reputation. It is important to deliver best quality.

As far as our relationship with public institutions is concerned, I would like to say that I was a willing lender to them even before the founding of the WAM. This will continue to be the case and the WAM is very interested in cooperating with other institutions. We are here definitely also thinking about large public museums.

What are WAM's specific plans for the future? What kind of exhibitions will you present?

We have more than enough ideas for exhibitions and we definitely don't want our scope to be too narrow. Of course, all of our projects should be related to Vienna Actionism in some way, but this offers a wide range of possibilities. In the first exhibition entitled *WHAT IS VIENNA ACTIONISM?* we provided an overview of the core period of this movement. We define this dating from 1957 to 1973, starting with the year when Nitsch had the first idea for his Orgien Mysterien Theater (Theatre of Orgies and Mysteries) and ending with the year in which Muehl carried out his last public action in Columbus, Ohio. At this point, Schwarzkogler was already dead and Brus had carried out his last action in 1970. After that, only Muehl and Nitsch were active and continued to pursue their individual paths, without the (loose) artistic cohesion that previously existed between the protagonists of this movement.

After this initial presentation, we want to highlight numerous individual aspects of the movement and examine them in more detail. We also want to continually re-contextualise Vienna Actionism from many perspectives, for example put it in relation to other artistic manifestations. And last but not least, we must and want to establish a connection to the present. This means that we will approach this movement from the perspective of the current discourse and, in connection with it, we also want to present young artistic positions whose approaches we, or the artists themselves, see in relation to those of the Vienna Actionists.

Last question, what will happen to your private collection in the future?

I also want to keep it together and hope that it can stay that way after my death.

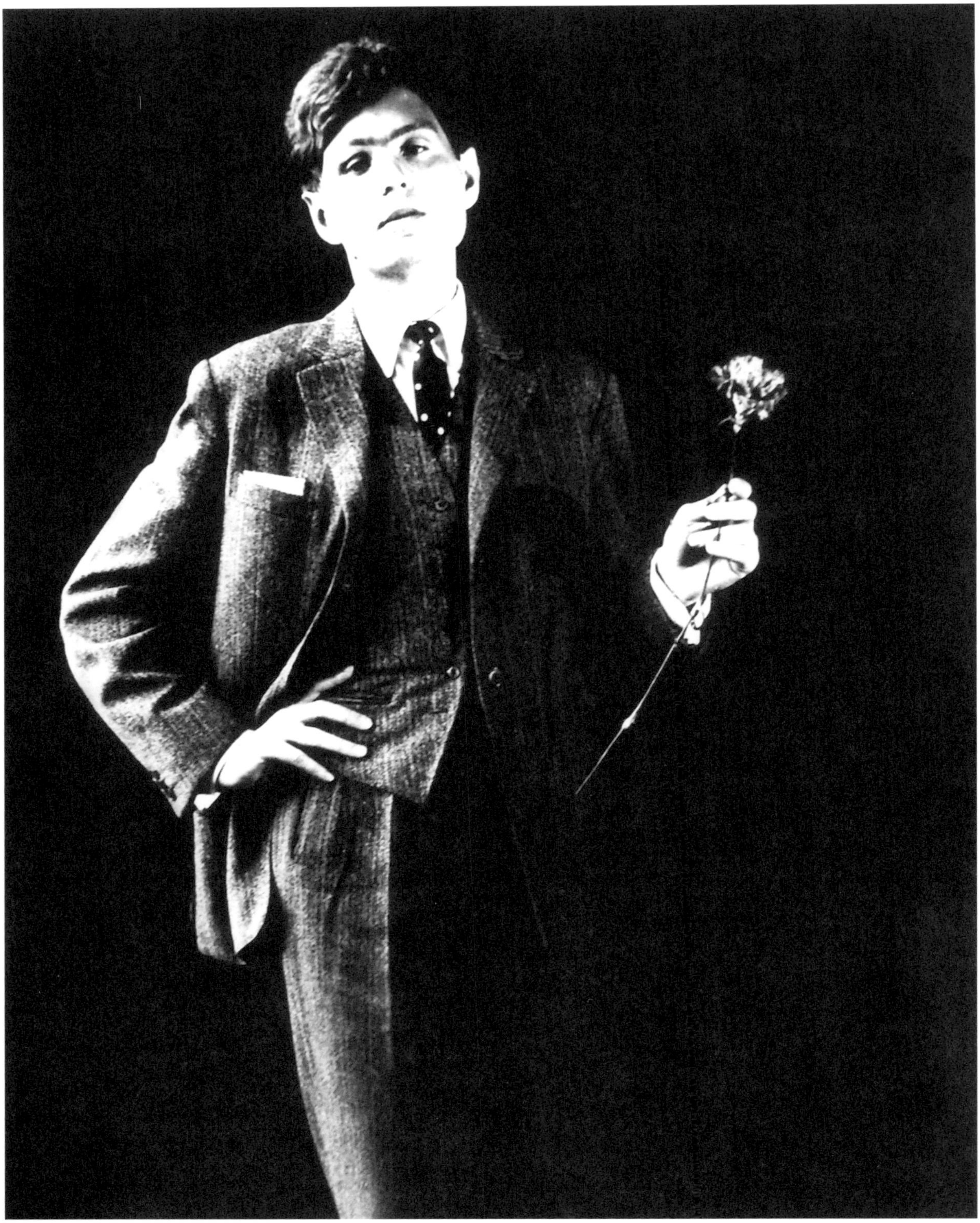

Fig. 1
Wilfried Klanjsek-Bratke
From a series of photographs with Rudolf Schwarzkogler, 1961/1962
B/W photograph
mumok – Museum moderner Kunst Stiftung Ludwig Wien

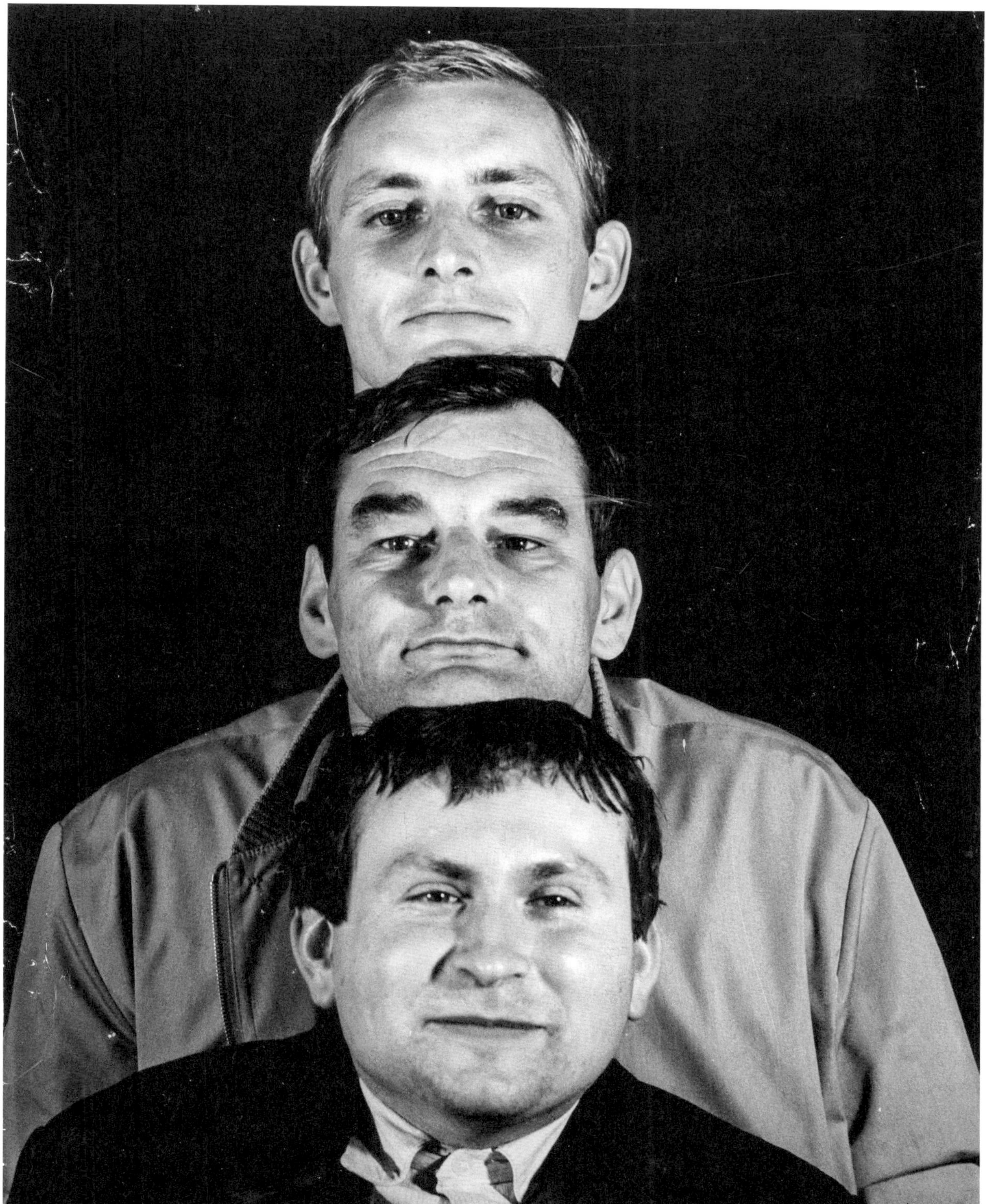

Fig. 2
Günter Brus, Otto Muehl, Hermann Nitsch, 1965
B/W photograph
photo: Ludwig Hoffenreich

Eva Badura-Triska

WHAT IS VIENNA ACTIONISM? ON THE MANY ASPECTS OF THIS MOVEMENT—QUESTIONS AND ANSWERS

Still regarded as a nightmare of the bourgeoisie, it is now out of the question that Vienna Actionism not only constitutes one of the most important and finest achievements of Austrian art, but also from an international perspective, made a highly significant contribution to the developments of the avantgarde of the 1960s that expanded the concept of art.

What Vienna Actionism exactly was can however not be said quickly or easily, and certainly not in a generalising way. This term describes a multi-layered and multi-faceted artistic movement that encompasses numerous aspects within a wide range of manifestations–in painting, action, photography, film and various printed works. In addition, it was operated by four artists who, despite numerous common concerns, each set their own priorities, cultivated different artistic styles and whose contents and formal solutions have also undergone constant–and individual–developments since the beginnings in the early 1960s. If one wants to do justice to Vienna Actionism one needs a differentiated approach that takes its different facets into account.

Who were the artists of Vienna Actionism?

Günter Brus (1938–2024), Otto Muehl (1925–2013), Hermann Nitsch (1938–2022) and Rudolf Schwarzkogler (1940–1969) were the central figures of this movement. It is a characteristic of Vienna Actionism that its protagonists repeatedly cooperated with each other and with others in different constellations, as well as being in artistic exchange with other artists.

In the early phase, when they were still making pictures, Brus was intensively in contact with Alfons Schilling (Fig. 45,46), as was Muehl with Adolf Frohner. Although these two artist friends also developed forms of transgressing the traditional panel painting into object-like three-dimensional works and Frohner, like Muehl, created sculptures out of junk (Fig. 133), they both did not take the step into making actions, but developed their work in different directions. From 1962 onwards, they no longer belonged to the inner circle of the Actionists. In turn, from that year on, the composer Anestis Logothetis became involved in several actions by Muehl, Nitsch and Brus; with Muehl then also taking part in one of his (noise) concerts in 1967[1]. Important friendships were maintained with the writers (and musicians) of the Wiener Gruppe (Vienna Group), in particular with Oswald Wiener, Gerhard Rühm and Friedrich Achleitner which led to several collaborations in the second half of the 1960s in Vienna, as well as in Berlin where Brus and some artists from the Wiener Gruppe lived at the end of the 1960s and

1 See: Eva Badura-Triska, Hubert Klocker (eds.), *Vienna Actionism. Art and Upheaval in 1960s'* Vienna, Vienna / Cologne (mumok, Museum moderner Kunst Stiftung Ludwig Wien / Verlag der Buchhandlung Walther König), 2012, p. 56.

the beginning of the 1970s. Other Vienna-based artists who took part in collectively realised actions included Christian Ludwig Attersee, Otto Kobalek, Hermann Schürrer, Reinhard Priessnitz, Franz Kaltenbäck, Dominik Steiger and Peter Weibel.

Were women artists also part of Vienna Actionism?

Women artists did not form part of the movement. This question is often asked against the backdrop of current and legitimate concerns to draw well-deserved attention to women artists as they have often been overlooked. In fact, Vienna Actionism was a movement entirely determined by male artists. In this context, the name VALIE EXPORT comes up time and again. In the second half of the 1960s, she was–through her partner at that time Peter Weibel–in contact with the circle of Brus, Muehl, Nitsch and Schwarzkogler. She however never cooperated with them[2] and did not regard herself as part of this group; instead she developed her own position, which nevertheless shared some of their intentions.

What were the artistic intentions?

All four artists of Vienna Actionism shared the basic aim of an immediate and taboo-free confrontation with both sensual and psychological experiences, in an artistically intensified manner, that thus created awareness. To this end, they worked with bodies, objects, and substances through actions in space and time.

Their art is situated within the context of international trends of the 1960s that brought the concrete reality of life back into the focus of artistic creation, responding to the abstraction that had dominated the visual arts in the (Western) world after 1945. In reaction to the atrocities of World War II, the latter had rejected any involvement with figurative content.

Likewise, Vienna Actionism was part of the developments at the time that transcended the traditional media of painting and sculpture in favour of "direct" (not media-translated) work with concrete bodies, objects and substances. Within this historical framework, they occupied extreme positions in every respect to which little can be compared.

While English and American Pop Art addressed the consumer and advertising world of Western civilisation, the French Nouveaux Réalistes dealt with the sphere of man-made objects on a broad basis, Joseph Beuys and the artists of Arte Povera worked with "natural" materials, the Vienna Actionists used both human and animal bodies, along with various objects and substances, as both the material and content of their actions. In particular, a ruthlessly taboo-free

2 In 1968, Valie EXPORT was asked if she wanted to take part in the event *Kunst und Revolution* (Art and Revolution). Sensing that this deliberately provocative evening would have consequences, she declined, citing her responsibility towards her child, but also for artistic reasons. She was only involved in so far that she operated a spotlight during Peter Weibel's speech which was linked to the microphone which she switched on and off via shouts from the audience this way fragmenting Weibel's speech. This was intended as a critical statement on the possibilities of communication.

approach to the human body, which was deployed in different ways, was a central concern. Initially, the artists predominantly used it as material for their actions; however, in the latter half of the decade, they increasingly engaged in analytical exploration of it per se, its functions, as well as its societal dimension. This included thematising bodily processes that are socially disapproved of such as urinating, defecating or menstruating, but also elementary life-events (some of which were even more tabooed at the time than today) such as conception, birth, injury or illness. It also encompassed sexuality in hetero- or homoerotic form, transgender tendencies as well as the question of how a differently equipped body would change our perception of the world. The (all male) artists did not only intend to place themselves in female bodily experiences—for example when Brus simulated a birth process—but generally considered the potentials of a differently constructed body in their texts and drawings.

The inclusion of the psychological dimension, also free of taboos, was of the same importance whereby particularly the unacknowledged and repressed human drives and levels of experience—such as (primal) fears, aggression, destructive or death instincts—were mercilessly addressed. An intellectual foundation for this was found in the theories of psychoanalysis, which the artists read intensively, in particular those of Sigmund Freud and C. G. Jung, and in Muehl's case of Wilhelm Reich. Above all, the Vienna Actionists derived their central concerns of abreaction and catharsis from psychoanalytic thought, seeing these as means of discharging, overcoming, and eliminating repressed urges. Each in their own way, they all aimed at cleansing and healing in their art, thus generating therapeutic effects.

Hermann Nitsch stated this most explicitly in the writings of his *Orgien Mysterien Theater* (Theatre of Orgies and Mysteries), where he referred to the catharsis concept of all sacrificial religions as well as of Greek tragedy. Both regard experiencing psychologically extremely stressful situations—in cult actions as well as in proceedings on a stage—as a way of abreacting unacknowledged and repressed drives and affects. These intentions live on in the liturgies of Western churches and the theatre, but only in a weakened or abstracted form—which Nitsch conceived of as a loss that he wanted to counteract with his actions.

Brus and Muehl also strove for cathartic, which means cleansing and purifying effects in their actions through excessive, disturbing and shocking events, although they did not explicitly use this vocabulary—but then Brus hardly wrote any programmatic texts at all. Muehl's particularly strong belief in the positive, clarifying,

3
Rudolf Schwarzkogler, *manifest PANORAMA I / der totale Akt*, 1965, in: Eva Badura-Triska, Hubert Klocker, Rudolf Schwarzkogler. Leben und Werk, Klagenfurt (Ritter Verlag), 1992, p. 245..

even constructive effect of destruction is clearly connected to these therapeutic intentions aimed at renewal. He propagated destruction as a way to expose what had been repressed, and to overcome it in order to allow positive energies to come into play. This idea of the cleansing effect of destruction was shared by numerous artists in the 1960s, including Nam June Paik, Jean Tinguely, Arman, Niki de Saint Phalle, Joseph Beuys, Dieter Roth and Ralph Ortiz. It is no coincidence that the German artist Gustav Metzger named an event he organised in London in 1966 the *Destruction in Art Symposium*. Brus, Muehl and Nitsch were among the participants.

Schwarzkogler's approach was generally much calmer, more distant and cooler. Accordingly, he pursued the therapeutically cathartic concern in his work differently. Cleansing and healing were his terms. These were reflected both in the content and motifs of his only six actions in total, as well as in his late work, where he took a very specific, unique path within Vienna Actionism, focusing exclusively on the creation of concepts. (Fig. 213–220)

The intention of addressing and involving all senses was another central concern of the Vienna Actionists. Nitsch explicitly describes his *Orgien Mysterien Theater* as a *Gesamtkunstwerk* (a total work of art) and Schwarzkogler speaks of a "total act [...] which can be experienced through all senses"[3] of an "aesthetic panorama" as an "effective total work of art". (Fig. 212) In the same spirit, Brus and Muehl titled two joint performances in 1966 Totalaktion (Total Action). (Fig. 155, 156)

With what media did these artists work and how significant was the issue of form for them?

For the Vienna Actionists, the formal aspect of their work was always extremely important. The relevance of their art lies not only in its critical and controversial content, but equally, and perhaps even more so, in the high aesthetic qualities of their entire production. Contrary to the popular belief, the actions–which undoubtedly play a central role in their work–were not the only medium in which Brus, Muehl, Nitsch and Schwarzkogler worked. Like almost all artists making actions, happenings or performances, the four Viennese began as painters and gradually transcended panel painting in favour of "direct" work with concrete bodies, objects and substances. In addition to and accompanying their actions, they have continued to produce artefacts at all times–primarily collages as well as drawings and prints–both as autonomous art and as preparatory work for the actions, as well as for announcements or documentation. Schwarzkogler, who completed his actionist work already in the spring of 1966, then only created concepts in the form of drawings and texts (Fig. 236–243) and Brus, after his last action in June 1970, devoted himself entirely to drawing (Fig. 112–119). In the 1970s, Muehl and Nitsch began to paint again. (Fig. 40, 184, 185)

The actions were precisely planned–mostly through sketches and sometimes elaborately drawn and/or written scores–and always executed with their formal qualities in mind. As a result, photographers and filmmakers were provided with subjects for aesthetic pictorial recordings and shots from the outset.

What is the position of Vienna Actionism in relation to other art forms in space and time?

In the 1960s (and afterwards), the Vienna Actionists shared their work with concrete bodies, objects and substances in space and time with the representatives of Happening and Fluxus, as well as with those of Performance and Body Art. On a structural level, it is not always easy to clearly distinguish between these terms and often it was a matter of self-definition or cultural context which designations particular artists preferred for their work. What these art forms all have in common is that they encompass both manifestations that took place live before an audience and such that were solely staged for photo or film. American Happenings, as those by Allan Kaprow (who coined the expression in 1958), Claes Oldenburg, Jim Dine, Robert Whitman and Carolee Schneemann, developed–unlike Vienna Actionism–not only from painting or sculpture, but also from environments, music as well as from New Dance. Partly understood as a new form of theatre and thus seen as re-enactable, various events were staged here, in which–in keeping with the literal meaning of the word “happening”–the people involved did not embody figures, but stood for what they were. Compared to the stirringly dramatic experiences to which the Vienna artists exposed their audience, however, their content–like that of the German Wolf Vostell, who also used the term Happening–was much more moderate. The same applies to Joseph Beuys’s actions, which operated to a large extent on a symbolic level. The performative concepts of the Fluxus movement in turn were set out to be muchmore playful from the beginning and relied heavily on the participation of the audience, something that rarely played a role in Vienna Actionism.

The term Performance Art, which was only later used in the visual arts, cannot be clearly distinguished from Actionism either, but it is predominantly chosen when the creators of a time-based artwork also perform it themselves. This is why Brus, who unlike his artist colleagues always acted himself in all his actions, is repeatedly apostrophised as the first performance artist, particularly with regard to his Body-Analytical Actions from the second half of the 1960s.

Body Art, understood as art that deals with the human body, likewise subsumes a broad spectrum of artistic expressions, predominantly those that actually operate with the body (and do not just depict it). In comparison to the notions of Happening and action, it became later established as a term for works made by visual artists. In retrospective, however, it can be said that the work of the Vienna Actionists prefigured much of what was later regarded and addressed as Body Art, and therefore some of it can also be considered Body Art.

Are there successors?

One cannot speak of a direct succession of Vienna Actionism–in the sense of a school. However, towards the end of the 1960s and in the 1970s, hence after the core period of this movement, artists such as Marina Abramović, Vito Acconci, Chris Burden, Paul McCarthy, VALIE EXPORT, Terry Fox, Tomislav Gotovac, Ion Grigorescu, Michel Journiac, Natalia LL, Ana Mendieta, Bruce Nauman, Gina Pane or Hanna Wilke, on the one hand, explored the human body and its functions performatively, and on the other hand, they exposed it to extreme experiences in a way akin to the uncompromising manner the Vienna Actionists. In her feminist art, EXPORT, who due to her partner at the time, Peter Weibel, moved in the circles of the Vienna Actionists, thematised, among other things, the bodily process of menstruation, which Nitsch had already addressed in his art before–albeit in a different form. Extreme actions, involving self-harm and/or working with (one's own) blood, can also be found in the 1970s in the case of EXPORT and in the international field with Abramović, Burden, Journiac, Pane or Mendieta–thus strikingly often with women who increasingly and self-confidently raised their voices in the art world from this decade onwards. This next generation has almost always operated with their own bodies and predominantly without other actors, which is why their work also runs under the label of performance.

Is it justified to speak of "Vienna" Actionism and how did this term come about?

The movement rightfully carries the name of the Austrian capital, as it was the place where this art form took shape, had its centre, and where most of the actions took place. Unlike today, post-World War II Vienna was the unchallenged centre in which cultural life

4 weibel/export (eds.), *wien. bildkompendium wiener aktionismus und film*, Frankfurt am Main (Kohlkunstverlag), 1970.

was concentrated. In no other city of this country did events of the Vienna Actionists take place in the 1960s.

However, work and life of these artists were not confined to Vienna. In June 1964, an action of Muehl presented at the Haro Lauhus gallery in Düsseldorf was the first foreign appearance of one of the artists, which was followed by a number of others, primarily in Germany, Italy and the United States of America in the second half of the 1960s. Of particular importance was the prominent and successful participation of Brus, Muehl and Nitsch in the *Destruction in Art Symposium* in London in September 1966 (Fig. 33, 34, 159–164), where the artists appeared together for the first time outside of Austria and received considerable attention–albeit primarily in artistic circles. Hermann Nitsch moved to Munich in 1967 for (mainly) private reasons and only returned to Austria in 1971, where he acquired Prinzendorf Castle, located north of Vienna, and made it his main residence and centre of his *Orgien Mysterien Theater*. Günter Brus fled to Berlin at the beginning of 1969, after being sentenced to five months in prison following his scandalised appearance at the event *Kunst und Revolution* (Art and Revolution) on 7 June 1968 at the University of Vienna (Fig. 97, 98, 179, 180). He only returned to Austria in 1979 and lived in Graz until his death. Otto Muehl, who for the same action was only convicted to two months in prison, which he had served with his pre-trial detention, remained in Vienna, but only made appearances in private locations here and moved most of his public work to Germany.

The mention of Vienna in the name of this movement is also appropriate because it has strong roots in Austrian art, primarily in art made at the turn of the century, which was also concentrated in Vienna.

The term Vienna Actionism was coined by the artist Peter Weibel only in 1970–that is after the most important manifestations of this movement in the 1960s. Together with VALIE EXPORT, his partner, at the time, he had moved in the circles of these artists and wrote a retrospective publication with her that provided the first overview. It is titled *wien. bildkompendium wiener aktionismus und film*[4] (vienna. image compendium vienna actionism and film) and places the movement in a larger context of contemporary artistic developments in Austria. To this day, it is considered an important standard work. The artists themselves only once called themselves the Wiener Aktionsgruppe (Vienna Action Group). This was in their first joint publication, a thin hectographed booklet created in 1965 on the occasion of Brus's first gallery exhibition. (Fig. 221–224) With regard to their participation in the *Destruction in Art Symposium* in London in 1966, Günter Brus and Otto Muehl coined the term Direkte Kunst / Direct Art (Fig. 159) for their activities, which the other artists did not take on–Schwarzkogler only mentions it in one note[5]. Nitsch subsumed his entire work under the name *Orgien Mysterien Theater* throughout his life. All these terms were chosen by the artists to set themselves apart and emphasise their special position within the simultaneous developments of Happening and Fluxus, with which they shared their work in space and time[6].

5
Rudolf Schwarzkogler, text 48, around 1966/67, in: *Schwarzkogler. Leben und Werk* (see note 3), p. 246.

6
Muehl and Brus, however, also used the term Happening on a few occasions, for example Muehl used it in 1964 on the invitation card of his Materialaktion Nr. 6, Destruktion eines weiblichen Körpers (Material Action No. 6, Destruction of a Female Body) (cf. Badura-Triska, Klocker, Vienna Actionism [see note 1], Fig. 462). In 1967 Muehl and Brus used it on the poster and the invitation cards of the Direct Art Festival which they organised together (cf. Badura-Triska, Klocker, Vienna Actionism [see note 1], Fig. 288, 292 and 296).

Who was part of the field of persons that facilitated the work of the Vienna Actionists? Who were the actors, photographers, filmmakers, and the organisers?

An art like that of the Vienna Actionists requires a broad spectrum of people who make its realisation possible. This includes the actors as well as the photographers and filmmakers and, last but not least, those who provided spaces, resources, assistance or propagated their work in various other forms. As it is always the case with the supportive environments of avant-garde art, these persons backed the artists' content and objectives, and were committed to them out of conviction and enthusiasm.

All of the actors interviewed stated that they considered taking part in the actions as a personally profitable and emancipatory act of rebellion against the extremely conservative social climate of their time, especially in Austria. This refutes the repeated claim that the Actionists exploited women in particular, which is made regardless of the fact that as many men as women were among their participants. While the involved people were initially recruited from the personal circle of friends and acquaintances of Brus, Muehl, Nitsch and Schwarzkogler, this field expanded over the years. The most frequently appearing actors in the early days were Anna Brus and Heinz Cibulka. The former was the partner and, from 1966, wife of Günter Brus who in his solo actions only performed alone or with her (and once with the inclusion of their baby). She in turn also took part in Muehl and Schwarzkogler actions. Cibulka, a fellow student of Nitsch and Schwarzkogler, actively participated in numerous actions of his friends and also took photographs of Nitsch actions from the 1970s onward. His wife at the time, Franziska Cibulka, also photographed at Nitsch's actions several times and actively participated in one. She also recorded Schwarzkogler's *4th Action*. Dieter Haupt, who appeared frequently at Muehl events, was a pupil from the care home where Muehl worked. In contrast, nothing other than her name is known about Zimie Schieb, who was

7
The four architecture students withdrew again in 1967. In 1968, at the event Kunst und Revolution, the group's last performance, Josef Kainz (called Antanas) was part of the formation.

one of Muehl's most frequent performers between 1963 and 1966. It is interesting that four architecture students (Otmar Bauer, Timo Huber, W.M. Pühringer, and Hermann Simböck) were so fascinated by a lecture given by Muehl at their university that they together with the philosophy student Herbert Stumpfl and the art printer Kurt Zein took part in his actions under the name Direct Art Group, also called "Muehl-Hunde" (Muehl-Dogs), between 1967 and 1968[7]. From the second half of the 1960s, when the artists increasingly appeared abroad, local people–very often fellow artists–repeatedly agreed to participate as actors. These included Juan Hidalgo, Susan Cahn, Robin Page, Al Hansen, Günter Sarée, Jon and Geoffrey Hendricks as well as Charlotte Moorman, who participated as cellist in many performative events of the avant-garde.

The individual scope of the actors was limited. Essentially, they had to do what the artists or their action scores demanded. In many cases, especially during the photo sessions, their role was also a very passive one. Exceptions were the fashion designer Hanel Koeck and her husband, the art historian Peter Gorsen, who had a strong influence on the content of Muehl's action *Scheisskerl* (Shithead, 1969) in which they both appeared. Koeck also played an active creative role that went beyond the original score in Nitsch's *31. Aktion, Maria Empfängnis* (31st Action, Immaculate Conception, 1969, Fig. 36) and in his *32nd Action* at Kunstraum 1 in Munich (1970).

In the early days of the movement, the photographers and filmmakers came from the artists' circle of friends until the professionals Ludwig Hoffenreich (from 1963 onwards) and Siegfried Klein (pseudonym: Khasaq, from 1964) became their main photographers. As to the moving images with Kurt Kren (who joined in 1964) and Ernst Schmidt Jr. (who joined in 1965) two of the most important international avantgarde filmmakers became actively involved. In addition, numerous other people took up photo and/or film cameras for the Vienna Actionists. The role of photography and film in Vienna Actionism is an extremely complex topic that requires a differentiated consideration (see p. 234–265 in this book).

Equally open-minded were the people and institutions that invited the artists to present actions and organised these or made space available to them. With their commitment, they often took personal risks, or paid for this with inconveniences which in some cases even included police prosecution. Important figures here were the psychoanalyst Josef Dvorak, in whose basement gallery in Vienna's Lagergasse with Nitsch's *2nd Action* in March 1963 (Fig. 13) the first public manifestation of Vienna Actionism took place, Uzzi Förster, in whose nightclub Chattanooga Muehl carried out his *Materialaktion Nr. 6, Destruktion eines weiblichen Körpers*

(Material Action No. 6, Destruction of a Female Body) in 1964 (even though it had been prohibited in advance by the police), the architecture student Bertram Mayer, who through his connections organised the inn Grünes Tor as a location for the *Zock-Fest* (Zock-Festival) which ended with a police operation, or those students who were persuaded by Wiener and Weibel to invite the Actionists to the *Kunst und Revolution* (Art and Revolution) event at the University of Vienna on 7 June 1968 (Fig. 97, 98, 179, 180), which resulted in the movement's biggest scandal and legal consequences for many of those involved.

The organisers abroad included the Düsseldorf gallerist Haro Lauhus who invited Muehl to show his first action outside of Austria, Gustav Metzger who brought the artists to the *Destruction in Art Symposium* in London in 1966 (Fig. 33, 34, 159–164), the architecture students Valdiš Abolinš and Gerd Vorhoff who organised an action by Brus at the Technische Hochschule Aachen (Fig 92–96), the writer, critic and gallery owner Adam Seide and the gallery owner Margot Ostheimer who made their spaces in Frankfurt available to Muehl for staging his actions on the occasion of Germany's first sex fair in 1970, the curator Harald Szeemann who included them in his exhibition *Happening and Fluxus* at the Kölnischer Kunstverein (Fig. 182) in autumn 1970, Gerd Settje, co-founder and managing director of the first arthouse cinema in Germany, who organised Muehl's action *Advent, Advent!* (1970) in Bremen, or Eva Madelung, Alfred Gulden and Peter Nemetschek, the highly committed operators of Aktionsraum 1 in Munich where with Nitsch's *32nd Action* and Brus's last action *Zerreißprobe* (Stress Test, Fig. 106) two of the most radical actions of Vienna Actionism took place in 1970. Also worth mentioning are several American universities and other places for avant-garde art where Nitsch and Muehl were able to perform, as well as the film and music promoter and collector Karlheinz Hein who organised screenings of Muehl's films.

What police measures, charges, convictions, and penalties did the Vienna Actionists and their supporters face?

It is not surprising that the radical content of Vienna Actionism and its implementation in the form of actions–which were not accepted as art by the general public–met with resistance. The public appearances of this movement repeatedly led to intervention by the authorities and also to criminal prosecution of the artists and their supporters, with the charges generally being "public indecency" and "disorderly conduct". Starting with the *Fest des Psychophysischen Naturalismus* (Festival of Psychophysical Naturalism,

1963, Fig. 134, 135) all the way through to Brus's *Wiener Spaziergang* (Vienna Walk, 1965, Fig. 73) or the *Zock-Fest* (Zock-Festival, 1967, Fig. 165, 166), several individual performances and collaborative events by Brus, Muehl and Nitsch were dissolved by the police, and all three artists faced fines or imprisonment on various occasions. Only the shy Rudolf Schwarzkogler, who avoided the lime-light, was spared from such measures. The highlight of the criminal prosecution was the trial of Brus, Muehl, Wiener and Weibel in 1968 after the action *Kunst und Revolution* at the University of Vienna (Fig. 97, 98, 179, 180). The events of that evening were leaked to the press due to the presence of a tabloid journalist, and sparked a major public scandal that resulted in legal convictions and prison sentences for several of those involved. Brus received the maximum sentence of six months, which was reduced to five after the appeal; and which he avoided by fleeing to Berlin in early 1969. Muehl received two months, which he had served with his pre-trial detention, while Wiener was acquitted after two months in pre-trial detention and did not receive compensation for his imprisonment. Weibel (temporarily) fled to Sweden in time and was sentenced in absentia to fourteen days of arrest which he never served. The students Bauer and Stumpfl, who had taken part in Muehl's Direct Art Group, were not prosecuted but they were temporarily excluded from their universities, which ultimately led to the discontinuation of their studies in both cases.

The artists were confronted with harassment and prosecution not only in Austria but also abroad. At the *Destruction in Art Symposium* in London (1966, Fig. 33, 34, 159–164), the police stormed the hall and the organiser Gustav Metzger had to pay a fine. Actions by Brus in Aachen (1968, Fig. 92–96) and by Muehl in Braunschweig (1969) were scandalised and led to criminal charges, though the proceedings were later dropped.

The supporters of the artists also faced significant inconveniences and even penalties. Josef Dvorak whose gallery showed Nitsch's painting *Erste Heilige Kommunion* (First Holy Communion), containing a bloody menstrual pad, in 1966 was sentenced along with the artist. The book, *wien. bildkompendium wiener aktionismus und film*, compiled by Weibel and EXPORT in 1970 was confiscated at the border during its transport to Austria, its sale was banned, the two editors were charged and conditionally sentenced for "producing an indecent brochure with profit-seeking intent". In 1970 the film-maker Kurt Kren was suspended from his position as an employee of the Österreichische National Bank after a house search. Karlheinz Hein was charged for distributing pornography in 1970 after showing Muehl films in Munich, and the material was confiscated.

His trial went through four instances in which he was convicted twice and then had to pay his legal costs after a settlement in court. He only got the films back after he agreed to censor parts of them.

Who are the artistic ancestors of Vienna Actionism?

Both in terms of their extreme, relentlessly taboo-breaking content, as well as their formal qualities and aesthetic precision, the Vienna Actionists have predecessors in early twentieth-century Austrian painting, particularly in that of its main representatives Gustav Klimt, Egon Schiele and Oskar Kokoschka, to whom they explicitly refer. Still working in the medium of easel painting, these artists already addressed the human body in a radical manner, sometimes even going further than Brus, Muehl, Nitsch and Schwarzkogler with their display of the naked body and elementary life processes, such as pregnancy, birth and death or erotic content. Through these themes and the form of their depictions, they also affected the psychological level to a high degree. Like their later colleagues, they therefore came into conflict with the state and society and were not only defamed, but also imprisoned and sentenced, as it happened to Schiele.

In addition to that, the Vienna Actionists had role models and kindred spirits in the entire history of art. They saw their work in the context of art dealing with elementary existential conditions, especially their tragic and disturbing aspects, across the ages. In this sense they referred to old-masters paintings, such as Matthias Grünewald's or Rembrandt's crucifixions, Dutch representations of slaughtered animals or to the cruelties depicted by Hieronymus Bosch, Pablo Picasso and others.

In the painting of their early phase, Brus, Muehl and Nitsch drew on Informal Art and Action Painting, while Schwarzkogler's distanced and cooler approach was rather inspired by artists such as Luigi Fontana, Yves Klein and Piero Manzoni.

Which historical backdrop should Vienna Actionism be viewed against?

Like all artistic movements, Vienna Actionism has to be considered within the context of the specific political and social situation at its place and time of origin. In general, the 1960s mark a time of upheaval and change after the catastrophe of World War II, which had ended (more than) 15 years ago and whose material damage had largely been repaired. The successful reconstruction, which took place in Europe to a great extent with American support (Marshall Plan), was part of an economic upswing ("Wirtschaftswunder"), which enabled the spread of prosperity–and with it the participation of more and more people in the achievements of the rapid technological developments. Accordingly, this decade, at the end of which the first man set foot on the moon, was characterised by a strong belief in progress.

In the social sphere, developments were however ambivalent. Many young people questioned the values of their parents or wanted to throw them overboard–such as the student and Hippie movement, which grew particularly strong towards the end of the decade, but in Austria was significantly less pronounced than in other Western states. Especially (but not only) in this country, the spirit of optimism among young people was countered by a pronounced and persistently defended value conservatism in broad realms of society which met the demands for rethinking, and thinking differently, with sometimes bitter resistance and strict rejection.

In Germany, but even more so in Austria, this has not least to be seen against the backdrop of the pending and unfinished process of coming to terms with the country's connection with the Nazi regime and its associated participation in World War II, as well as of course with its status as a defeated nation. While Germany could not deny its responsibility in this regard, Austria took refuge in the so-called "Opferthese" (victim theory), according to which this country had been the first victim of Hitler's aggression and therefore bore no guilt. This view was even supported by the Allies who were primarily interested in economic and democratic reconstruction and the resurgence of Europe as a reliable partner of the Western world. The victim theory was an essential, actually decisive factor that prevented the willingness to confront the not insignificant involvement of Austrians in the crimes of the Nazi regime. What was ignored here was the fact that this country had already had its own right-wing authoritarian regime with its "Ständestaat" (corporate state)–also known as Austrofascism–before Hitler's invasion (which was hailed by many!). Accordingly, in many cases, denazification was superficial and many perpetrators and escaped relatively unscathed, allowing them to once again hold influential positions. As a result, the political, social, and cultural climate of the post-war decades often still had traits of post-fascism.

Vienna Actionism is undoubtedly to be seen against this background or rather as a reaction to this denial of any guilt, even the subcutaneous survival of Nazi ideas as well as the pronounced conservatism of values. The personal fates of all four artists were impacted by this burdened past: Muehl, Nitsch and Schwarzkogler had lost their fathers in the war. Those of Muehl and Brus had favoured the Nazis and Muehl, who was more than ten years older than the others, had been called up for military service himself in 1944, where he had made traumatic experiences. Undoubtedly, all of this was a major trigger for the desire for purification and reformation that was so dominant in Vienna Actionism. Likewise, the need to reveal what has been repressed and tabooed must be seen against this background, as well as Vienna Actionism's addressing of (elementary) psychological experiences such as the fear of injury, illness and death or the desire for healing.

In Muehl's case only, in the second-half of the 1960s an additional enthusiasm for pop culture phenomena emerged. This manifested itself in various ways in his work–such as in his brightly coloured silkscreen series, which satirically and critically portrayed prominent politicians and other personalities of the time (Fig. 169–173), but also in his design of various announcement posters and flyers as well as his use of mass consumer goods as materials in his actions. (Fig. 153)

How political was the art of the Vienna Actionists?

If one regards Vienna Actionism as a strong reaction to the social and political situation in post-war Austria, this art was of major political relevance. It is no coincidence that it has been repeatedly seen as the most significant manifestation of the 1968 movement in this country–especially with respect to the event *Kunst und Revolution* (Art and Revolution) which took place on 7 June 1968 in Hörsaal 1 (Lecture Hall 1) at the University of Vienna (Fig. 97, 98, 179, 180). This was, in fact, the event where the artists took a stand against the political conditions of the time in the most radical and explicit manner, with the sharpest verbal statements made by Muehl and Weibel. The latter had initiated the event together with Wiener and participated in it alongside him and others. Brus and Muehl carried out actions which were essentially consistent with their engagement with the body and its functions that they had been pursuing since the middle of the decade, but here they took the breaking of taboos to new extremes, and Brus also combined this with political provocation: Standing on the table next to the lectern in the lecture hall, he urinated and defecated and finally masturbated while singing the Austrian national anthem. This was his most explicit political statement. According to his own words, he deliberately wanted to provoke–which does not apply to his other work.

In principle the Vienna Actionists–with very rare exceptions–did not comment on current political issues in their art. Rather, they offer a cross-temporally relevant commentary on human nature–its physical constitution with all its functions but also its weaknesses and vulnerabilities, as well as its psychological processes, especially traumas and fears but also the capacity for cruelty. Their work is therefore not explicitly but only indirectly political.

How can Vienna Actionism be circumscribed in time? What happened after the 1960s?

Like many aspects of Vienna Actionism, the question as to its time-frame cannot be answered easily, and once again not in general terms. Depending on where one wants to place the emphasis, its beginning can either be determined in 1957 when Hermann Nitsch had the idea and first developed the concept for his *Orgien Mysterien Theater*, or in 1960, the year of Nitsch's first Painting Action, or in 1962, when he used his body in an action for the first time. (Fig. 12) In any case, the first manifestations of this movement were by Nitsch.

What is more difficult—and ultimately a matter of opinion—is to determine an end. The 1960s constitute undisputedly the core period of this movement, insofar as its four main representatives were all artistically active and also in a number of cases cooperated with each other. Schwarzkogler died in June 1969, Brus carried out his last action in June 1970 and then focused on the medium of drawing—in which he also, but not only, dealt with topics related to Vienna Actionism. Nitsch continued to develop his *Orgien Mysterien Theater* until his death in 2022. After the "scandal event" *Kunst und Revolution*, Muehl no longer appeared in public in Austria and instead moved his activities abroad, mainly to Germany. In April 1973, during a trip to the United States of America, he carried out his last public action in Ohio.

In 1968 he started a living community that gradually developed into a commune and in 1975 moved to the Friedrichshof, around 60 km east of Vienna. With branches in numerous European cities, including Zurich, Düsseldorf, Munich, London and Paris, as well as a kind of holiday colony on La Gomera, it had at times over 600 members. It fell apart when Muehl was sentenced to seven years in prison for various offences (amongst them statuary rape and drug offences), which he served. While he was still in prison, a new much smaller commune was formed in southern Portugal, where he then lived after his release until his death in 2013. A number of action-based activities in the commune were structurally related to his previous work. These included so-called Selbstdarstellungen (Self-Presentations), where the communards had to reveal themselves to the group in individual performances. Films were produced in which prominent artists and art world personalities appeared, such as Christian Ludwig Attersee, Georg Jiri Dokoupil, Kurt Kalb, Maria Lassnig, Oswald Oberhuber, Nam June Paik, Raphael Ortiz, Norman

Rosenthal or Harald Szeemann. Muehl also took up painting again and created a large oeuvre of oil paintings and prints. (Fig. 184, 185) Whether all of these activities should be subsumed under Vienna Actionism or viewed as another separate development is ultimately a matter of opinion or definition.

What remains? What is the significance of Vienna Actionism in retrospect?

This question is frequently asked. Just as the actions of Brus, Muehl, Nitsch and Schwarzkogler are often superficially associated primarily with keywords such as “radical”, “taboo-breaking”, “socially critical”, or “scandalous”, many expect that the answer to this should primarily refer to the role of this art as a cry against the social rigidity and non-reflection of the Nazi past in Vienna in the 1960s.

But will this still be of relevance in 300 years and will it be of interest to everyone around the world? The answer should rather be a different one: What remains is great art of high aesthetic quality that transcends time and is universally valid. Vienna Actionism is part of the long and still unbroken history of artistic engagement with existential questions, in particular about the tragedy of life as well as the dark sides of human nature, its traumas, fears and its potential for cruelty. It is part of a worldwide tradition that includes depictions of crucifixions and martyrs of saints in Christian art, as well as the topic of war, injuries, killings and deaths in paintings and sculptures from early times right up to Francisco de Goya, Pablo Picasso, Max Beckmann and many others.

At the same time, with its formal solutions–especially the breakout from panel painting–Vienna Actionism was at the forefront of the avant-garde of its time.

Julia Moebus-Puck

FROM PAINTING TO ACTION. FOUR INDIVIDUAL PATHS

The four main protagonists of Vienna Actionism began as painters and gradually transgressed the panel picture to finally arrive at actions with concrete bodies, objects and substances. The driving force behind this was the desire to convey intensified sensual experiences and thereby to more directly connect with reality. In terms of content, topics were addressed in a ruthless manner that had been tabooed and suppressed by post-war (Austrian) society.

These artists did not regard their work with concrete materials, that included the human body, as the overcoming of painting, but rather as a new, expanded form of it, and never gave up their pictorial thinking. It is therefore not contradictory that, in addition to their actions, they continued to create artefacts such as drawings, collages, prints, and even canvas paintings and, after the heyday of Vienna Actionism in the 1960s, they increasingly turned to classical media again, starting to work with them each in their own way: From his last action in spring 1966, until his death in the summer of 1969, Rudolf Schwarzkogler exclusively created concepts in the form of sketches and texts (Fig. 213–220), and Günter Brus returned to drawing after his last action in June 1970 (Fig. 112–119). Otto Muehl and Hermann Nitsch both started to paint again on a larger scale in the 1970s, while continuing to perform actions. (Fig. 40, 184, 185)

Retrospectively, it becomes clear that the Vienna Actionists were four artists who, although they shared essential basic concerns and worldviews–which is why they were in close contact with each other–have also developed different signatures and priorities. Their developmental moves from panel painting to action were already different and their paths remained individual; yet, these differences did not prevent them from repeatedly cooperating with each other in a variety of constellations.

Hermann Nitsch

Of the four artists, Nitsch was the first to take the step from panel painting to action, and he was the only one who also regarded his actions as a new form of theatre. Accordingly, his path not only began in painting, but also led through literature with literary texts always remaining a part of the comprehensive *Gesamtkunstwerk* concept that he developed.

Nitsch's artistic beginnings lay in figurative religious painting. (Fig. 3–5) He referred to old masters, in particular to Rembrandt who, throughout his life, aimed to faithfully reproduce the emotions, affects, and facial expressions of his figures in order to express feelings in which the viewers should see themselves reflected. The understanding and awareness of placing

1 Hermann Nitsch, „Zur Theorie des OM Theaters“, in: ders. *das orgien mysterien theater 2, theoretische schriften, partiturentwurf des 6 tagespiels*, Neapel, Reggio Emilia, München 1976, S. 32.

his work and its content in the tradition of Western art, and expanding this into a contemporary language, has accompanied Nitsch throughout his life.

The *Gesamtkunstwerk*

The idea for his *Orgien Mysterien Theater* (Theatre of Orgies and Mysteries), which he developed in 1957 while still studying at the Grafische Lehr- und Versuchsanstalt (Graphic Arts Teaching and Research Institute) before he turned twenty, was crucial for his further path. This is a *Gesamtkunstwerk* concept, in which Nitsch wanted to bring all aspects of life into an artistic form; including pain, suffering, and violence, whose conscious experience he understood as an indispensable prerequisite for the experience of increased joy in existence that he ultimately strived for.

A key reference point in his approach was ancient theater, particularly Greek tragedy. The latter's intention to achieve a form of purification (catharsis) by living through tragic situations within the realm of art was a concern that he shared. Based on this concept, Nitsch himself wrote plays in which he wanted to convey not only disturbing psychological experiences, but also extremely strong sensory ones. (Fig. 6, 7) This led him to overload his language so lavishly with adjectives that the word was no longer sufficient for him and he wanted to incorporate concrete sensory perceptions into his theatre–such as the spilling of substances and the spreading of scents or creating loud noise.

Action Painting

As a next step, Nitsch discovered informal Action Painting. It fascinated him as a theatrical act of painting, in which physical and psychological energies can be activated or abreacted in equal measure, as well as a possibility for a sensual interaction with colour matter. He saw a way in it to realise the intention underlying his *Orgien Mysterien Theater* of bringing to the fore repressed drives, by going through extreme physical and psychological states, in order to ultimately overcome them, and achieve an intensified experience of existence: “The innermost, perhaps unrecognized concern of Tachism lay in the Dionysian-dynamic, in a consciousness-raising abreaction that grasp fundamental psychic layers. Excitement, the surge of lust, disinhibition, ecstasy, the release of deeply pent-up matter are to be shown.”[1]

The first three Painting Actions took place in the Technical Museum in Vienna, where Nitsch was working as a graphic designer at the time. They were each documented photographically and/or filmed. During the excessive work process, the artist threw or poured

2
Hermann Nitsch, „Kreuzigung eines geschlachteten Lammes, durchgeführt am 4. Juni 1962",(Crucifixion of a Slaughtered Lamb, carried out on 4 June, 1962), in: idem, Frühe Aktionen, Naples n.d. p. 1.

red paint onto canvases, or let it run down from the top edge of the picture. He was fascinated by the substance of colour and, by presenting it as concretely as possible, aimed to achieve intensive emotional experiences for the viewers. The colour red, which he used exclusively between 1960 and 1979 with a few exceptions, was of particular importance because, in its analogy to the substance of blood, it is directly associated with life and death. (Fig. 8–11)

In the same year, he also took the next decisive step in expanding his theatre from painting to staging concrete events. This happened as part of a working retreat that he held with Muehl and Adolf Frohner, which they entitled *Blutorgel* (Blood Organ)–the first collaborative project of Vienna Actionism. For three days and three nights, the artists were walled up in Muehl's basement studio in Vienna's Perinetgasse (Perinetkeller / Perinetcellar), without audience, while they each created their own artworks independently. Nitsch produced a large action painting, his so-called *Blutorgelbild* (Blood Organ Painting), and on the last day, he took a decisive further step by using an animal carcass and its blood as artistic material for the first time. He hung a skinned dead lamb, as if crucified, on the wall with its head down in front of a white cloth and placed a table, covered with a white cloth underneath it, onto which he placed the bloody innards and intestines which he showered with blood and hot water. In reference to this work, he still spoke of a "display of concrete objects"[2] as part of a painting action.

The Actions

Only when Nitsch positioned himself crucified in front of a white screen for 30 minutes on 19 December 1962 and had Muehl pour blood on him (Fig. 12), he described this as his *1st Action*. The painting surface was no longer the canvas but his own body. The *2nd Action* took place on 18 March in 1963 and was open to the public in Josef Dvorak's basement gallery in Lagergasse (Vienna); it moved away from painting. Here, a slaughtered and skinned lamb, hanging upside down from the ceiling, was doused with blood and swung around the room over a white cloth on the floor, which had entrails on it. (Fig.13)

From the *8th Action* on, which took place on 22 January 1965, Nitsch entered into a phase of formal reflection. Until August 1966, with this and his *10th* to *15th* and *20th Actions*, he carried out a series of so-called Body Actions, which he regarded as a "body grammar" and collection of motifs for his later larger actions. In each case, a naked male body, only visible as a torso in the photos, was covered with entrails and animal bodily fluids and also marked with various symbols, such as arrows or circles. All of these actions were deliberately staged solely to be photographed and illustrate Nitsch's pictorial thinking. (Fig. 29, 30)

The Body Actions were preceeded and followed by numerous others in the 1960s, in which the artist increasingly differentiated the concept of his *Orgien Mysterien Theater*. In his *7th Action (for Dr. Wolfgang Tunner)*, which he carried out at the request and on the occasion of a friend's graduation at two locations, namely in his studio and his apartment, and in several rooms at each, he realised a Table Action for the first time. For this purpose, he laid out different objects and substances on tables and handled them in various ways, including pouring liquids over them. The audience was encouraged to participate–an opportunity which was taken up by Schwarzkogler (Fig. 19, 20), who a month later began his own *1. Aktion, Hochzeit* (1st Action, Wedding) also with a Table Action. This type of action subsequently became part of the lifelong repertoire of Nitsch's work. Among others, a Table Action took place at the press conference organised by the Actionists in Vienna before they travelled to London for the *Destruction in Art Symposium*. (Fig. 31, 32) In 1966, Nitsch was able to include music in the form of a so-called screaming choir for the first time during his actions at the *Destruction in Art Symposium* (Fig. 33, 34) in London – something he had planned for his theatre from the very beginning. In 1967, he and Muehl were invited by the open-minded editor Wolfgang Kudrnofsky to realise actions for the Austrian Broadcasting Corporation (ORF). However, the finished films were not broadcast due to a ban by the television director at that time Helmut Zilk. Partly out of disappointment with this, but mainly for personal reasons, Nitsch moved to Harmating near Munich in the same year, where he carried out several actions in the following. In 1968, his friend, the avant-garde filmmaker Peter Kubelka, who lived in New York from 1966, forwarded him an invitation to this city, where he gained recognition and fame in artistic circles. (Fig. 35) A second invitation to New York followed in 1970.

Nitsch's *31. Aktion, Maria Empfängnis* (31st Action, Immaculate Conception) (Fig. 36), which was carried out in Munich on 8 December 1969, is a special work as it was the first time he involved a woman, Hanel Koeck. In fact, she was not only an actress, but also worked as a co-director and had a significant influence on the course of the action. Nitsch's guiding motive of a crucified lamb was replaced here by her body. Strongly determined by her performance, the language of the *Orgien Mysterien Theater* became sexually charged in a way that was never to been seen again on this scale: While Koeck lay naked on the cross with her legs spread, Nitsch performed the sexual act with her—both in a stylised manner as well as by using a plastic penis. Also, during this action, Nitsch wore a priest's robe for the first time, used a priest's chalice, and included sacred symbols. Controversially discussed until today, this action was and still is perceived by Koeck as a deeply emancipatory act.

After 1970

In 1971, Nitsch and his second wife Beate (born König) managed to purchase Prinzendorf Castle in Lower Austria, where the artist lived and worked until his death in April 2022, and which from then on also served as the venue for his *Orgien Mysterien Theater*. This gave him the opportunity to expand the activities, which had previously been limited in terms of time and space. While he never abandoned the basic concept of his *Gesamtkunstwerk*, with respect to content or motifs, he continued to develop and change details and the respective structure of the course of an action. He progressively worked towards his long-held ambition of a six-day performance in stages. In 1975 his *50th Action* was a *24-Stunden-Spiel* (24-Hour-Play, Fig. 37) in Prinzendorf. A *Drei-Tage-Spiel* (Three-Day-Play, Fig. 38) was realized there in 1984, and finally, in 1998, a *Sechs-Tage-Spiel* (Six-Day-Play, Fig. 39) was achieved, which Nitsch considered the pinnacle of his entire body of work. Within these large-scale actions, which occupied the entire interior and exterior spaces as well as the surrounding area of the castle, all elements of the *Orgien Mysterien Theater* were brought to life by a variety of actors, slaughtered animals, their entrails and blood as well as other substances and objects. At this point, it should be emphasised that only once—during the *Sechs-Tage-Spiel*—a living ox was slaughtered directly on site by a master butcher, according to the standards of the time. Usually, Nitsch obtained his animals, which would otherwise have been processed for consumption, as cadavers from selected slaughterhouses. Regarding the motifs of his work, the focus in the *Sechs-Tage-Spiel* was, in addition to the tearing ritual, the pouring of blood and sometimes extensive disembowelments of the animals, as well as the merging of human bodies with those of dead animals. After the physically and psychologically demanding tearing and pouring actions, lavish feasts with processions and communal meals took place.

As part of these actions, which by then spanned many spaces and large periods of time, Nitsch was able to stage complex panoramas, which once again make evident how important the pictorial effects of an overall scenic composition, with precise details—for which he again quoted from the formal canon of

European painting–were to him. In the *Sechs-Tage-Spiel* in particular, the ritually recurring, dramatic phases were staged as images strictly organised according to a central perspective. (Fig. 39)

Pictorial Works and Music

From the outset, Nitsch preserved selected objects he had used in his actions (such as bloody cloths, chasubles, or wooden stretchers) as so-called "relics", which he either used in collages (Fig. 17, 18, 230) or exhibited per se. In this way, material artefacts were again created that could be transferred back into an exhibition context.

While Nitsch had almost completely turned away from his painting practice, after he had begun his actionist work, from the late 1970s onwards, it started to play an increasing role in his work again. He created numerous large-scale pictures in which he, towards the end of his life, made more and more use of the entire colour palette and applied the paint substance so lavishly that the works acquired an object-like three-dimensionality. (Fig. 40)

Likewise, in the last phase of his life, Nitsch increasingly turned to music and created a number of works in this field that could be performed per se–independently of actions–including string quartets and symphonies.

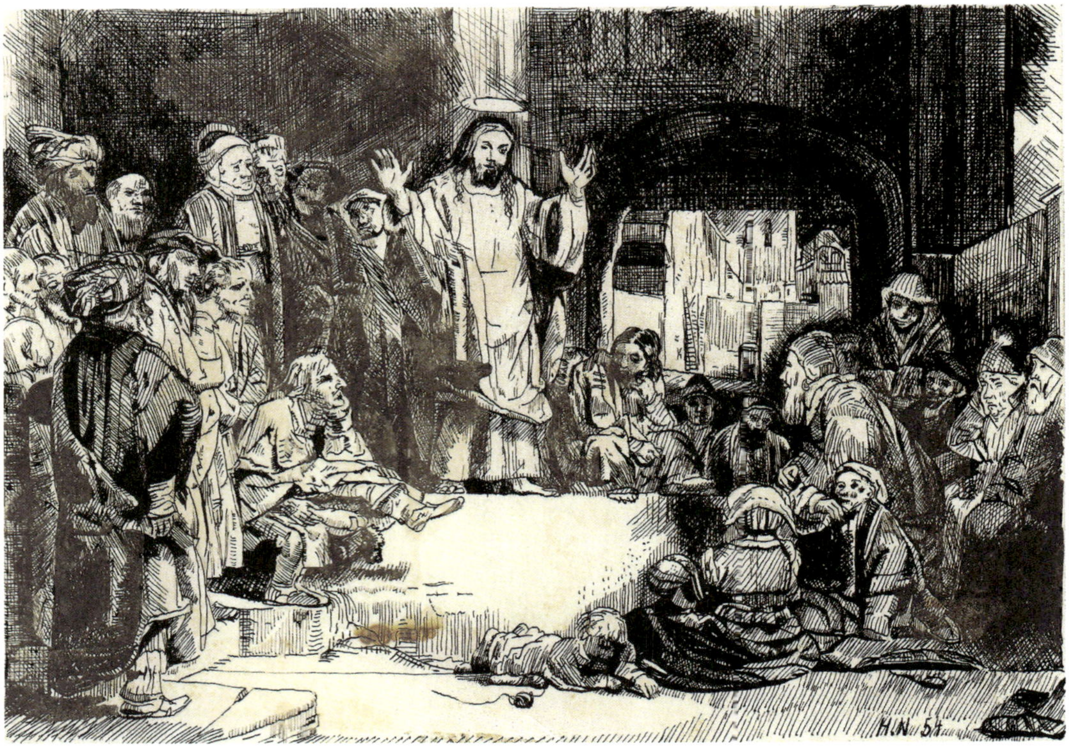

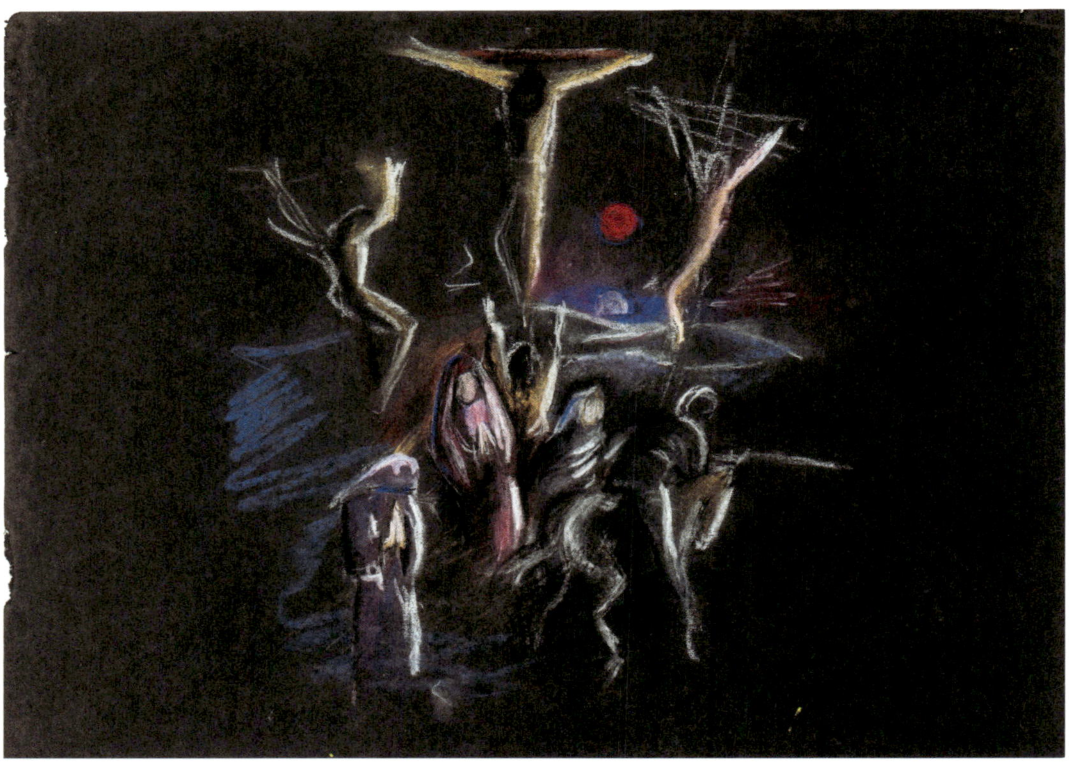

Fig. 3
Hermann Nitsch
Untitled, 1954
(Copy after Rembrandt, *Christus lehrend*, or: *La petite tombe*)[Copy after Rembrandt, *Christ teaching*, or: *La petite tombe*]
Ink on paper
15,5 x 20,8 cm
Collection Thomas Bachlechner

Fig. 4
Hermann Nitsch
Untitled, 1955
Oil crayon on black paper
35 x 50 cm
WAM – Wiener Aktionismus Museum, Vienna,

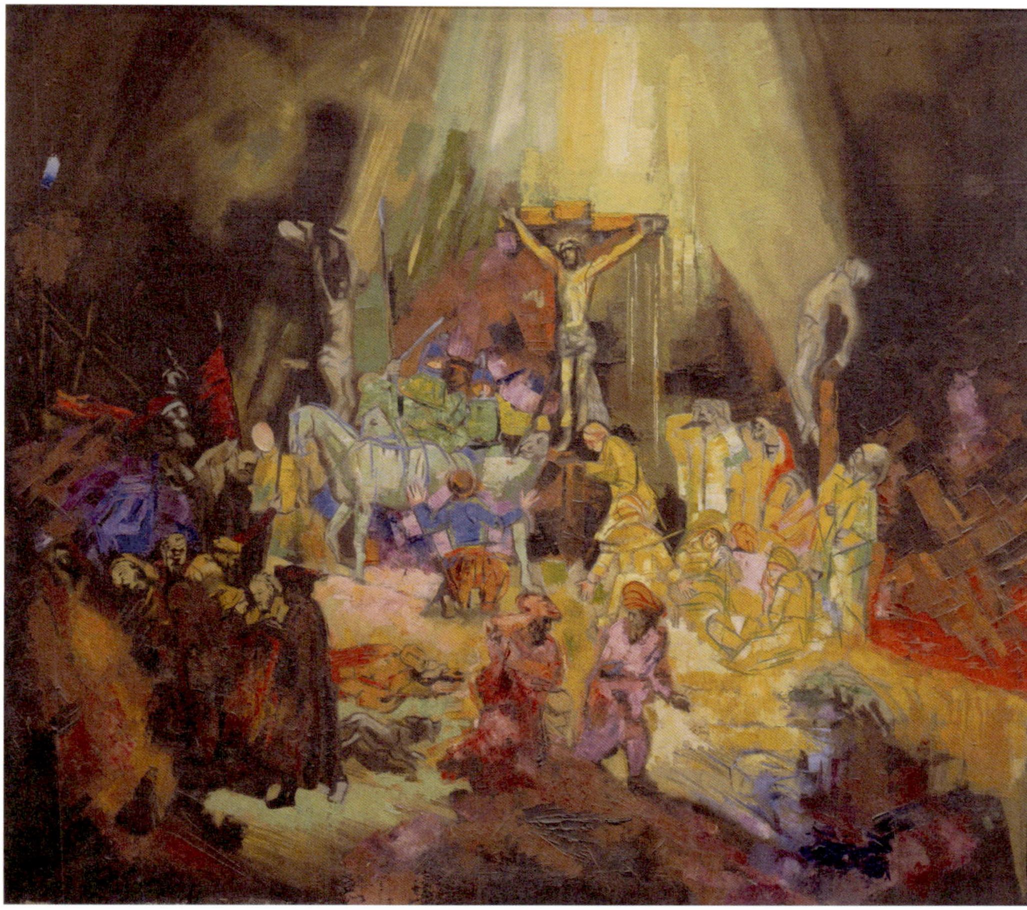

Fig. 5
Hermann Nitsch
Kreuzigung (nach Rembrandt) (Crucifixion [after Rembrandt]), 1955/1956
Oil on fibreboard
136 x 157 cm
Collection Rita Nitsch

stichworte zur entwicklung der theorie des o. m. theaters

$\frac{2}{10}\ \frac{2}{10}\ \frac{2}{10}\ \frac{2}{10}$

erregung aller sinne = orgie

exzess
wollust
schmerzqualwollust
wollustqual
qualwollust
lust wird zu schmerz
schmerz wird zu lust
schmerz = genuss
genuss = schmerz
zerreissung
lust wendet sich in den exzess
lust wendet sich in die destruktion
urexzess
grundexzess
die zerreissung des lammes
die zerreissung des schafes
die zerreissung der ziege
die zerreissung des ziegengestaltigen gottes
die zerreissung des stieres
die zerreissung des stiergestaltigen gottes
die zerreissung des gottes
die zerreissung des dionysos
der vom eber zerrissene
der getötete sonnengott
der gemarterte jesus christus
das kreuz

geburtstrauma
schrei der gebärenden

$\frac{100001634(b)a,a,a,23(414)5000ALa445900123(ABLM4)000}{504130180006000004591111163211594590000562347000523111500}$

Fig. 6
stichworte zur entwicklung der theorie des o.m. theaters (keywords on the development of the theory of the o.m. theatre), in: hermann nitsch, peter vei: (ed.), *hermann nitsch, die wortdichtung des orgien mysterien theaters* (the word poetry of the the thea:re of orgies and mysteries), Vienna-Prinzendorf, 1982, n.p.

1. runde

kemin erlebt trunken den frühling. voll lebensbejahender begeisterung wünscht sie sich, dass ein junger heidnischer gott sie liebt. ein als dionysos verkleideter jüngling liest ein brevier für die lebensekstase. hyldis, die mutter von kemin und celosis, verneint das leben, ihr ekelt vor dem leben. sie wünscht sich, dass sie celosis nie geboren hätte. der schwächliche celosis kommt, von einer krankheit genesen, und ist ebenfalls von dem frühlingsfieber ergriffen.

wenn nicht anders angegeben, tragen alle darsteller lange, weisse, kuttenartige hemden. die schädel sind kahl geschoren. vorne steht kemin, etwas weiter hinten sitzt auf einem trohnartigen podest ein verlebter jüngling. er ist nackt und zu einem kultischen spiel als dionysos angetan. seine stirn ist mit feuchten blüten umwunden.

KEMIN: milch rinnt über das regenheisse fleisch der erde. der hodenlose pan verstopft flötenlöcher mit abgebissenen keimen und schneidet weinnasse äpfel und birnen in zwei hälften. oft legt er seine schlafsüsse zunge auf die flachen schnittwunden des obstes. in bettwarme unterwäsche gekleidete weiber gehen in prozessionen über die hügel. sie tragen lila fahnen durch die nachheissem urin riechenden wochenbettgärten, sie atmen den urinsüssen föhn aus fliederwaschküchen, oft wälzen sie sich auf feldwegen und halten sich gegenseitig ihre hände in ihre behaarten achselhöhlen. ich will den schamlosen überfluss des lebens. der jubel, der rausch pfercht sich in die fleischkörbe der unbestrumpften sängerknaben, deren geruchsnerven in jasminüberfüllten turnsälen abgetötet wurden. ihre geschlechtsteile sind mit wasserstoffsuperoxyd gewaschen, in ihre münder hat man sacharingetränkte watte gestopft, aber sie singen iiiiiiiiiiiiiiiiiiiiiiiiiiiiii
ich bin krank, aufgereizt vom fieber der jahreszeit, brunst narkotisiert meinen schlaf in, mit weissen, geruchlosen tulpen bebauten nachgeburtenzimmern. ich will nackt sein und schreien. das weisse sexuelle bettbad in der cella, die rituelle blütenbefruchtung reizt die entzundene haut meiner handteller, weihrauchschmeckendes magnesiumlicht trifft die weichheit meines grosshirns und das weisse fleisch des geschlechtsteiles. aus den gartenwäldern der befruchtungsfeste rennen knabenbischöfe. sie haben ihr fieber gekühlt, indem sie in die holztröge stiegen, welche mit wasser gefüllt waren, in dem fleisch gewaschen wurde. die nacht vor der zeugung marterte ihre verwesenden glieder. jetzt jauchzen sie in der unzuchtliturgie, welche meine begierde ihnen abverlangt. der penis meines knaben ist weich, fühlt sich an wie eine nasse, föhnverblühte teerose. ich will die neumondwollust. meine hand wird sich in die haut unter seinen schamhaaren krallen.

bis zu ihrem nächsten einsatz singt kemin in frei erfundenen unsinnigen melodien hallelujahallelujahallelujahallelujahallelujahallelujahallelujahalleluja

JÜNGLING: sonne sonne sonne sonne sonne sonne sonne sonne sonne sonne ihre weingeistnassen münder kleben auf den weissen hemden der mädchen. nur dionysos sitzt müde unter ihnen (ich bin dionysos). die rauschfiebrige, von schweiss und erbrochenem nasse stirn ist mit verwesenden rosen umkränzt, die nackten füsse in warmem, süssem zuckerwasserbad (im lavoir mit warmem zuckerwasser). ich will den geilen honigtod der sakristeiembryozuckerwasserorgie im essignassen beichtstuhl sterben. mein

Fig. 7
First page from: *1. Teil* (first part) *BRUNSTSPIEL*, in: hermann nitsch, peter veit (ed.), *hermann nitsch. die wortdichtung des orgien mysterien theaters* (hermann nitsch. the word poetry of the theatre of orgies and mysteries), Vienna-Prinzendorf 1982, n.p.

Fig. 8
Hermann Nitsch
Untitled, 1960
(As one of seven individual paintings, this work became part of Nitsch's *Kleiner Existenzaltar* [Small Existence Altar] in 1981.)
Mixed media on wood
85 x 83 x 2,5 cm
mumok – Museum moderner Kunst Stiftung Ludwig Wien

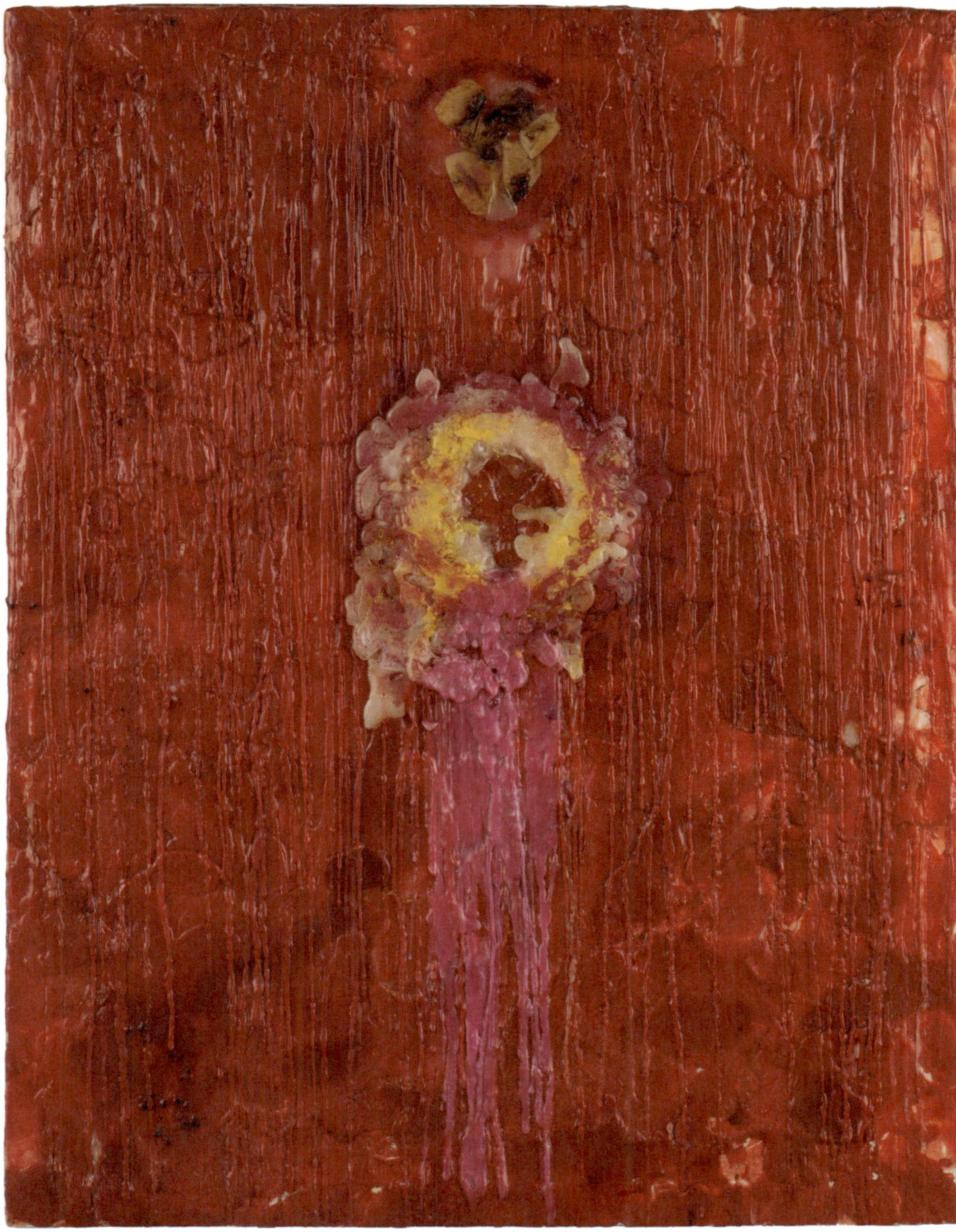

Fig. 9
Hermann Nitsch
Die Wunden des Ölbergs bluten (The Wounds of the Mount of Olives Bleeding), around 1960
Wax, incense, pieces of fabric, colour powder on cotton
75 x 60 x 5 cm
mumok – Museum moderner Kunst Stiftung Ludwig Wien,
former Collection Hahn, Cologne

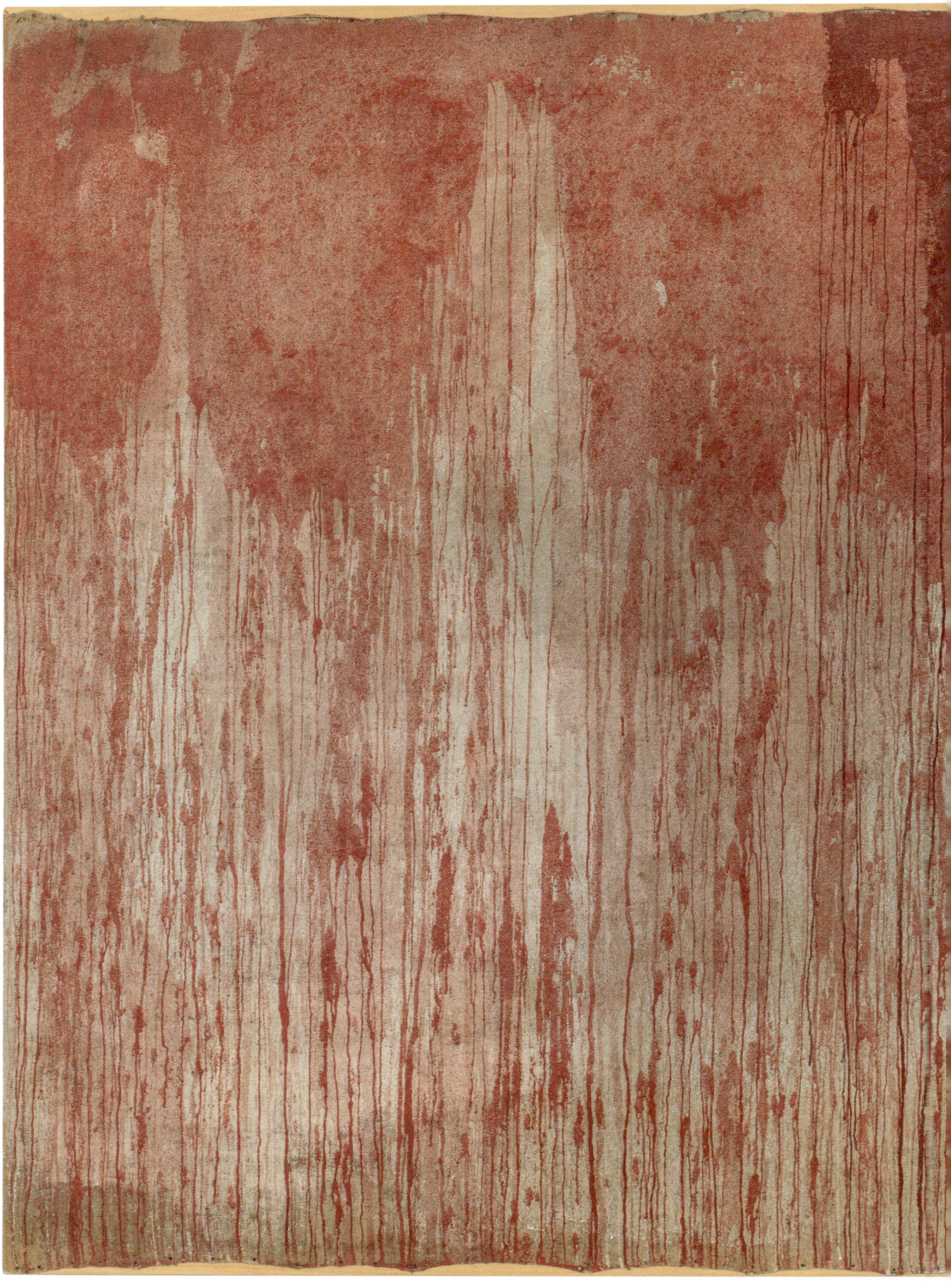

Fig. 10
Hermann Nitsch
Untitled, 1962
Mixed media on burlap
190 x 300 cm
WAM – Wiener Aktionismus Museum, Vienna

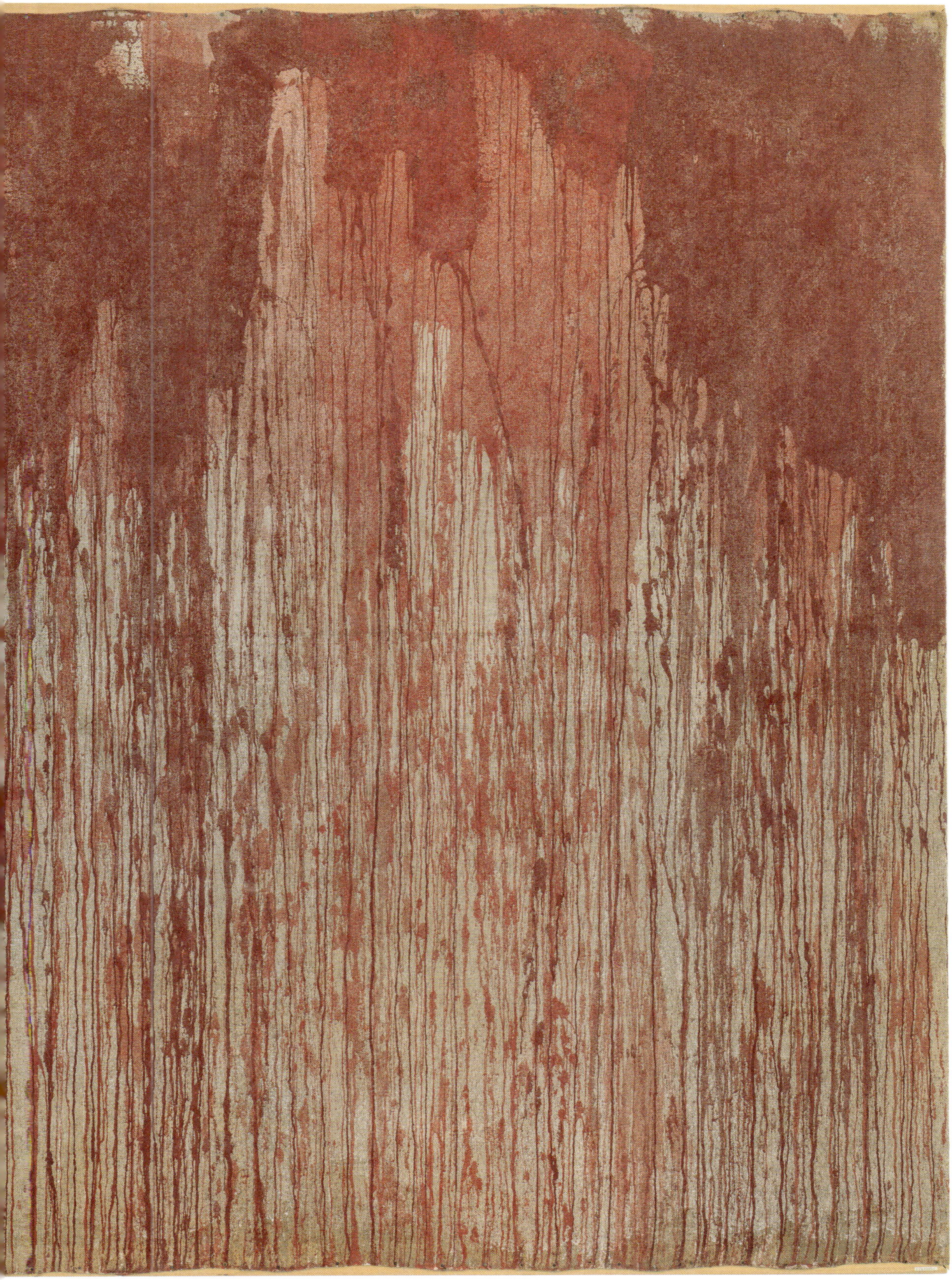

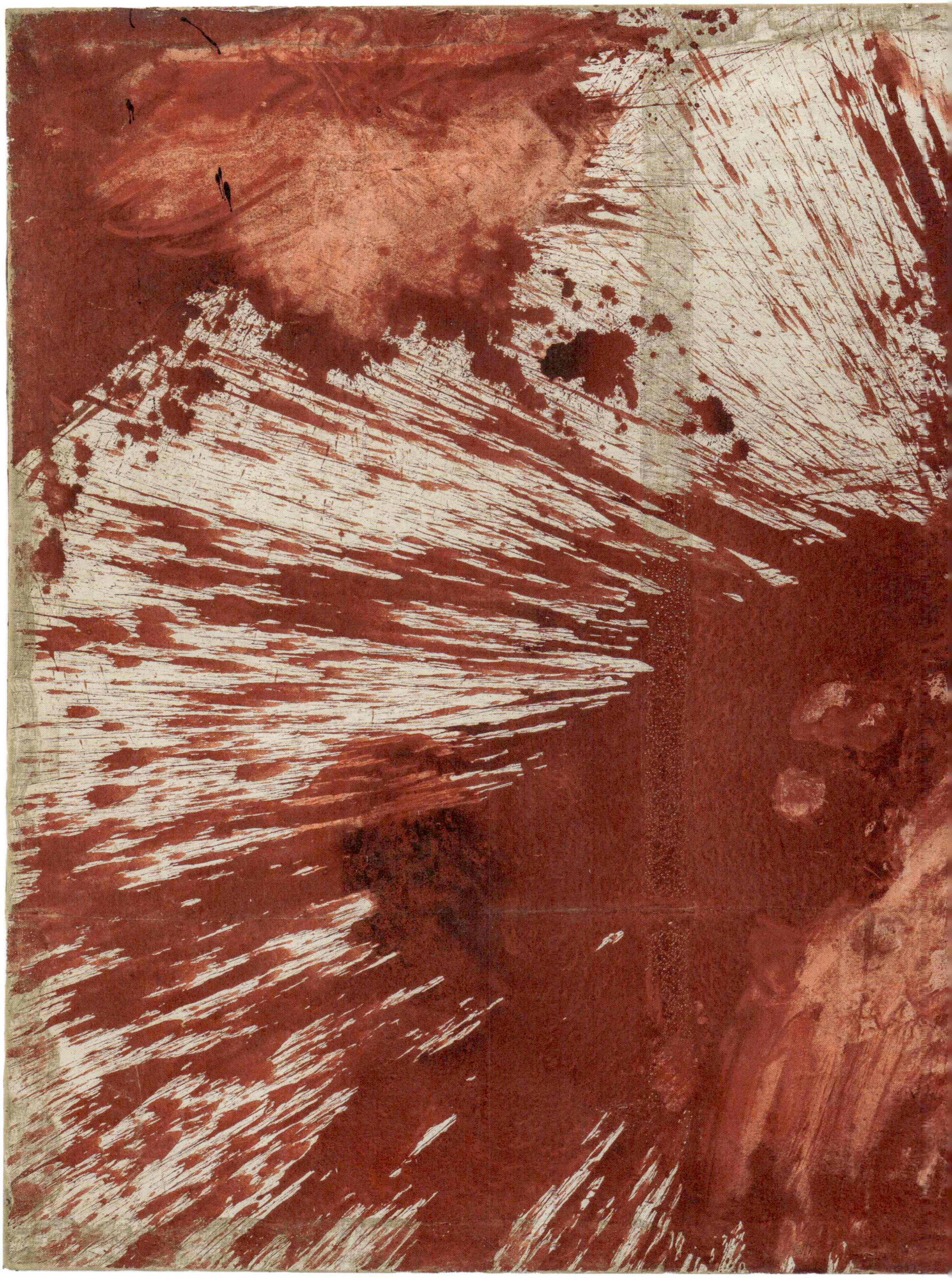

Fig. 11
Hermann Nitsch
Untitled, 1962
Mixed media on burlap
190 x 300 cm
WAM – Wiener Aktionismus Museum, Vienna, Collection K.

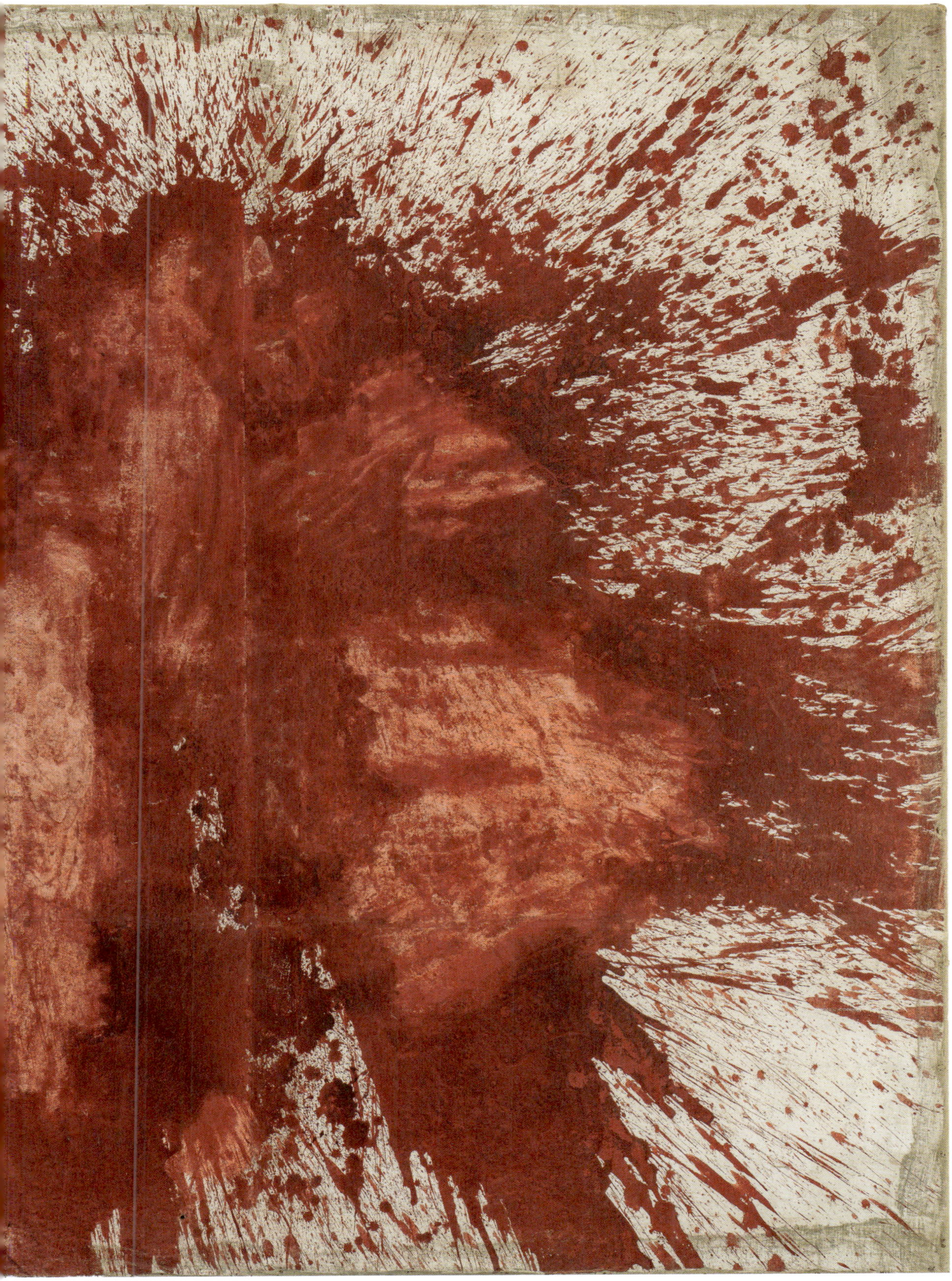

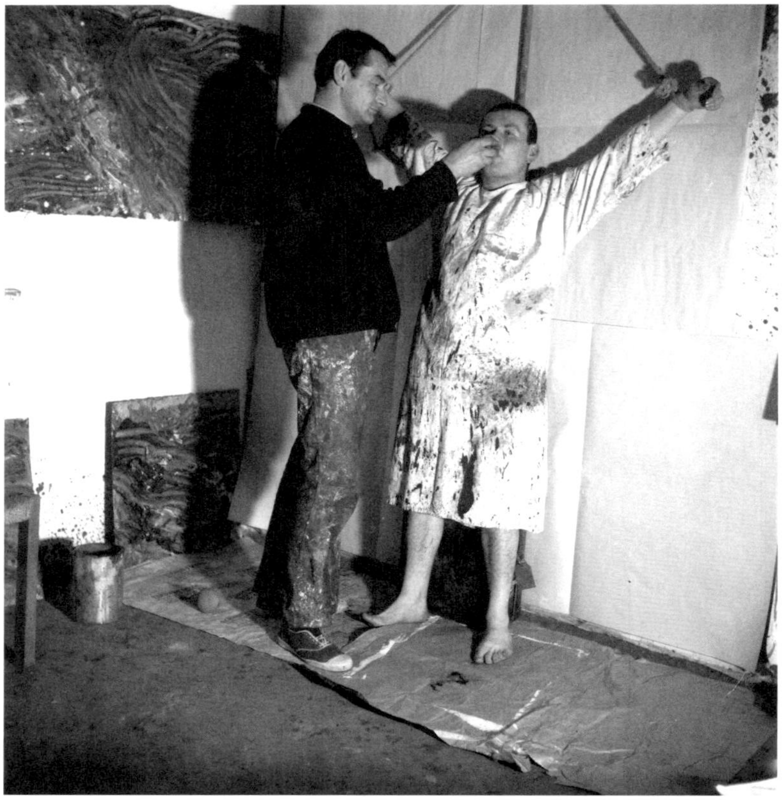

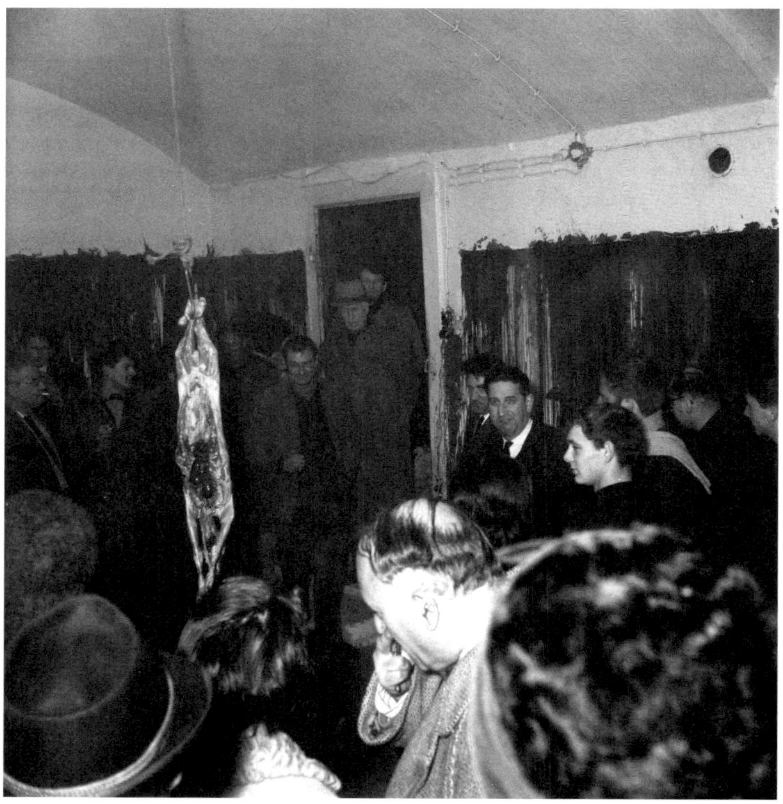

Fig. 12
Hermann Nitsch
1st Action, 19 December 1962
Muehl's apartment, Obere Augartenstraße 14a/20,
1020 Vienna
B/W photograph
photo: Hans Niederbacher
with: Otto Muehl

Fig. 13
Hermann Nitsch
2nd Action, 8 March 1963
Galerie Josef Dvorak, Lagergasse 2
1030 Vienna
B/W photograph
photo: Stangl
music: Anestis Logothetis

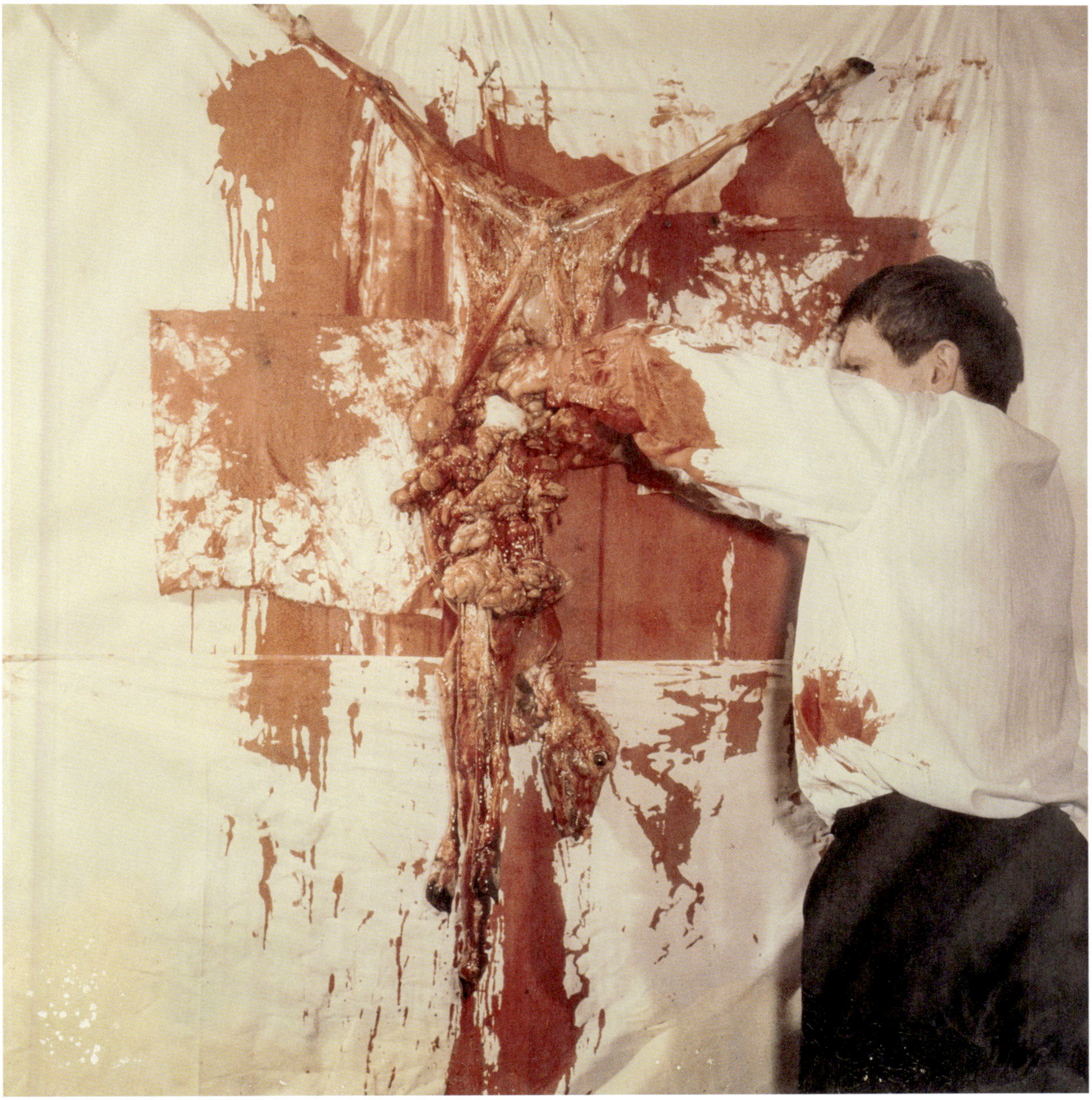

Fig. 14
Hermann Nitsch
4th Action, 21 November 1963
Nitsch's studio, Brünner Straße 132, 1210 Vienna
Colour photograph
photo: Ludwig Hoffenreich

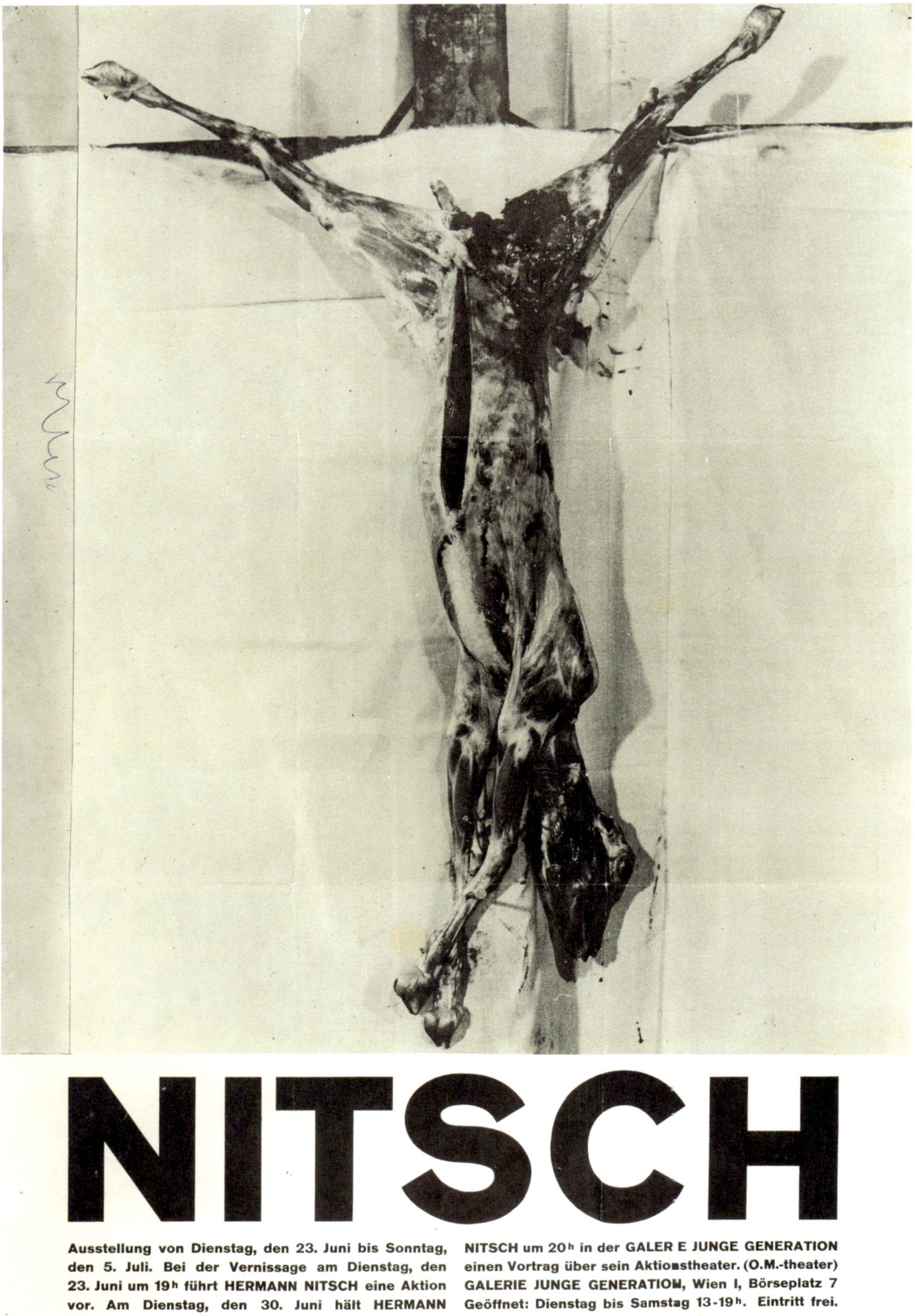

Fig. 15, 16
Hermann Nitsch
MANIFEST das lamm (*MANIFESTO the lamb*), 1964
6th *Action* and lecture in Galerie Junge Generation
Offset print
59 x 41 cm
WAM – Wiener Aktionismus Museum, Vienna, Collection K.

MANIFEST das lamm

Die entwicklung der kunst tendierte dahin, die wirklichkeit als direktes gestaltungsmittel zu benützen. Die kunst automatisierte sich, verwandelte sich zur reinen anschauung der wirklichkeit, befreite sich vom ursprünglich geringeren bewußtseinshorizont der traditionellen werkwertung. Das schöpferische wird aktivere mitformung der umwelt, wird zu einer mystik gegenüber der lebendigkeit.

Eine bewußtere, erweiterte, verfeinerte, sinnliche umweltregistration verbindet sich mit dem registrieren des symbolgehaltes, der jedem konkreten objekt bzw. jedem konkreten vorgang anhaftet, d. h. alle assoziationsmöglichkeiten, welche sich durch die durch die kunst zitierten teile der wirklichkeit auslösen, werden belebt, systematisch zerlegt und bewußt gemacht. Ein durchaus analytischer charakter der kunst aktiviert, geschult durch die zu regressionen lockenden sinnlichen mittel des informels, das unbewußte. Das arbeiten mit konkreten mitteln beansprucht mehr denn je die kontakte mit den unteren schichten der psyche, deren gegebenheiten zum eigentlichen darstellungsbereich werden. Die beanspruchten konkreten objekte sind nur chiffren einer innerpsychischen wirklichkeit, welche ausgelotet werden kann bis zu archetypischen kollektiven grundgegebenheiten des seelischen. Das menschliche begreift sich wesentlich umfänglicher, die symbolbelastung jedes realen objektes wird bewußt. Das gestaltete arrangement der wirklichkeit hat daher die zur kunst sich steigernde addition von symbolgruppen zur folge. Das innerhalb des traumes sich zeigende wirken der assoziationsverkettungen sowie die symbolsprache der unbewußten intentionen in traum und mythos werden durch die genannten produktionswege ans bewußtsein gebracht und entschlüsselt. Die durch die kunst arrangierten wirklichkeiten sind mit projektionen aus dem kollektiven unbewußten behaftet, es kehrt sich die realität des mythos nach außen. Es zeigen sich tief in der seele vorgezeichnete einordnungsprinzipien, diese durch die kunst erfaßten bezirke werden dem instinktbereich entzogen, wodurch sich ein konstruktives begreifen ihres vorhandenseins ermöglicht.

Das konkrete objekt des gekreuzigten lammes manifestiert demonstrativ die nachaußenkehrung der innerpsychischen realität des mythos, es kehrt eine das mythische durchziehende zentrale entwicklungslinie nach außen, welche stets das lamm als symbol benützt und berührt.

<u>Zur symbolik des lammes</u>

von der sinnlich empfundenen realität des blutnassen abgehäuteten kadavers ausgehend, läßt sich zu den anfängen des mythischen assoziieren. Der so ausgelöste assoziationskreis berührt sich sehr direkt mit der bewältigung der ständig zur orgiastik drängenden kollektiven vitalitätsaufwallungen des menschlichen. Mit deren endpunkten, sublimationen und verdrängungen, tritt das lamm meistens im symbolischen zusammenhang auf. Die dionysische aufwallung endet in der zerreißung des gottes dionysos (des ihn symbolisierenden stieres), endet im exzeß. Das negative abbild der dionysischen orgiastik, die passion, endet im masochistischen opferexzeß. Das informel, das konkrete durchbrechen des triebhaften in der kunst, hat unbedingte ähnlichkeit mit dem wesen des dionysischen, denn seine konsequenz ist äußerste erregung bis zum endpunkt des exzessiven.

das O. M. theater, aktionstheater, nützt dieses phänomen aus und erreicht so innerhalb der kunst eine regression, ein hervorbrechen des dionysischen.

Die lammzerfleischung ist im O. M. theater durchgeführte symbolhandlung für das urexzeßerlebnis (ekstatischer endpunkt der abreaktionsorgiastik). Die sinnlich reale sadomasochistische situation der zerfleischung ist identisch mit einem extremen triebdurchbruch.

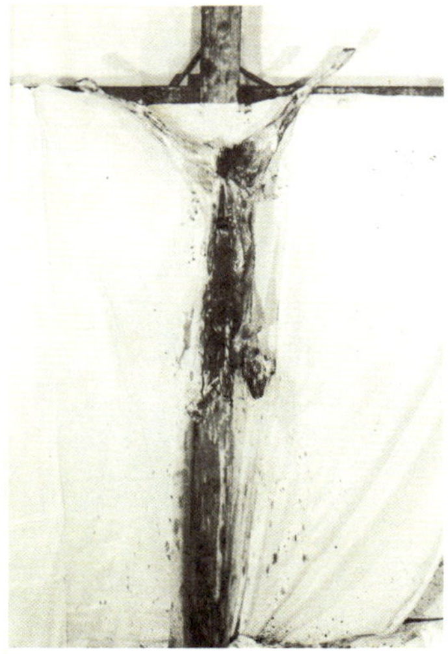

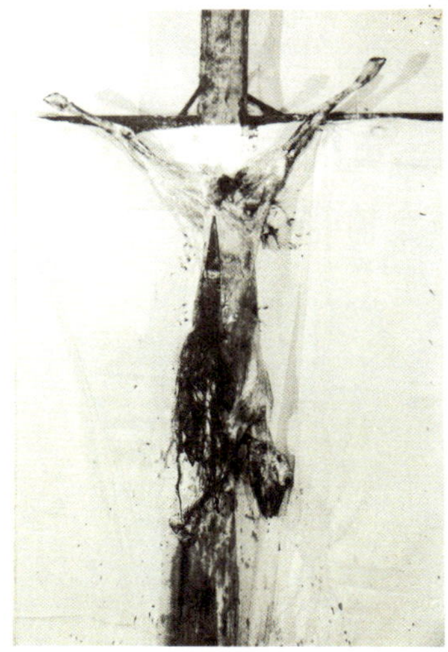

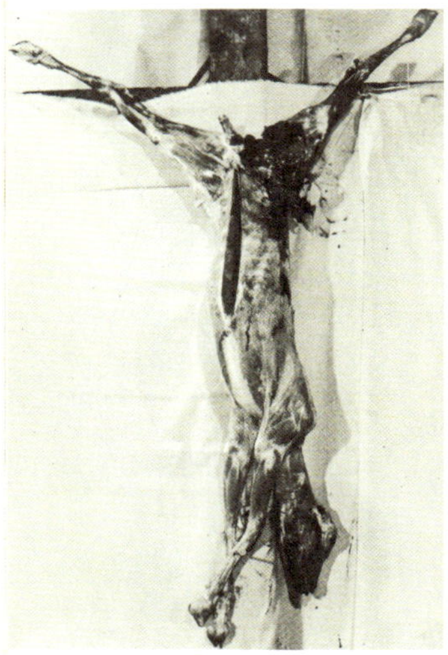

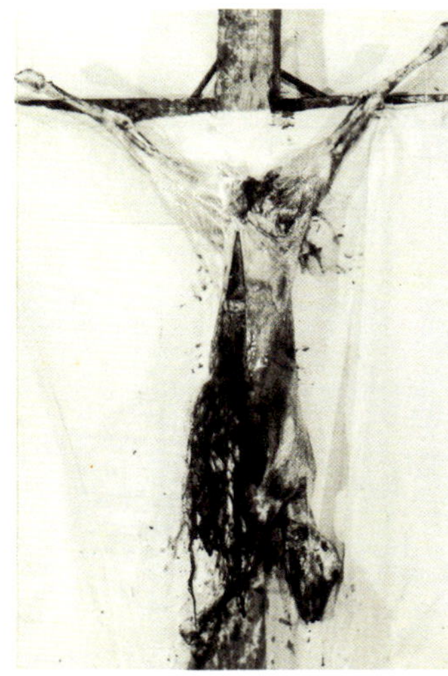

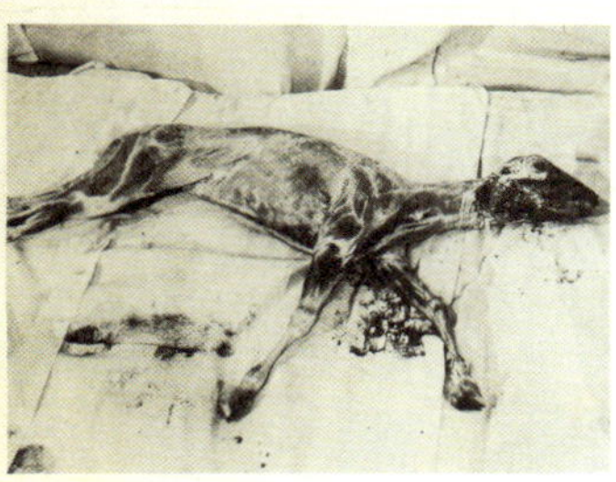

Nitsch
Wien XXI
Jedlersdorferstr. 171

Dieses manifest wird anläßlich der BIENNALE 1964 (VENEDIG) herausgegeben. Es wird an die bedeutendsten galerien und theater von europa und übersee gesendet.

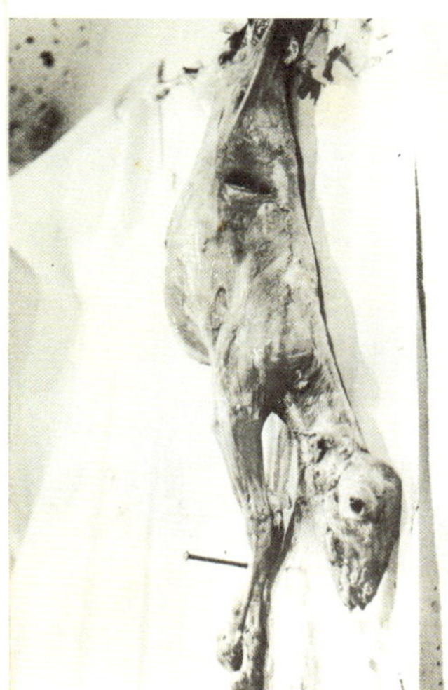

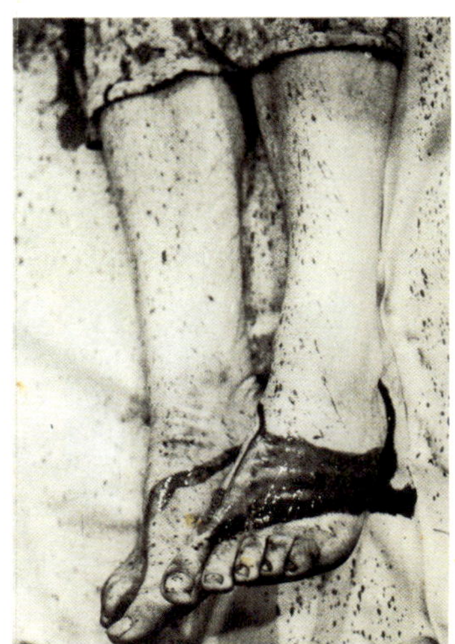

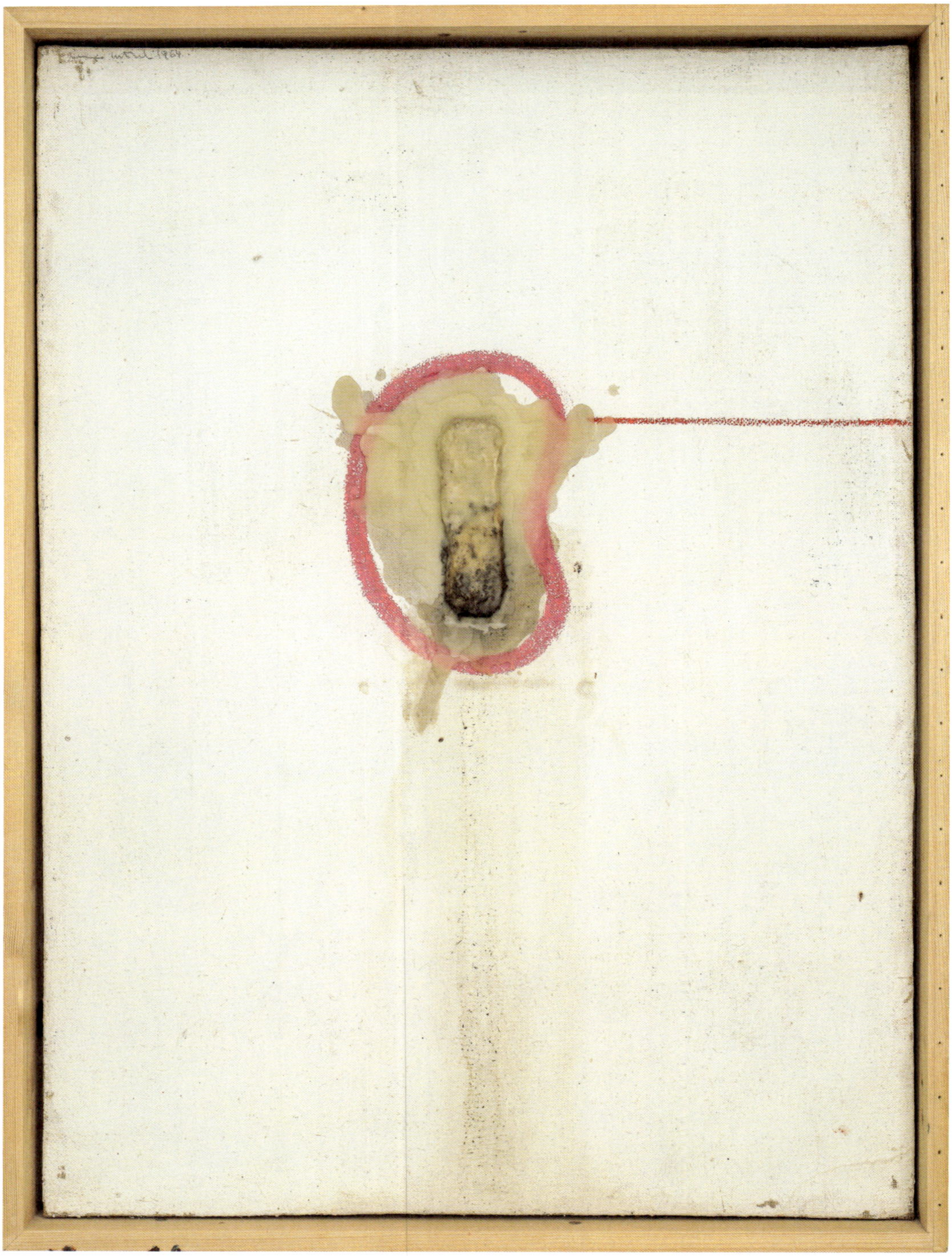

Fig. 17
Hermann Nitsch
Untitled, 1964
Wax, incense, oil crayon, menstrual pad on primed burlap
135 x 102 cm
WAM – Wiener Aktionismus Museum, Vienna

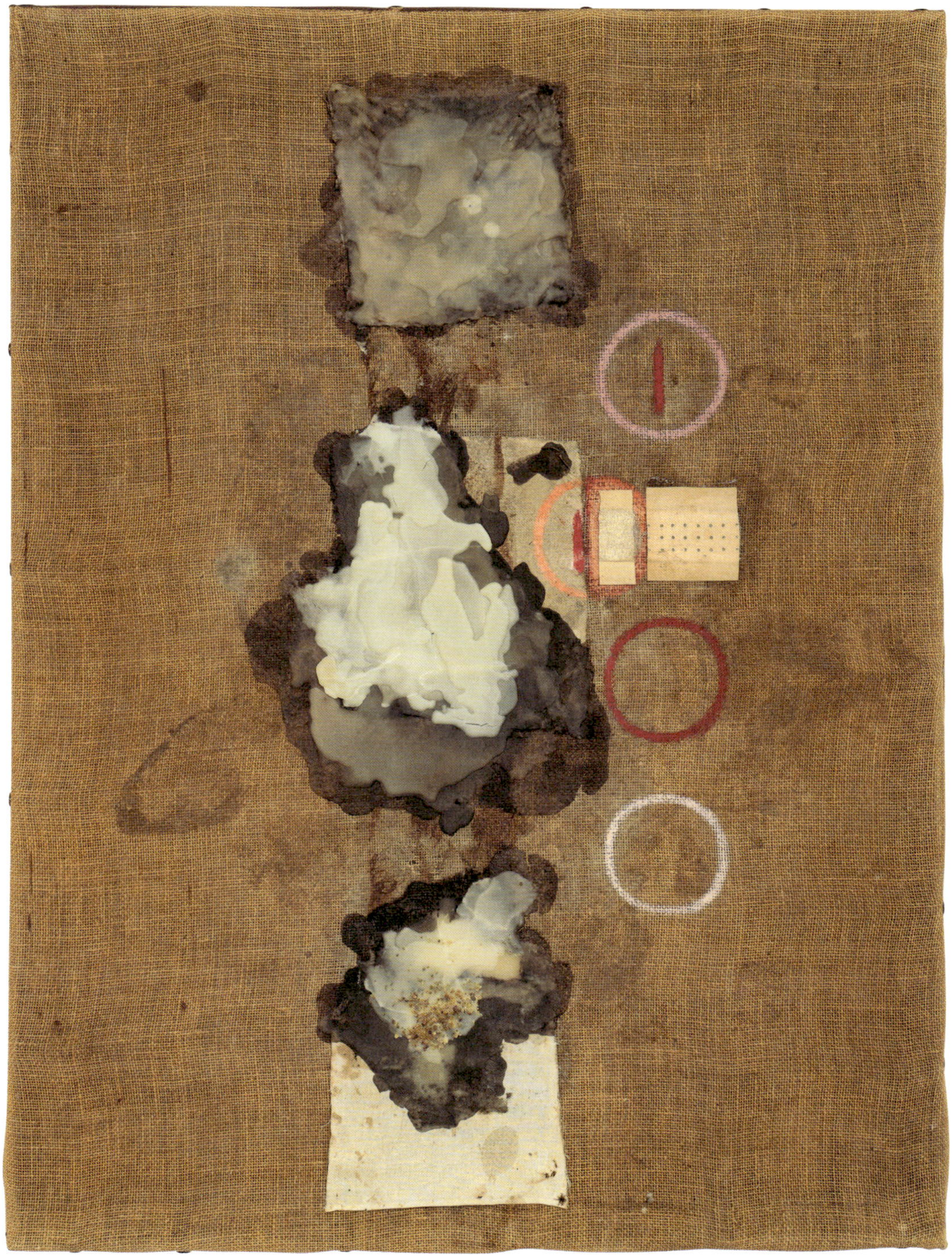

Fig. 18
Hermann Nitsch
Untitled, 1963
Blood, wax, tissues, oil crayon, plaster on burlap
106 x 80 cm
WAM – Wiener Aktionismus Museum, Vienna, Collection K.

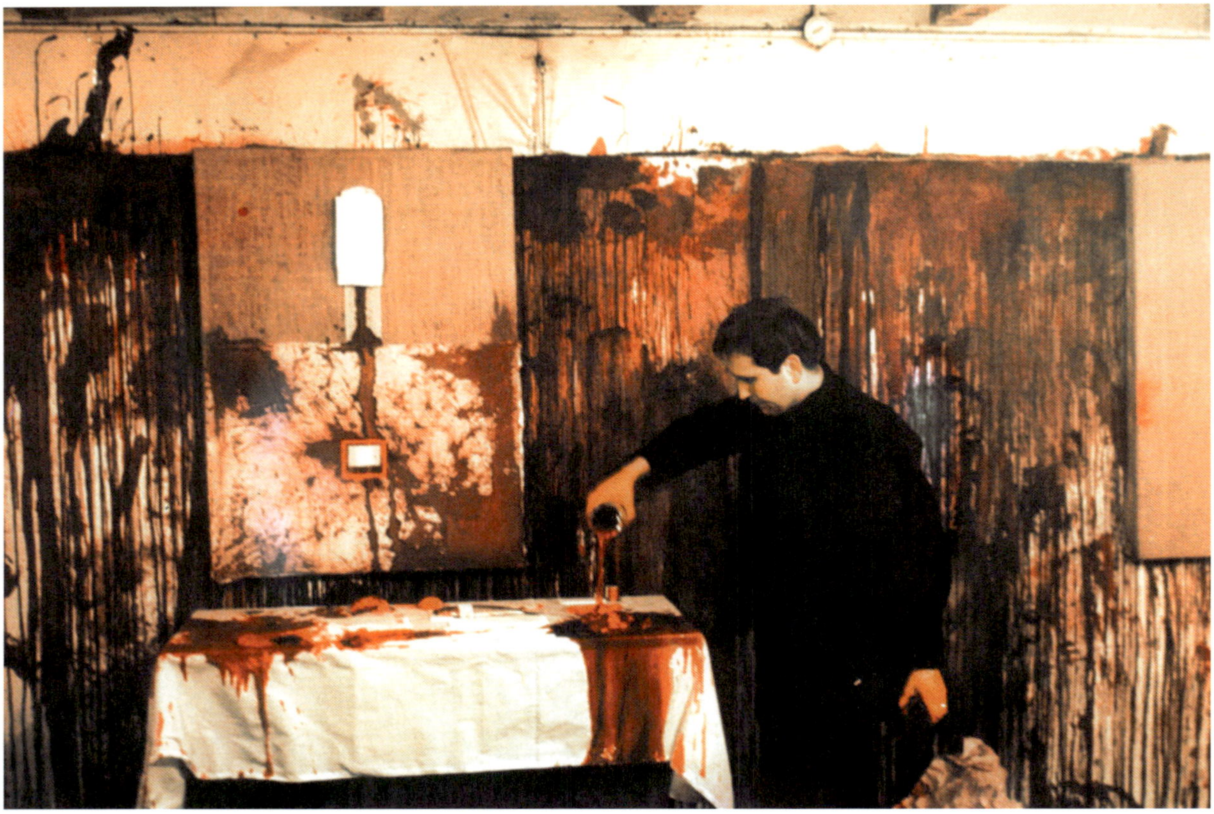

Fig. 19, 20
Hermann Nitsch
7. Aktion (für Dr. Wolfgang Tunner) (7th Action [for Dr. Wolfgang Tunner]), 16 January 1965
Nitsch's studio, Brünner Straße 132 and Nitsch's apartment, Jedlersdorfer Straße 171, 1210 Vienna
Colour photograph / b/w photograph
photo: Khasaq (Siegfried Klein)
with: Rudolf Schwarzkogler

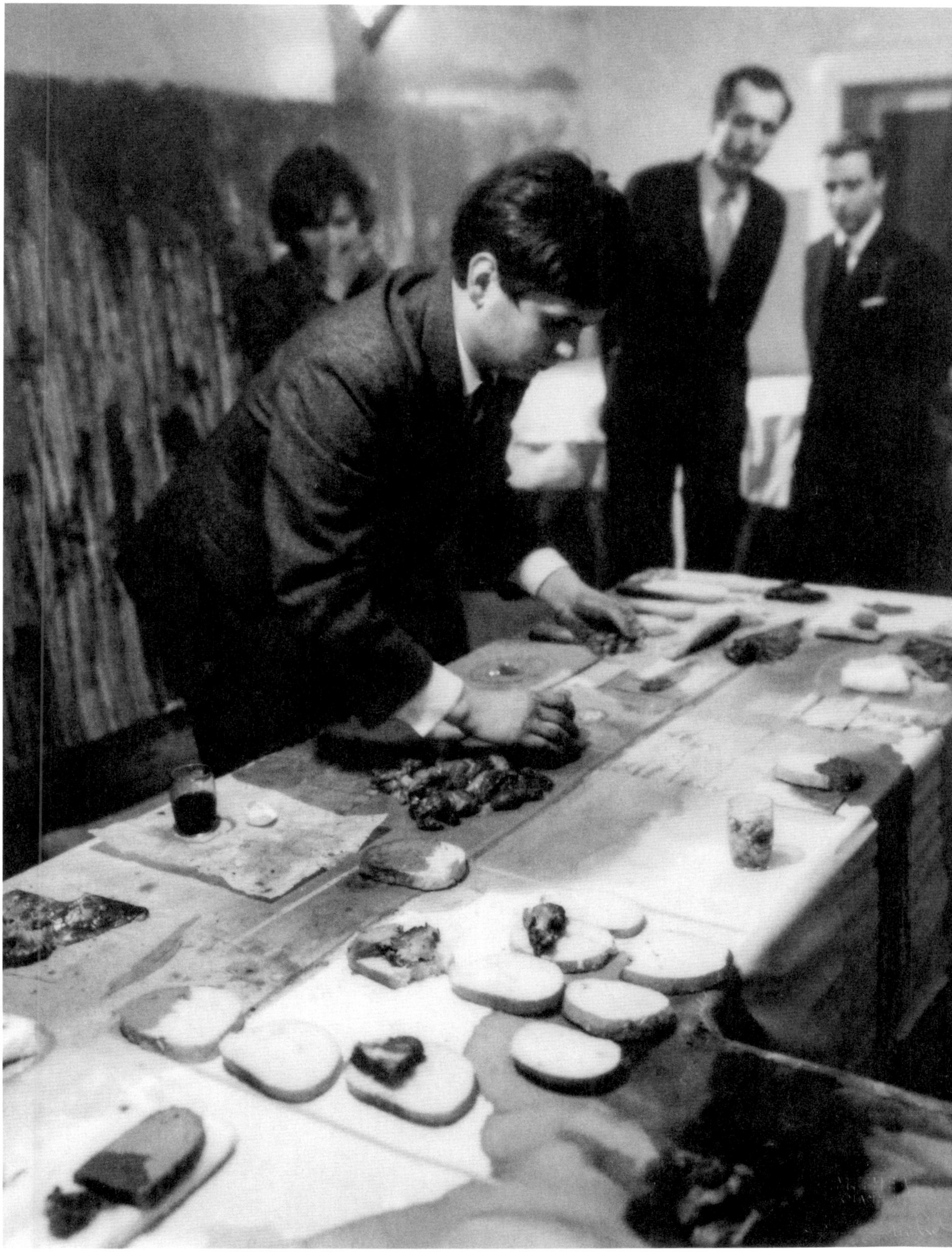

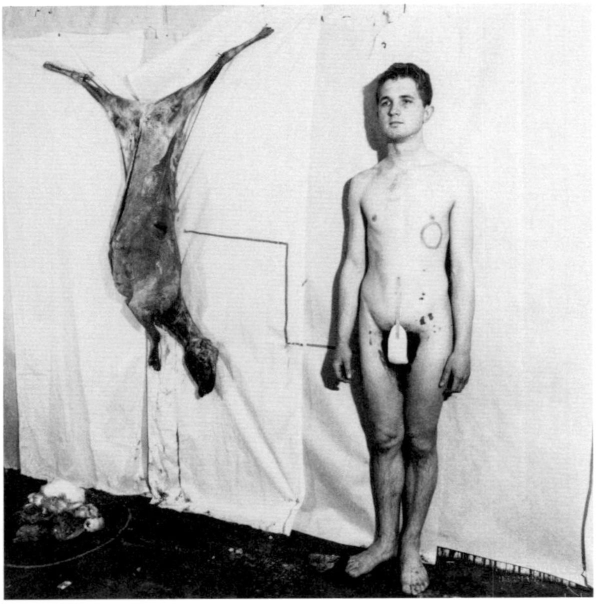

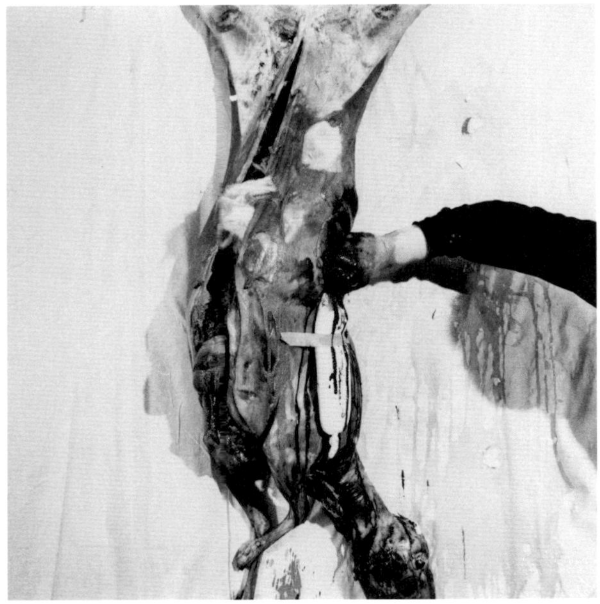

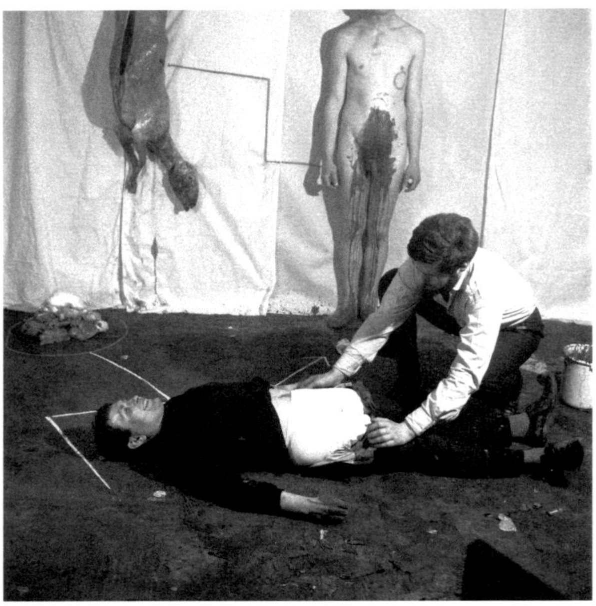

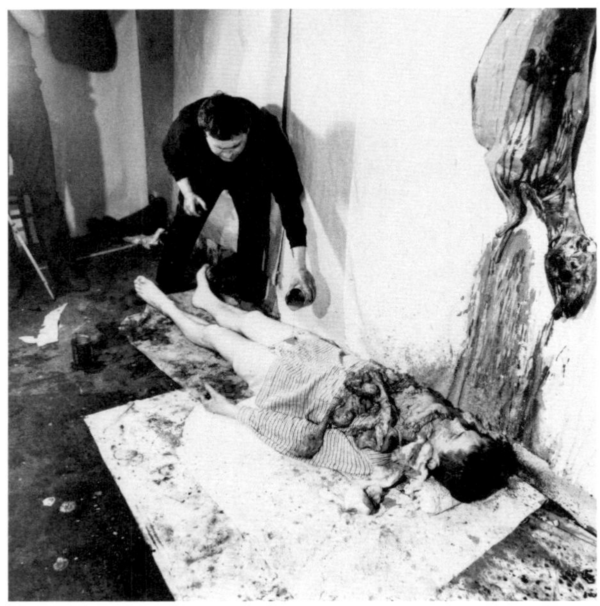

Fig. 21, 22, 23, 24, 25, 26, 27, 28
Hermann Nitsch
9th Action, 12 June 1965
Nitsch's studio, Brünner Straße 132, as well as in the fields and in a gravel pit in Stammersdorf, 1210 Vienna
B/W photographs
photo: Günter Brus, Ludwig Hoffenreich, Walter Kindler, Rudolf Schwarzkogler
with: Kari Bauer, Günter Brus, Heinz Cibulka, Otto Muehl, Reinhard Priessnitz, Rudolf Schwarzkogler

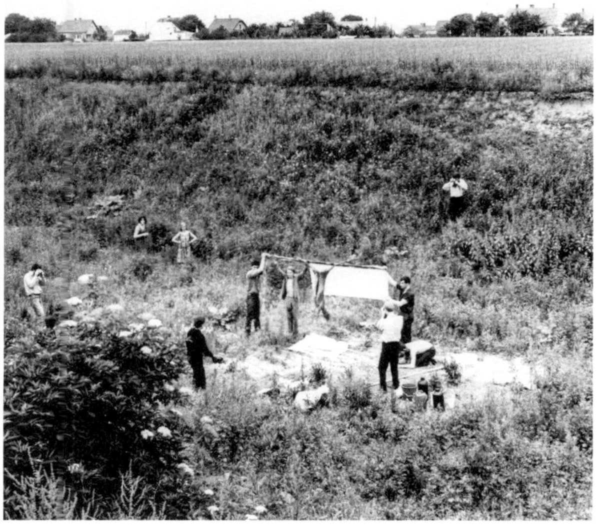

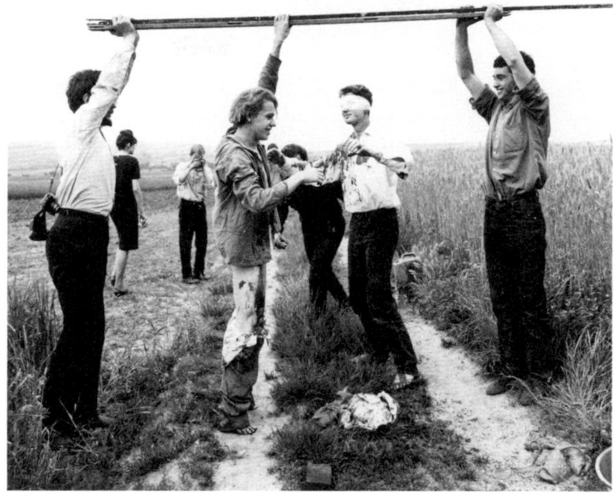

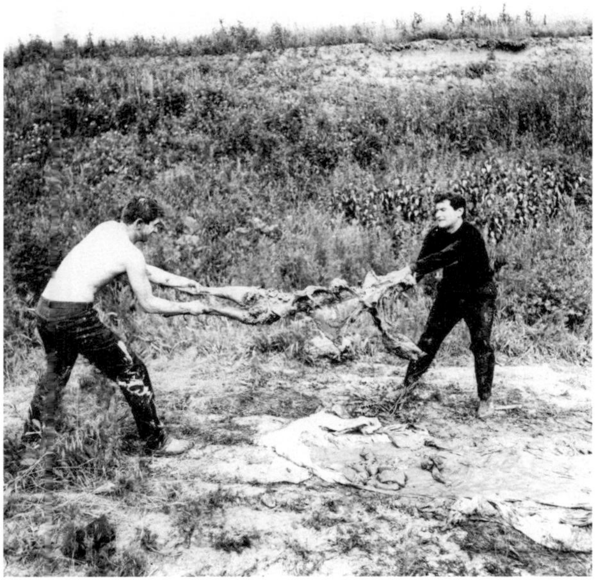

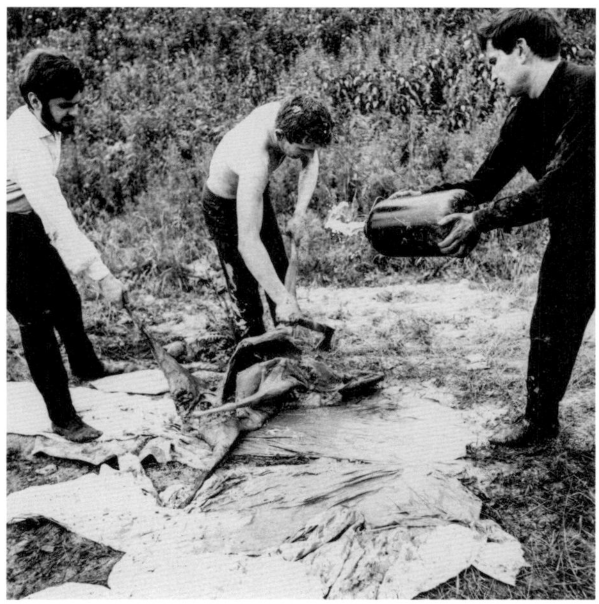

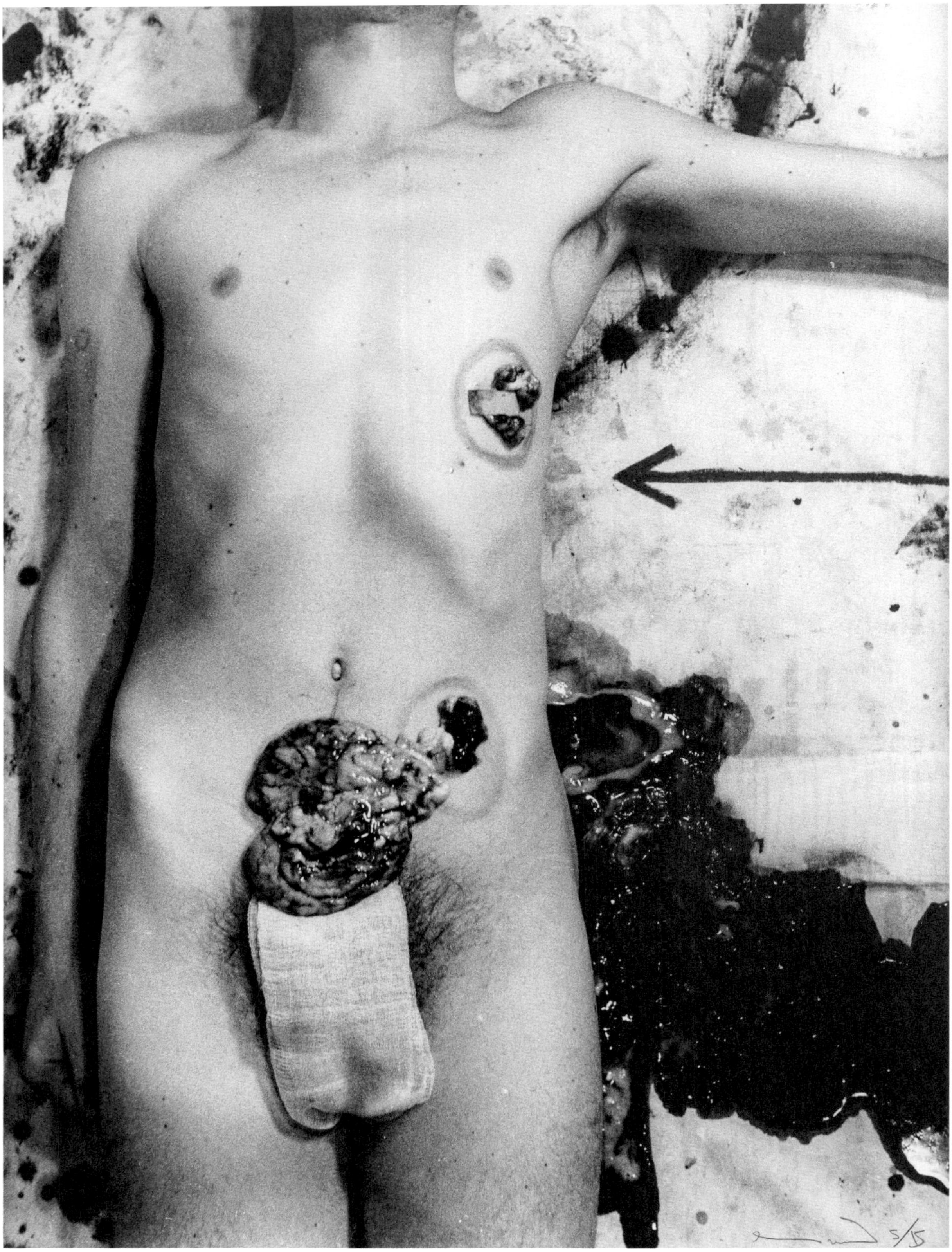

Fig. 29
Hermann Nitsch
12th Action, 6 September 1965
Heinz and Franziska Cibulka's apartment, Kaiserstraße 16, 1070 Vienna
B/W photograph
photo: Franziska Cibulka
with: Heinz Cibulka

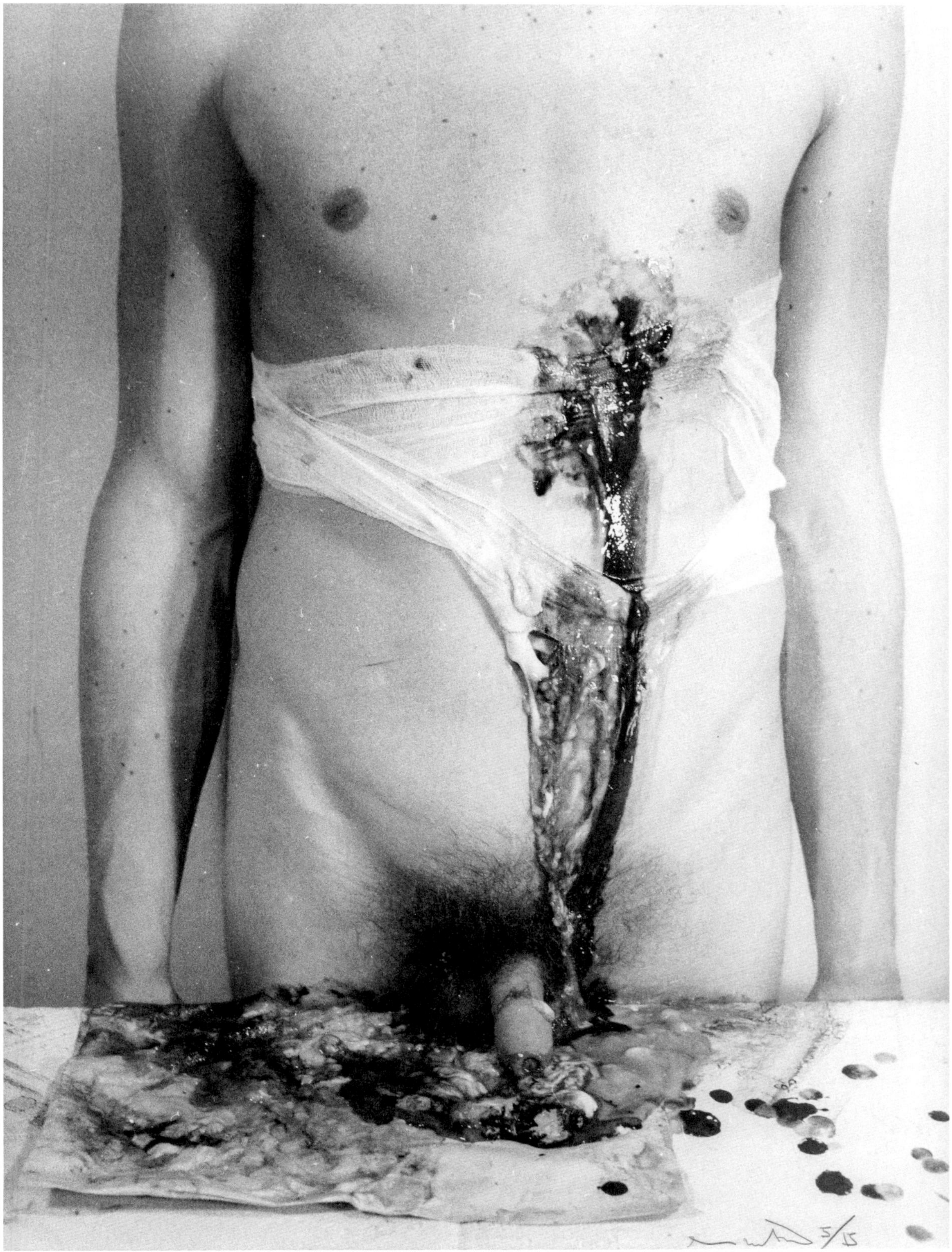

Fig. 30
Hermann Nitsch
14th Action, 29 September 1965
Heinz and Franziska Cibulka's apartment, Kaiserstraße 16, 1070 Vienna
B/W photograph
photo: Franziska Cibulka
with: Heinz Cibulka

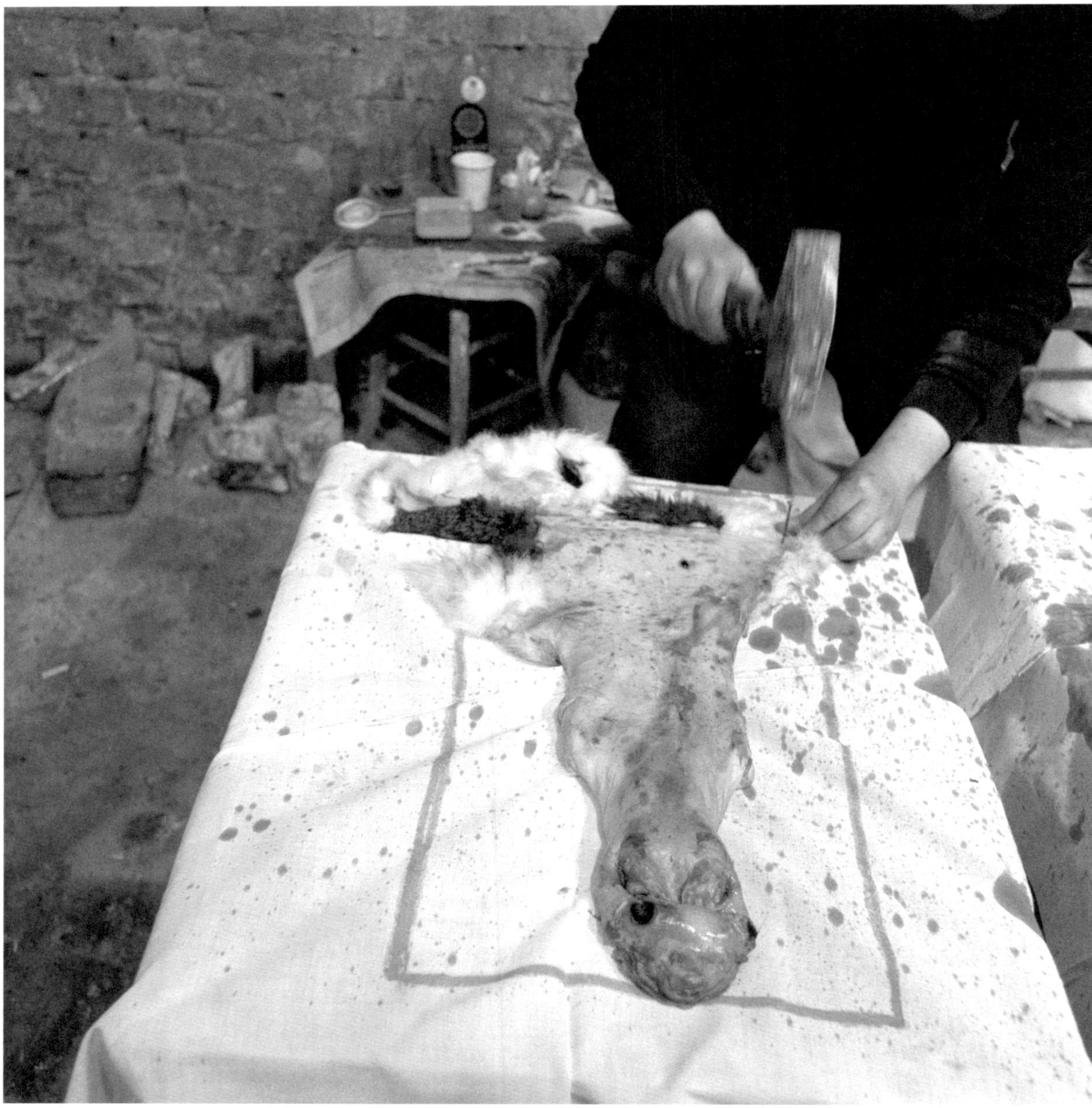

Fig. 31, 32
Hermann Nitsch
Action 20a, 2 September 1966 at the press conference for the *Destruction in Art Symposium*
Muehl's studio, Perinetgasse 1, 1200 Vienna
B/W photograph
photo: Ludwig Hoffenreich

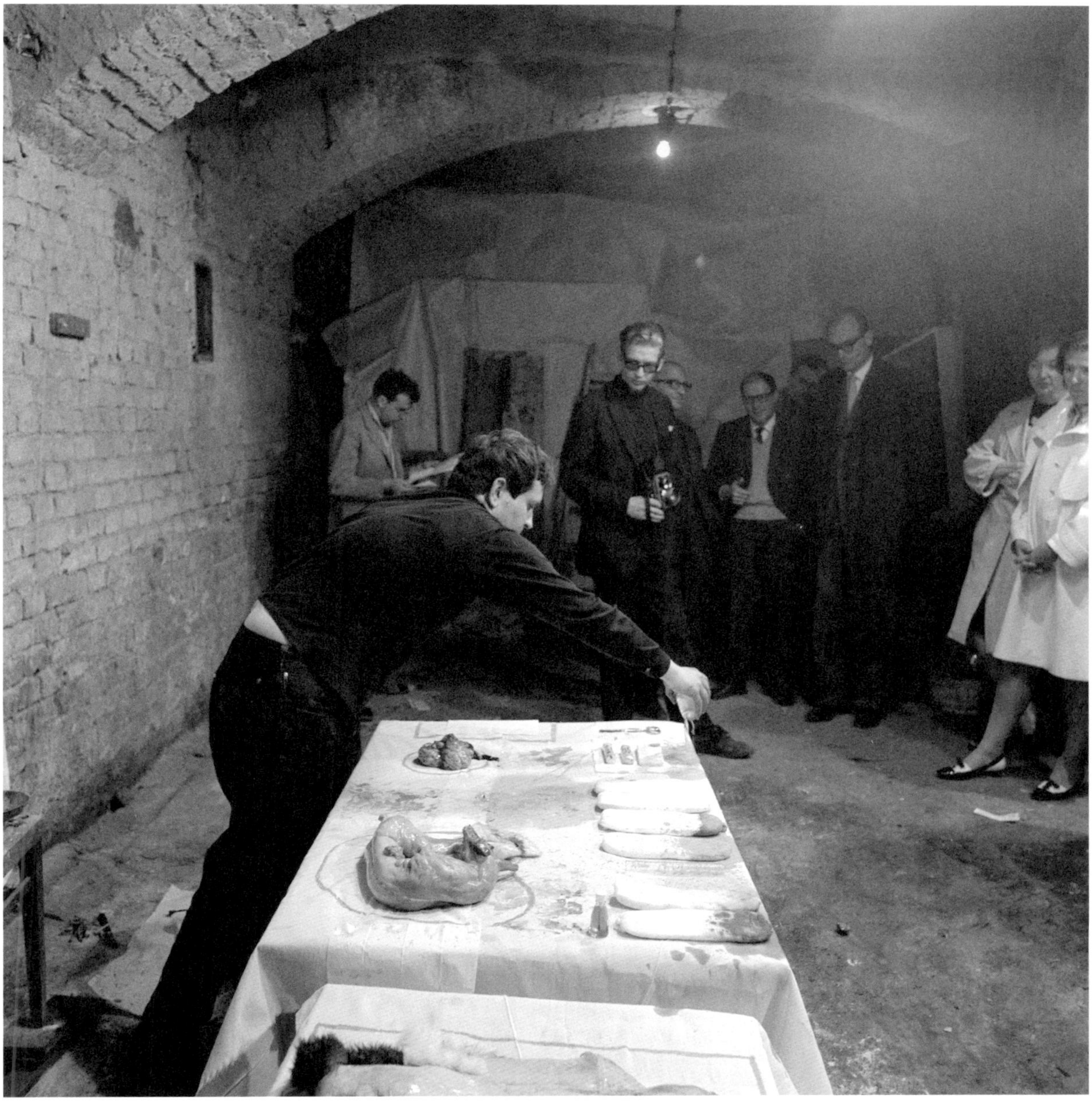

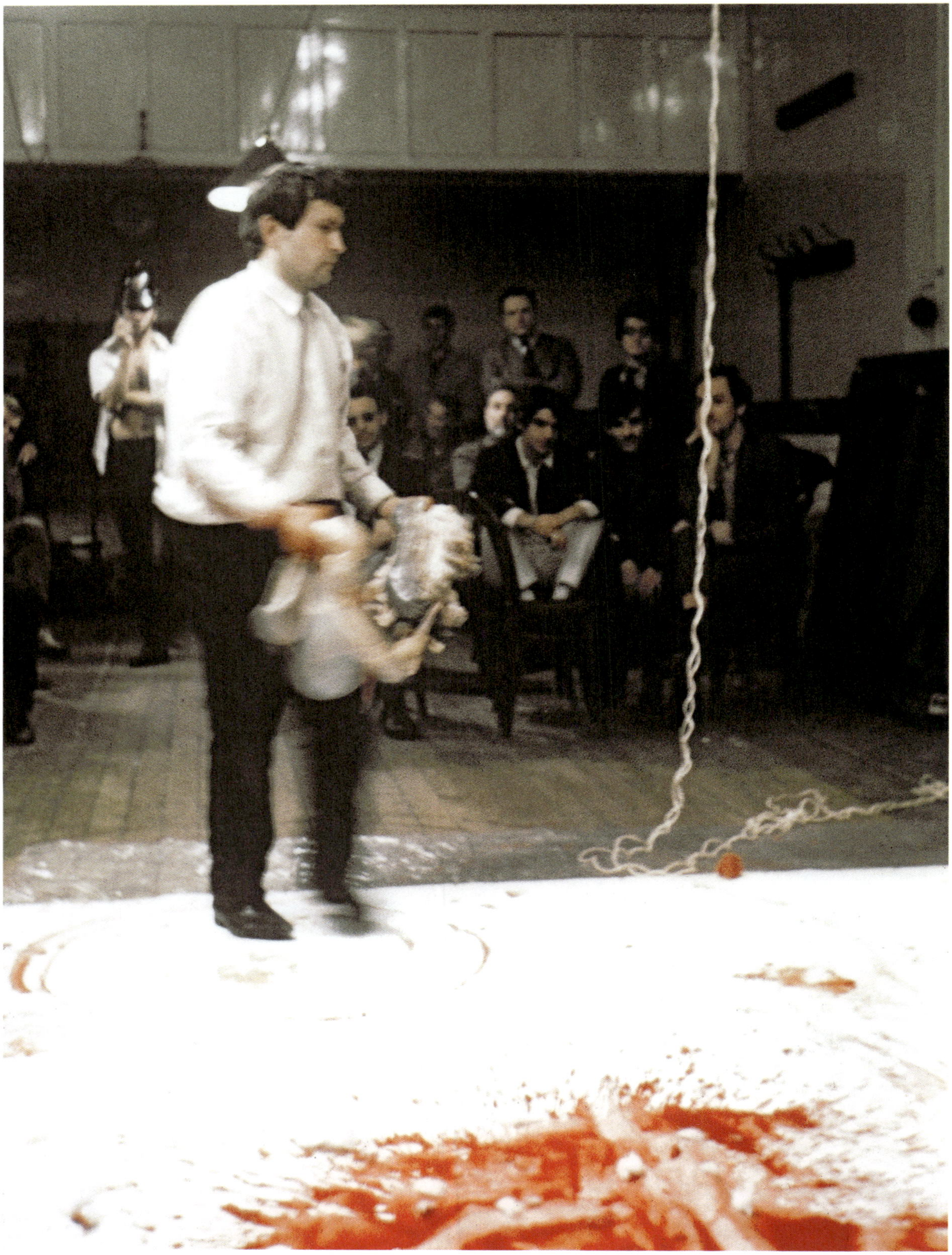

Fig. 33, 34
Hermann Nitsch
21st Action, 16 September 1966 at the *Destruction in Art Symposium*
St. Bride Institute, 14 Bride Lane, Fleet Street London EC4
Colour photographs
photo: Hanns Sohm
with: Günter Brus, Al Hansen, Kurt Kren, Otto Muehl, Robin Page, a ten-person shout choir and a sixteen-person orchestra (conducted by Peter Weibel)

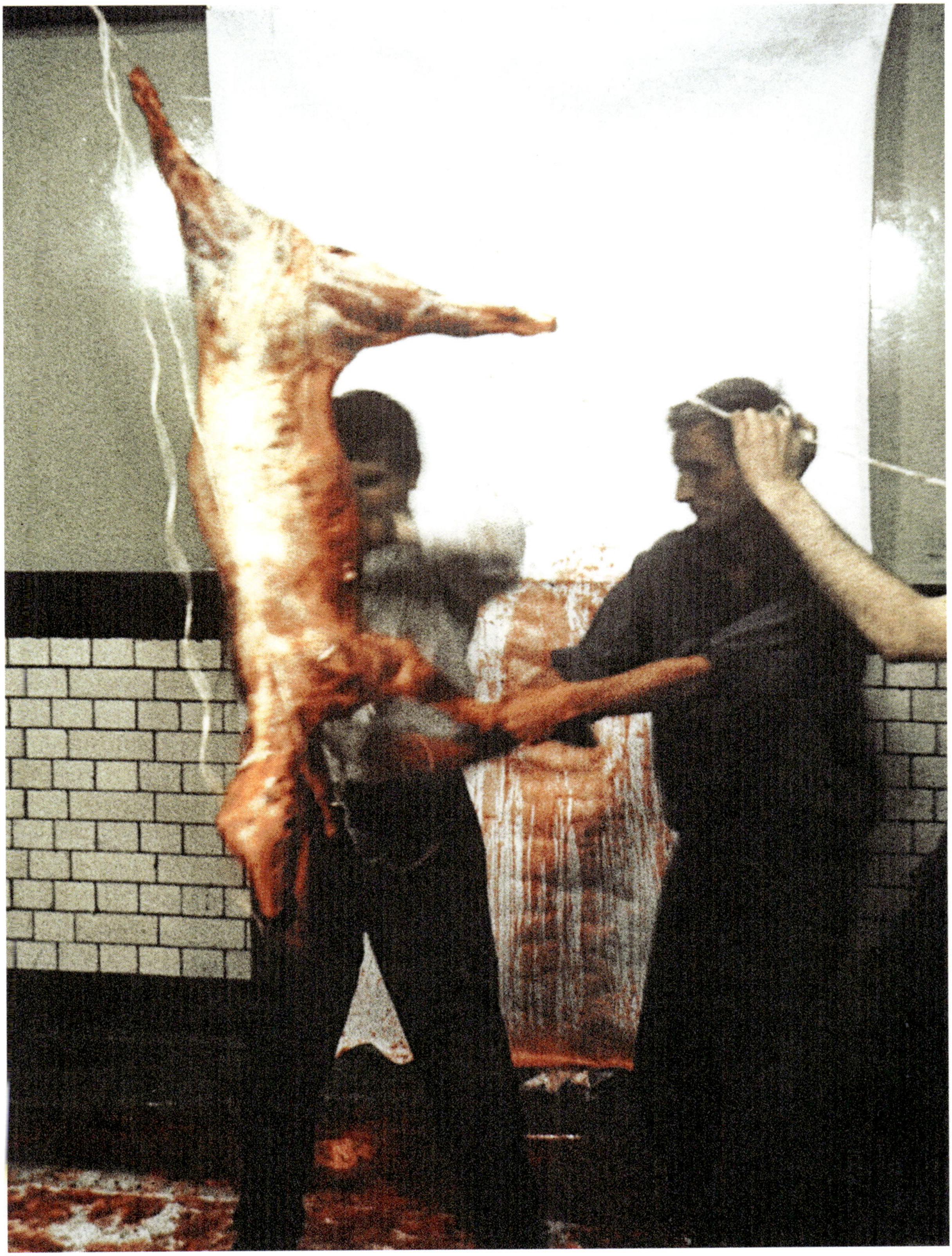

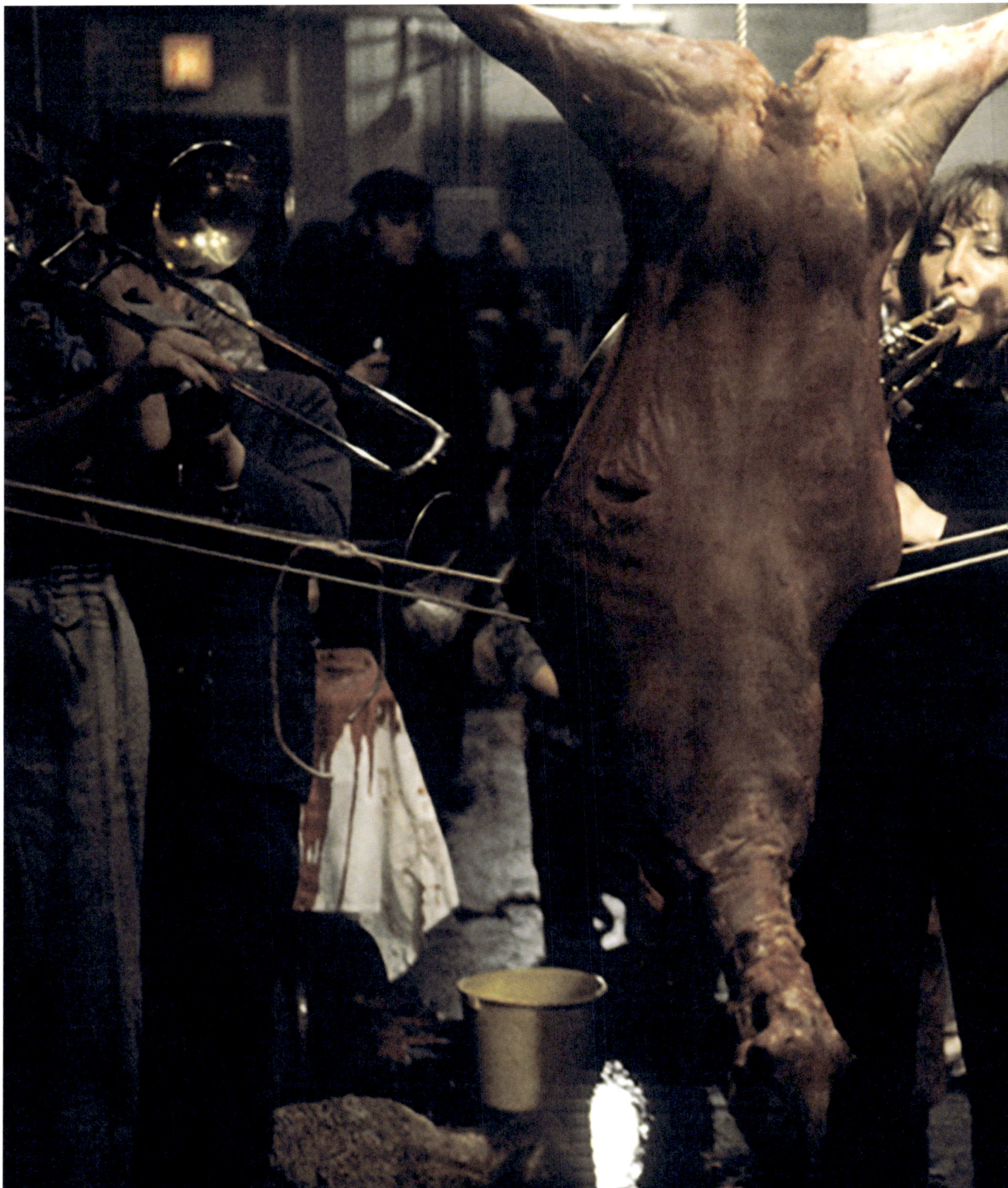

Fig. 35
Hermann Nitsch
25th Action, 2 March 1968
Film-Makers' Cinematheque, 80 Wooster Street, New York City
Colour photograph
photo: E. Dessentier
with: Al Hansen, Jon Hendricks, Ralph Ortiz, L. Perent, a ten-person shout choir and a twenty-person orchestra

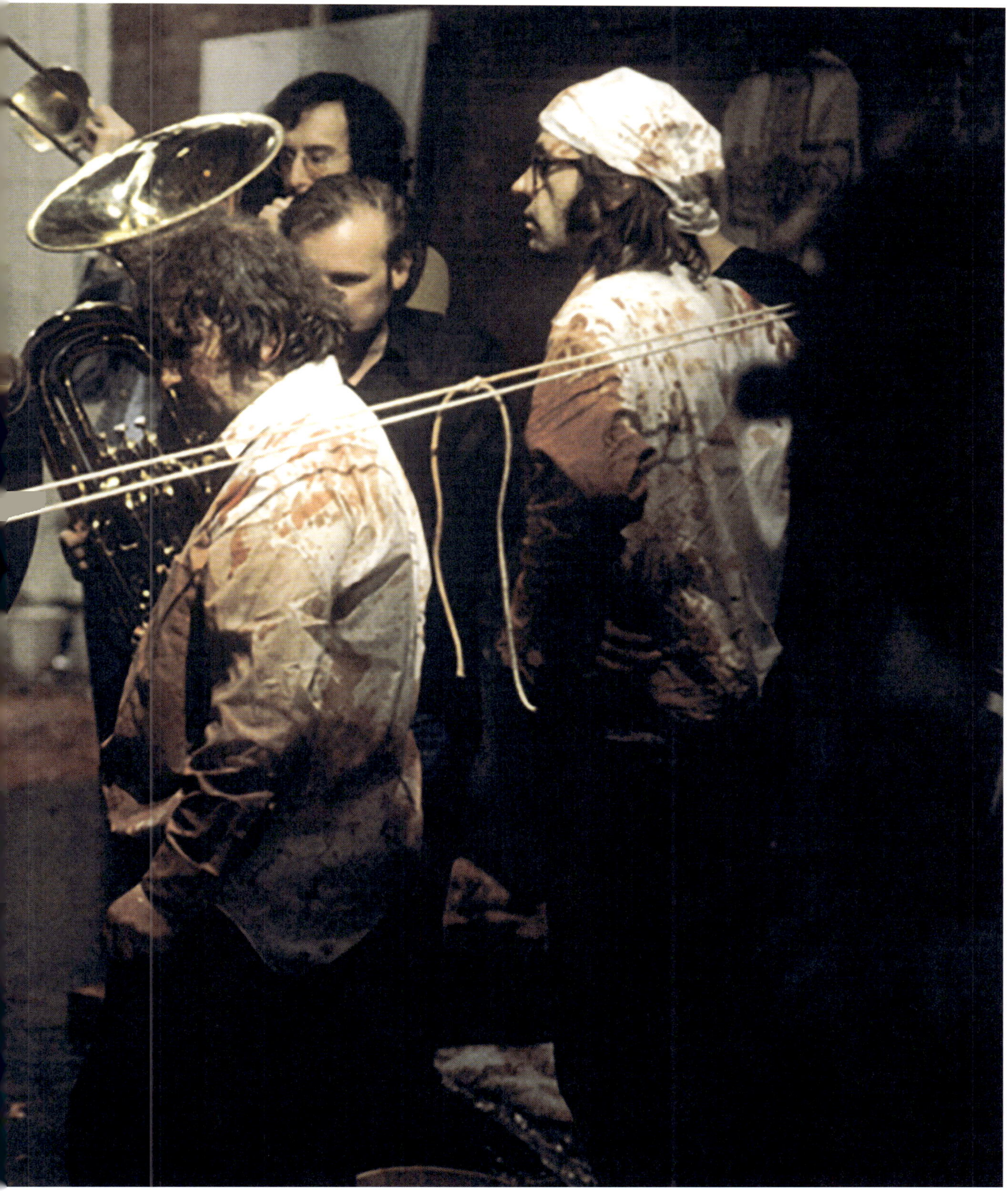

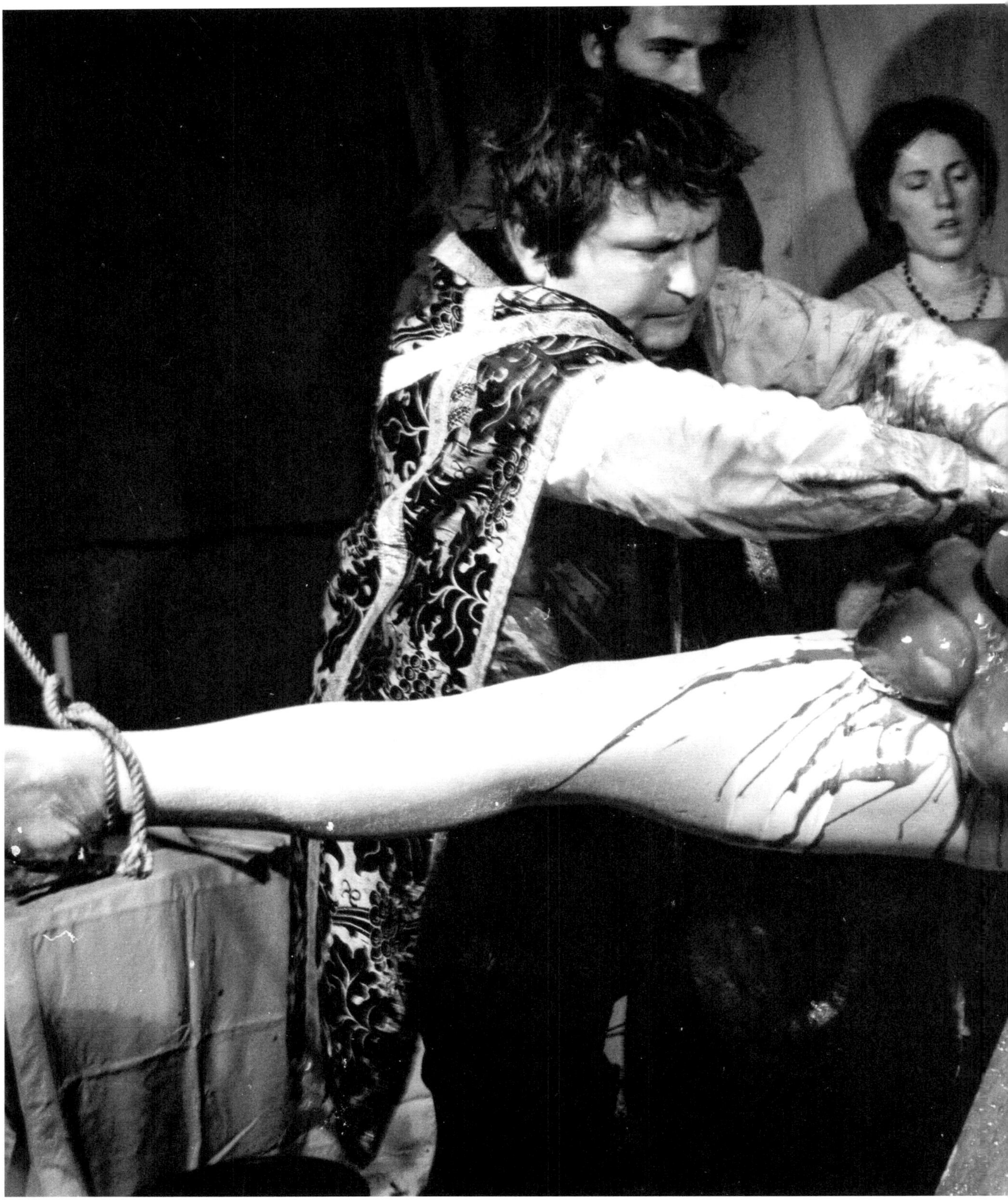

Fig. 36
Hermann Nitsch
31. Aktion, Maria Empfängnis (31st action, Immaculate Conception), 3 December 1969
Hans Peter Zimmer's studio, Munich
B/W photograph
with: Christian d'Orville, Peter Gorsen, Hanel Koeck, Peter Müller-Preuss

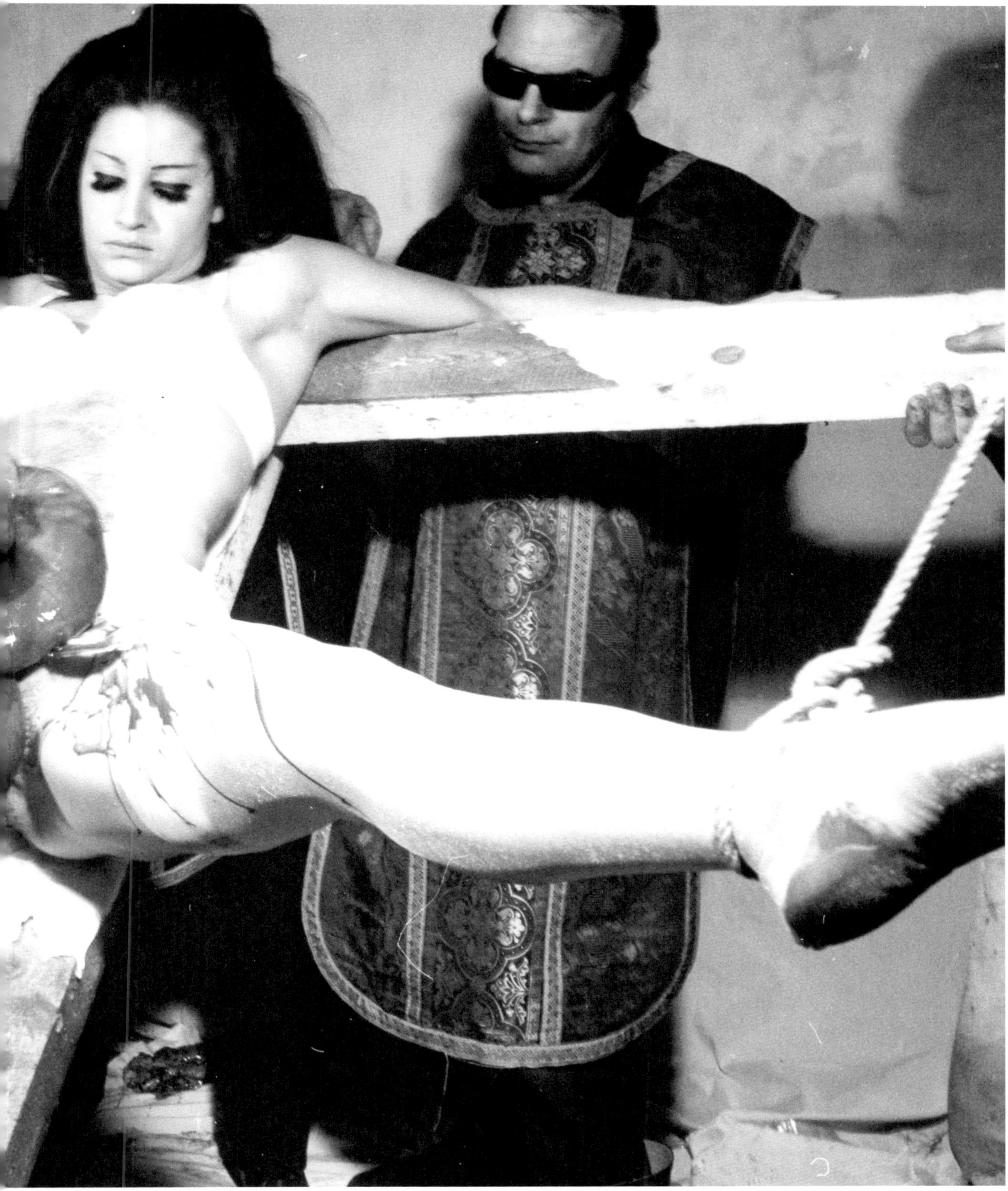

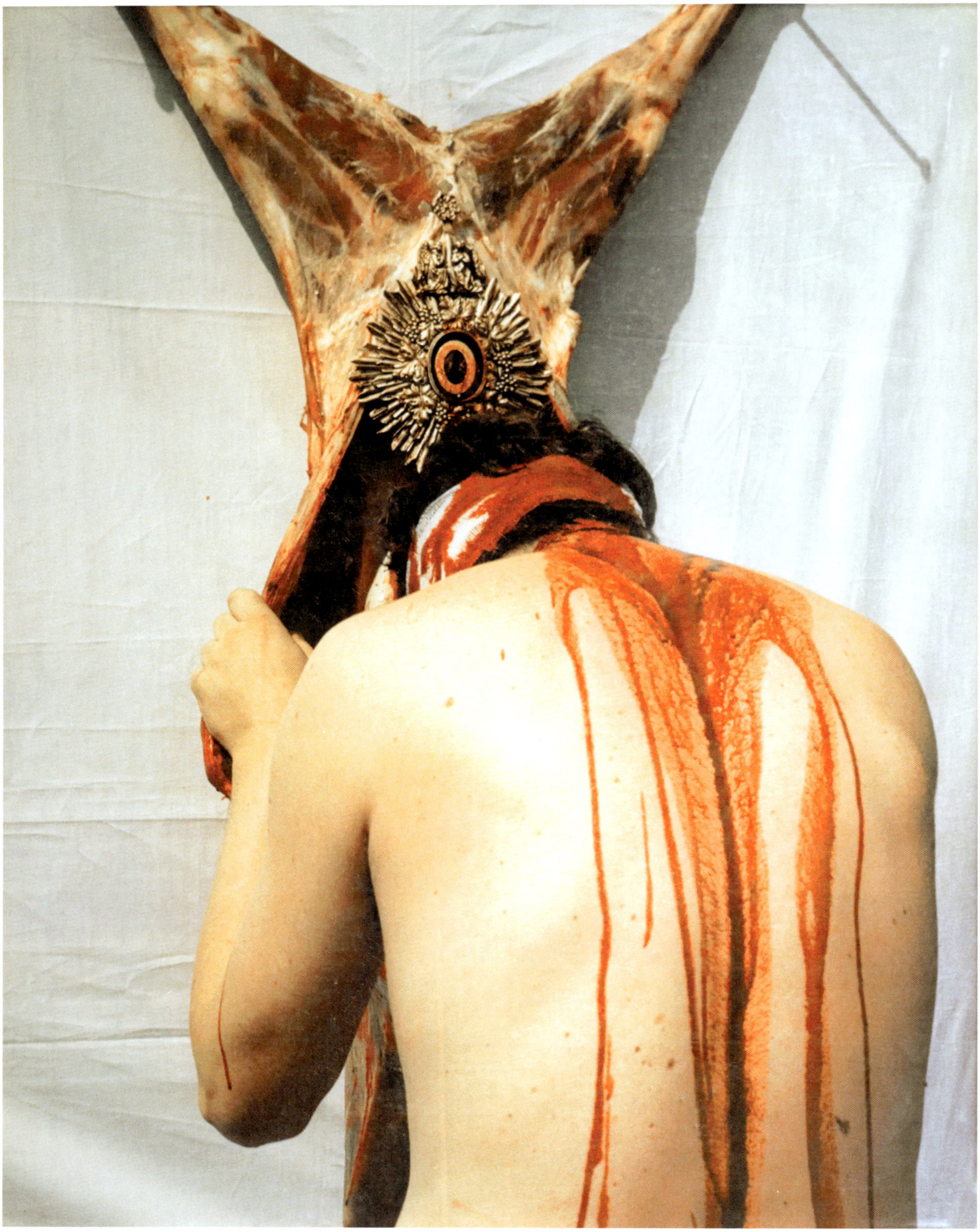

Fig. 37
Hermann Nitsch
50. Aktion, 24-Stunden-Spiel (50th Action, 24-Hour-Play), 26 July to 27 July 1975
Prinzendorf Castle
Colour photograph
photo: Beate Nitsch

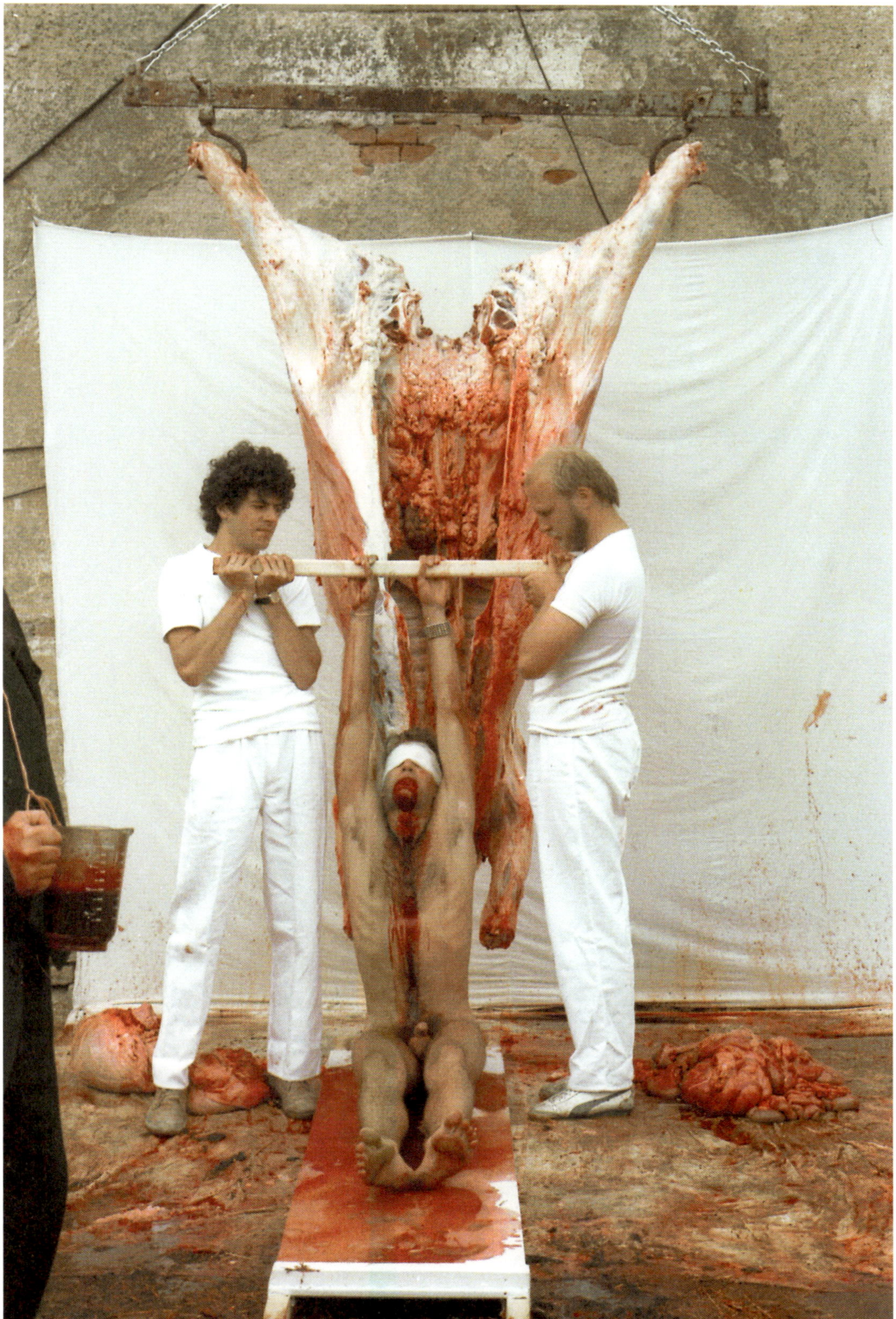

Fig. 38
Hermann Nitsch
50. Aktion, 3-Tage-Spiel (80th Action, Three-Day-Play), 27 July to 30 July 1984
Prinzendorf Castle
Colour photograph
photo: Heinz Cibulka

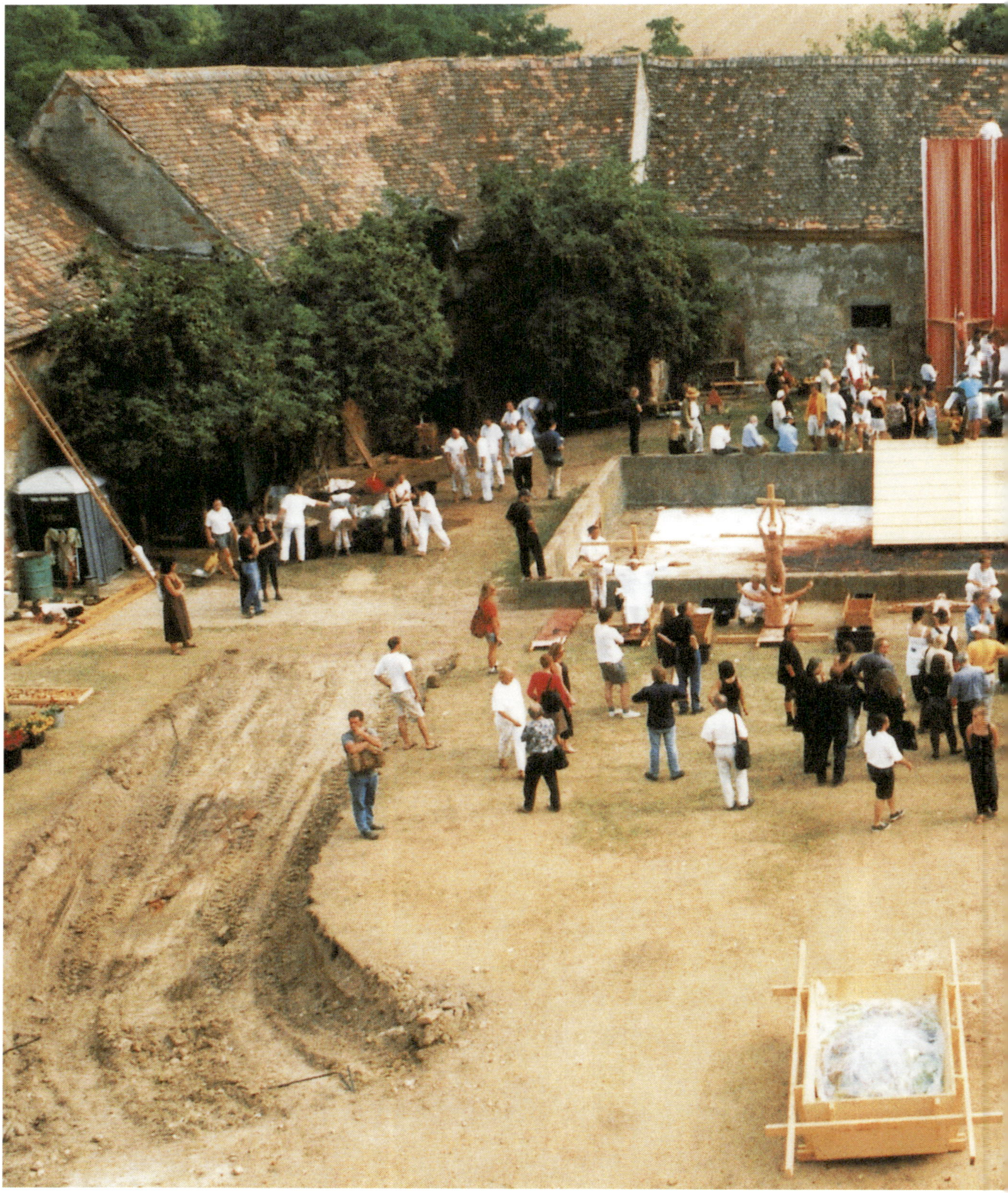

Fig. 39
Hermann Nitsch
100. Aktion, Sechs-Tage-Spiel (100th Action, Six-Day-Play), 3 August to 9 August 1998
Prinzendorf Castle
Colour photograph
photo: Heinz Cibulka

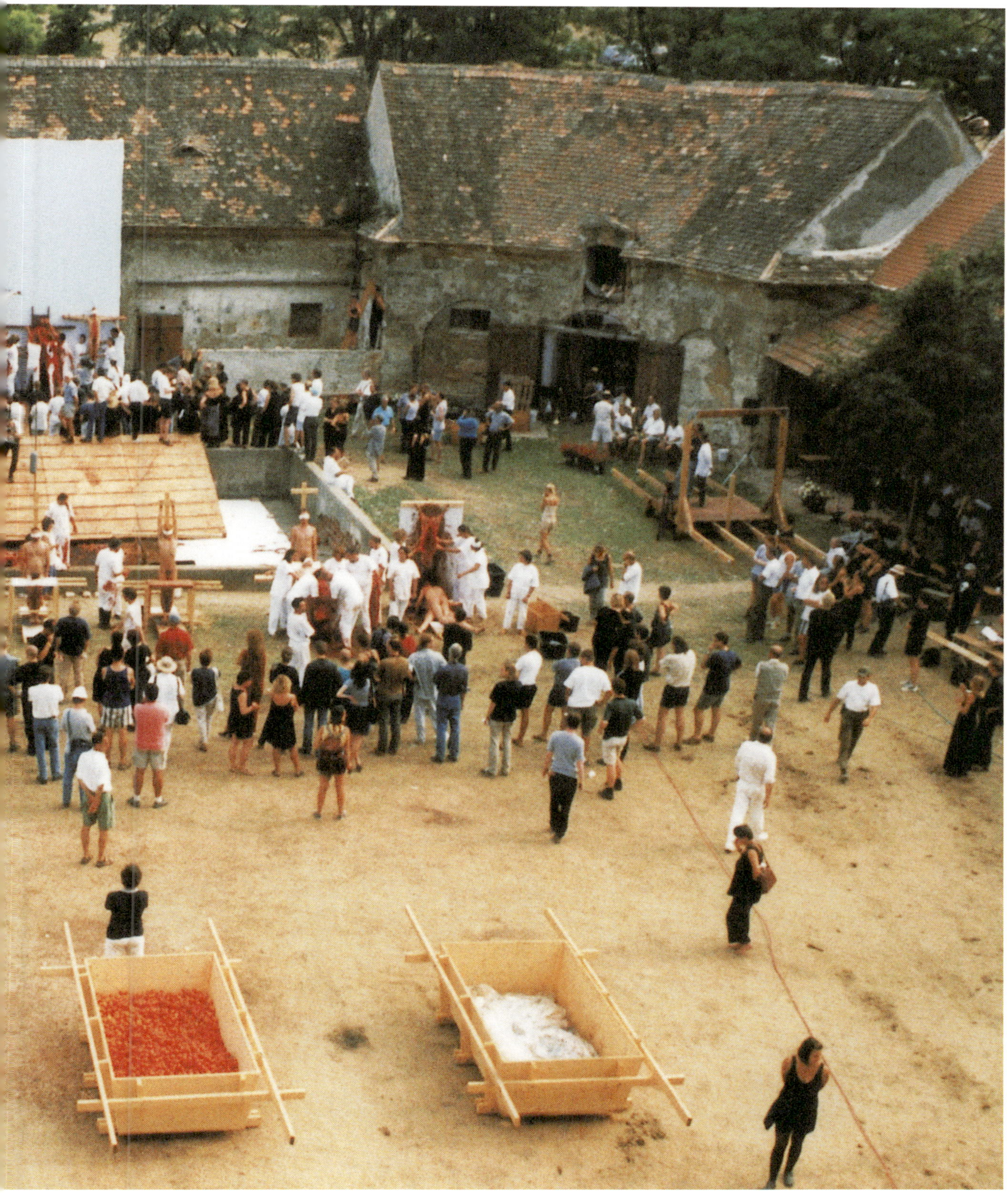

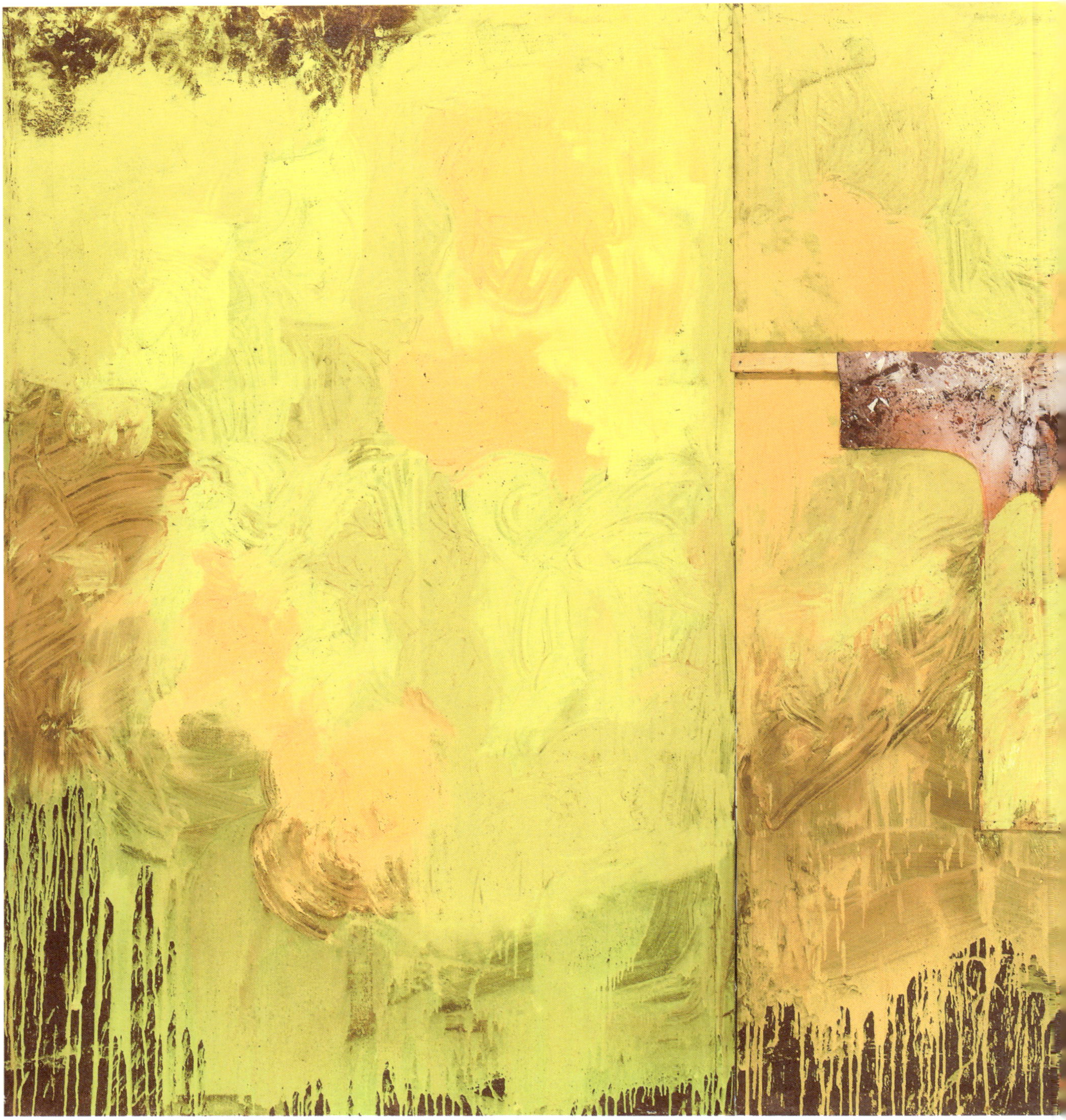

Fig. 40
Hermann Nitsch
Untitled *(Auferstehungstriptychon 1)* [Resurrection Triptych 1], 2003
Acrylic and fabric on burlap
300 x 600 cm
Collection Rita Nitsch

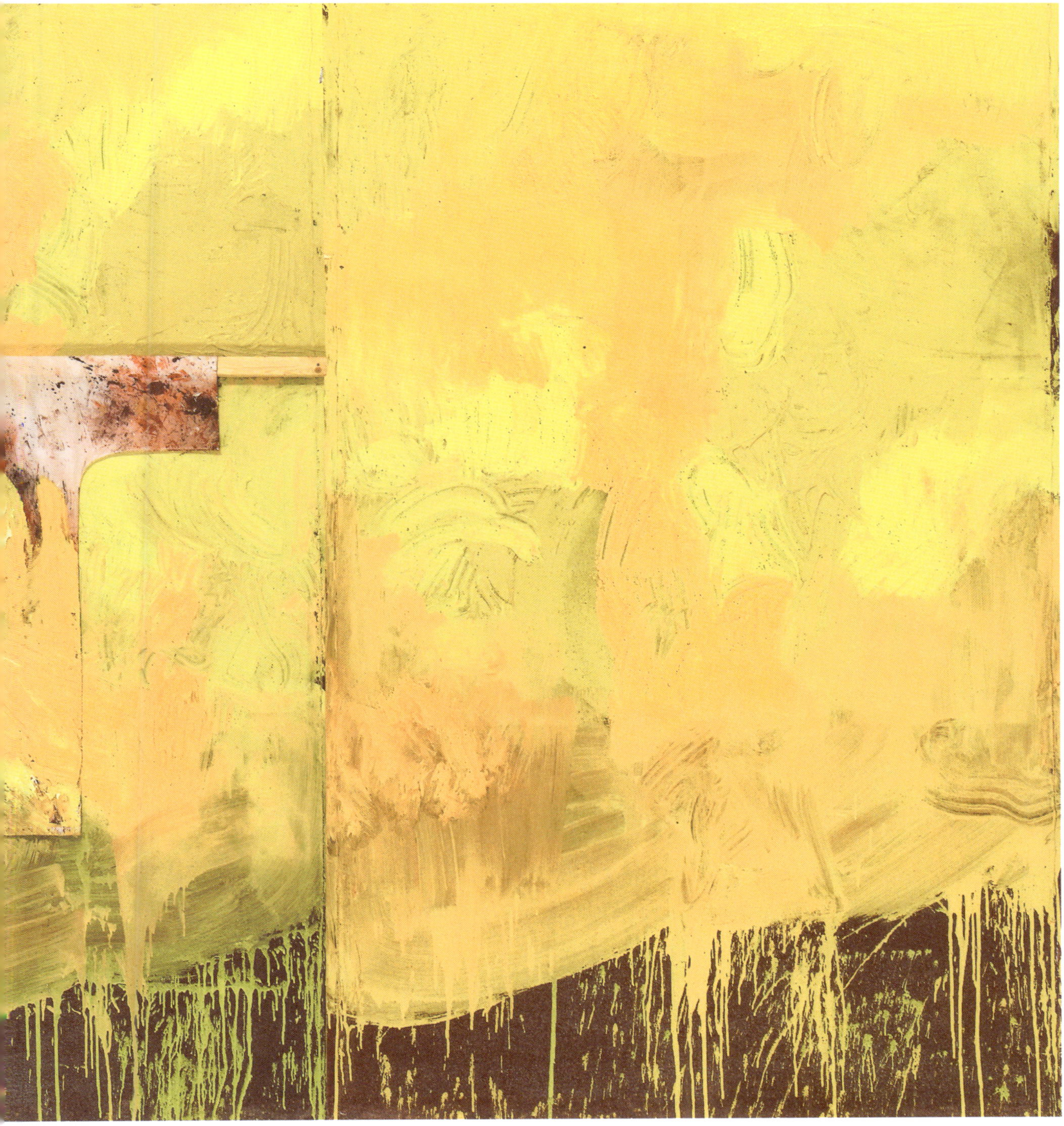

3 Günter Brus, "Extracts from the Viennese Diaries, Autumn 1960", as quoted in: Dieter Schwarz, "Chronology", in: Museum Fridericianum, Kassel, Kunstmuseum Winterthur und Scottish National Gallery of Modern Art, Edinburgh (ed.), *From Action Painting to Actionism*, Vienna 1960-1965, Klagenfurt (Ritter Verlag), 1988, p. 126/127. Translation: Lisa Moravec.

4 Ayrenhoffgasse 10, 1090 Vienna.

Günter Brus

Brus' artistic work began in the medium of drawing and here even his earliest–mainly trees and landscapes (Fig. 41)–are characterised by a particularly body-motoric ductus, which already foreshadows that his own body would subsequently become the central medium of his work and experience.

At the beginning of 1960, Brus went on a trip to Mallorca with his close friend Alfons Schilling, where they met the American artist Joan Merrit, who introduced them to the painting of the New York School and Abstract Expressionism. The two were enthusiastic about the powerful energy and radicalism of this process-based way of working and began, upon their return to Austria, to paint in a strongly gestural style of Informal Art. Brus involved his entire body in a working process, whose aim it was to overcome established principles of form and composition. "The most complete departure from the central point in the picture"[3], was his explicitly stated aim. At the end of 1960, he covered the walls of the small chamber, in which he lived and worked at the time[4], with wrapping paper and extended the act of painting to an entire room for the first time.

Still in 1960, Brus was called up for military service, which he had to do for over a year. After this, he entered a serious personal crisis and thought about giving up his artistic work. In 1962, however, he resumed and consistently pursued his aim of overcoming entrenched compositional patterns. In this context, he tried, amongst other things, to paint with his hands and legs tied together. With the same intention, he realised a very special, expansive form of Action Painting in 1963, in the basement of psychoanalyst Josef Dvorak's gallery, which he called *Malerei in einem labyrinthischen Raum* (Painting in a Labyrinthine Space): While he attached the molino fabric to be painted on to the walls, Brus braced the entire room with strings onto which he hung floor-length strips of wrapping paper. (Fig. 48) In this way, he created a labyrinth that disabled him to fully see the painting surfaces, hanging on the wall, when moving within the room. The intention was to irritate him in his gestural action painting and prevent a relapse into classical principles of composition and harmony. (Fig. 49) With the strong inclusion of space in this setting, he took a first step towards exiting panel painting, which he would complete with his first action in the following year.

Selbstbemalungen (Self-Paintings)

For his first action, Brus left the canvas aside and instead made an entire room–including all the objects in it, as well as his own body and that of his wife–his painting surfaces. (Fig. 50-57) This action, which he titled *Ana*, the Croatian name of his wife, took place in Muehl's apartment in November 1964.

While the latter was still strongly determined by highly painterly sequences, the artist developed a completely different concept for an action in December 1964, which was exclusively aimed at the photographic documentation of body-object constellations. With this he became the first artist of Vienna Actionism to turn to the action type of Staged Photography (see p. 237-238 in this book). Under the title *Selbstbemalung 1 (Handbemalung–Kopfbemalung–Kopfzumalung)* (Self-Painting 1 [Hand Painting–Head Painting–Total Head Painting]), Fig. 60-68), he successively staged highly pictorial still-life-like tableaux, each of which was photographed. In these, first his hand and then his head and upper body were painted in white and black and set in relation to various threatening objects such as razor blades, nails, scissors, and a saw. In *Selbstbemalung 2* (Self-Painting 2, Spring 1965, Fig. 69, 70), the arrangements that had previously been confined to the surface were expanded into space. In these early tableau-photographs, Brus created symbols for the deep-seated human fears of pain, violence, and injury. As his work progressed, this theme would become increasingly important, culminating in the artist's actual self-harm as part of his actions at the end of the 1960s.

In 1965 Brus was invited to present a solo exhibition at the Junge Generation gallery in Vienna. As an introduction to it, he realised his first public action, the *Wiener Spaziergang* (Vienna Walk, Fig. 73) on 5 July, the day before the vernissage, in which he moved through Vienna's city centre as a living painting. His suit-clad body was completely covered in white and an irregular black line, characterised by edges and small cross-strokes, ran like a cut or a seam across its front and back, dividing it into two halves. This can be read as an injury as well as an expression of a divided consciousness. Brus could not realise his original plan to walk from Heldenplatz to St. Stephen's Cathedral as he was stopped by the police and later sentenced to a fine for "causing public nuisance". The next day, at the opening of his exhibition of paintings and action photographs in the Galerie Junge Generation, the action *Malerei – Selbstbemalung – Selbstverstümmelung* (Painting–Self-Painting–Self-Mutilation) took place in front of an audience. (Fig. 74) Again surrounded by frightening objects, such as bricklayer's clamps, Brus once more performed a Self-Painting, drawing a vertical black line across his entire body. He then opened balloons, filled with white paint, hanging from his body, smeared the oozing substance, and then rolled on the floor until he finally crawled out of the gallery space.

5
In: Commentary on the action *Transfusion*, Graz, 1999, supplement to a portfolio of photographs of the action *Transfusion* (Galerie Heike Curtze, Wien 1999), Brus describes the process of birth as the central content.

In the fall of 1965, Brus realised *Transfusion* (Fig. 77–81), an action that, both in terms of form and content, is in many respects reminiscent of Egon Schiele. The latter's works, like those of the other important painters of early Austrian Modernism, were an essential reference point for him. These artists had already dealt with the human body, its functions, and its vulnerability without considering any social taboos and therefore, like the Vienna Actionists, had come into conflict with society and its authorities. Thematically, the focus of *Transfusion* was on the diverse forms of relationships between men and women.[5] Brus' wife Anna, who again served as a model, wore a blue high-heeled shoe and a pearl necklace. Various cables, scissors, nails, and metal objects were positioned on and around her naked body on a table. In the course of the action, her body was covered with a bright powder, which veiled this work in a splendour of colour, otherwise unusual for Brus. At the same time, this strongly contrasted his own white-painted body which repeatedly reconnected with the female in different poses.

From 1964 on, numerous small-scale drawings were created both before and alongside the actions, in which Brus sketched actionist scenarios. Some of these are preparatory works or subsequent visual reflections of concrete actions. (Fig. 58, 59, 75) However, many of these were never realised and could not have been realised as the artist imaginatively took the depiction of injuries and the human capacity for cruelty to extremes, without considering their feasibility. The bodies depicted here are brutalised, tortured, and mutilated in the most horrific ways through the use of various tools. (Fig. 76)

Body-Analytical Actions, Collaborations with Muehl

In 1966, a phase of multiple collaborations with Muehl began, which lasted until the event *Kunst und Revolution* (Art and Revolution) in June 1968. At its beginning, there were two so-called Total Actions in which the artists, with the inclusion of a female model, still operated in a very painterly manner. At the same time, however, they were, already concerned with the body and its functions, so that these actions were also subject to the body-analytical type that they both had initiated earlier and which was to play a central role in their work in the second half of the 1960s. In the *1. Totalaktion, Ornament ist ein Verbrechen* (1st Total Action, Ornament is a Crime, 1966, Fig. 156), the two artists appeared only in underwear and Muehl also wore a bra for the first time. In this way, female bodily experiences were addressed, something that had previously already been done in actions such as Muehl's

Nabelschnur – Darstellung einer Geburt (Umbilical Cord–Portrayal of a Birth) (1964, Fig. 143), or *Cosinus Alpha* (1964, Fig. 149) in which lesbian love was thematised, or Brus' *Transfusion* (1965, Fig. 77-81) and continued to be pursued by both. In the *1. Totalaktion*, the artists also dealt with the physical potential of sound production in the spectrum of speaking, screaming, shouting, stammering, wheezing, and thus also addressed the possibilities of communication through sounds and language, while otherwise Vienna Actionism was wordless and acted out purely through body language.

In 1966, Brus travelled with Muehl, Nitsch, Peter Weibel, and the filmmaker Kurt Kren to London for the *Destruction in Art Symposium*. The actions he carried out there again corresponded to the body-analytical type; the painterly element no longer played a role, but instead issues of body-motorics as well as language deconstruction. In his action, *Head Destruction*, (Fig. 161, 162), Brus started reading a text, then began to stutter, and subsequently to chew and swallow the paper until he finally hit his head several times on a sack filled with paper that was lying on the table, and then fell backwards to the ground. In the action, *Breath Exercises*, (Fig. 164), carried out with Muehl, the two performed action music using breathing, screaming, panting, and moaning.

In the time before the birth of his daughter on 29 March 1967, Brus was particularly concerned with the delivery process, a physical experience that is not possible for men. This resulted in the filmic action trilogy *Pullover, Osmose, Einatmen und Ausatmen* (Pullover, Osmosis, Breathing In and Breathing Out). (Fig. 261-264) Its sequences, each shot from a static position, initially show the naked upper body of Brus' heavily pregnant wife Anna, who is knitting–supposedly the clichéd idea of the occupation of a woman expecting a child. Brus then fakes a birth by having a balloon (apparently) emerging from his buttocks inflated by Anna off-camera. The final shot focuses on the artist's upper body breathing in and out–which is probably a reference to every human being's first and last breath.

In September of the same year, Brus carried out *Aktion mit Diana* (Action with Diana) (Fig. 84-86) into which he integrated his six-month-old daughter in a very sensitive way. In tableau-style, he arranged his body, once again painted completely white and thus neutralised, for the camera together with that of the baby, which lay protected on a pillow, surrounded by various objects, including aggressive ones, but also children's toys.

Afterwards, Brus irrevocably turned away from the painterly elements and material symbolism of his early actions and focused on

6
Günter Brus, invitation to the action *Der Staatsbürger Günter Brus betrachtet seinen Körper* (Citizen Günter Brus Observes His Body), Vienna 1968.

an analytical examination of the body per se, aimed at a liberation from prevailing social control mechanisms and taboos. This must be seen against the background of the extremely conservative climate in post-war Austria and ultimately led to the scandals that Brus' work caused in the late 1960s.

On 6 February 1968, the artist realised his action *"Der helle Wahnsinn" für Aachen: "Die Architektur des hellen Wahnsinns"* ("Sheer Madness" for Aachen: "The Architecture of Sheer Madness") in Aachen in which he—now in everyday clothes—publicly urinated, defecated, and finally cut his upper body with a razor blade through his shirt, causing his blood to flow. (Fig. 92-96) While the theme of injury was only symbolically hinted at in his early Self-Painting and Self-Mutilation Actions, it was now actually carried out.

Body Analysis as a Form of Politicisation

The explosive power of Brus' taboo-free Body-Analytical Actions and the inevitably associated conflict with the norms and morals of society led to an increasing willingness of the artist to confront this very society and in this sense also politicised his work. In May 1968—at the height of the student revolts in many countries—he realised his action, *Der Staatsbürger Günter Brus betrachtet seinen Körper* (Citizen Günter Brus Observes His Body), which was announced by a poster. In a text published on this subject, Brus wrote:

> "Art with exactly formulated goals arouses my suspicions: 'Manifestos'.
> But I certainly know how to describe what gets on my nerves:
> The Austrian with his Metternich in his trousers.
> The Austrian as a childish village idiot.
> The Austrian as a liberal patron not only of old but also of modern, even recent art (Protokolle 68).
> Art Nouveau fooling around.
> The Austrian as a religious nut.
> The Austrian who supports the mentally ill with state prizes and eradicates level-headed perversion."[6]

Shortly afterwards, on 7 June, at the invitation of the Sozialistischer Österreichischer Studentenverband (SÖS) (Socialist Austrian Student Union), the legendary *Kunst und Revolution* event took place in Lecture Hall 1 at the University of Vienna. It became the most pronounced political statement of Vienna Actionism. (Fig. 97, 98, 179, 180) In addition to Brus and Muehl, Oswald Wiener, Weibel, Franz Kaltenbäck, and others took part with radical actions that led to criminal prosecutions. The political situation (not only) in Austria was harshly attacked by the artists. Brus' contribution to this evening consisted of particularly uncompromising Body-Analytical Actions, which he combined with an explicitly political statement: he undressed, cut his chest and thigh with a razor blade, urinated into his hand, drank his urine, and vomited. He then struck up the national anthem, defecated, smeared feces on his body, vomited again, laid down on the lecture hall desk, and masturbated.

Due to the reporting of a tabloid journalist, a wave of protest broke out after this action, which resulted in Brus being imprisoned and ultimately sentenced to six months of aggravated arrest for degrading state symbols. After the appeal against this verdict was rejected on 25 February 1968, he fled to Berlin with his family.

While still in Vienna he had prepared two pamphlets, *Patent urinoir* (Fig. 104) and *Patent merde* (Fig. 99-103), in which he dealt with the events surrounding and following the event of *Kunst und Revolution* and published the corresponding documents. Another magazine was created in Berlin under the title *Unter dem Ladentisch* (Under the Counter). (Fig. 105)

In Berlin, Brus met up with fellow artists Wiener and Gerhard Rühm, who already lived there, as well as a number of international colleagues who stayed here for longer or shorter periods, including Friedrich Achleitner, Arnulf Rainer, and Dieter Roth. Among them, an artistic collective formed, which referred to their joint literary activities as *Dichterworkshops* (Poet Workshops). They also engaged in deliberately amateurish musical pursuits, organising concerts and recording records. This circle of artists also founded an *Österreichische Exilregierung* (Austrian Exile Government). As their organ, a series of magazines, self-published by Brus under the name *Die Schastrommel* (The Old Gossip Monger), appeared in twelve issues between 1969 and 1974, with the objective of retrospectively making the events of Vienna Actionism known and historically reviewing them. It was continued in five editions under the title *Die Drossel* (The Song Trush) until 1976. (Fig. 107-111)

After smaller actions in Berlin–only one of which took place in front of an audience of friends, while the others wererealised solely for film–Brus performed a pre-program for Nitsch's *32nd Action* in Aktionsraum 1 in Munich on 28 February 1970. This was a ten-minute action, entitled *Psychodramolett*, in which he appeared wearing a bra and a suspender belt. It was the first of his actions to be recorded for television (Hessischer Rundfunk), but was not broadcast.

Brus' last action, *Zerreißprobe* (Stress Test), on 19 June 1970 also took place in Aktionsraum 1 in Munich. (Fig. 106) Here he initially appeared in underpants and suspender belt which he soon cut up and then maltreated his body in a very radical way by various forms of self-harming, drinking urine, and also feigned seizures. The action culminated in a cut into the clean-shaved back of his head, from which blood ran down his back.

Zerreißprobe was Brus' most extreme action, marking a point where any continuation of his physical explorations, particularly those involving self-harm, was no longer possible. Consequently, the artist ended his actionist activity and from then on devoted himself to drawing—the form of artistic expression that was closest to him from the outset. Through this medium, he continued to explore themes related to Vienna Actionism, among others. He increasingly integrated longer and shorter literary texts into specific series of his drawings and thus arrived at a genre that he called *Bilddichtungen* (Pictorial Texts). (Fig. 112–119) Furthermore, he also wrote independent literary texts and plays.

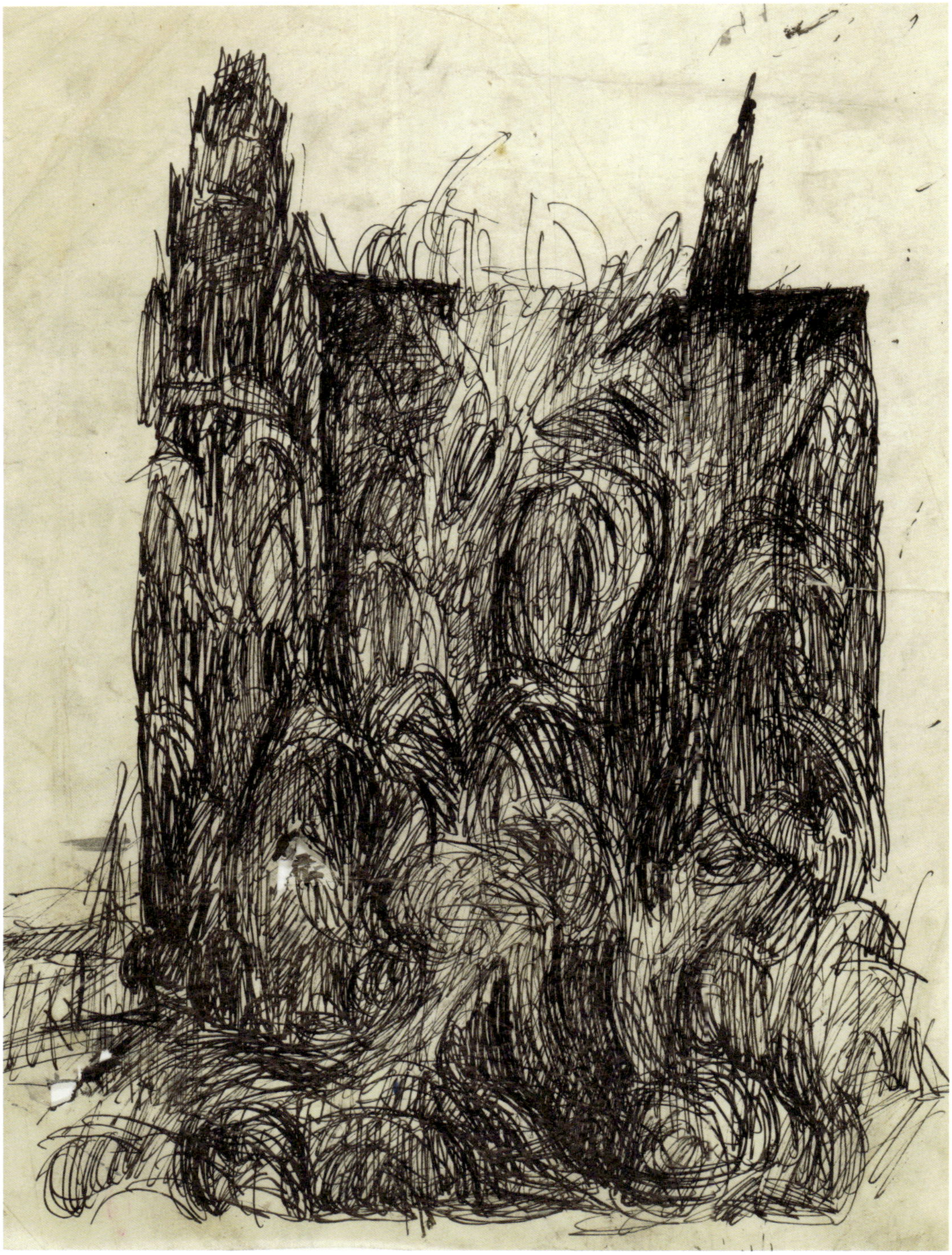

Fig. 41
Günter Brus
Untitled (Church with tree), 1958/59
Ink on transparent paper,
34 x 26 cm
Private collection

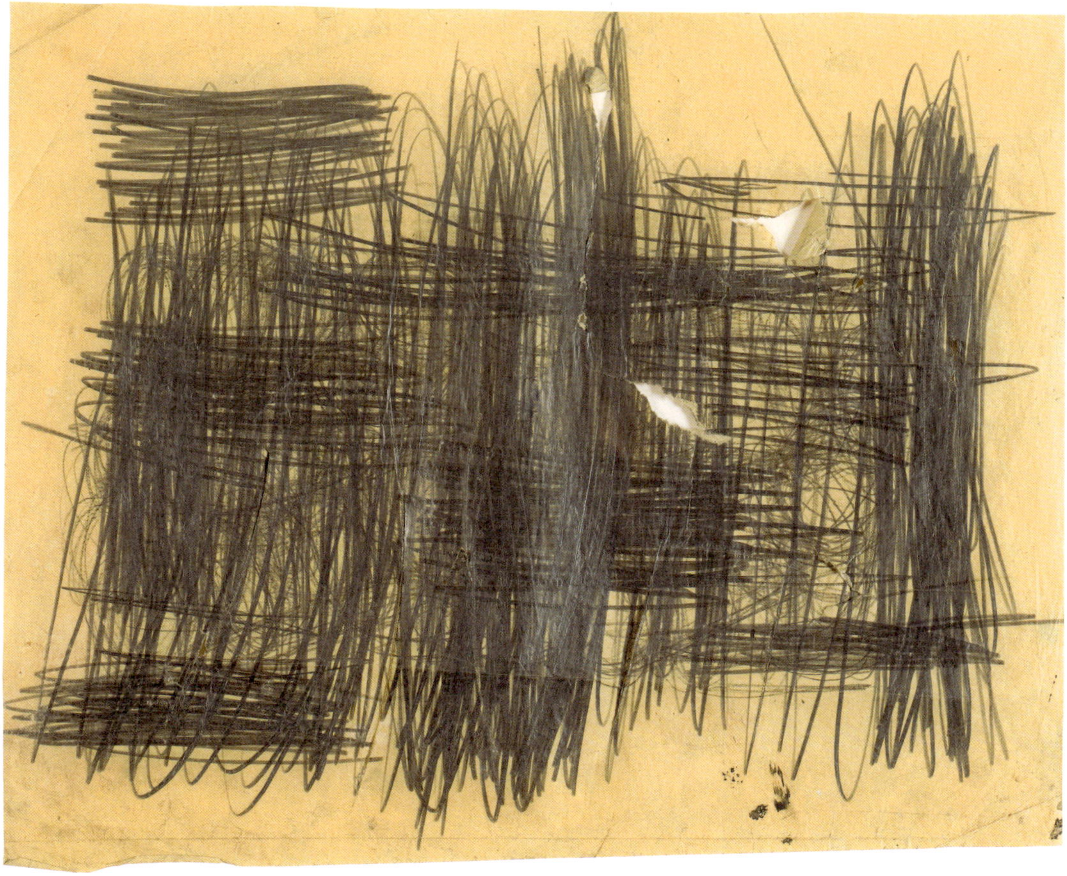

Fig. 42
Günter Brus
Untitled, 1960
Pencil on paper
46,5 cm x 55 cm
BRUSEUM/Neue Galerie Graz, Universalmuseum Joanneum

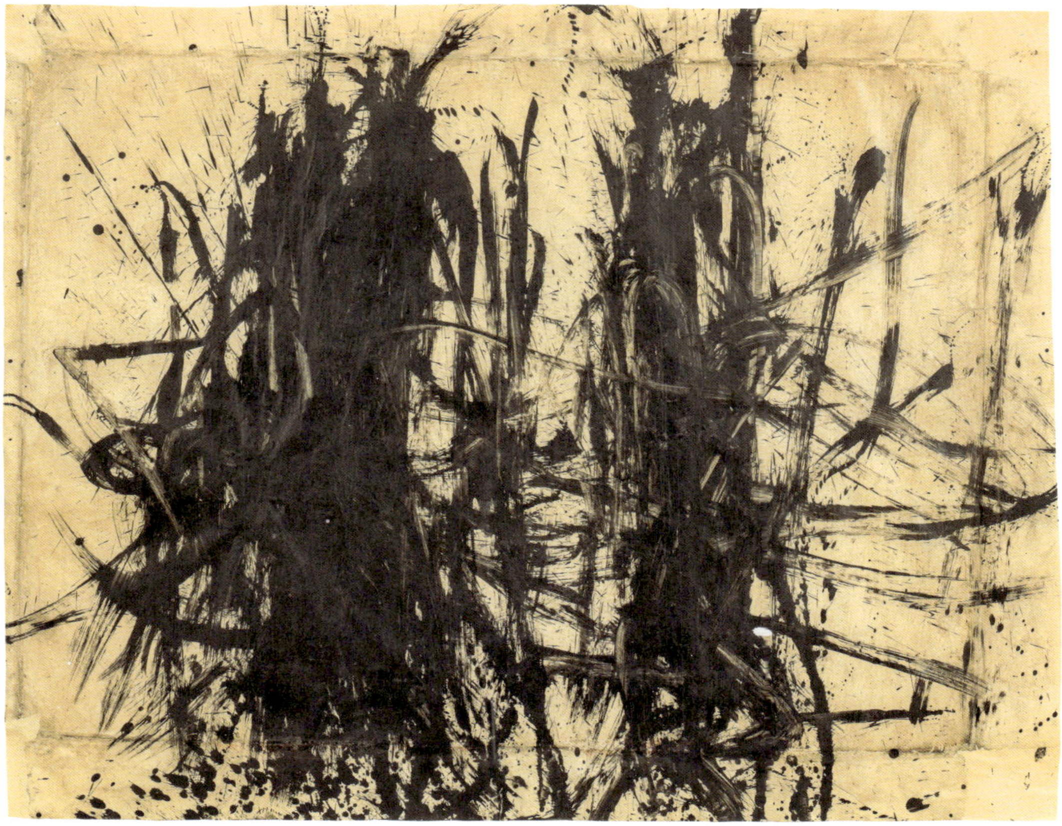

Fig. 43
Günter Brus
Untitled, 1961
Dispersion on paper
85 x 110,5 cm
WAM – Wiener Aktionismus Museum, Vienna

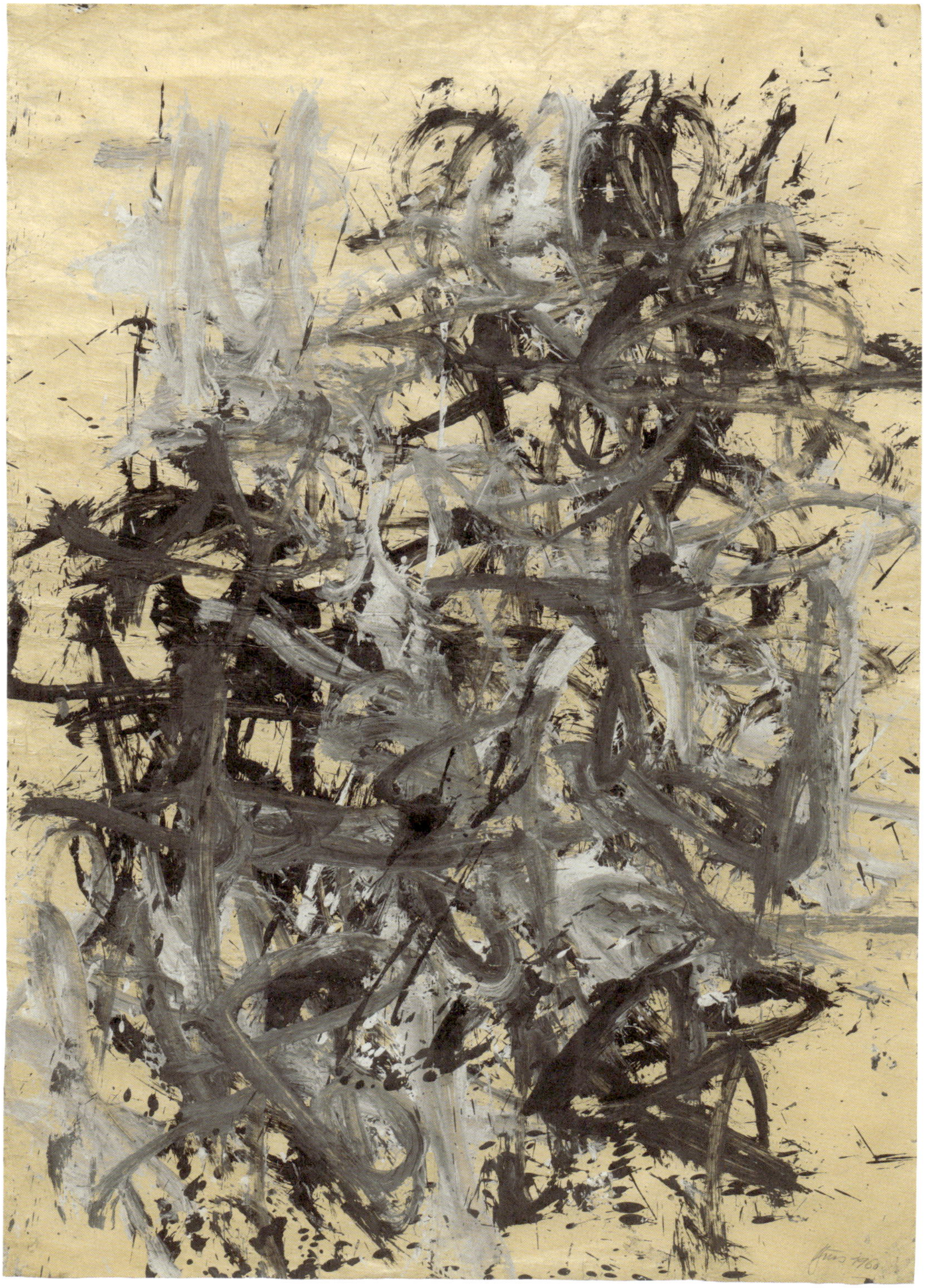

Fig. 44
Günter Brus
Untitled, 1960
Dispersion on paper
125 x 84 cm
THP Privatstiftung

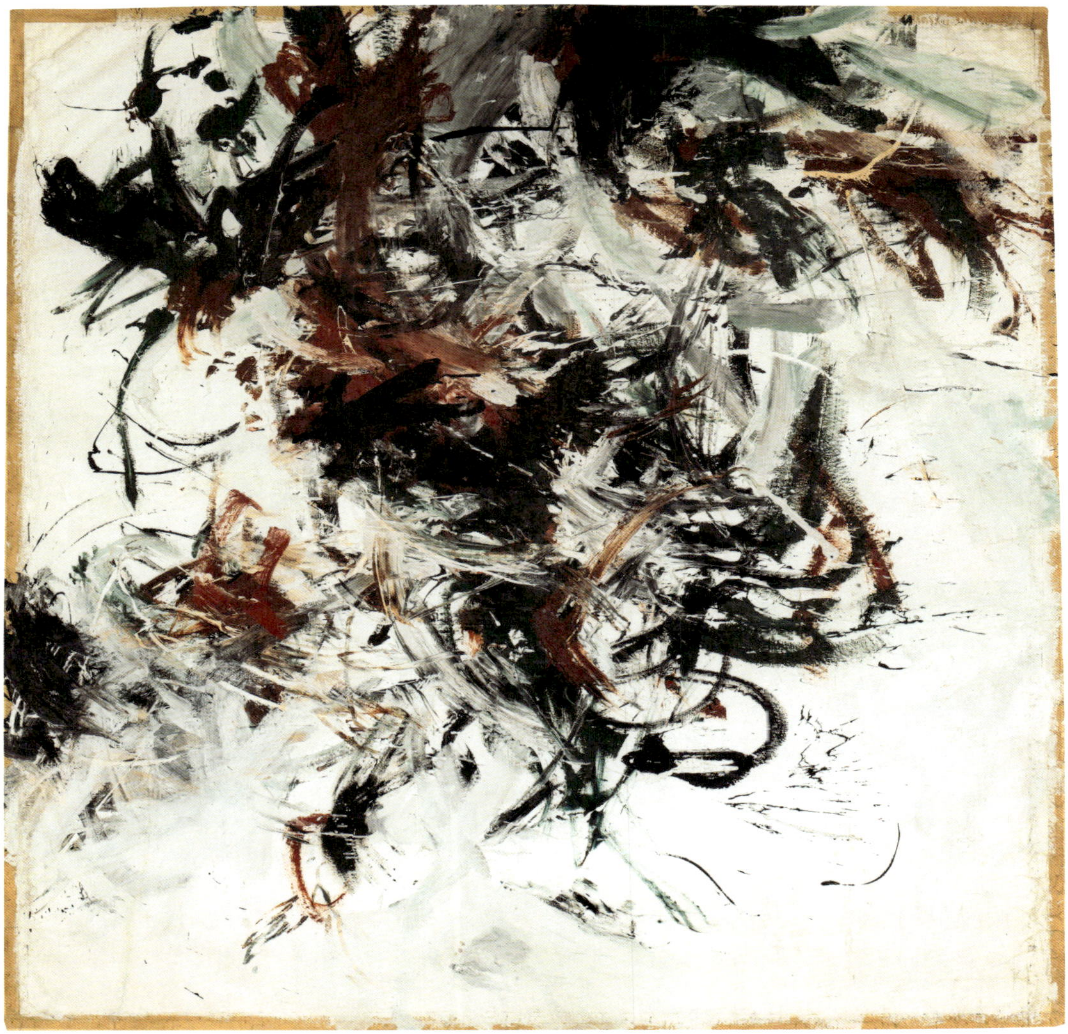

Fig. 45
Alfons Schilling
Untitled, 1961
Dispersion on paper
297 x 285 cm
WAM – Wiener Aktionismus Museum, Vienna

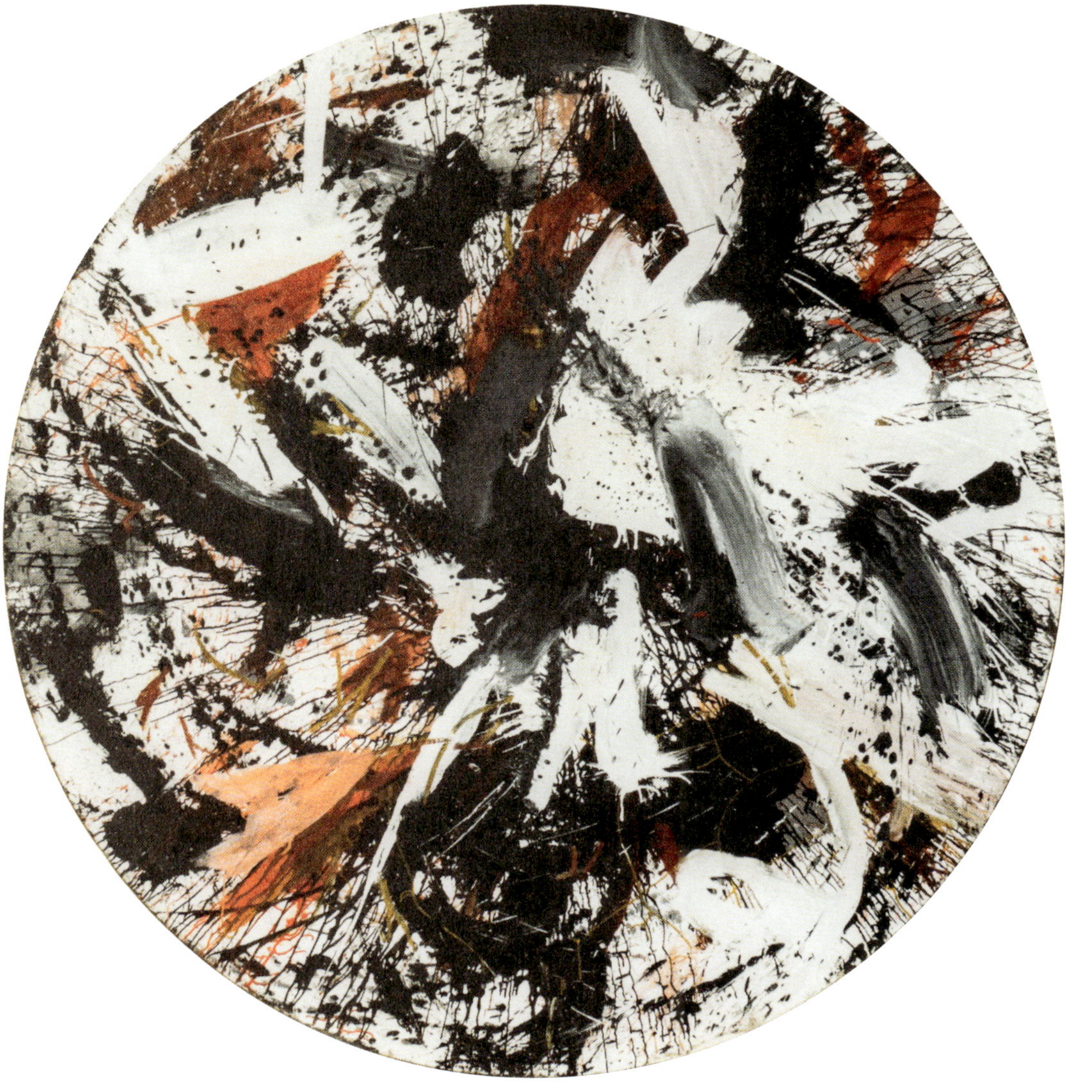

Fig. 46
Alfons Schilling
Untitled, Spin Painting, 1962
Acrylic, powder colour on molino fabric, flywheel belt, electric motor
Diameter 221,5 cm
mumok – Museum moderner Kunst Stiftung Ludwig Wien

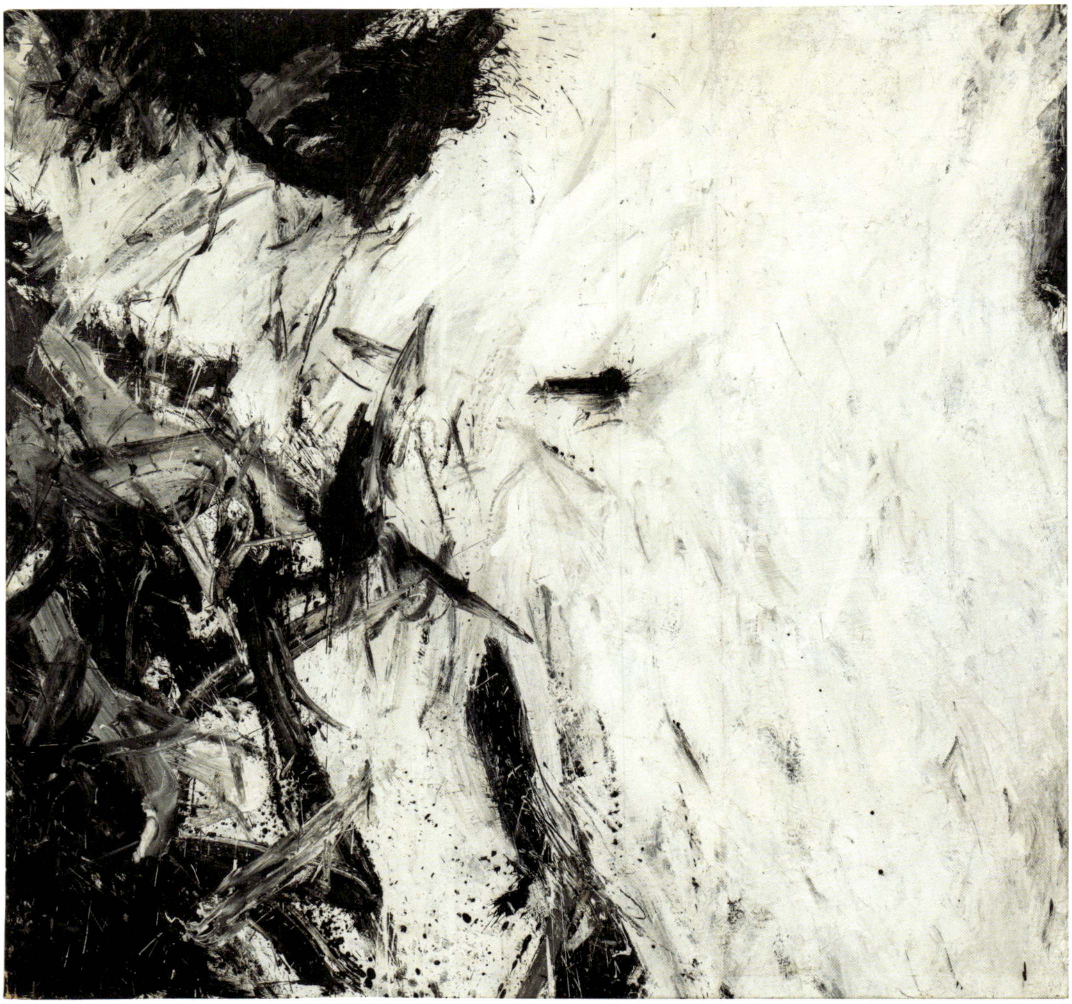

Fig. 47
Günter Brus
Untitled, 1961
Dispersion on nettle
222,5 x 239,5 cm
private collection Graz, Theodor Poppmeier

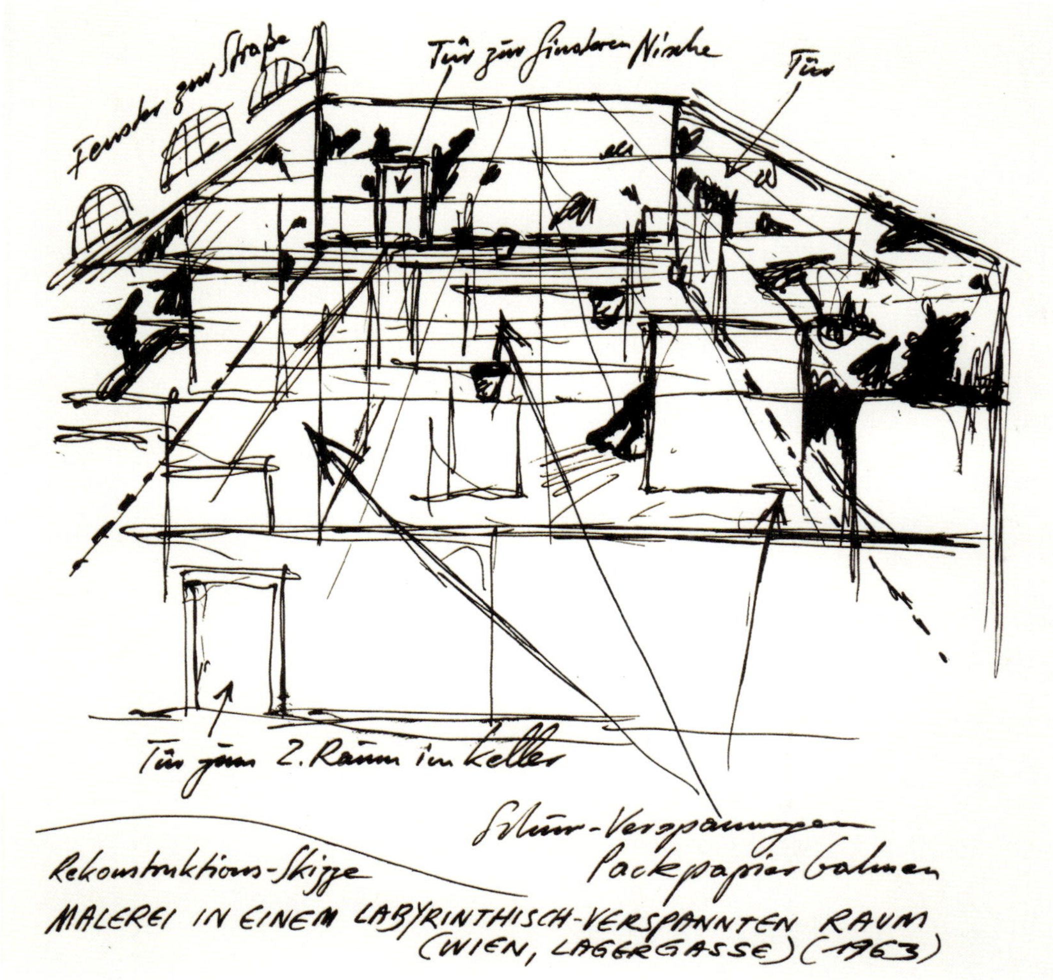

Fig. 48
Günter Brus
Rekonstruktions-Skizze Malerei in einem labyrinthisch-verspannten Raum (Wien, Lagergasse) (1963)
(Reconstruction-Sketch Painting in a Labyrinthine Spanned Room [Vienna, Lagergasse] [1963])
Supplement to the portfolio Günter Brus, *Ana*, Galerie Heike Curtze, Galerie Krinzinger, Vienna 1985

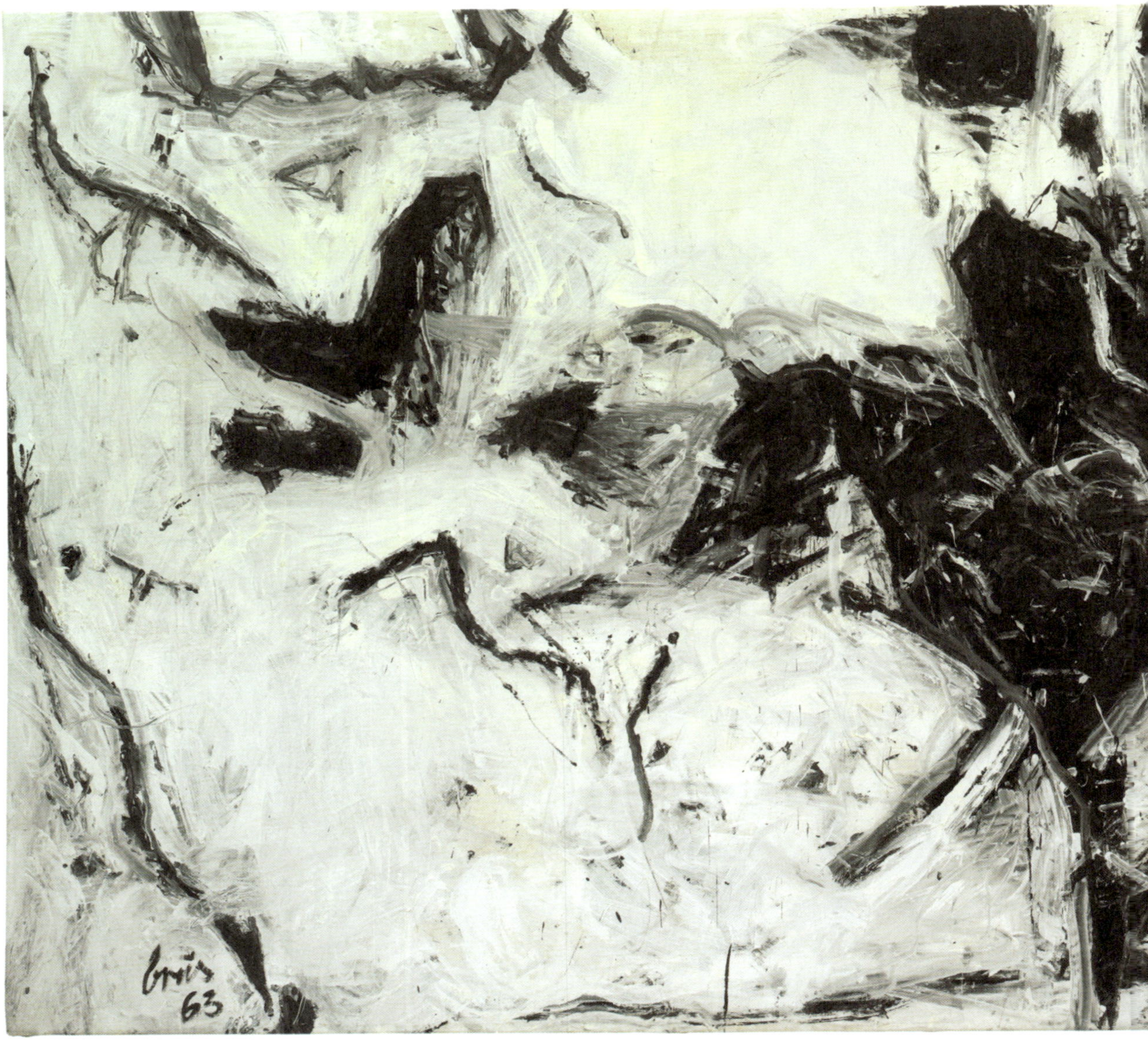

Fig. 49
Günter Brus
Untitled, 1963
Emulsion on canvas
196.5 x 466.1 x 3.5 cm
Glenstone Museum, Potomac, Maryland

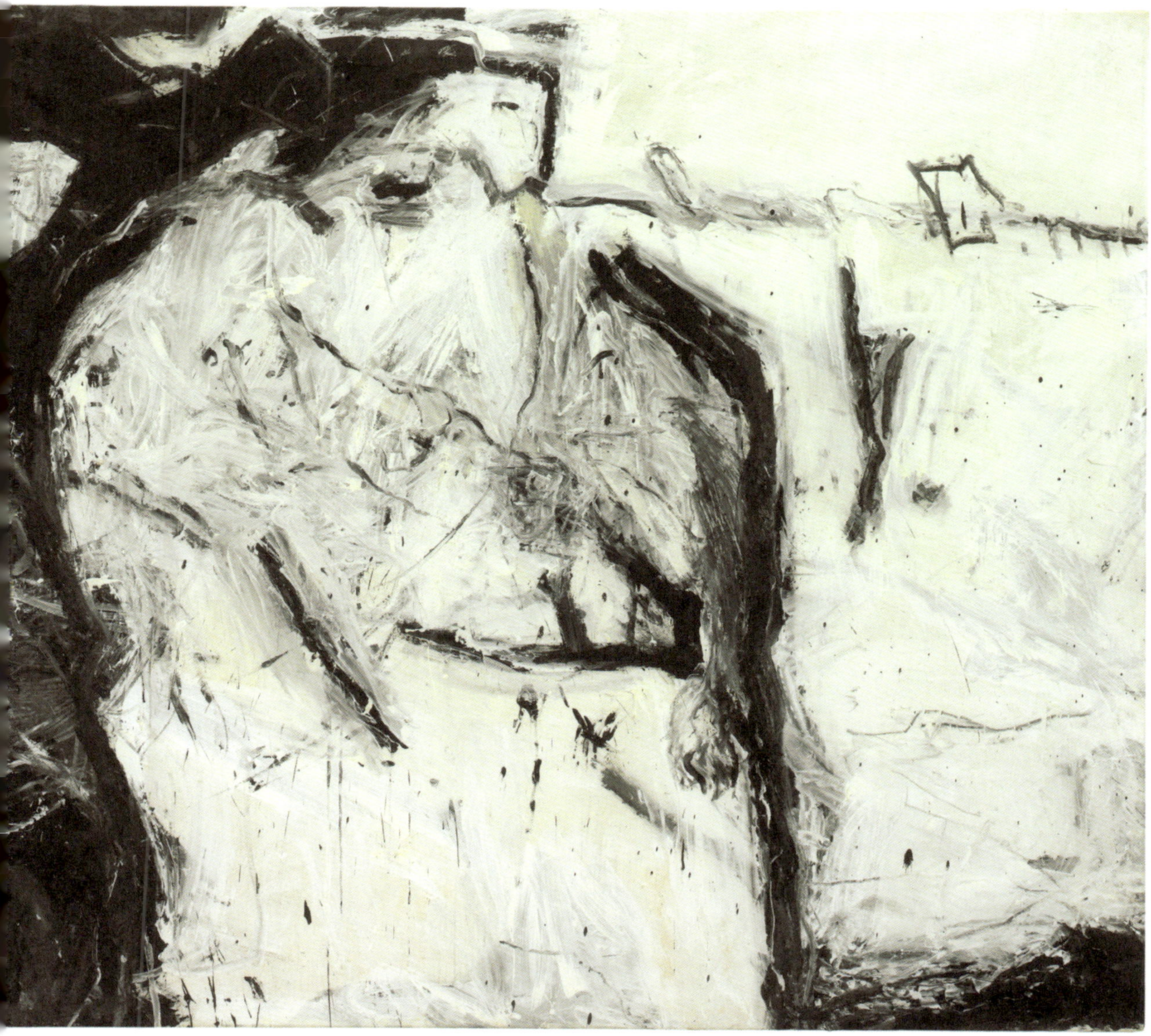

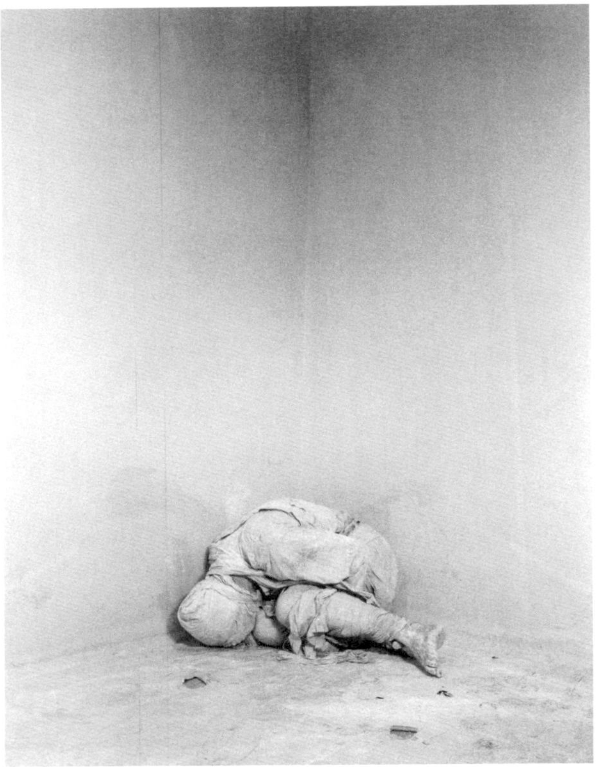
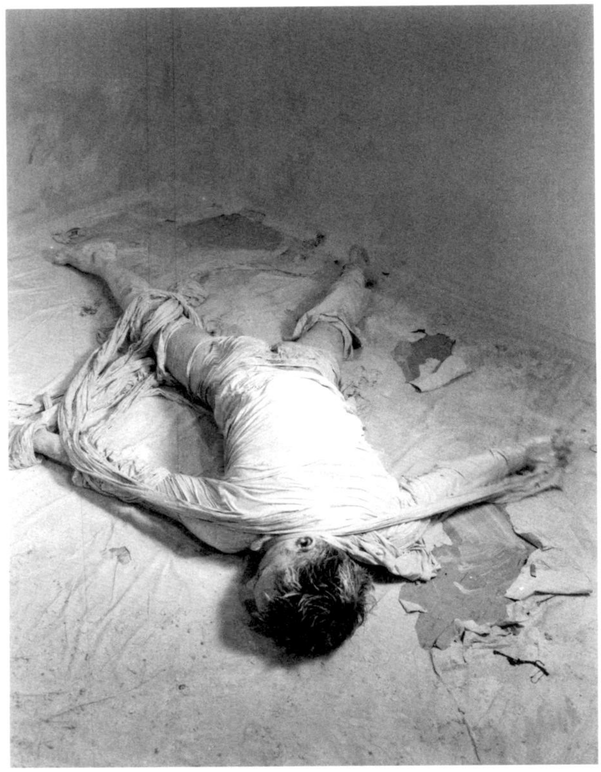
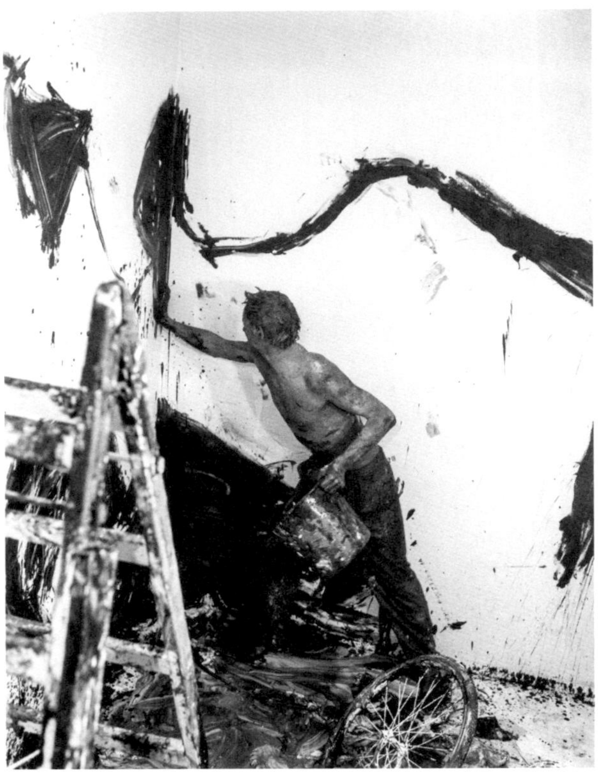
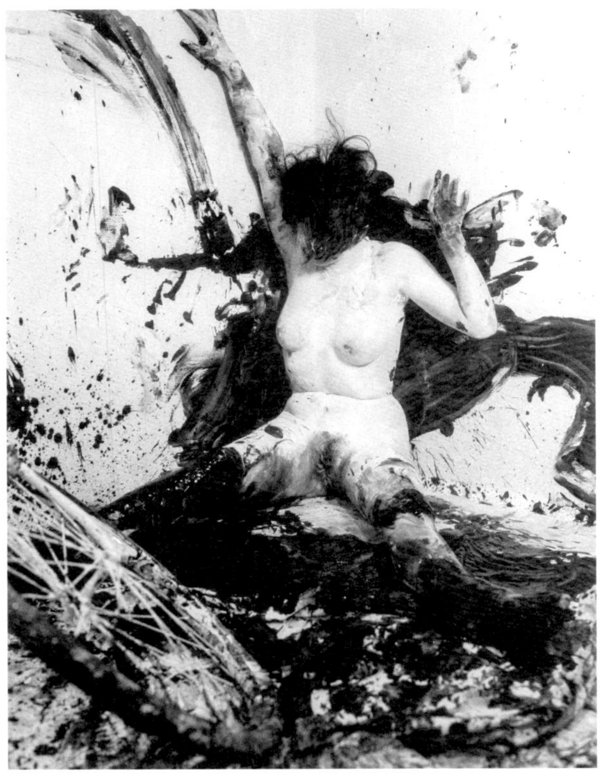

Fig. 50, 51, 52, 53, 54, 55, 56, 57
Günter Brus
1st Action, Ana, November 1964
Muehl's apartment, Obere Augartenstraße 14 a/20, 1020 Vienna
B/W photographs
photo: Khasaq (Siegfried Klein)
with: Anna Brus

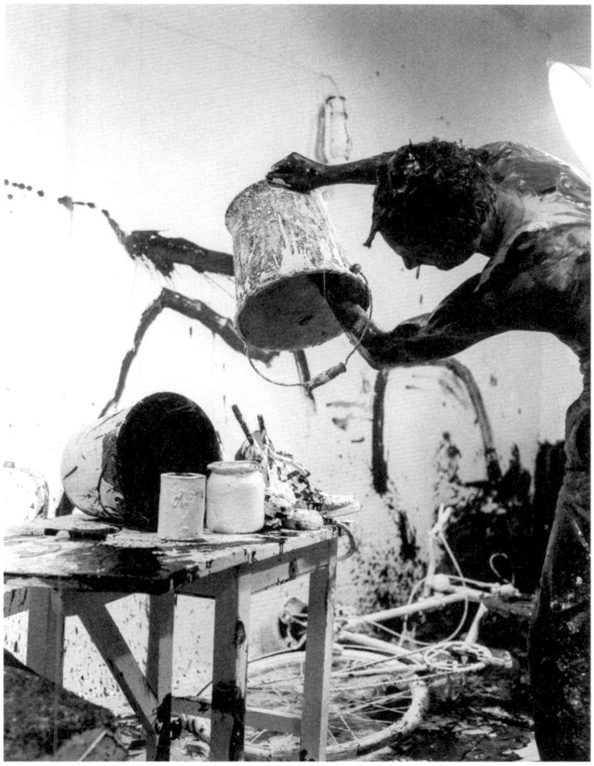

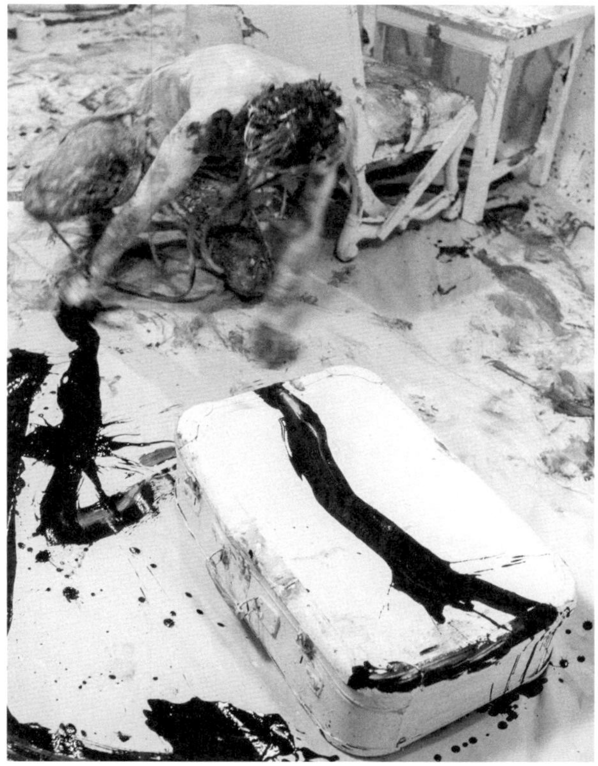

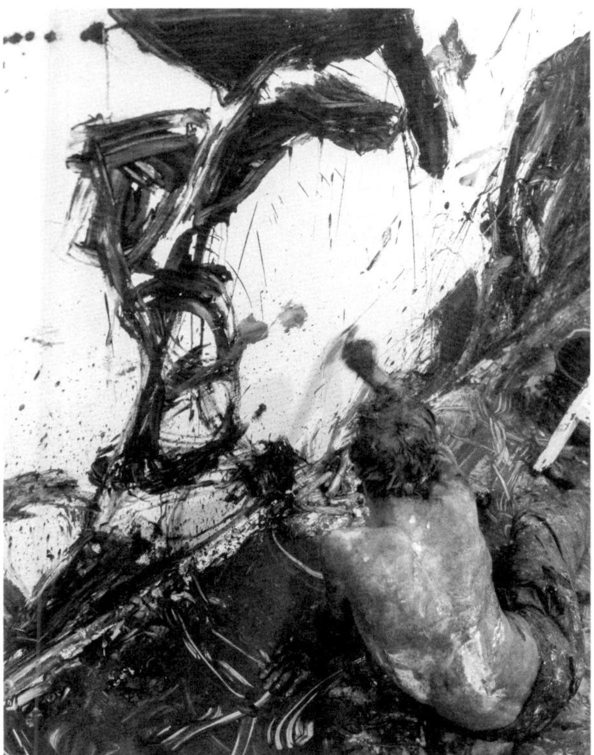

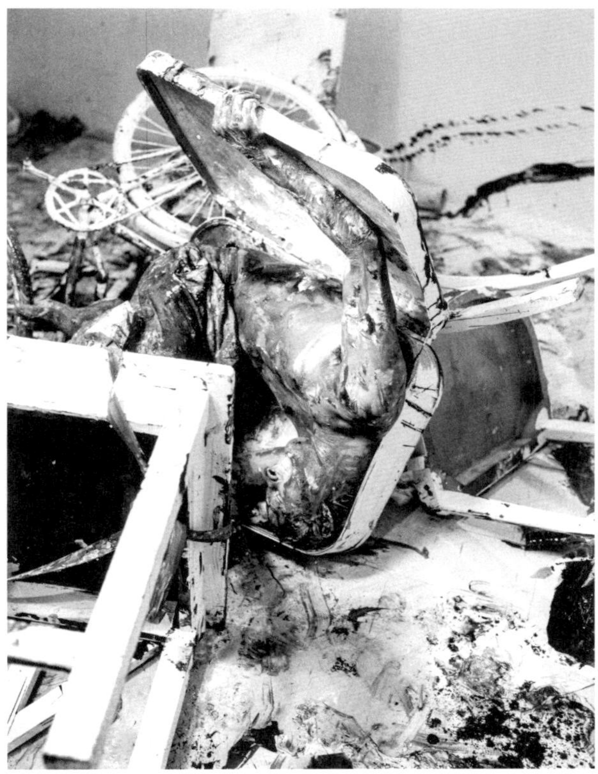

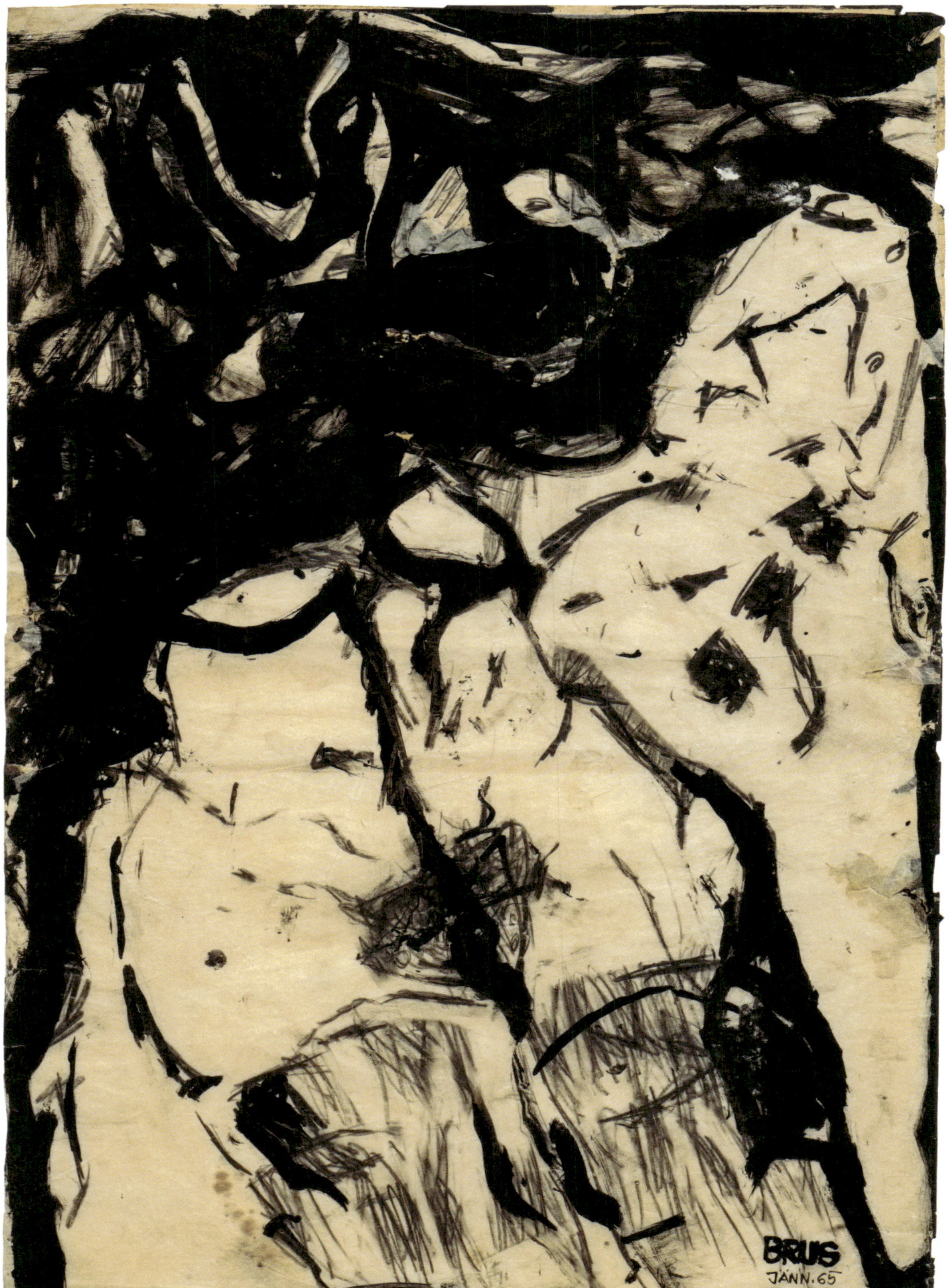

Fig. 58
Günter Brus
Ana 9, Jänner 1965 (Ana 9, January 1965)
Pencil and ink on transparent paper
62,5 x 44,5 cm
THP Privatstiftung

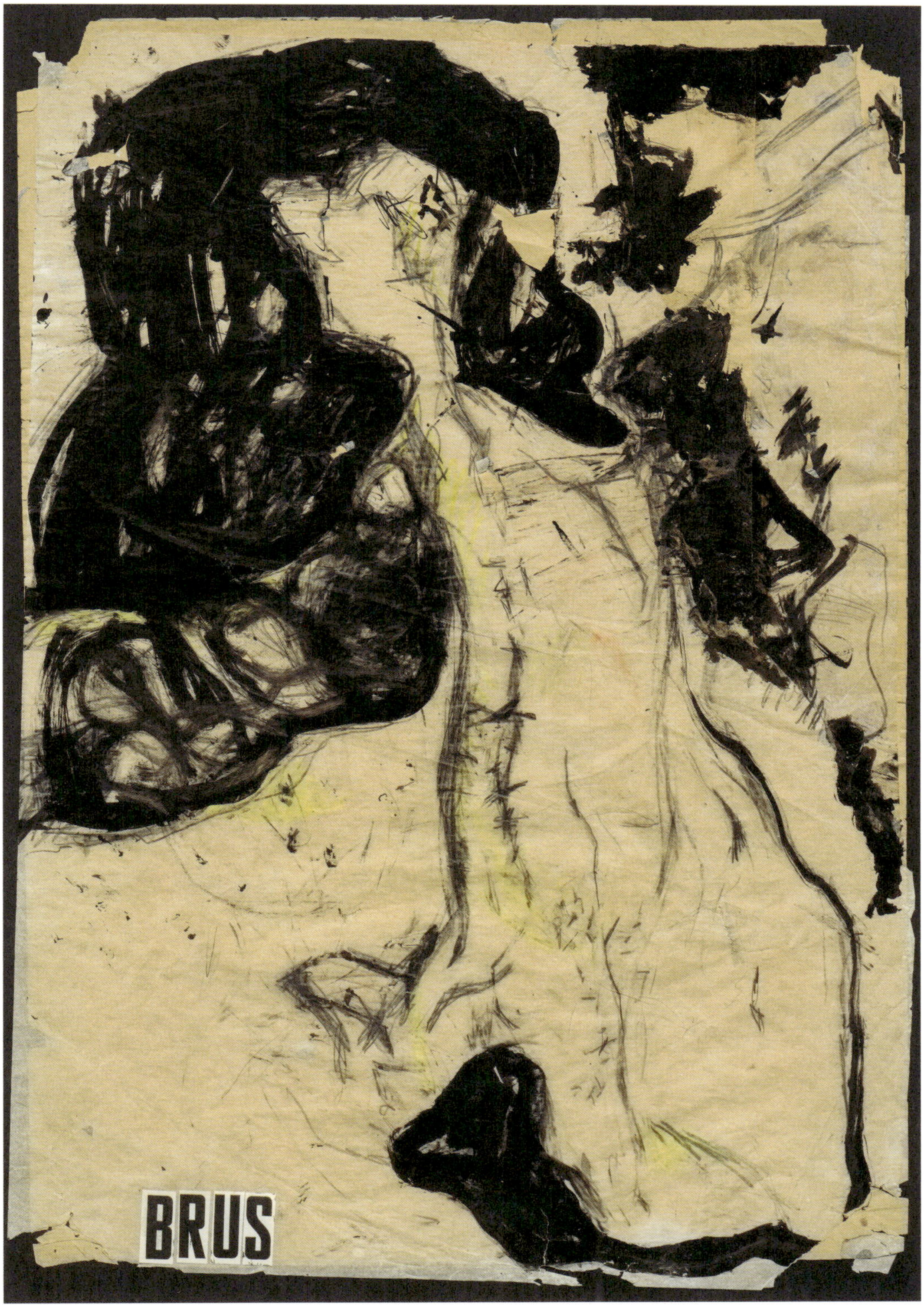

Fig. 59
Günter Brus
Untitled *(Ana)*, 1964
Pencil, ink and tempera on transparent paper
62,5 x 43,5 cm
THP Privatstiftung

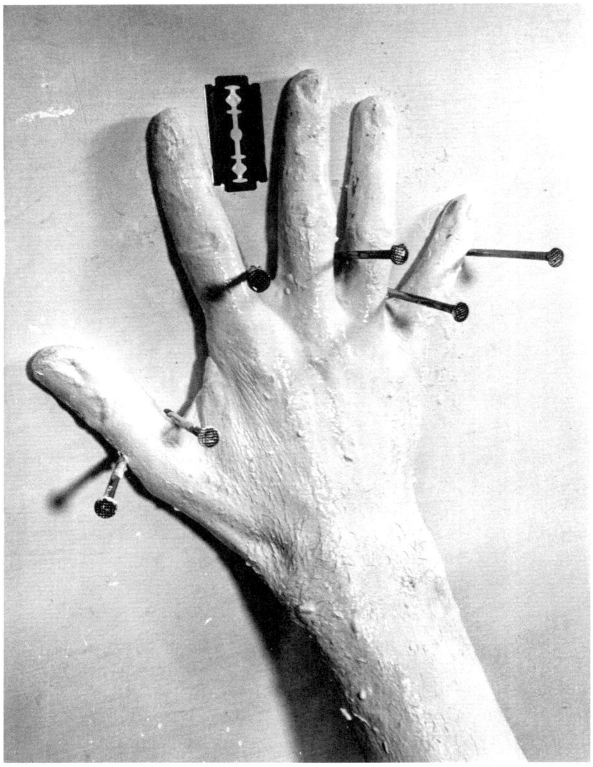

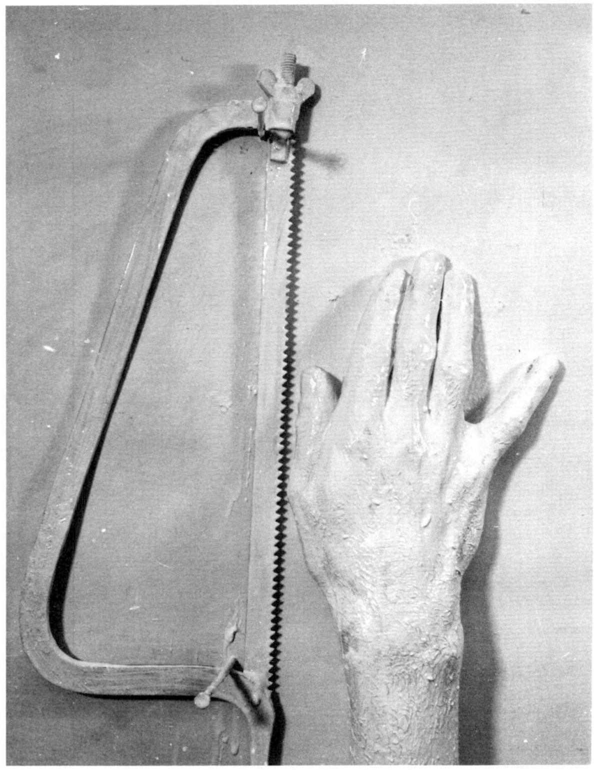

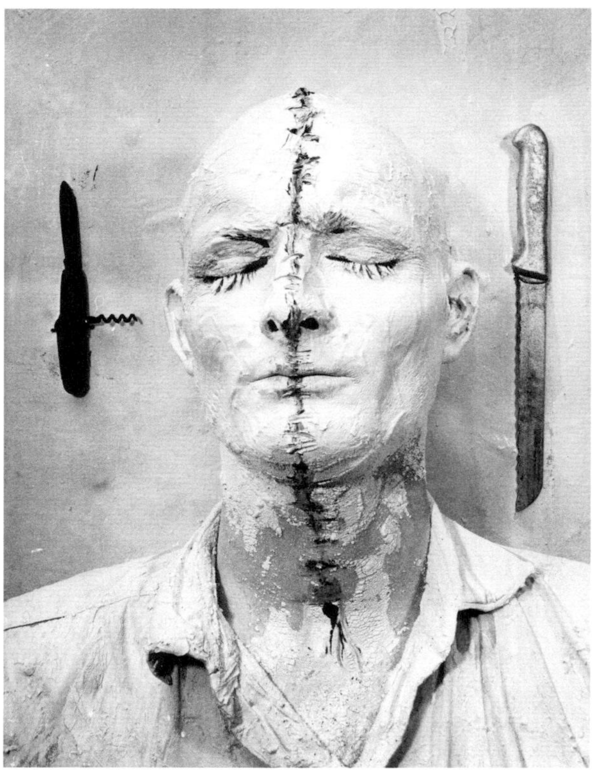

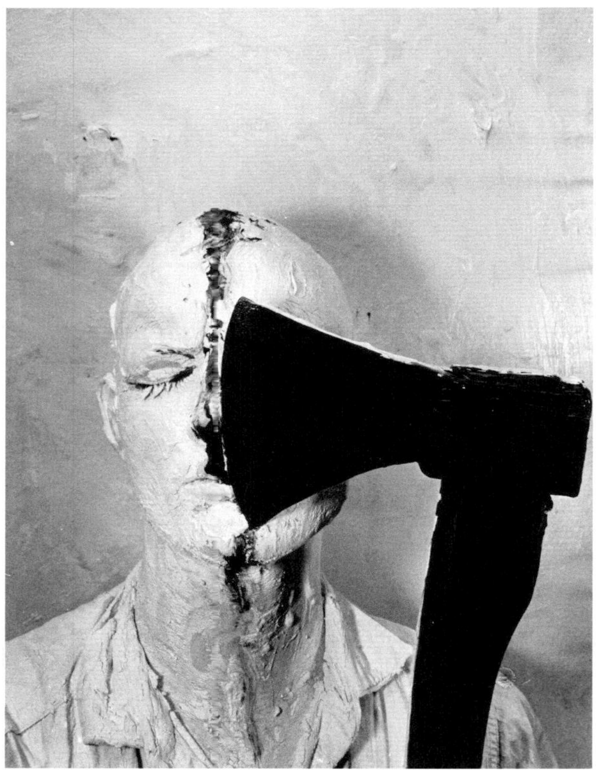

Fig. 60, 61, 62, 63, 64, 65, 67, 68
Günter Brus
Selbstbemalung 1 (Handbemalung – Kopfbemalung – Kopfzumalung)
(Self-Painting 1 [Hand Painting–Head Painting–Total Head Painting]), December 1964
John Sailer's studio, Opernring 21, 1010 Vienna
B/W photographs
photo: Ludwig Hoffenreich

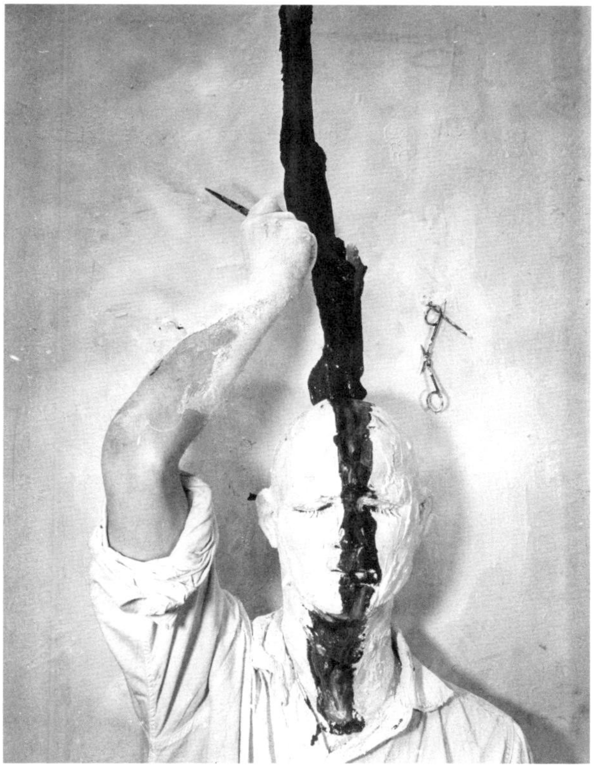

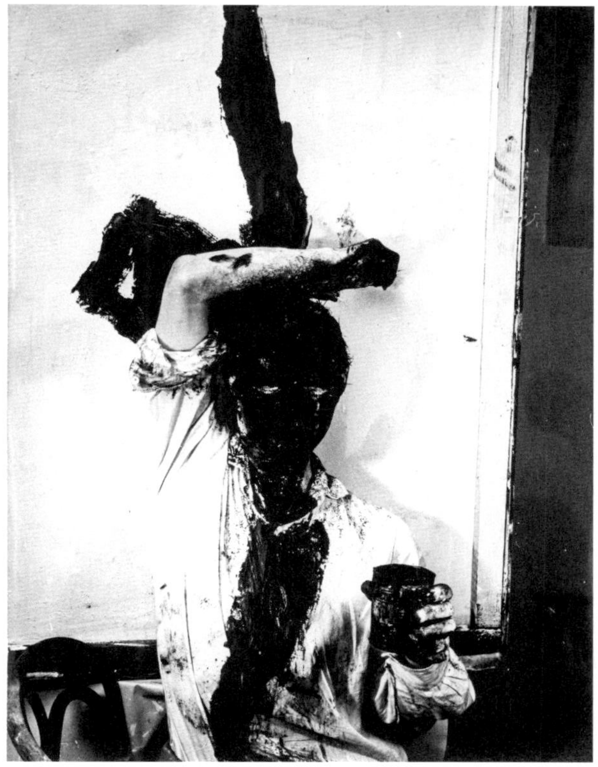

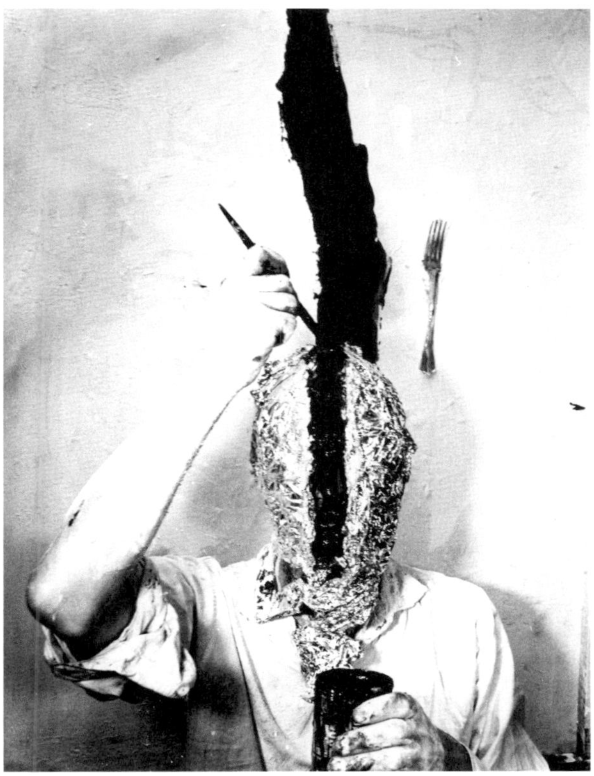

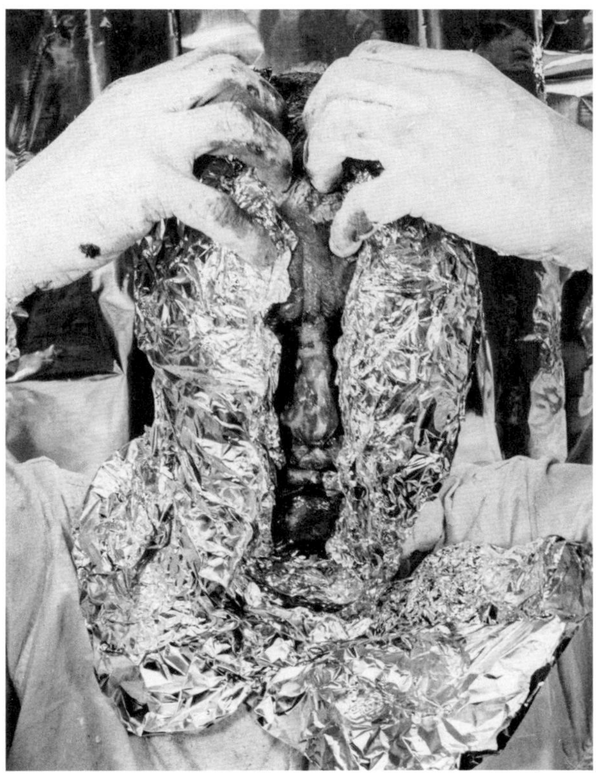

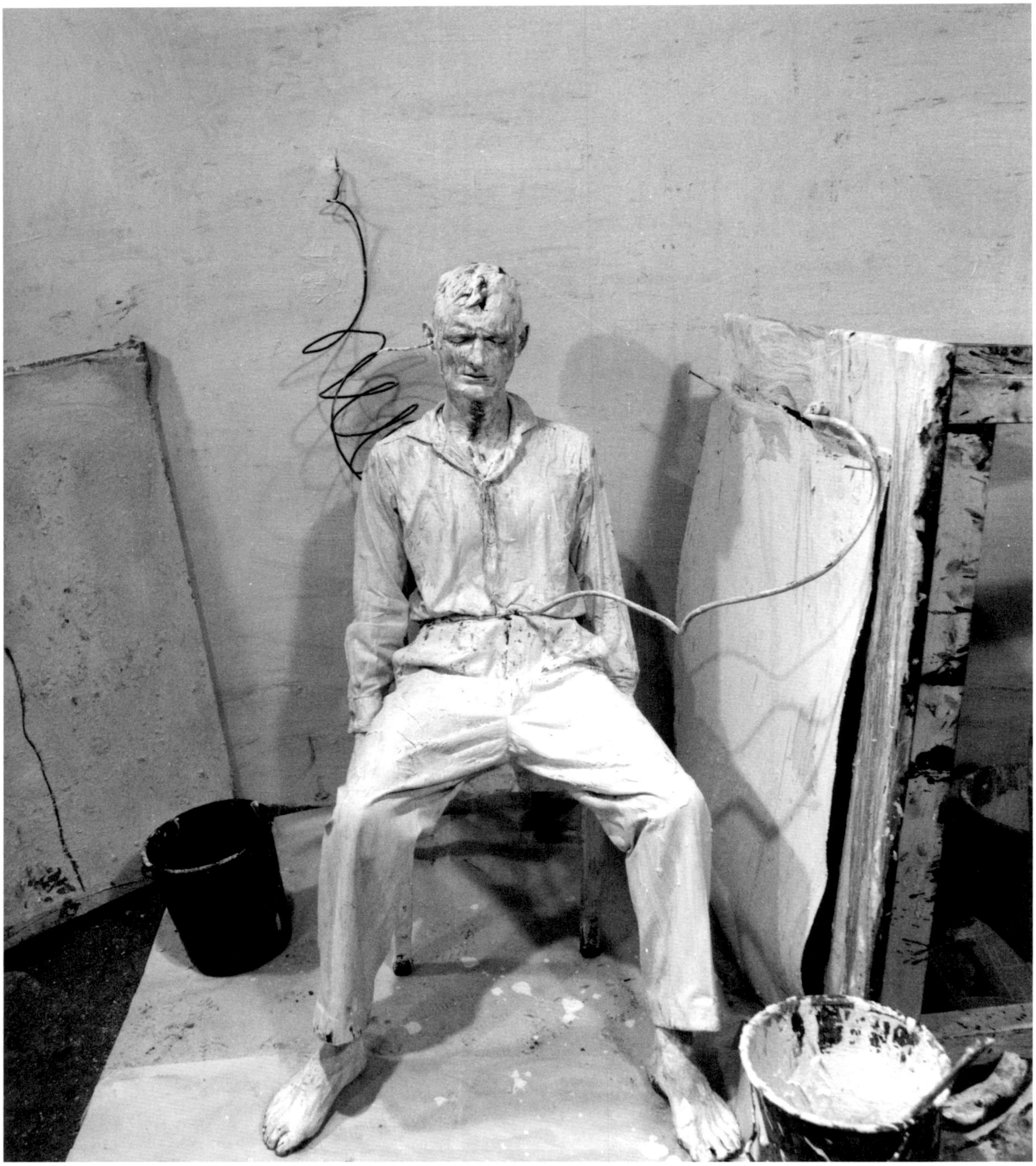

Fig. 69, 70
Günter Brus
Selbstbemalung 2 (Self-Painting 2), spring 1965
Muehl's studio, Perinetgasse 1, 1200 Vienna
B/W photographs
photo: Ludwig Hoffenreich

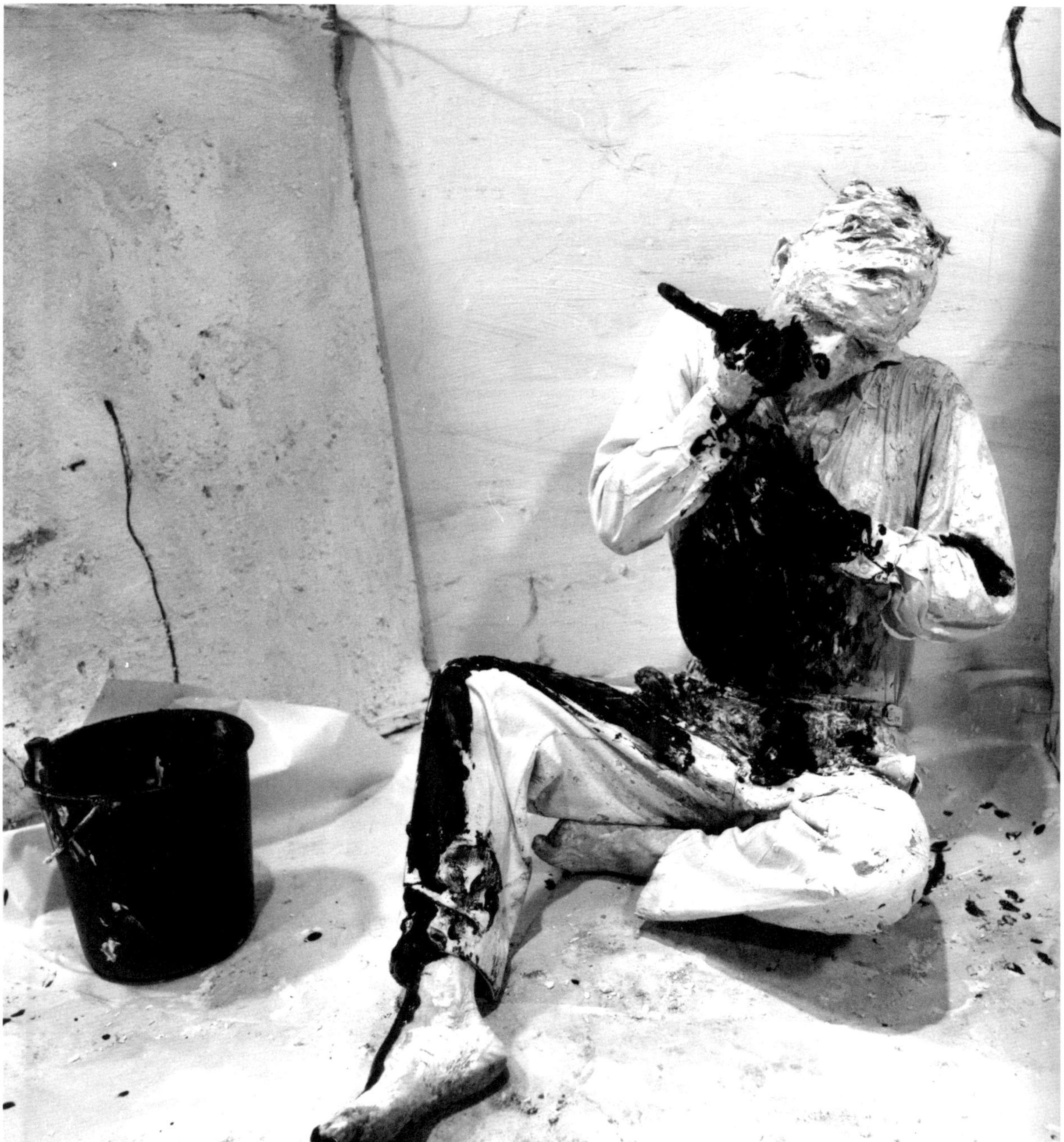

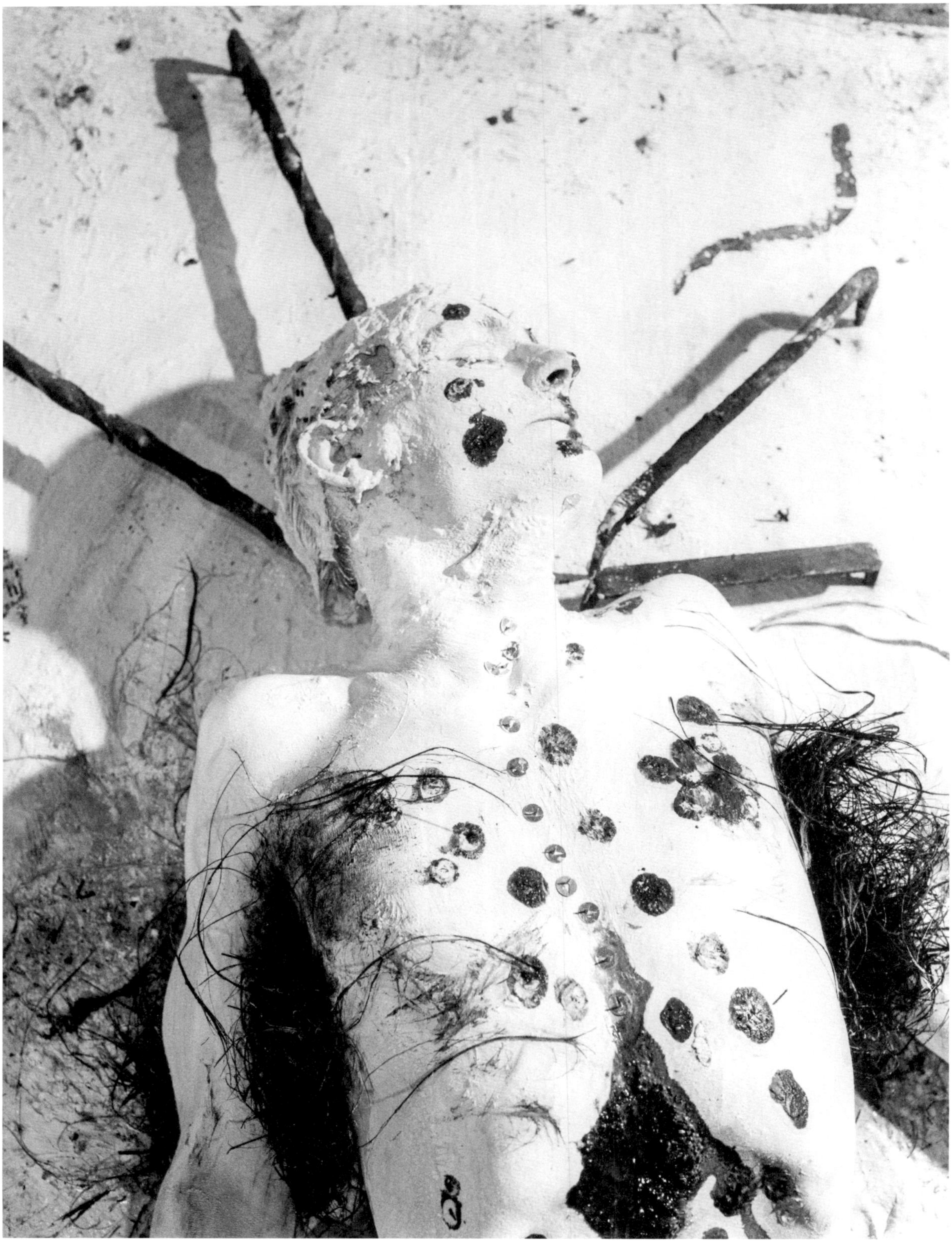

Fig. 71, 72
Günter Brus
Selbstverstümmelungen (Self-Mutilations), spring 1965
Muehl's studio, Perinetgasse 1, 1200 Vienna
B/W photographs
photo: Ludwig Hoffenreich

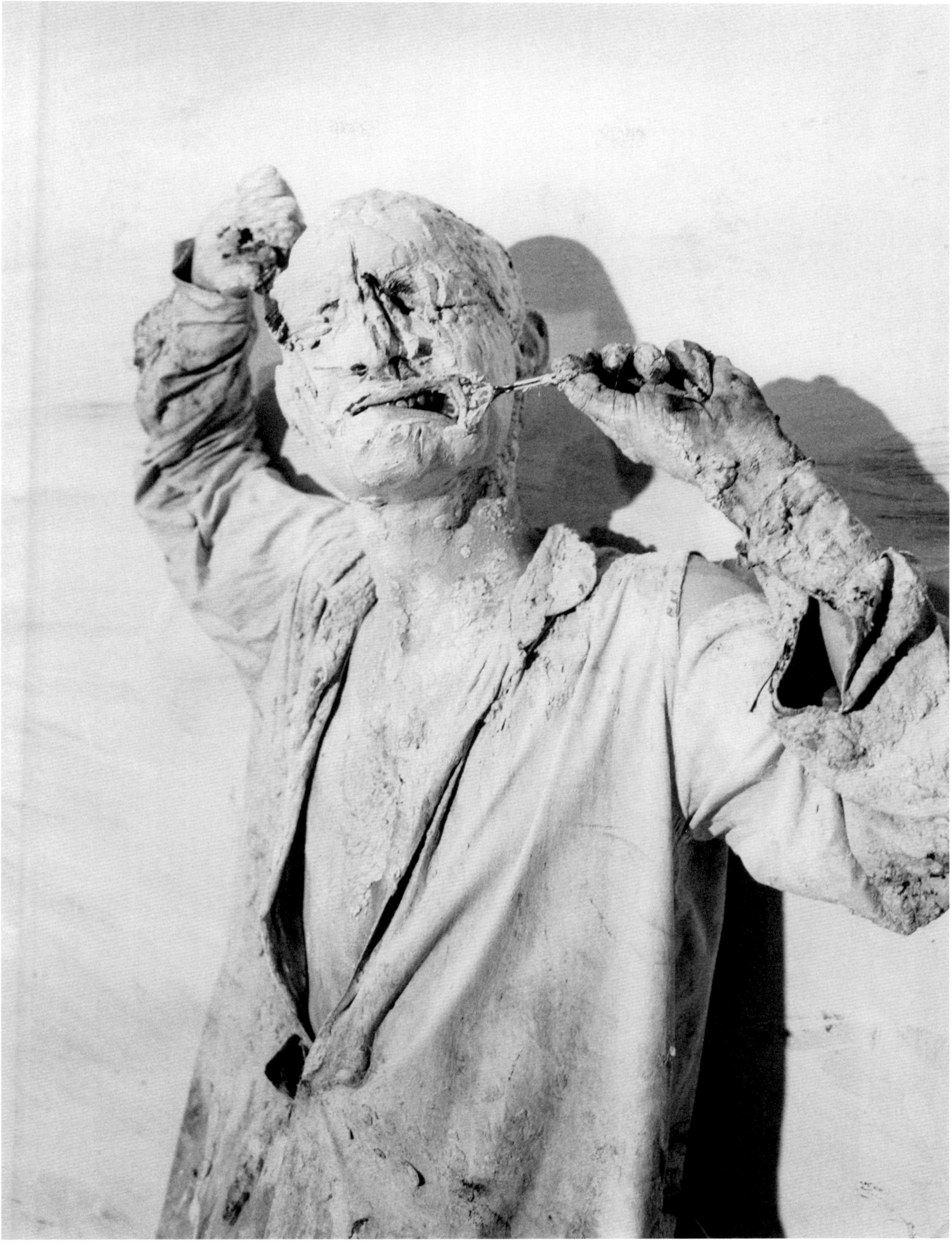

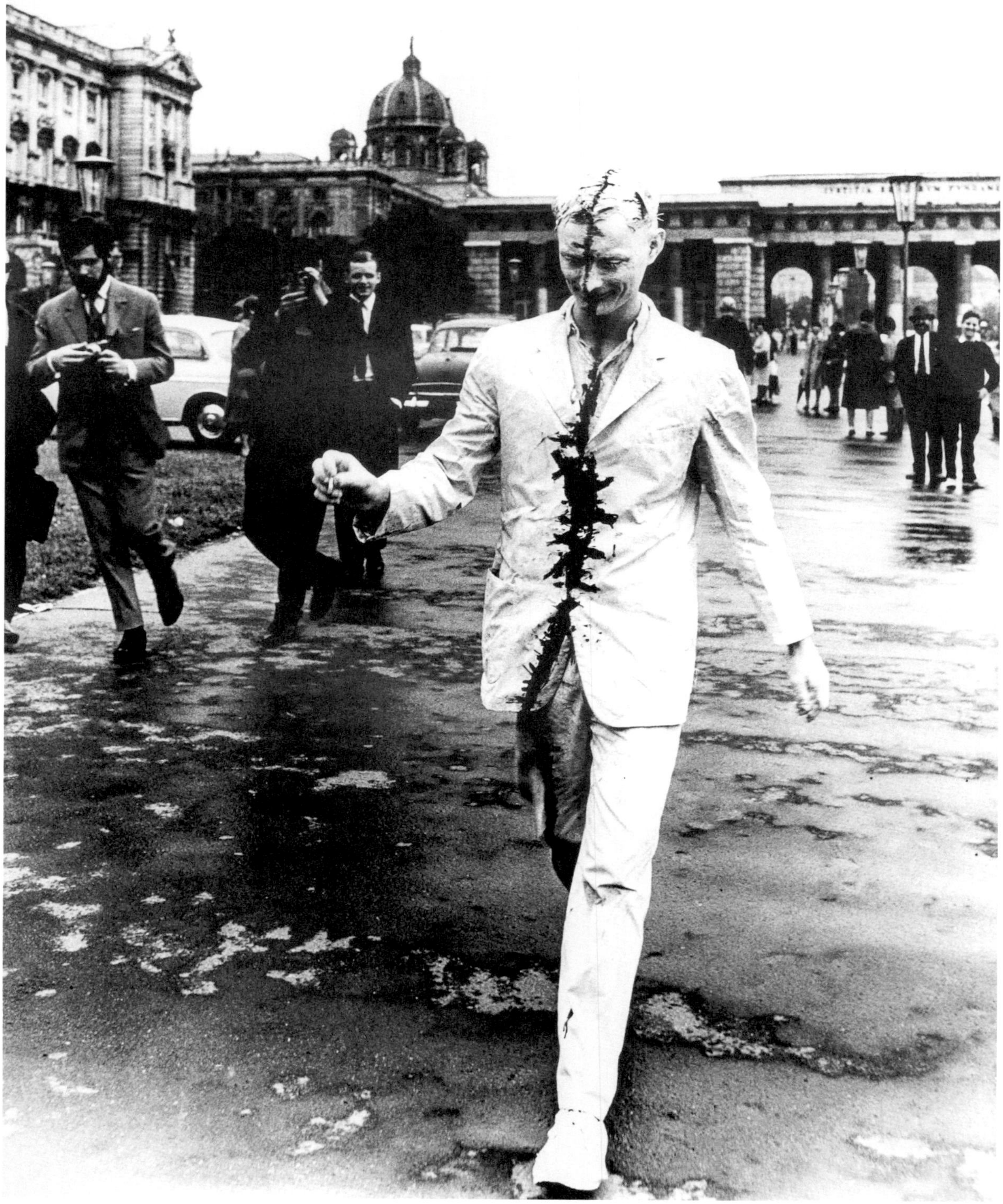

Fig. 73
Günter Brus
Wiener Spaziergang (Vienna Walk), 5 July 1965
Heldenplatz and city-center, 1010 Vienna
B/W photograph
photo: Ludwig Hoffenreich

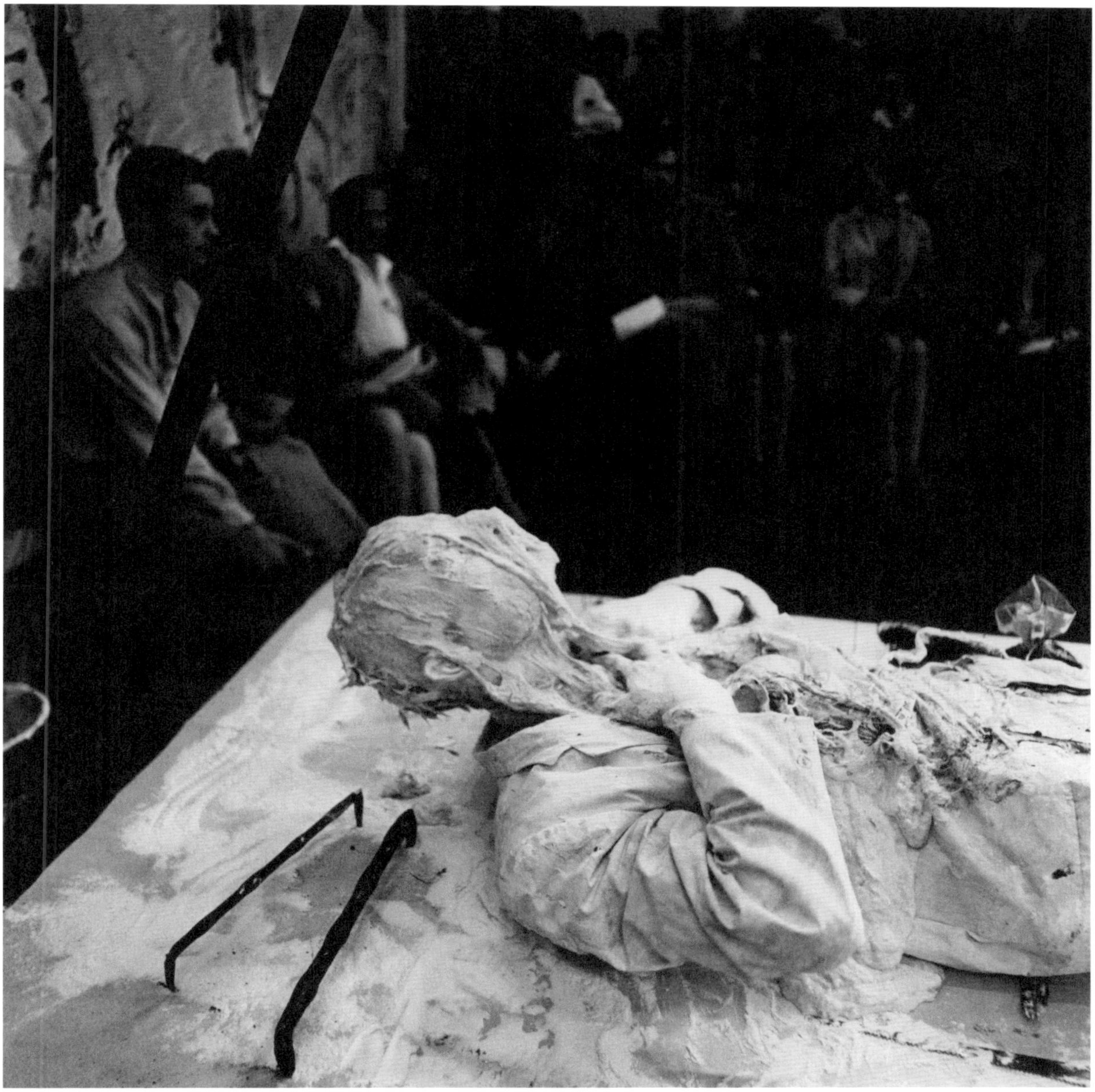

Fig. 74
Günter Brus
Malerei – Selbstbemalung – Selbstverstümmelung
(Painting–Self-Painting–Self-Mutilation), 6 July 1965
Galerie Junge Generation, Börseplatz 7, 1010 Vienna
B/W photograph
photo: Ludwig Hoffenreich

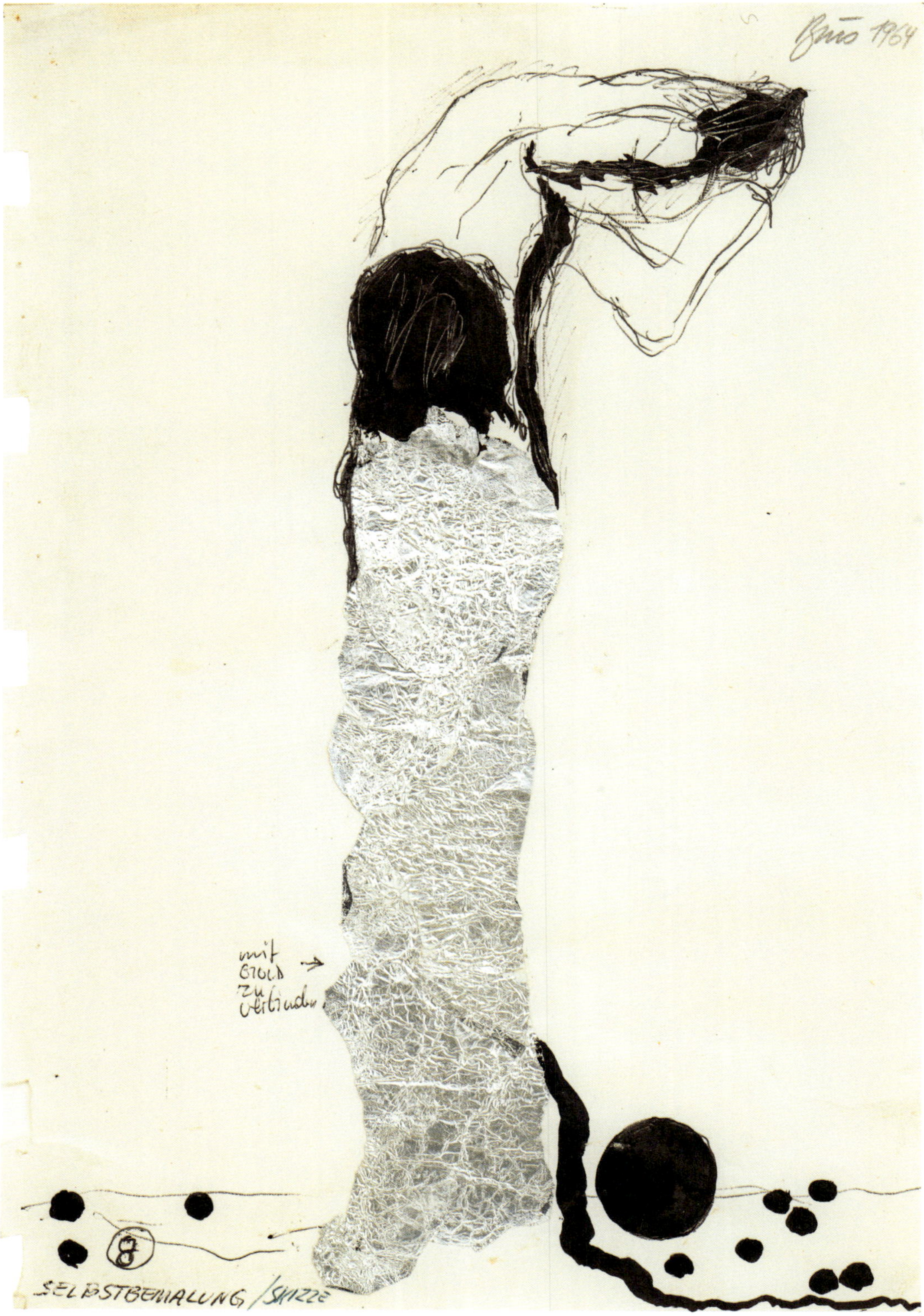

Fig. 75
Günter Brus
Selbstbemalung/Skizze (Self-Painting/Sketch), 1964
Ink, ballpoint pen, tin foil on paper
29 x 20 cm
WAM – Wiener Aktionismus Museum, Vienna, Collection K.

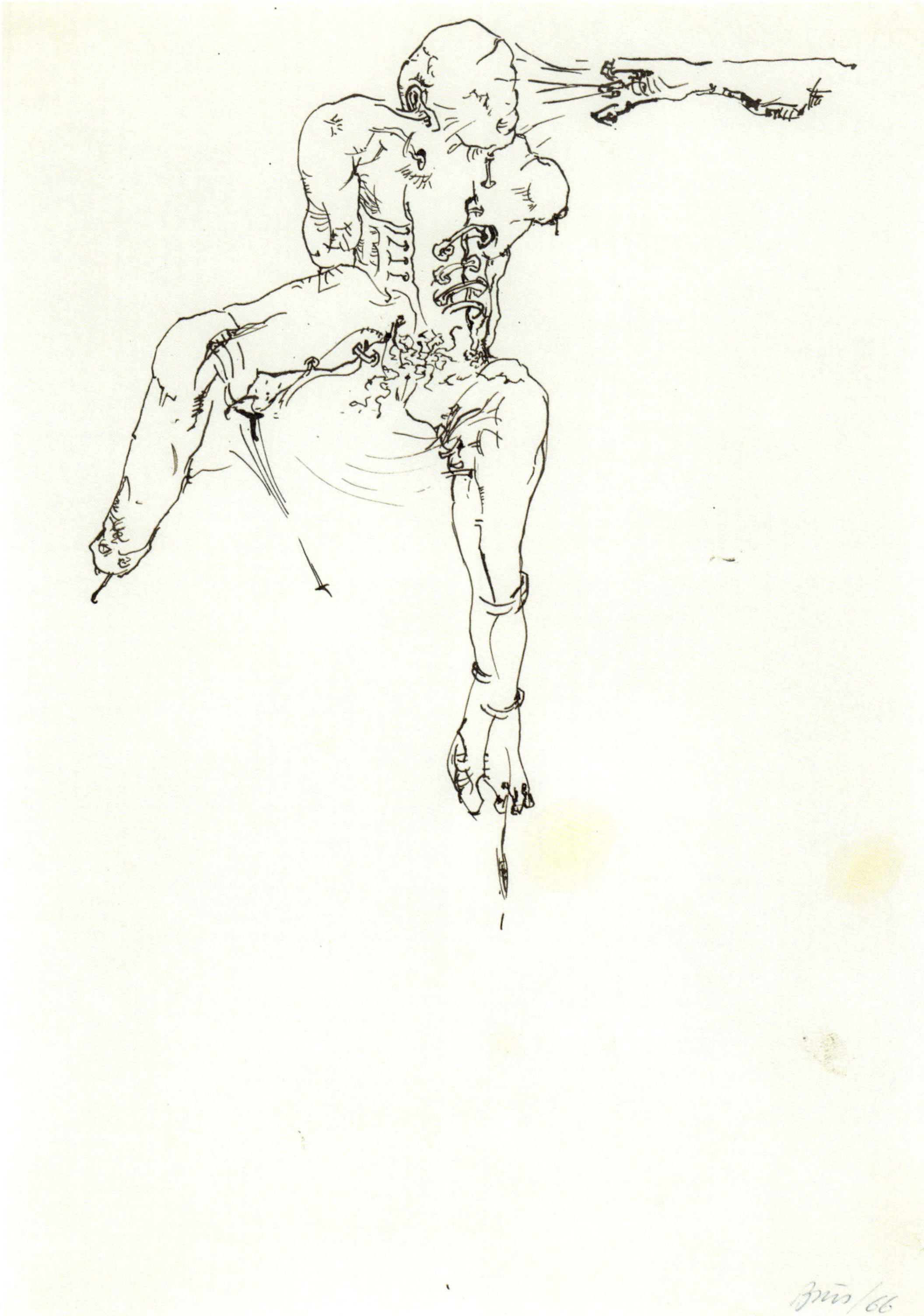

Fig. 76
Günter Brus
Untitled, 1966
Ink on paper
29 x 21 cm
WAM – Wiener Aktionismus Museum, Vienna

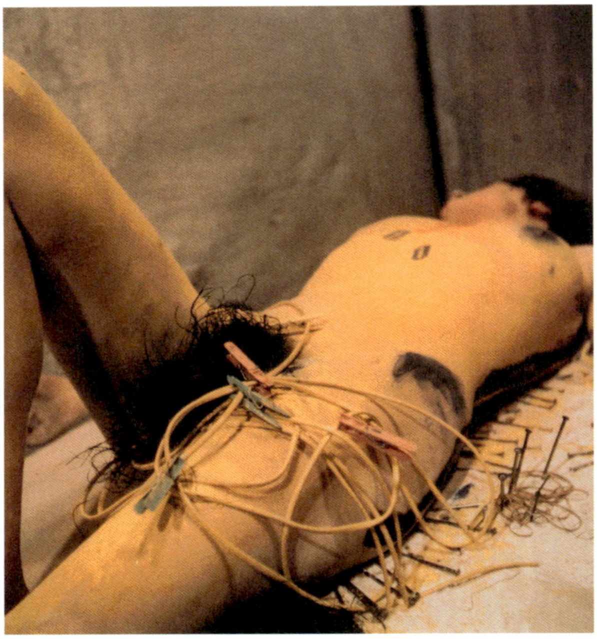

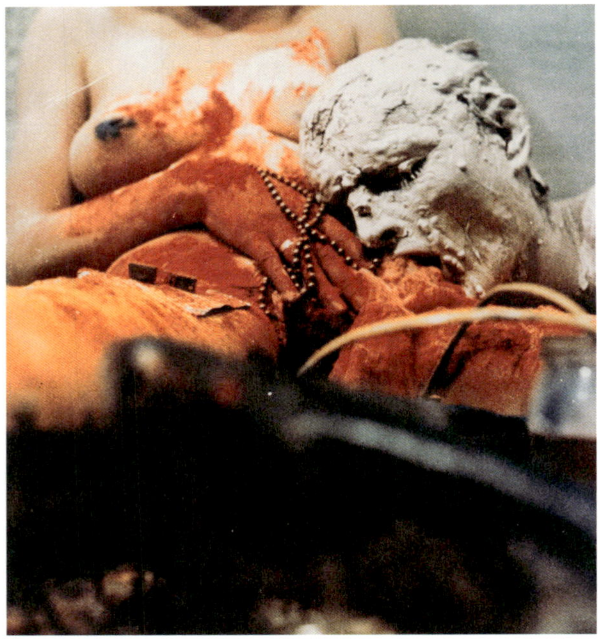

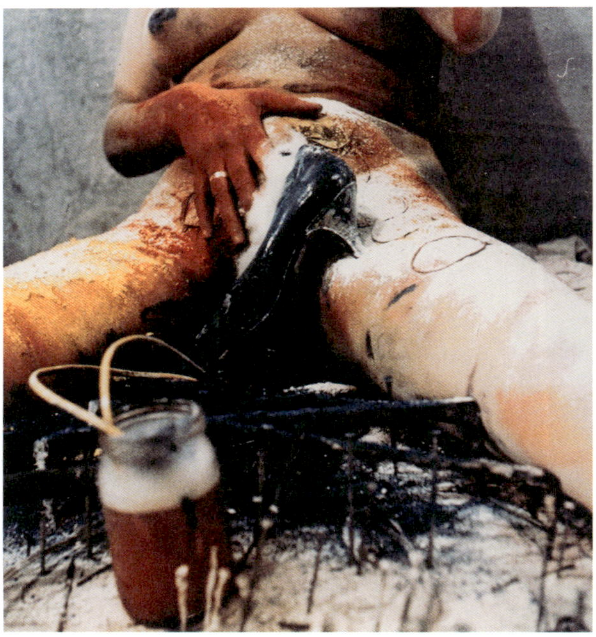

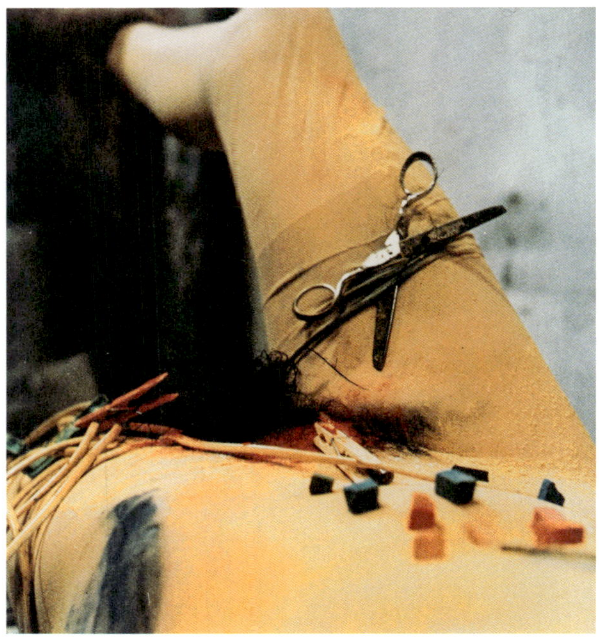

Fig. 77, 78, 79, 80, 81
Günter Brus
Transfusion, fall 1965
Muehl's studio, Perinetgasse 1, 1200 Vienna
Colour photographs
photo: Ludwig Hoffenreich
with: Anna Brus

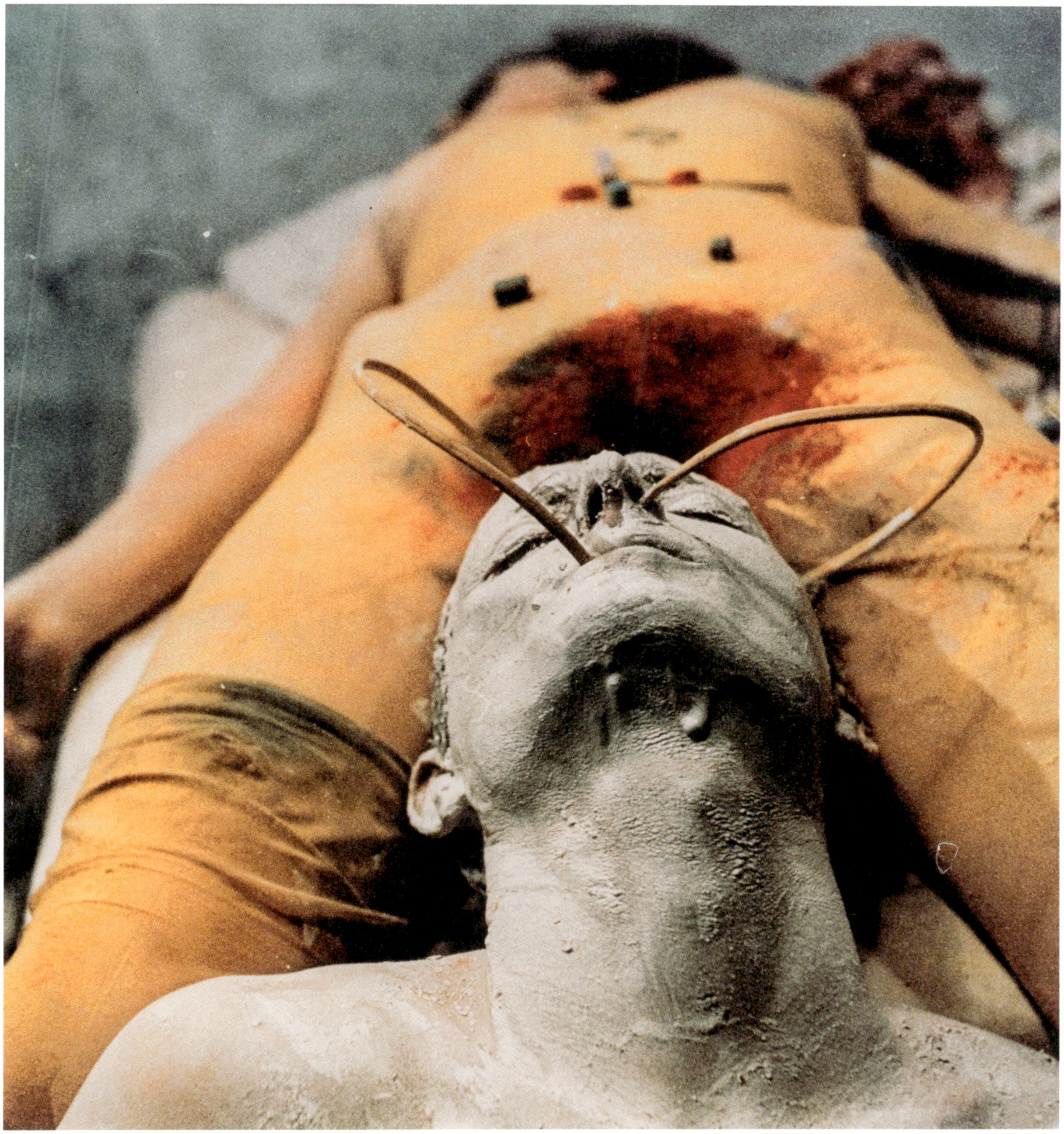

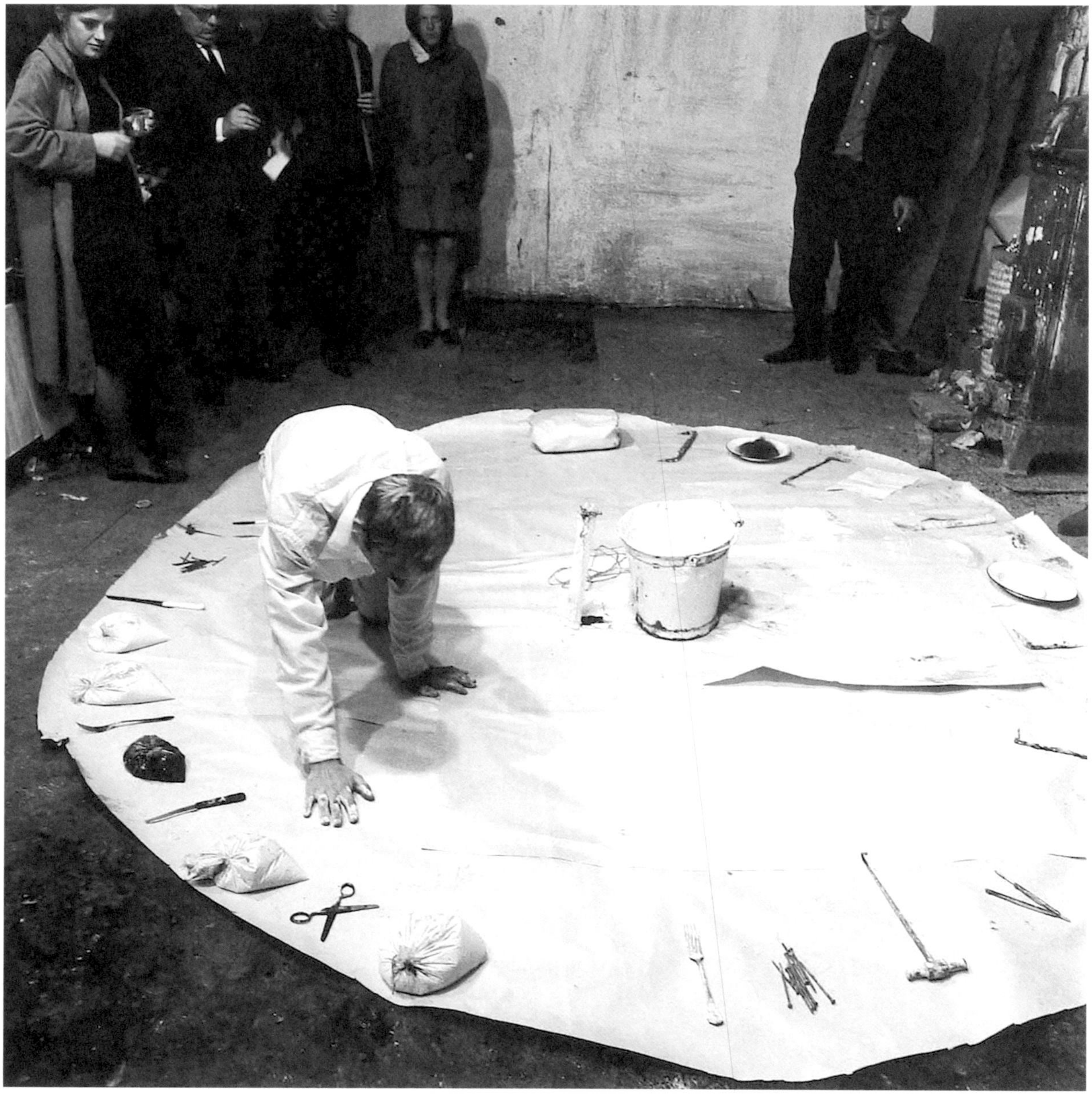

Fig. 82, 83
Günter Brus
Aktion in einem Kreis (Action in a Circle), 2 September 1966,
at the press conference for the *Destruction in Art Symposium*
Muehl's studio, Perinetgasse 1, 1200 Vienna
B/W photographs
photo: Ludwig Hoffenreich

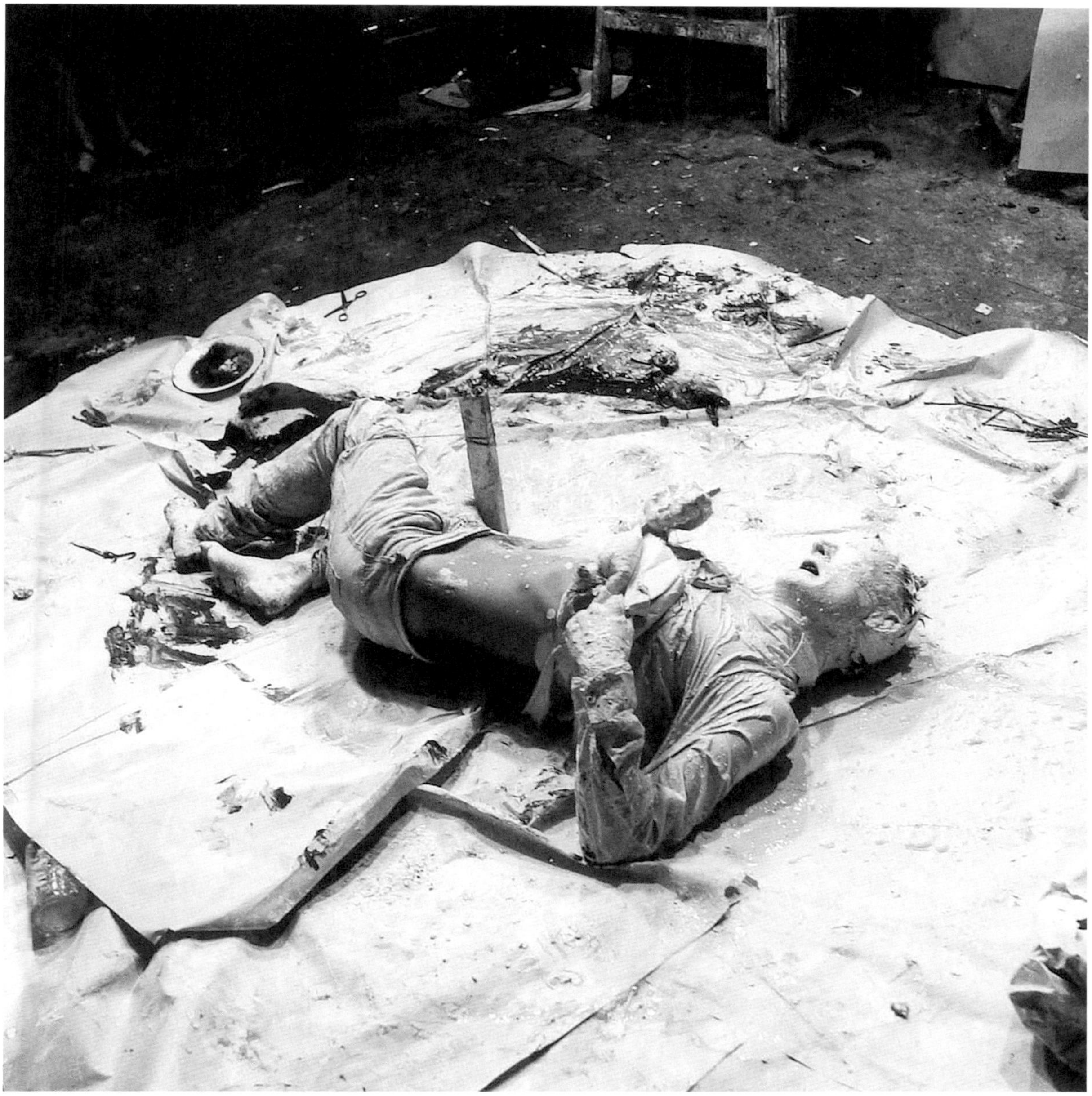

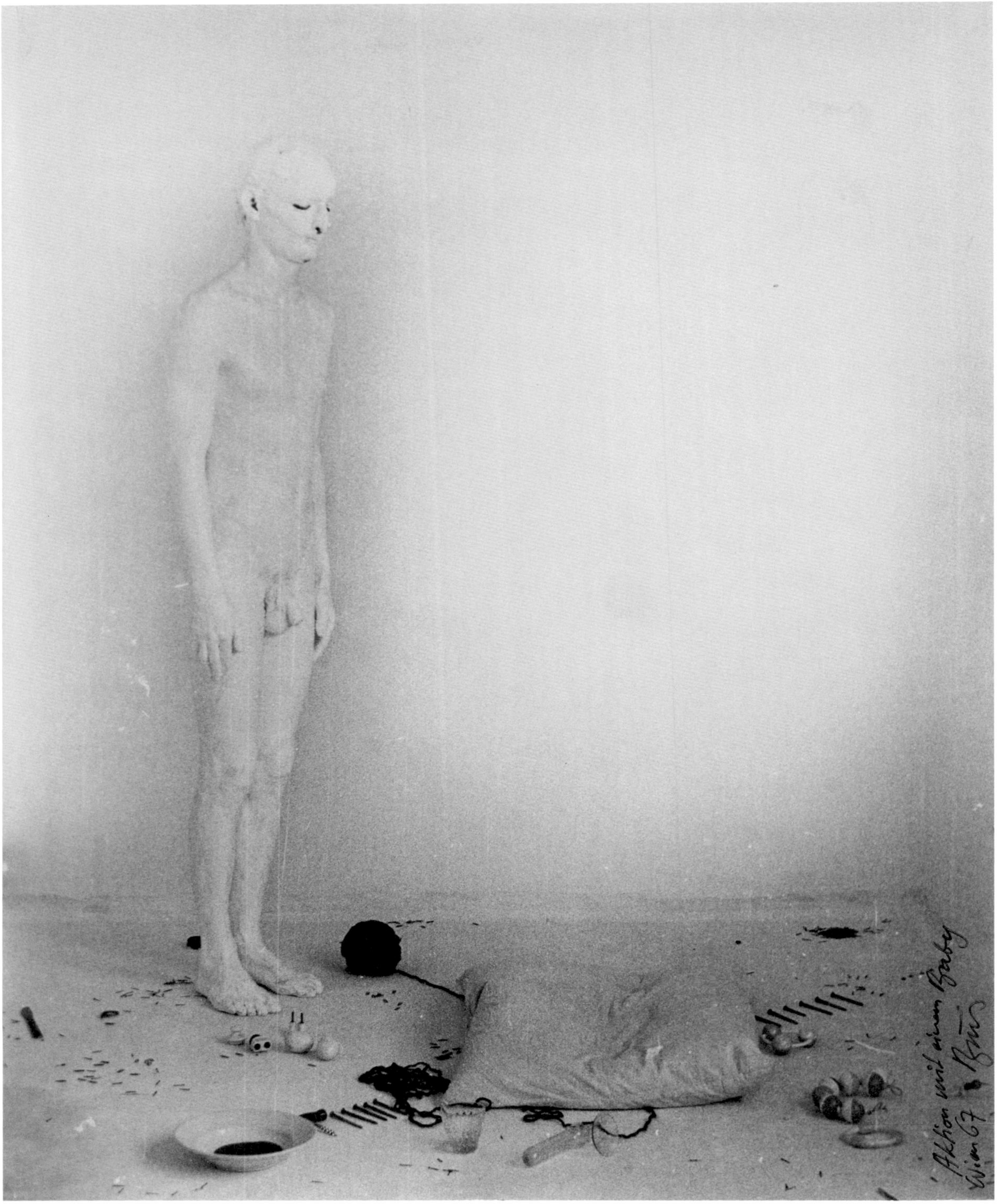

Fig. 84, 85, 86
Günter Brus
Aktion mit Diana (Action with Diana), September 1967
Brus's apartment, Adalbert-Stifter-Straße 31/20/40, 1200 Vienna
B/W photographs
photo: Kurt Kren
with: Diana Brus

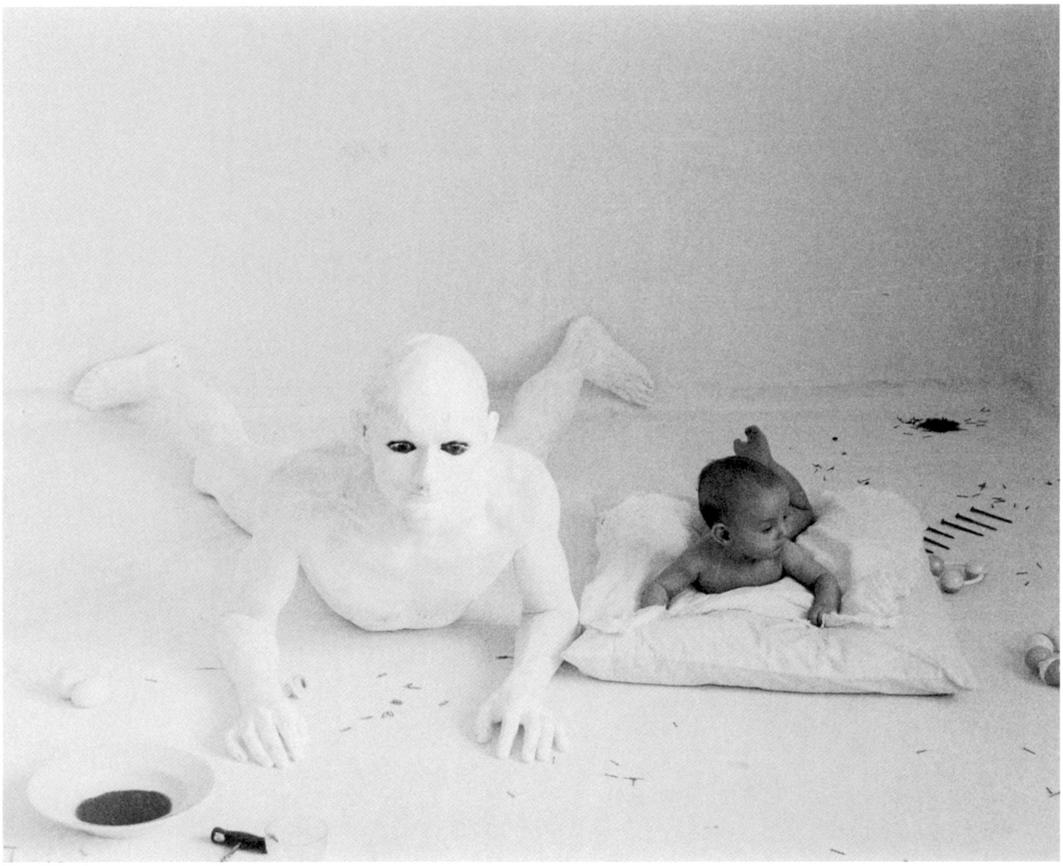

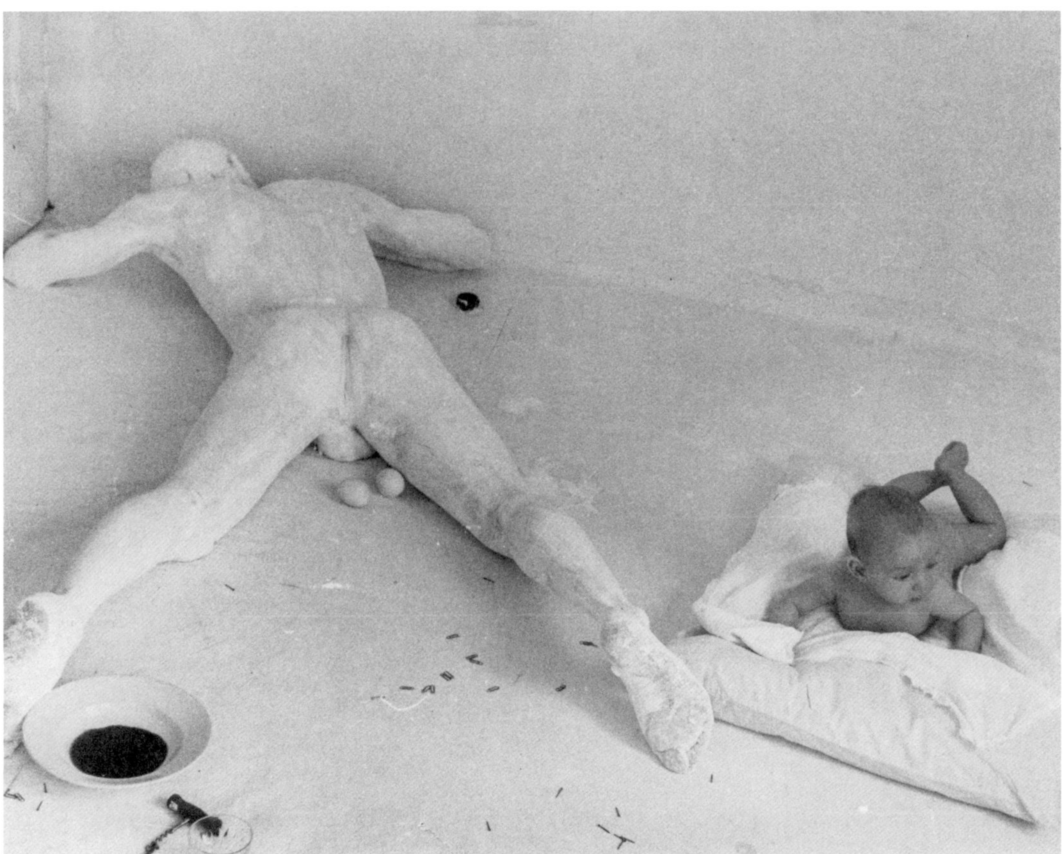

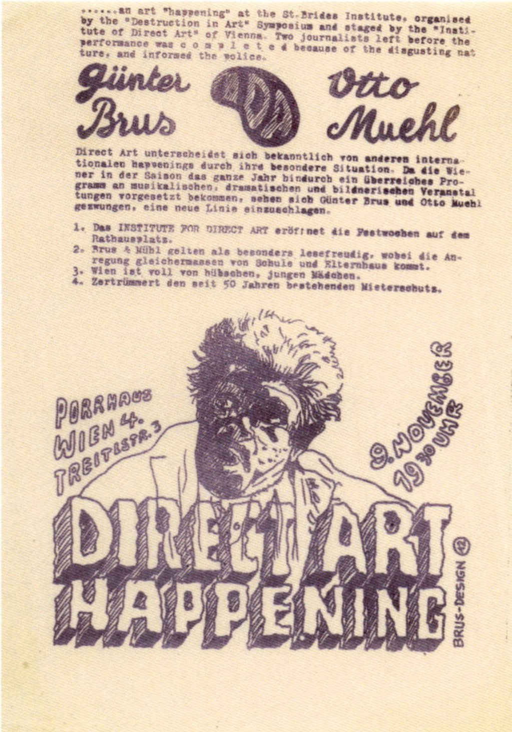

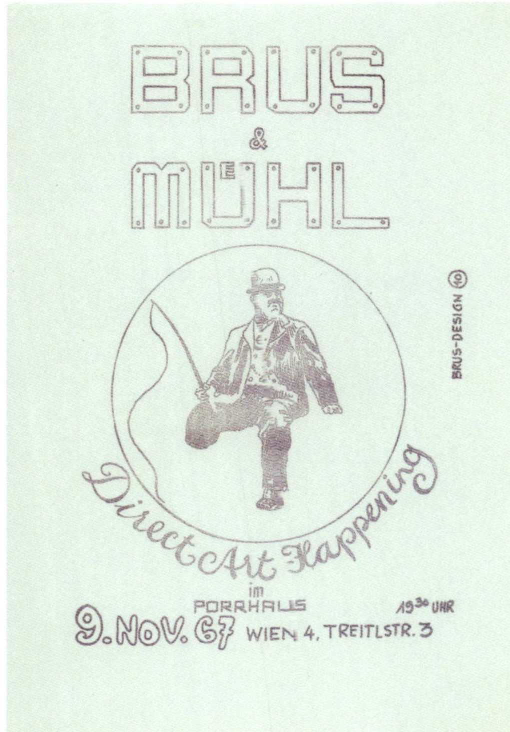

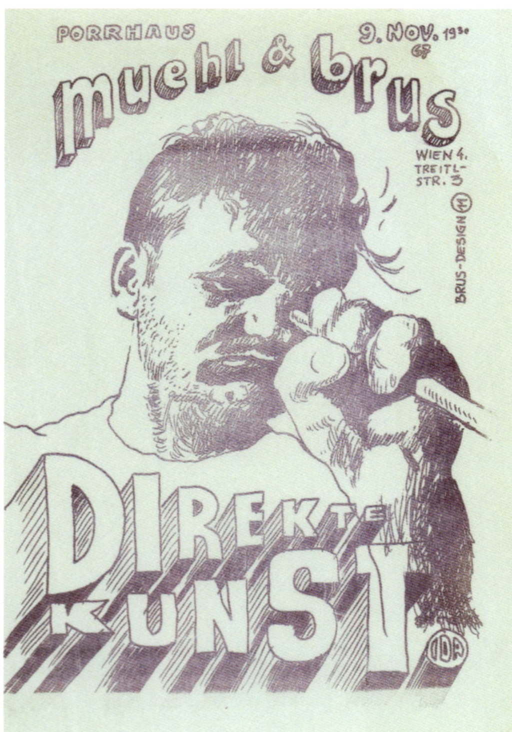

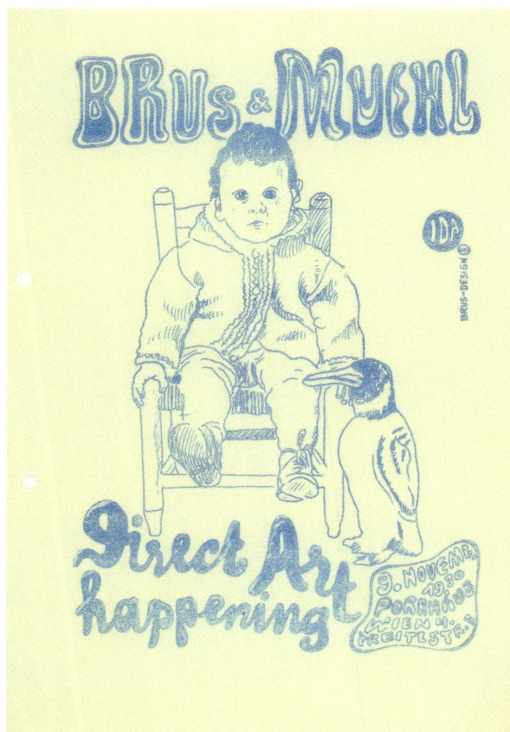

Fig. 87, 88, 89, 90
Günter Brus
Announcements for the *Direct Art Festival (Direct Art Happening)*, 1967
Matrix prints
29,7 x 21 cm
WAM – Wiener Aktionismus Museum, Vienna, Collection K.

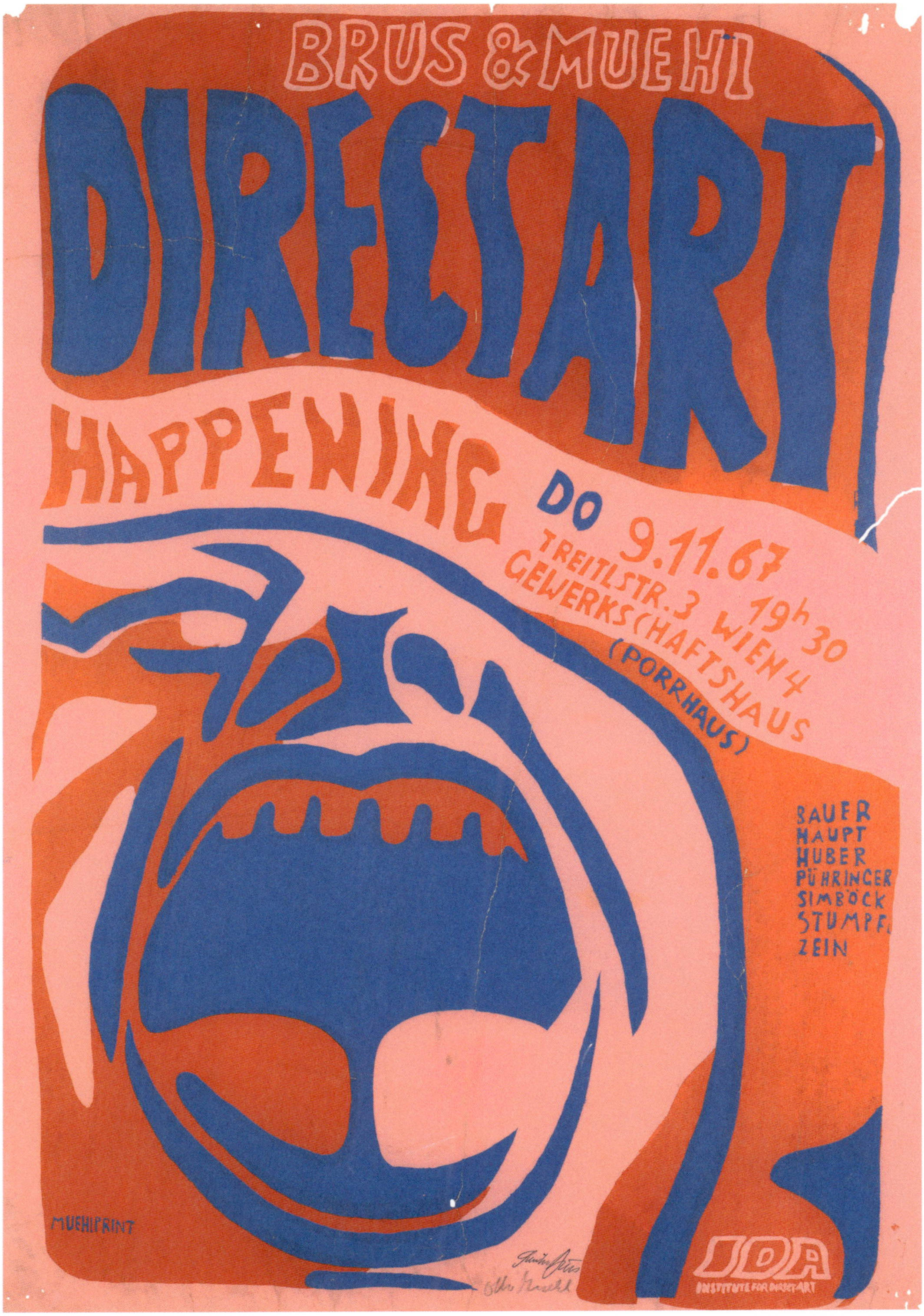

Fig. 91
Günter Brus
Poster for the *Direct Art Festival (Direct Art Happening)*, 1967
Silkscreen on paper
86,5 x 62 cm
WAM – Wiener Aktionismus Museum, Vienna, Collection K.

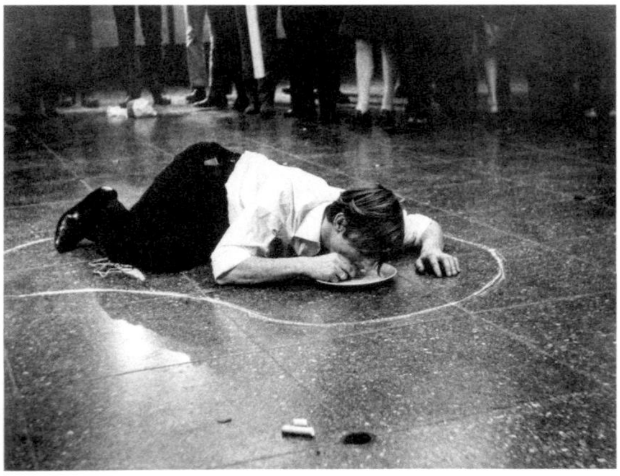

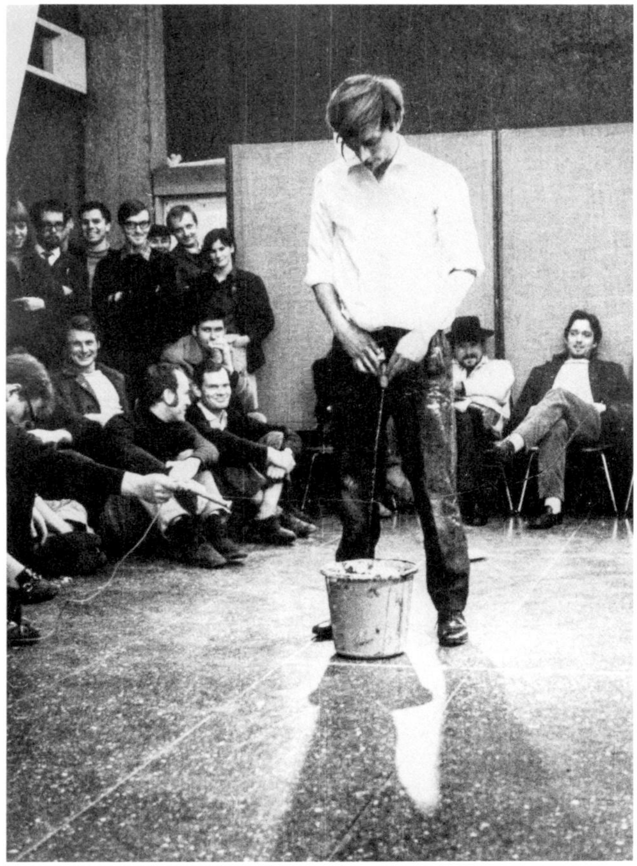

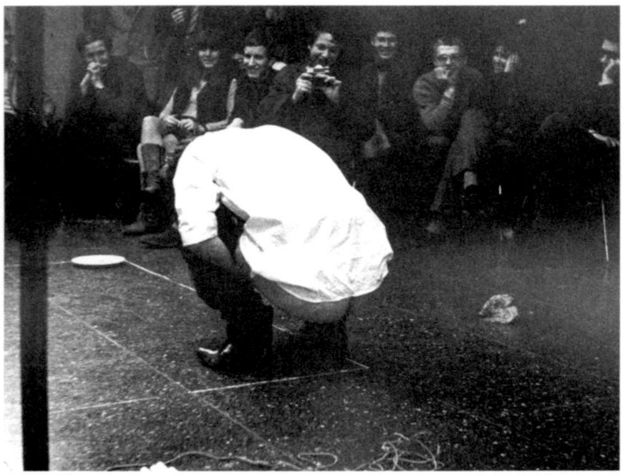

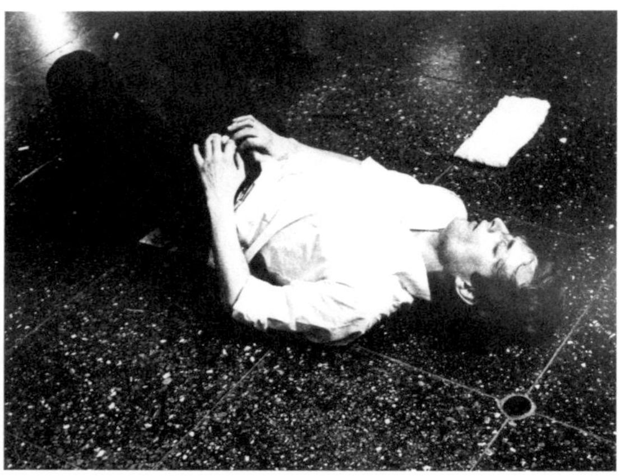

Fig. 92, 93, 94, 95, 96
Günter Brus
„Der helle Wahnsinn", für Aachen: „Die Architektur des hellen Wahnsinns"
("Sheer Madness", for Aachen: "The Architecture of Sheer Madness"), 6 February 1968
Reiff-Museum (Rheinisch-Westfälische Technische Hochschule),
Schinkelstraße 1, Aachen
B/W photographs
photo: Henning Wolters

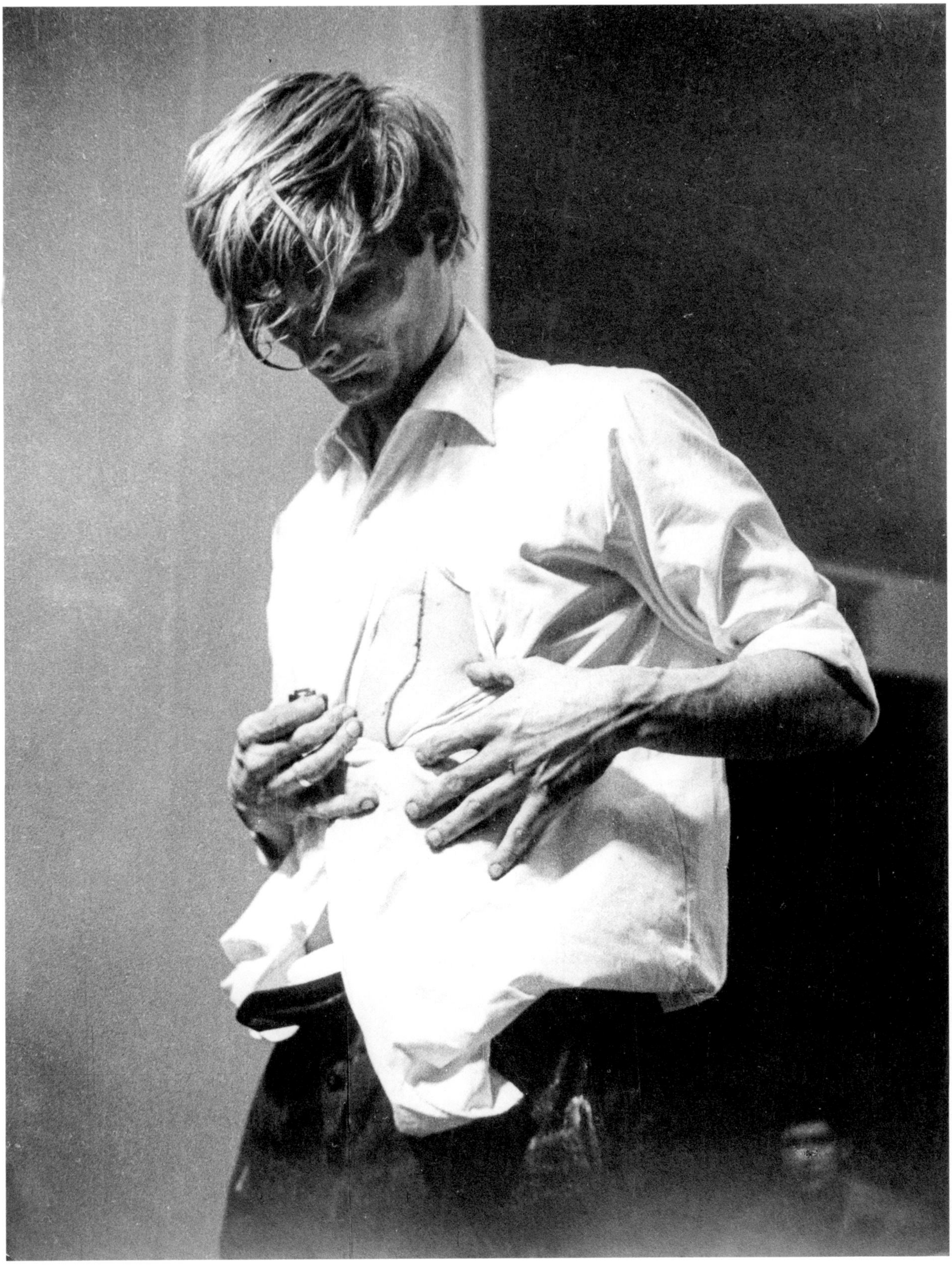

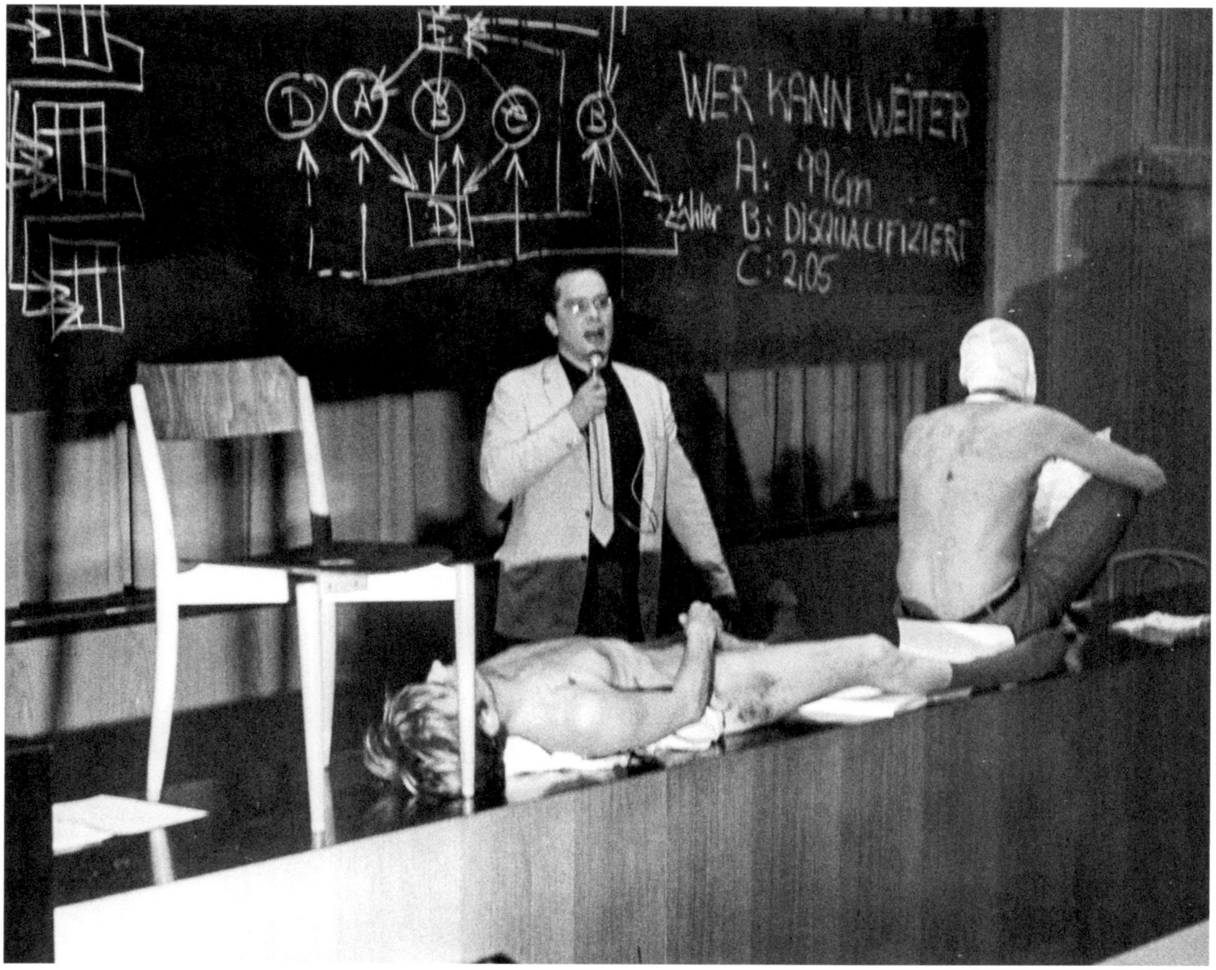

Fig. 97, 98
Günter Brus, Otto Muehl, Peter Weibel, Oswald Wiener and others
Kunst und Revolution (Art and Revolution), 7 June 1968
Universiy of Vienna, Lecture Hall 1 of the Neue Institutsgebäude, Universitätsstraße 7, 1010 Vienna
B/W photographs
photo: Khasaq (Siegfried Klein)
with: Direct Art Group (Otmar Bauer, Dieter Haupt, Herbert Stumpfl, Anastas [Josef Kainz], Franz Kaltenbäck, Malte Olschewski [Laurids])

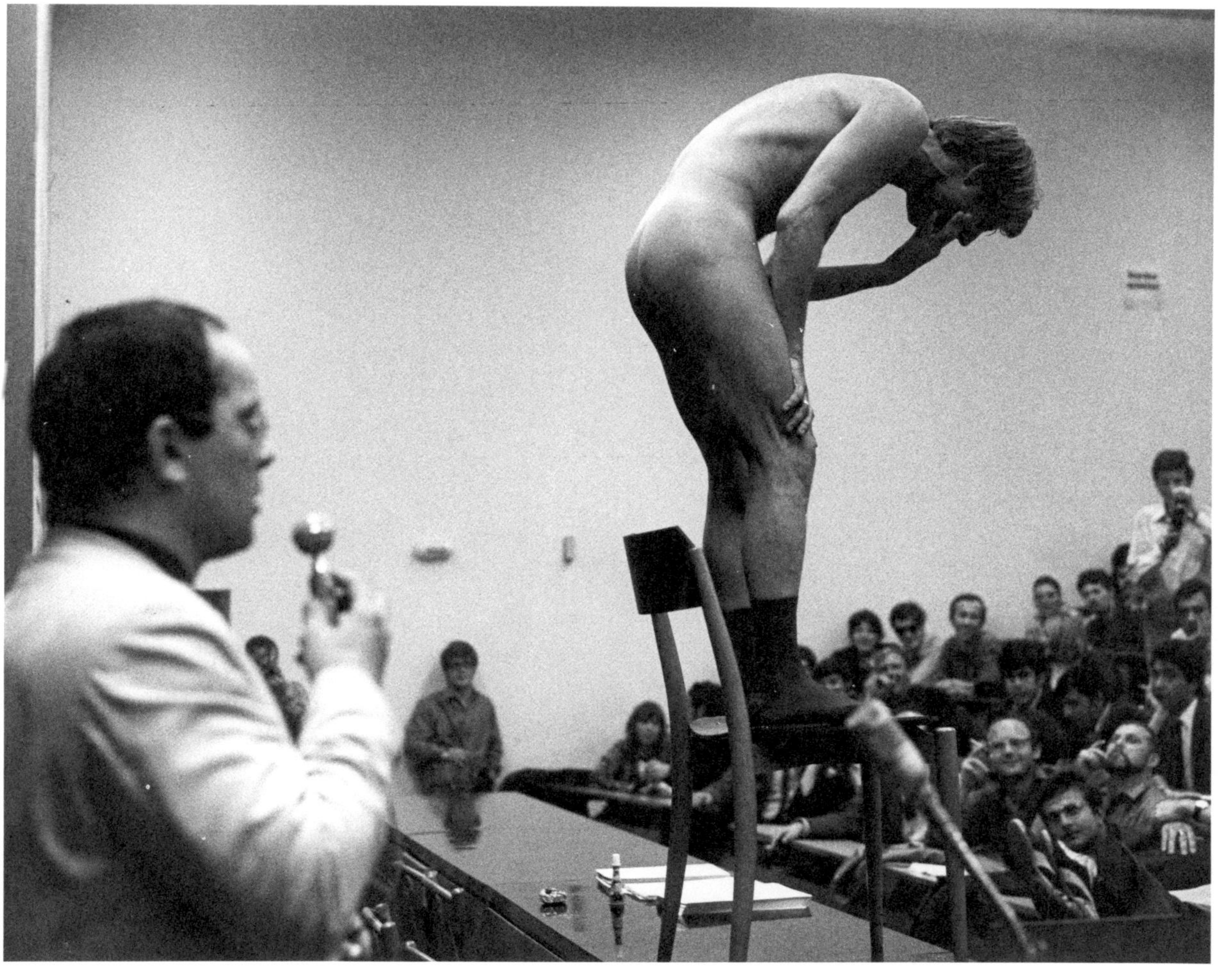

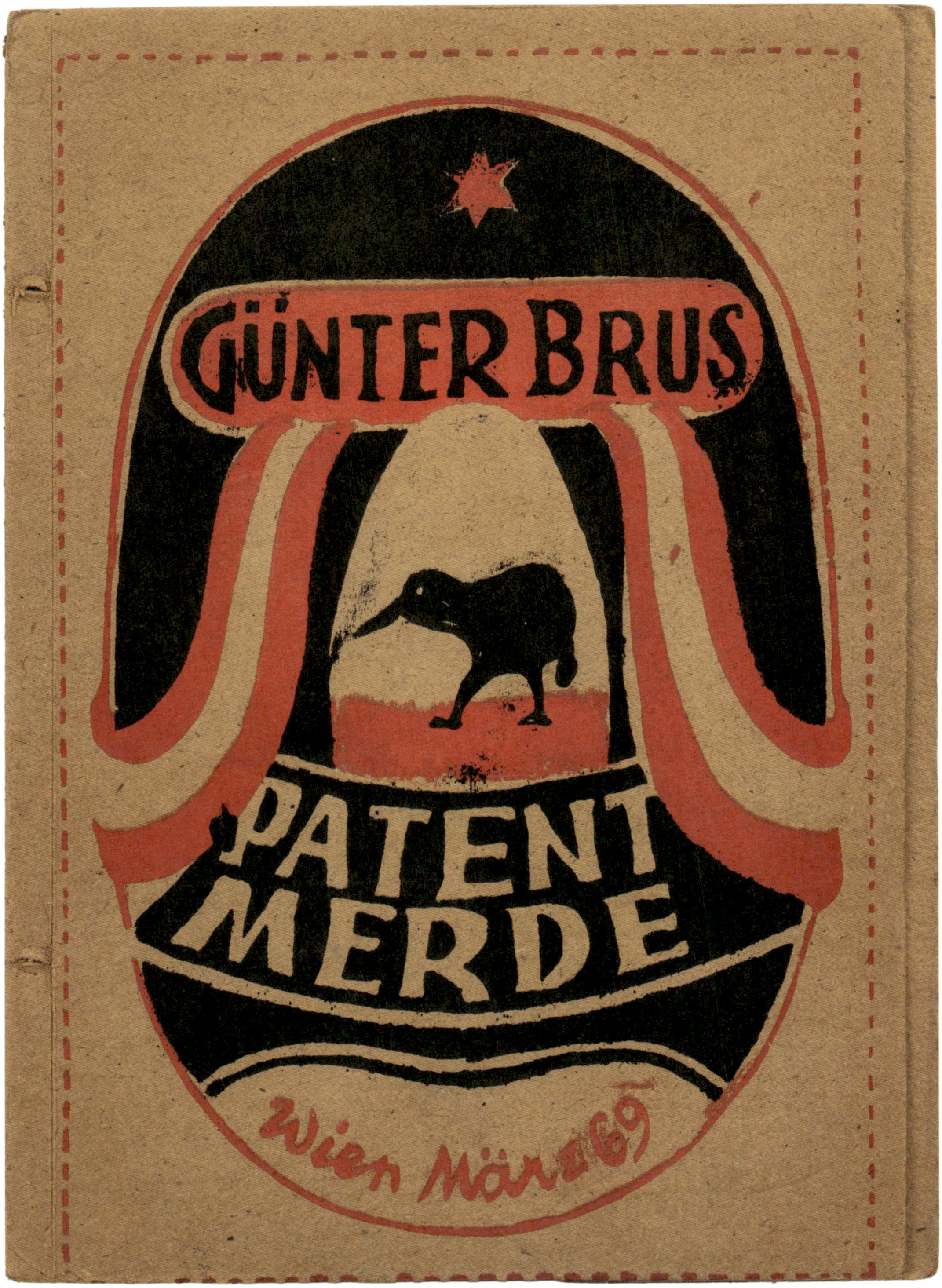

Fig. 99, 100, 101, 102, 103
Günter Brus
Cover and pages from: *Patent merde*, March 1969
Silkscreen and matrix print on cardboard and magazine pages
29,9 x 21,3 cm
WAM – Wiener Aktionismus Museum, Vienna

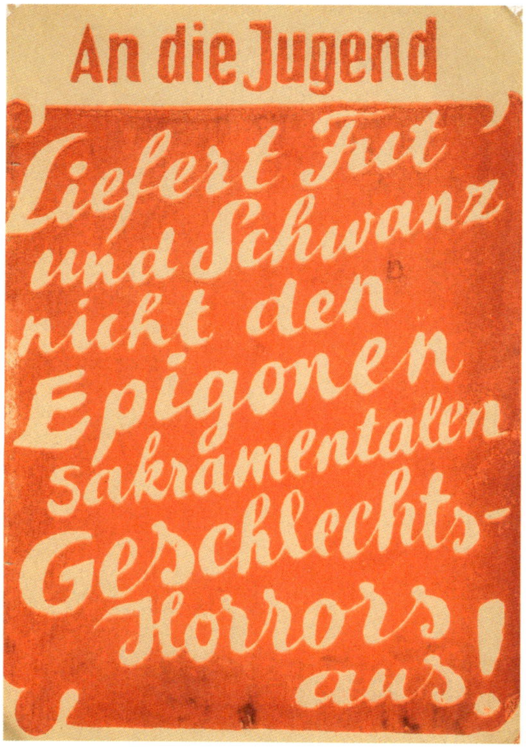
An die Jugend
Liefert Fut
und Schwanz
nicht den
Epigonen
sakramentalen
Geschlechts-
Horrors
aus!

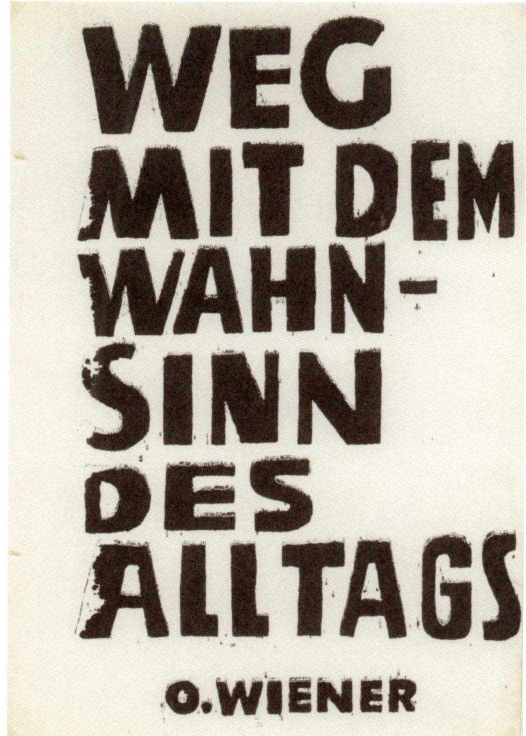
WEG
MIT DEM
WAHN-
SINN
DES
ALLTAGS
O. WIENER

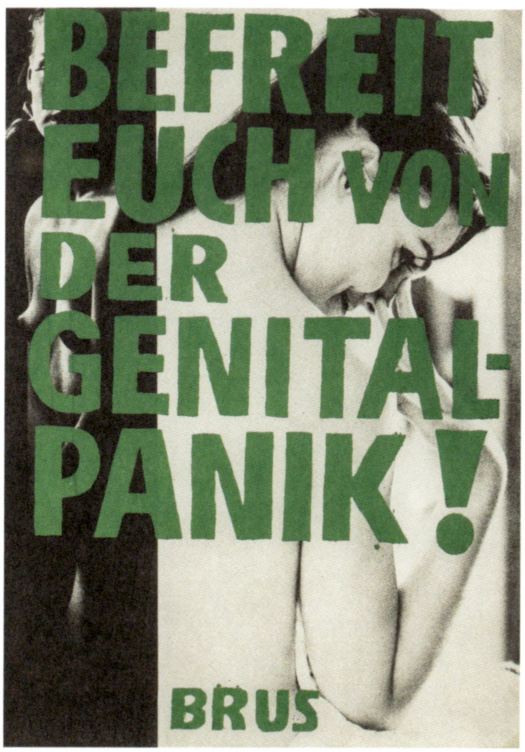
BEFREIT
EUCH VON
DER
GENITAL-
PANIK!
BRUS

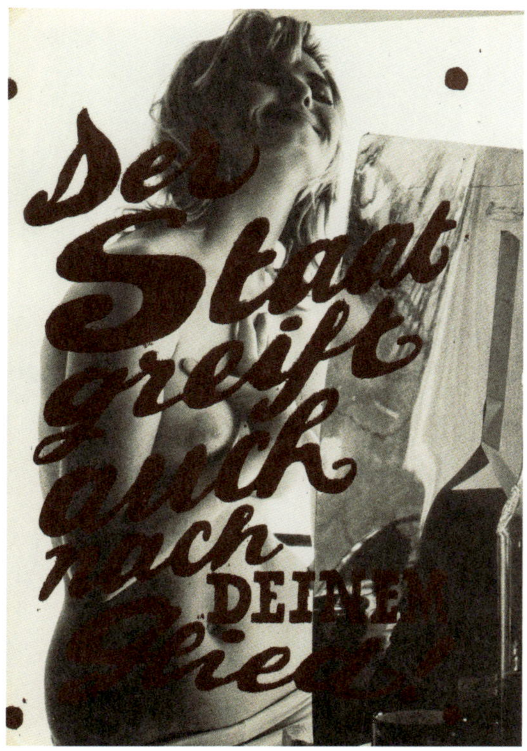
Der
Staat
greift
auch
nach

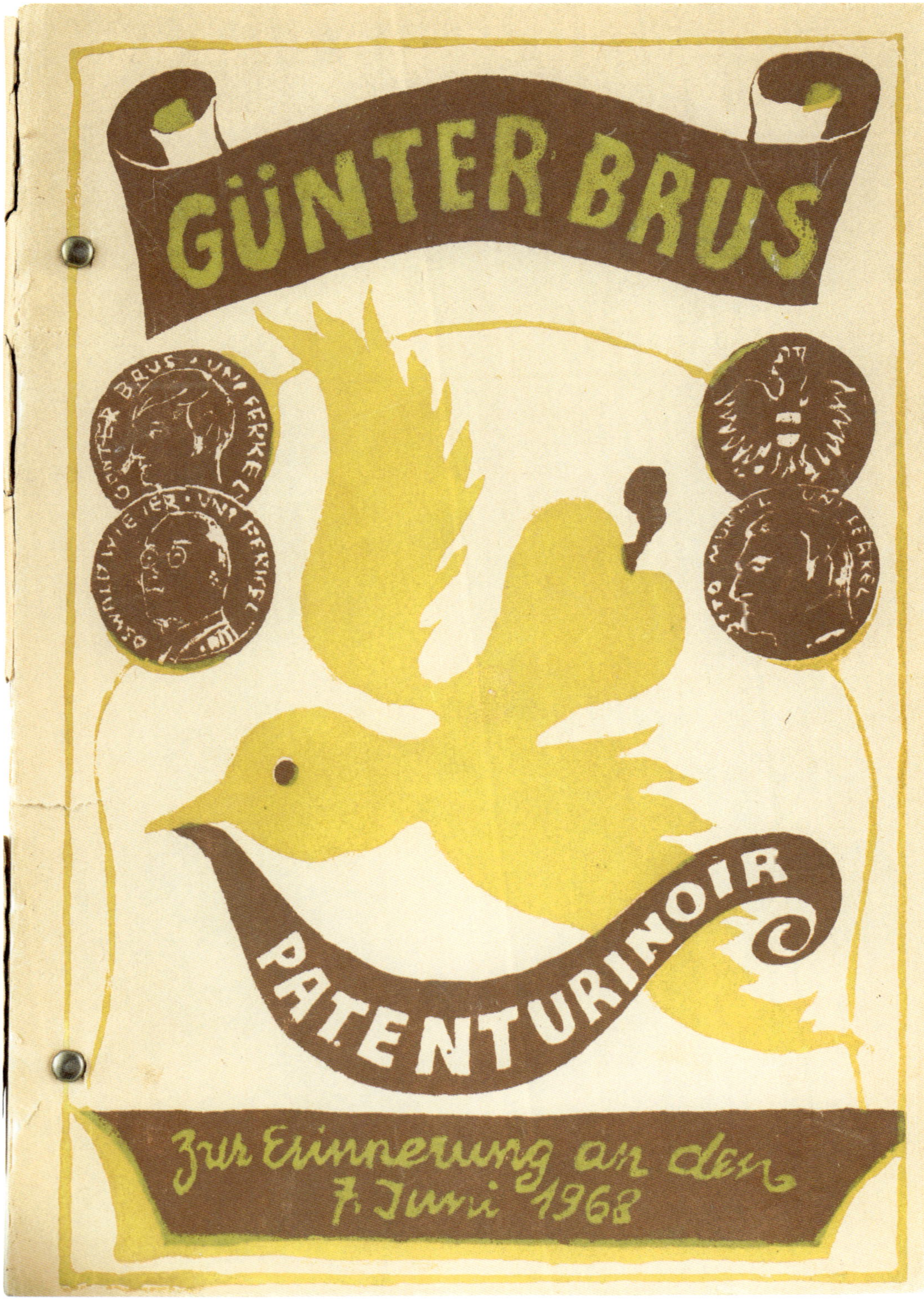

Fig. 104
Günter Brus
Cover, *Patent urinoir*, 1968
Silkscreen and matrix print on cardboard and paper, stapled
29,9 x 21,3 cm
WAM – Wiener Aktionismus Museum, Vienna, Collection K.

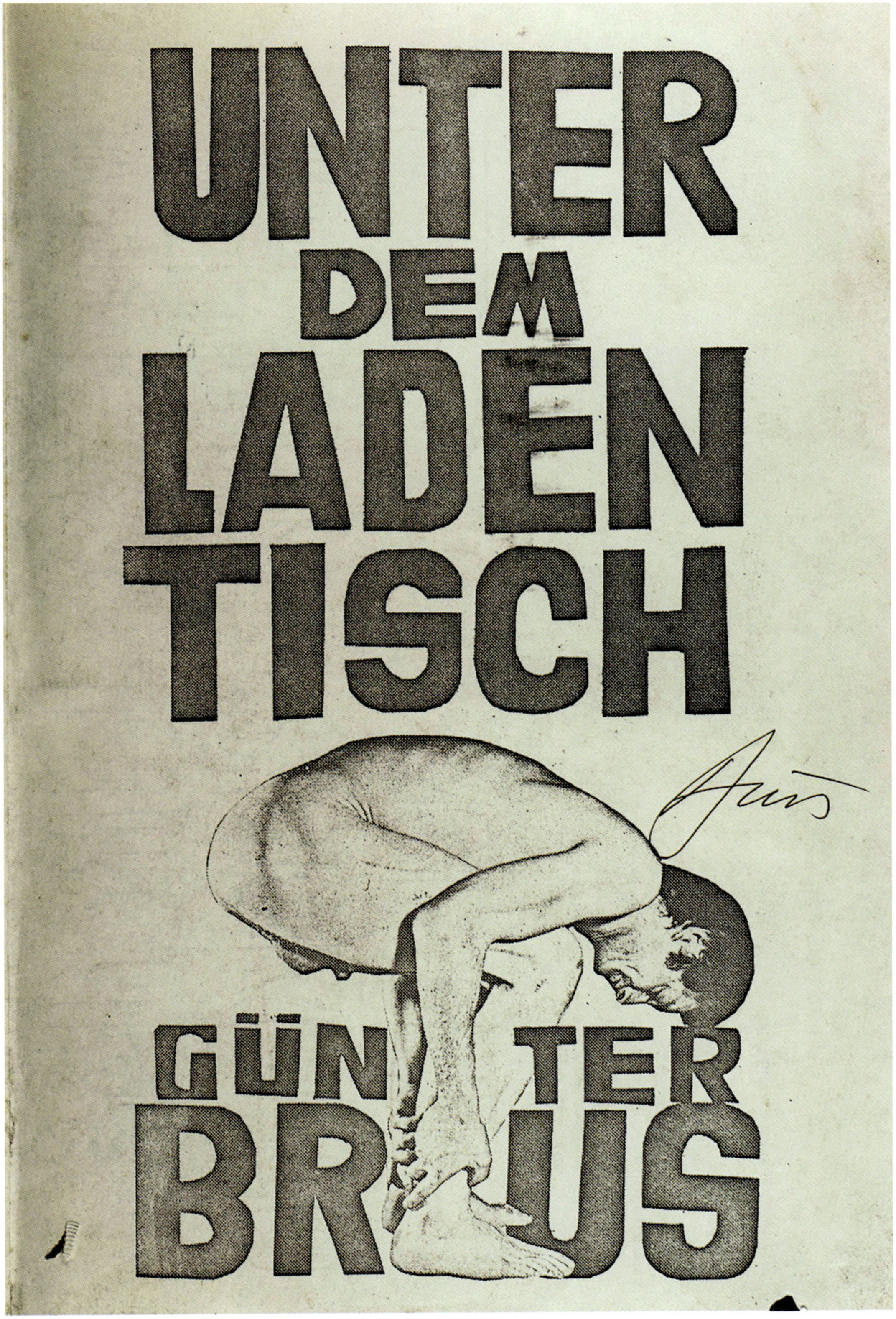

Fig. 105
Günter Brus
Cover of *Unter dem Ladentisch* (Under the Counter), 1969
Matrix print on paper, stapled
29,7 x 21 cm
WAM – Wiener Aktionismus Museum, Vienna

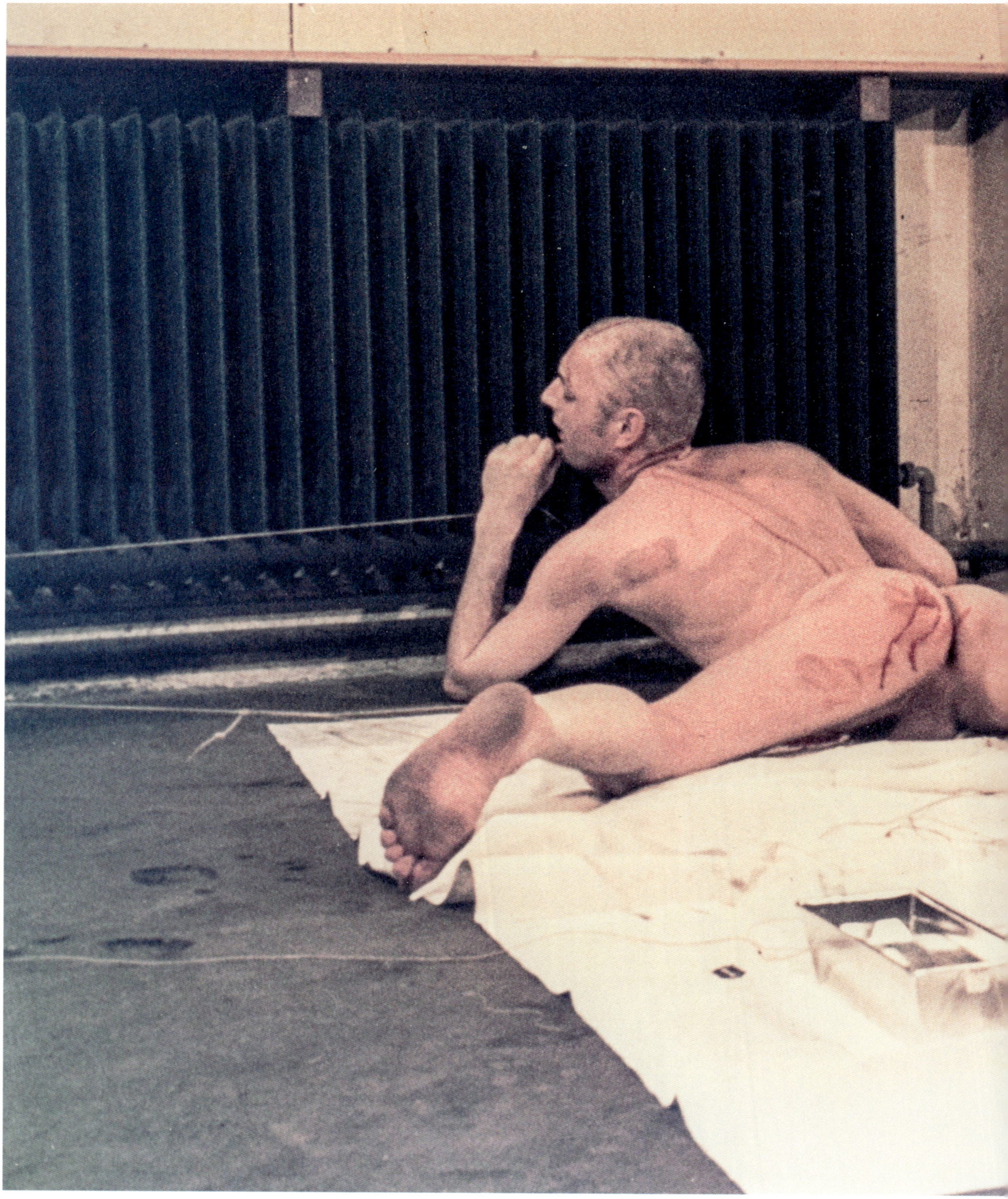

Fig. 106
Günter Brus
Zerreißprobe (Stress Test), 1970
Aktionsraum 1, Waltherstraße 25, Munich 15
Colour photograph
photo: Klaus Eschen

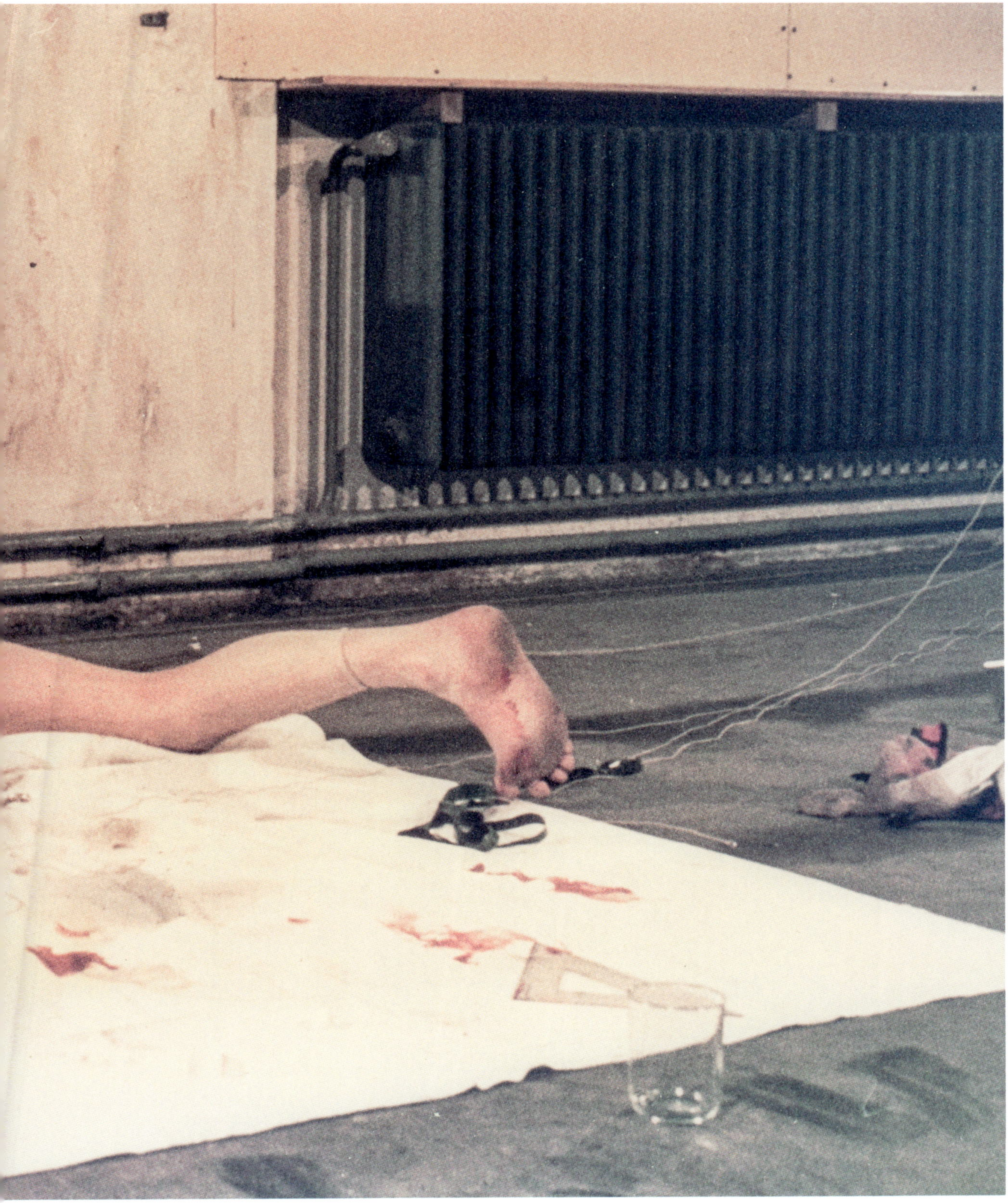

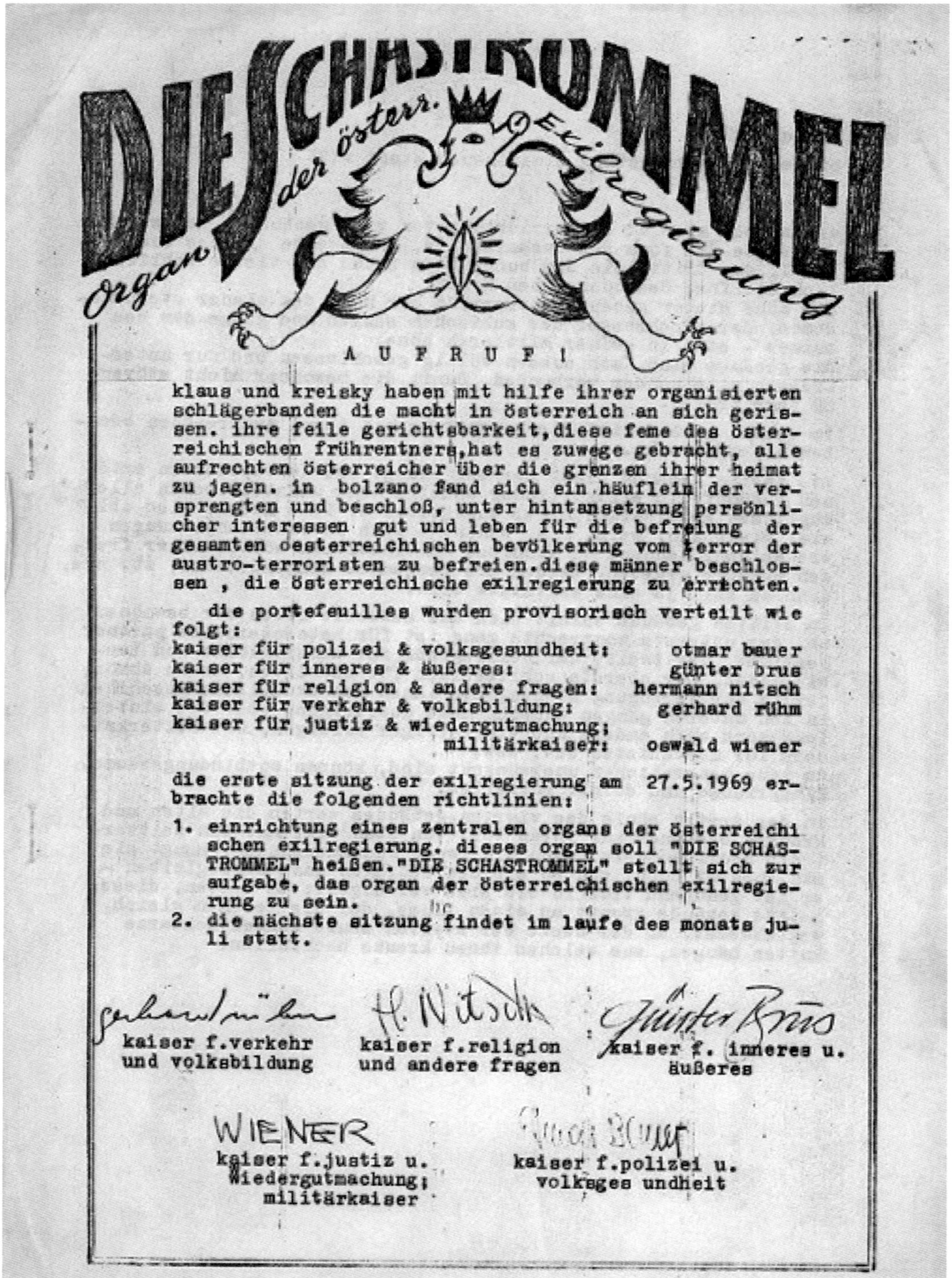

DIE SCHASTROMMEL

Organ der österr. Exilregierung

A U F R U F !

klaus und kreisky haben mit hilfe ihrer organisierten schlägerbanden die macht in österreich an sich gerissen. ihre feile gerichtsbarkeit, diese feme des österreichischen frührentners, hat es zuwege gebracht, alle aufrechten österreicher über die grenzen ihrer heimat zu jagen. in bolzano fand sich ein häuflein der versprengten und beschloß, unter hintansetzung persönlicher interessen gut und leben für die befreiung der gesamten oesterreichischen bevölkerung vom terror der austro-terroristen zu befreien. diese männer beschlossen , die österreichische exilregierung zu errichten.

die portefeuilles wurden provisorisch verteilt wie folgt:

kaiser für polizei & volksgesundheit: otmar bauer
kaiser für inneres & äußeres: günter brus
kaiser für religion & andere fragen: hermann nitsch
kaiser für verkehr & volksbildung: gerhard rühm
kaiser für justiz & wiedergutmachung;
militärkaiser: oswald wiener

die erste sitzung der exilregierung am 27.5.1969 erbrachte die folgenden richtlinien:

1. einrichtung eines zentralen organs der österreichischen exilregierung. dieses organ soll "DIE SCHASTROMMEL" heißen. "DIE SCHASTROMMEL" stellt sich zur aufgabe, das organ der österreichischen exilregierung zu sein.
2. die nächste sitzung findet im laufe des monats juli statt.

gerhard rühm
kaiser f.verkehr und volksbildung

H. Nitsch
kaiser f.religion und andere fragen

Günter Brus
kaiser f. inneres u. äußeres

WIENER
kaiser f.justiz u. wiedergutmachung; militärkaiser

kaiser f.polizei u. volksges undheit

Fig. 107
Günter Brus
Die Schastrommel (The Old Gossipmonger), no. 1, 1969
Matrix print on paper, stapled
29,7 x 21 cm
WAM – Wiener Aktionismus Museum, Vienna, Collection K.

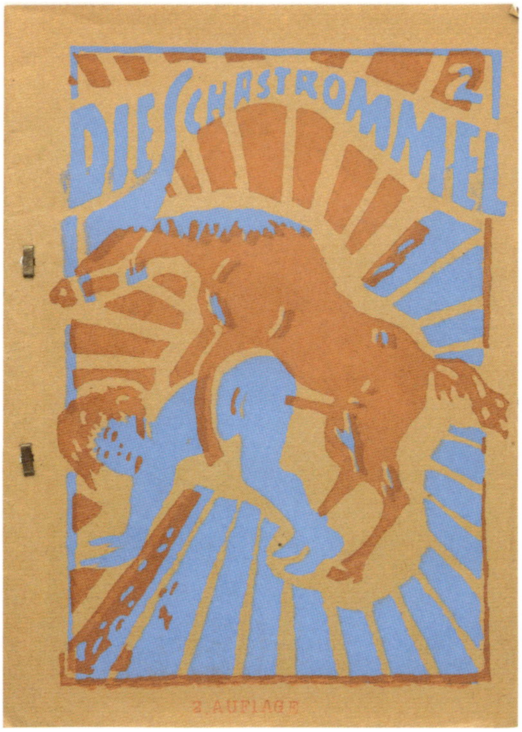

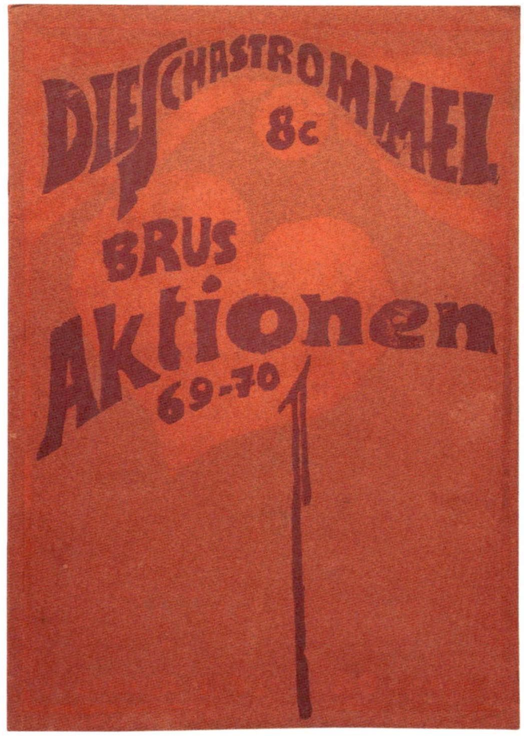

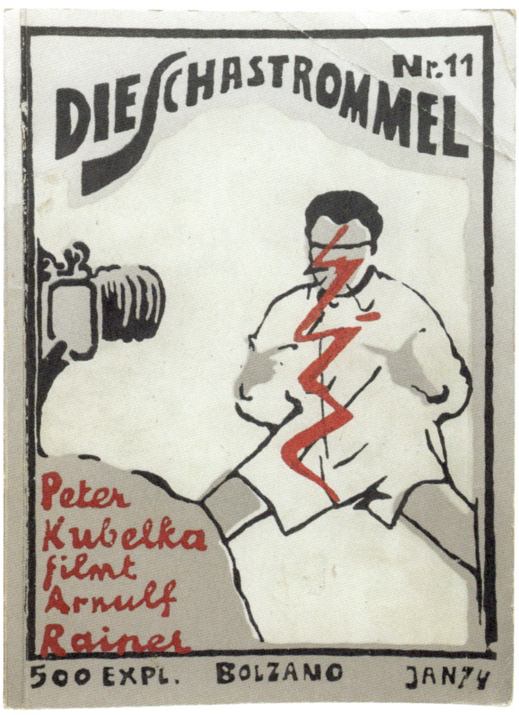

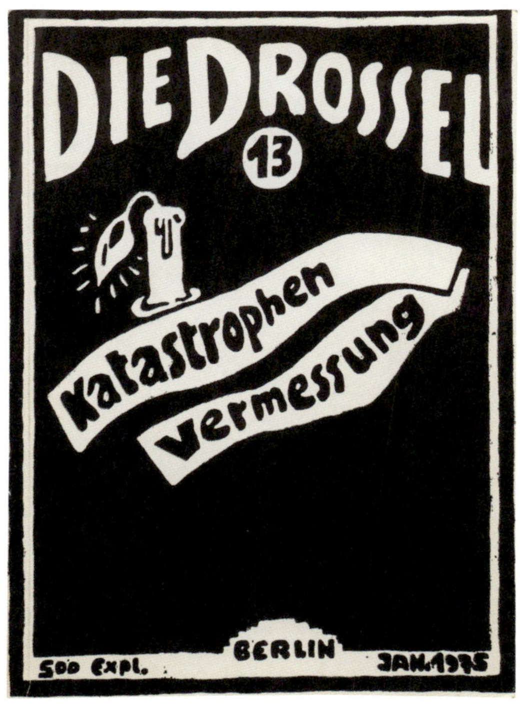

Fig. 108, 109, 110, 111
Günter Brus
Die Schastrommel (The Old Gossipmonger), no. 2, May 1970, 29,3 x 21,5 cm,
no. 8c, December 1972, 29,5 x 21 cm; no. 11, January 1974, 23 x 17,3 cm,
Die Drossel (The Song Trush), no. 13, January 1975, 23 x 17 cm
Silkscreen, matrix print on cardboard and paper
WAM – Wiener Aktionismus Museum, Vienna

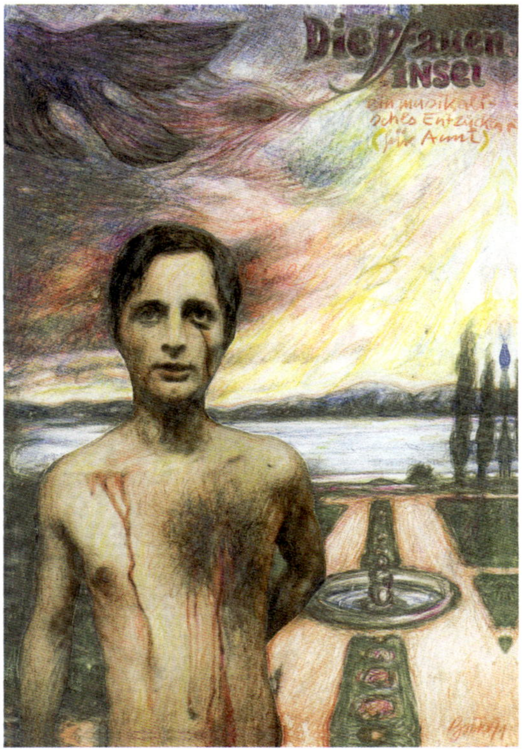

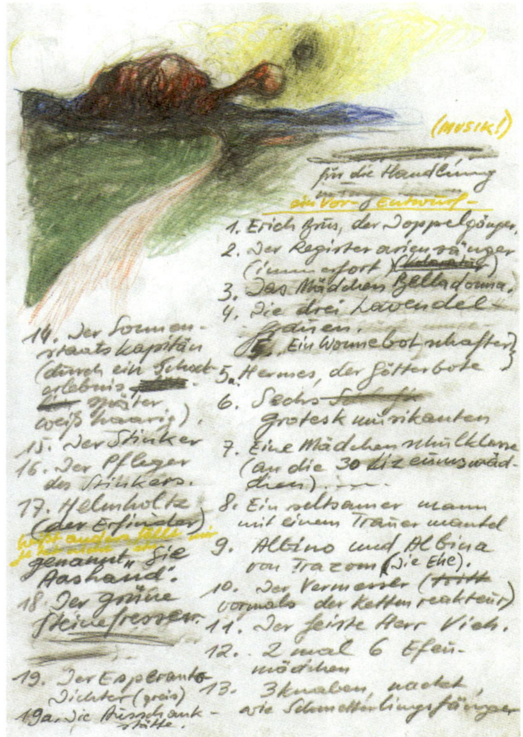

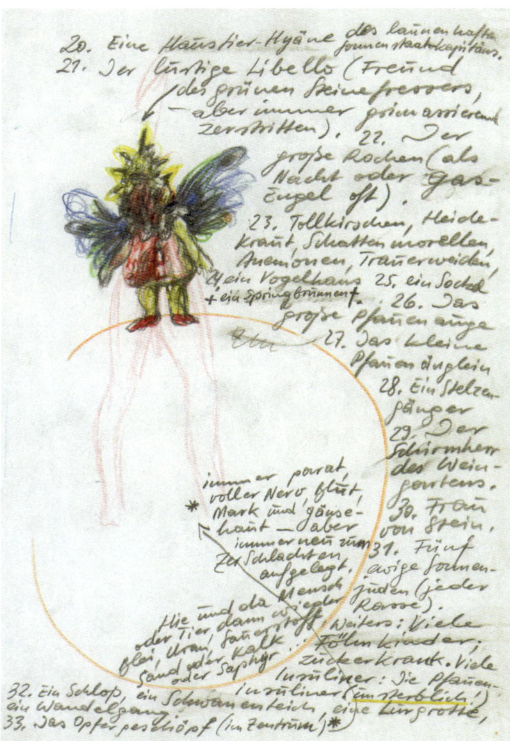

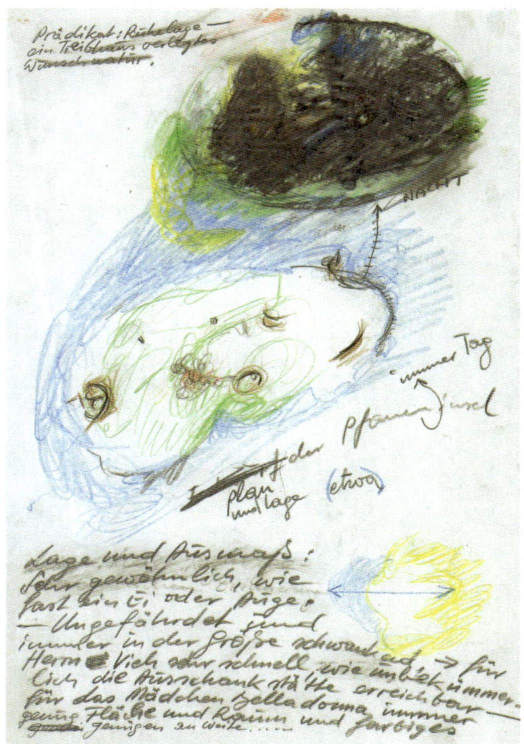

Fig. 112, 113, 114, 115, 116, 117, 118, 119
Günter Brus
Die Pfaueninsel (The Peacock Island), pages from the manuscript *Irrwisch* (Will-o'-the-Wisp), 1971
Typescript, pencil, coloured pencil on paper
29,7 x 21 cm
Walther König, Köln

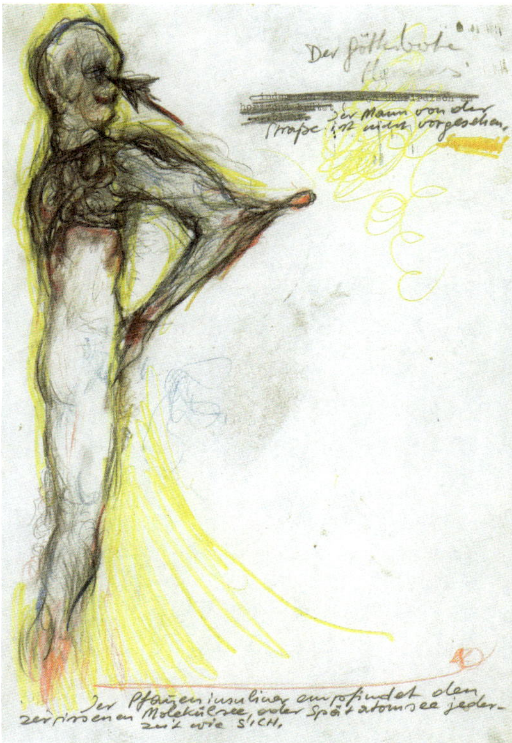
Der Mann von der Straße ist nicht vorgesehen.
Der Pflanzeninsuliner empfindet den zerrissenen Molekülsee, oder Spätatomsee jederzeit wie SICH.

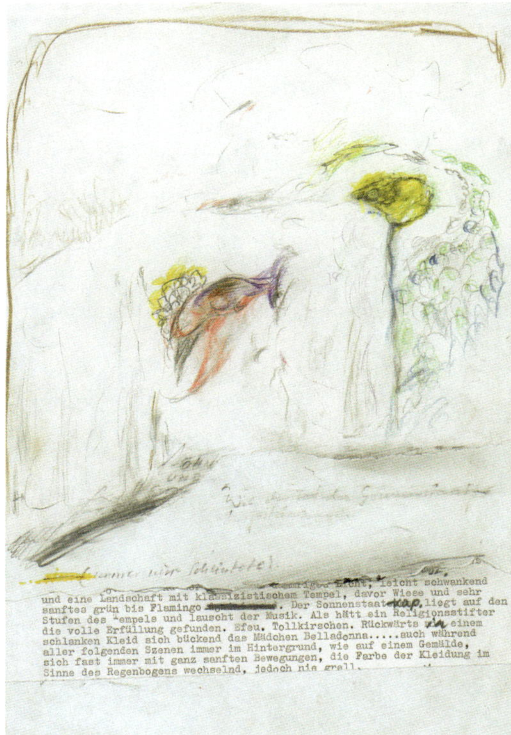
leicht schwankend und eine Landschaft mit klassizistischem Tempel, davor Wiese und sehr sanftes grün bis Flamingo. Der Sonnenstaat kap. liegt auf den Stufen des Tempels und lauscht der Musik. Als hätt ein Religionsstifter die volle Erfüllung gefunden. Efeu. Tollkirschen. Rückwärts einem schlanken Kleid sich bückend das Mädchen Belladonna.....auch während aller folgenden Szenen immer im Hintergrund, wie auf einem Gemälde, sich fast immer mit ganz sanften Bewegungen, die Farbe der Kleidung im Sinne des Regenbogens wechselnd, jedoch nie grell.

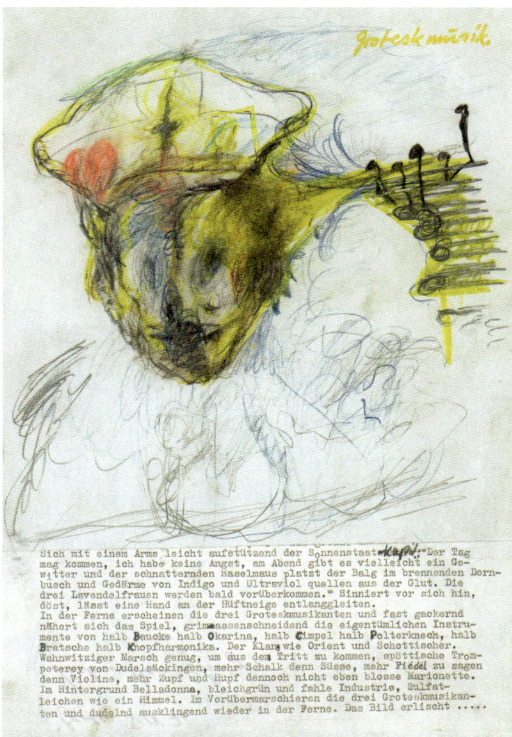
Groteskmusik.
Sich mit einem Arme leicht aufstützend der Sonnenstaat kapi.: "Der Tag mag kommen, ich habe keine Angst, am Abend gibt es vielleicht ein Gewitter und der schnatternden Haselmaus platzt der Balg im brennenden Dornbusch und Gedärme von Indigo und Ultraviol quellen aus der Glut. Die drei Lavendelfrauen werden bald vorüberkommen." Sinniert vor sich hin, döst, lässt eine Hand an der Hüftneige entlanggleiten.
In der Ferne erscheinen die drei Groteskmusikanten und fast gackernd nähert sich das Spiel, grimassenschneidend die eigentümlichen Instrumente von halb Baucke halb Okarina, halb Cimpel halb Polterknech, halb Bratsche halb Knopfharmonika. Der Klang wie Orient und Schottischer. Wahnwitziger Marsch genug, um aus dem Tritt zu kommen, spöttische Trompeterey von Dudelsäckingen, mehr Schalk denn Süsse, mehr Fiedel zu sagen denn Violine, mehr Zupf und Hupf dennoch nicht eben blosse Marionette. Im Hintergrund Belladonna, bleichgrün und fahle Industrie, Sulfatleichen wie ein Himmel. Im Vorübermarschieren die drei Groteskmusikanten und dudelnd ausklingend wieder in der Ferne. Das Bild erlischt .....

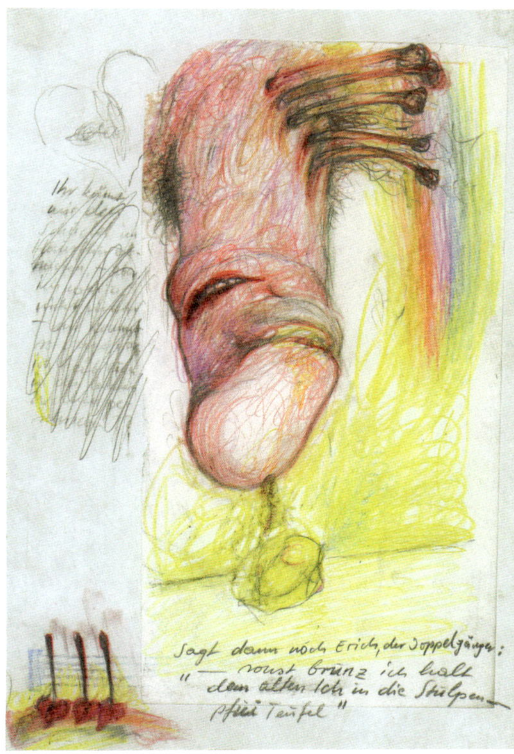
Sagt dann noch Erich, der Doppelgänger:
"— sonst brunz ich halt dem alten Ich in die Stulpen — pfüat Teufel"

7
Otto Muehl, letter to Erika Stocker, 14 January 1962, mumok Vienna.

8
Otto Muehl, *Weg aus dem Sumpf*, Nuremberg 1977, p. 148.

Otto Muehl

While Brus, Nitsch, and Schwarzkogler each attended graphic art colleges, Muehl, who was more than ten years older than the other artists, studied visual arts education at the Academy of Fine Arts in Vienna, after initially studying history and German, to become a school teacher.

His artistic beginnings consisted of figurative, partly expressive, partly cubist painting. (Fig. 120, 121) The material—which he understood in a broader sense as the tangible as well as being in general, including the human body—was to become the central element and vehicle of expression in his further work. "Material is the actual object of our works. It is a matter of representing the material: purely and simply matter."[7]

Material Pictures and Material Objects

The pivotal experience for Muehl came in late 1960, when he encountered the informal painting style of the significantly younger Brus, characterised by intense bodily motions and an excessive use of paint. This fascinated Muehl greatly, giving way to a new approach to his own artistic work. Retrospectively, he later enthusiastically recalled Brus's "total creative excess [...]. The whole room was flecked with paint. The dried pigment sludge was centimetres high on the floor. There was no point trying to wash it away. The floor was littered with stubs of paint-encrusted brushes with which he used to scratch into his pictures."[8]

Soon afterwards, Muehl started to pour materials—such as pure pigment—directly onto painting grounds, spread it out on the floor, mix it with cement and lime and add various waste-objects and substances, which rendered his works increasingly relief-like. (Fig. 122, 123, 130) Similar to Nitsch's Painting Actions, physical and psychological acting out played a central role during the work process for him. He would stand directly on the canvas, throw the paints, step onto them, and roll around in them.

His next step was to gradually destroy the canvas. He slit it open, smashed the stretcher frame, and tied the two elements together, this way creating sculptural works. (Fig. 124) Muehl understood destruction as a constructive design principle—a conviction that he also transferred onto society: in his opinion, its norms and conventions, which he perceived as restrictive, could only be changed through the willingness to destroy. This way, energies should be released to bring about renewal. (Fig. 126–127)

Around the same time, Muehl also made material objects that in addition to waste items incorporated mirrors, among other reasons to include the surrounding space. (Fig. 125) After that, his works became increasingly expansive in terms of space leading him to his *Gerümpelplastiken* (Junk Sculptures). One of these was produced with his, back then, close artist friend Adolf Frohner during the three-day working retreat *Die Blutorgel* (The Blood Organ), whereby each of them began working in a different corner of the room, until their works finally met. (Fig. 131)

Material Actions

The next step for Muehl was to plan his first action as a public appearance from the outset. As part of a joint event that he realised together with Nitsch on 23 June 1963 under the title, *Fest des psychophysischen Naturalismus* (Festival of Psychophysical Naturalism) (Fig. 134, 135), a large-format material-picture was to be created, as the result of an actionist event. For this, he wanted to throw a kitchen credenza with all its contents of food, dishes, and utensils onto the street from the fourth floor of the house on Vienna's Perinetgasse, in which his basement studio was located. Everything was supposed to spread out on the ground and be smashed by Muehl with a hoe. However, the event was broken up by the police after Nitsch's action, so that Muehl was not able to carry out his intended part.

Finally, he realised his first action a few months later in his studio on Obere Augartenstrasse, behind closed doors. Entitled *Versumpfung eines weiblichen Körpers – Versumpfung einer Venus* (Bogging Down a Female Body–Bogging Down a Venus), he covered a woman's naked body with paint, wrapped it with cloths soaked in paint and knotted it with strings. (Fig. 136–139) In this way he combined his painterly and sculptural practice within the framework of a pictorial event in space and time. The title of this action can be read in multiple ways: on the one hand, the term "bog" stands for the different, mostly waste-like, dirty materials that he used, and on the other hand, it serves as a metaphor for the repressed "dirty" aspects of human nature, which Muehl wanted to reveal and free from taboos in order to change society. "Venus" alluded to a traditional motif that was often taken as a pretext for erotic depictions. Like Nitsch, he saw his work operating across time, in a larger context of art history, to which he repeatedly referred in his works.

Starting with this *1st Action*, Muehl referred to his actionist works until 1966 as Material Actions–a term that corresponded to his fascination with the material and which he reflected on theoretically in numerous texts. At first, more actions followed in which female bodies were formed into sculptural objects by wrapping them in foil, tying them with strings, and smearing them with various substances. (Fig. 140)

9
Schwarzkogler did not take up the offer to accompany them.

10
Nitsch kept the term *Orgien Mysterien Theater* for his work, but had already used the expression "direct" in 1964 in his manifesto *Das Lamm* (The Lamb, Fig. 15, 16): "the development of art tended to use reality as a direct means of creation".

As another form of connection to historical art, he then moved on to staging still lives, in which he–contrary to traditional still life painting–involved human bodies. He had their heads, as well as various animal skulls, protrude from table tops and arranged them together with food, plants, and other objects in an aesthetic way. (Fig. 141, 142)

At the same time, Muehl began to address elementary life functions, or rather to re-enact them within the frame of his Material Actions. In this way, socially tabooed events, which usually took place "behind closed doors" (and partly still take place there today), should be experienced and lived through in an artistically heightened form, including birth (*Nabelschnur – Darstellung einer Geburt* [Umbilical cord–Portrayal of a Birth], 1964, Fig. 143) or hetero- and homosexual sexuality (*Mama und Papa* [Mama and Papa], 1964, Fig. 144–147, *Leda mit dem Schwan* [Leda with the Swan], 1964, Fig. 148, *Cosinus Alpha*, 1964, Fig. 149). The same category includes the engagement with events, that are not only tabooed but also frightening, such as a brain surgery, which the artist presented in the form of an action, after he had had the opportunity to witness one himself. While Muehl initially used the human body as artistic material, treating it with painterly and sculptural techniques, his focus here shifted to the body as an organism, exploring both its functions and its social implications.

Direct Art

In the spring of 1966, Muehl along with Brus, Nitsch, Weibel and the filmer Kren accepted an invitation to the *Destruction in Art Symposium* in London (Fig. 33, 34, 159–164), a vital step towards international success.[9] There, Brus and he also carried out Body-Analytical Actions (some together, but also with the Spanish artist Juan Hidalgo), in which they, among other things, addressed breathing, but also possibilities (and impossibilities) of phonetic and linguistic expression.

To differentiate themselves from other performative tendencies of the 1960s, with names such as Happening or Fluxus, Brus and Muehl chose the term Direkte Kunst / Direct Art for their work and founded the Wiener Institut für Direkte Kunst / Vienna Institute for Direct Art. Through this self-description, they emphasised their concern for "directly" working with concrete bodies, objects, and substances–both in the context of eventful actions as well as in actions solely staged to be photographed–in contrast to traditional artistic translation of content via painting or sculpture.[10]

Social Criticism and Politicisation

Their confrontations with the tabooed issues led the Vienna Actionists to conflict with society, which in turn resulted in their increasingly sharp criticism of its normative moral and value concepts, as well as

11
There were two invitations to the *Vietnam Party* action, one for 6 April 1966 (Fig. 157) and one for 4 July 1966 (illustrated in: Eva Badura-Triska, Hubert Klocker, *Vienna Actionism*. Art and Upheaval in 1960s' Vienna, Vienna / Cologne [mumok, Museum moderner Kunst Stiftung Ludwig Wien / Verlag der Buchhandlung Walther König], 2012, p. 166). The action actually took place on 4 July, the American National Holiday.

in a fundamental critique of human nature itself. This was the case for Muehl from the very beginning–amongst other things, in that he made the bog, which means the dirt and waste, the material of his art thereby also metaphorically referring to people's physical and psychological processes, as well as to society as a whole. Furthermore, of the four Vienna Actionists, he was the one who denounced the political and social situation in his art more and more explicitly, and also staged this in the form of actions.

It already began in the first half of the 1960s with actions such as *Oh Tannenbaum* (Oh Christmas Tree, 1964) which critically examined bourgeois Christmas celebrations, or *Bodybuilding* (1965, Fig. 152) which was about body optimisation, or *Turnstunde in Lebensmitteln* (Gym Lesson in Foodstuffs, 1965) and *Nahrungsmitteltest* (Food Test, 1966, Fig. 153) which both criticised the consumer craze that emerged in the 1960s.

Vietnam Party (1966, Fig. 157, 158), a joint action by Muehl and Brus, was explicitly political in a particularly provocative way, as it ironically turned the occurring international protests against the Vietnam War into a "party". The artists wanted to express that they considered human nature to be so bestial, making the anti-war demonstrations and peace efforts appear unpromising, even naive. Here again, a frightening event involving physical and psychological injury was re-enacted in a grotesquely carnivalesque way. According to the invitation, the audience of that evening should only consist of "invited guests". An "obligatory costume" ruled, which included suggestions such as "head bandages, chest, arm, leg, and belly bandages, corsets, girdles, neck supports, splints, prosthetics, plaster casts [...]". Additionally, one was asked to bring "2 kg of flour per person [...] and various foodstuffs suitable for the artistic representation of torture and atrocities [...]" as well as "old clothes and a coat for the way home." (Fig. 157)[11]

In 1967, Muehl's political thinking was reflected in a radical anarchic program that he developed together with Oswald Wiener and entitled with the crisp, made-up word *Zock*. It was reflected in three pamphlets entitled *Zock–Aspekte einer Totalrevolution* (Zock–Aspects of a Total Revolution), which Muehl self-produced in 1968, 1970, and 1971 in the form of small booklets in limited numbers. (Fig. 167, 168) These contain a ruthless reckoning with the bestial nature of humans in an overexaggerated manner, as well as the idea of a complete destruction of extant social forms.

Muehl's portraits of politicians were also related to the *Zock*-concept: a series of screen prints and painted pictures, in which public figures are shown in a brightly coloured pop style based on models from magazines, including Konrad Adenauer (Fig. 173),

Ho Chi Minh (Fig. 170), Mao Tsedong, Prince Charles (Fig. 171), Adolf Hitler, the Shah of Persia Mohammad Reza Pahlavi and his wife Farah Diba (Fig. 172), Charles de Gaulle, Lyndon B. Johnson, or Gamal Abdel Nasser (Fig. 169). Muehl described his selection as a "blacklist of personalities found suspicious by Zock".[12]

On 17 April in 1967, Muehl carried out an action, entitled *Zock Exercises*, together with Weibel and Wiener, in the Galerie nächst St. Stephan, during which, among other things, a manifesto entitled *Zock an alle* (Zock to All) was read aloud and subsequently destroyed. Four days later, on 21 April, the now legendary, although not explicitly political, *Zock-Fest* (Zock-Festival) (Fig. 165, 166) took place at *Gasthaus Grünes Tor*–a revue-like evening, divided into "numbers", in a heated atmosphere, that was ended by a police raid. In addition to Muehl and Nitsch, numerous Viennese artists close to the Vienna Actionists took part, including Ludwig Christian Attersee, Wolfgang Bauer, Otto Kobalek, Gerhard Rühm, Dominik Steiger, and Oswald Wiener.

On 7 June in 1968, Muehl – alongside Brus, Weibel, Wiener, and a few other actors – took part in an event in Lecture Hall 1 at the University of Vienna, that went down in history as the most political manifestation of this art movement. (Fig. 97, 98, 179, 180) There, in his speech, he insulted Robert Kennedy, who had just been murdered, and his family while Weibel then lambasted the Austrian Finance Minister Stephan Koren. Then, Muehl carried out taboo-breaking Body-Analytical Actions with sexual content: he whipped the self-confessed masochist Malte Olschewski, who was taking part in a mask, with a leather belt. The latter visibly enjoyed this while at the same time reading aloud from pornographic texts. Muehl also organised a urination competition with a group of actors[13], which ended with simulated masturbation movements.

The scandal caused by this action led to Muehl's imprisonment and a sentencing of two months in jail, which he had already served during pre-trial detention.

The Actions after *Art and Revolution*

After this conviction, Muehl no longer appeared publicly in Austria. The only exception was an action in the fall of 1968, in a Viennese nightclub, in which he staged a comparatively harmless still life Table Action of the same kind he had realised in 1964. Formally and thematically radical actions were carried out in this city only in the private realm of his apartment on Praterstrasse, where they were documented photographically and on film. In return, Muehl increasingly received invitations to perform abroad–to Germany, the Netherlands, Italy, Switzerland, Belgium, and to the USA, where he

12 Otto Muehl, Zock – *Aspekte einer Totalrevolution* (1967), Vienna 1968 (2nd edition), n.p.

13 It was his Direct Art Group.

carried out his last action in April 1973 at the State University of Columbus in Ohio. However, also here he did not continue with his radical actions but instead carried out another table-based one.

Apart from these "tamer" public appearances in Vienna and Ohio, Muehl took his social criticism and his general examination of human nature to extremes in a cynical and grotesque manner in his actions of the late 1960s and early 1970s. They focused on topics such as sexuality in various forms–including those that are not socially accepted–as well as on generally breaking physical and psychological rules, going beyond the norm, not least in a psychotic way.[14] Noteworthy is the strongly erotic action *Oh Sensibility* (1970, Fig. 181), which involved the killing of a goose and which, unlike his earlier actions, Muehl performed several times in different places during his travels. Formally, he here again drew on motifs and compositional schemes of historic art by staging towers of human bodies in the manner of the *figurae serpentinatae* of Mannerism.

The Commune

In the 1970s, Muehl's socio-critical discourses culminated in the founding of a Commune, which, after its beginnings in his apartment on Praterstrasse in Vienna, had its headquarters on the Friedrichshof estate, located about 60 km east of Vienna, from around 1975 and over time included over 600 members.[15] (Fig. 183) On the theoretical basis of Jean-Jacques Rousseau, Karl Marx, and Wilhelm Reich, among others, conventional relationship patterns within the family were to be dissolved and new models of life and society were to be developed. Methods such as Action Analysis were applied, in which Muehl appeared as a self-appointed therapist. Over time, these resulted in Selbstdarstellungen (Self-Presentations) in which the Communards had to reveal themselves to the group in individual performances. In addition, free sexuality and the rejection of two-person relationships were essential aspects of this social experiment.

In 1988, criminal proceedings were opened against Muehl, accusing him of sexual abuse and also drug offences. Three years later, in 1991, he was convicted of "having sexual intercourse with a minor, fornication with a minor, rape (in one case), abuse of authority, moral endangerment of persons under 16 years of age, giving false evidence in court and suppressing evidence"[16] and was sentenced to seven years in prison, which he served in full.

After his release in 1998, he settled in Portugal with a group of fourteen adults and their children,[17] where he lived and worked until his death on 26 May 2013.

14
Muehl coined the term Manopsychotik (Manopsychotics) for this and founded an Institut für Manopsychotik (Institute for Manopsychotics) in 1970. See Hubert Klocker, "Biography Muehl", in: Badura-Triska, Klocker, *Vienna Actionism* (see note 11), p. 382. In 1970, Muehl organised the actions *Mano-Test* as well as *Manopsychotisches Ballett* 1 (Manopsychotic Ballet 1, Fig. 182) and *Manopsychotisches Ballet 2* (Manopsychotic Ballet 2).

15
The commune had various names. From 1970 onwards, outsiders spoke of the 'Muehl Commune',but the self-designations included *Therapiekommune* (Therapy Commune, 1973), P.P.Rep.Ko (*Psycho-Physische ReparaturKommune*) (Psycho-Physical Repair Commune, 1974), *Kommune Friedrichshof* Friedrichshof Commune), *AA Kommune (Aktionsanalytische Kommune)* (AA Commune (Action-Analytical Commune) and *Aktionsanalytische Kulturvereinigung* (AAKV/Action-Analytical Cultural Association AAKV, 1975), and *Aktionsanalytische Organisation AAO* (Action-Analytical Organisation AAO, 1976). In 1977, the association *AAO für bewusste Lebenspraxis* (AAO Association for Conscious Life Practice) was founded. In the spring of 1978, the AAO was dissolved and the Friedrichshof became the center of the *Verein für Lebens- und Gesellschaftsgestaltung* (Association for the Design of Life and Society.) In 1981, a cooperative in Burgenland that was in liquidation was taken over and revitalised: the „Gemeinschaftsbau" a housing, construction, and settlement cooperative, became the new legal entity of Friedrichshof. The last name of the community was *Cooperation Friedrichshof*, a society under civil law (GesbR), founded in April 1990, under which the community dissolved on 31 December 1990.

16
Verdict against Otto Muehl, November 1991.

17
This community was called *Art-Life-Algarve* and located in Moncarapacho.

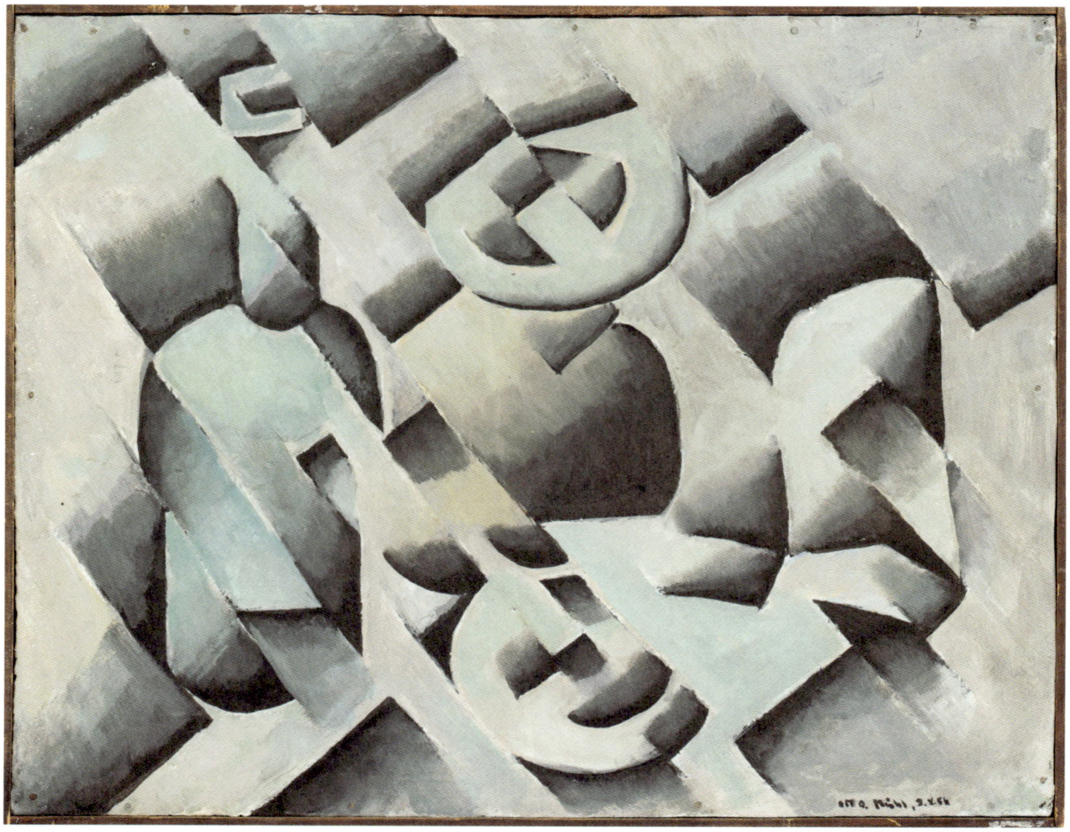

Fig. 120
Otto Muehl
Untitled, 1956
Oil on hard fibreboard
40 x 52 cm
WAM – Wiener Aktionismus Museum, Vienna

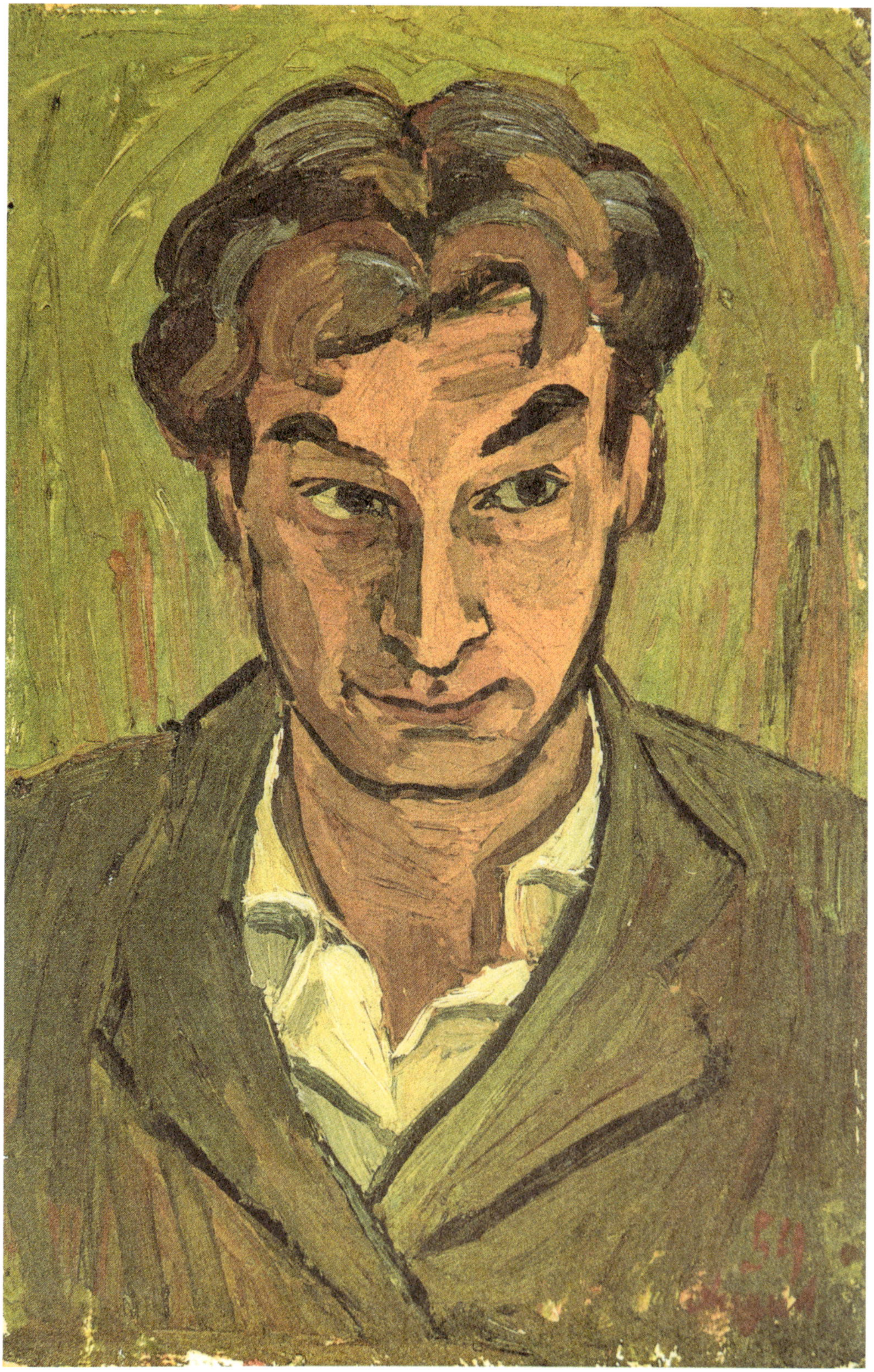

Fig. 121
Otto Muehl
Selbstportrait (Self-Portrait), 1954
Oil on cardboard
50,5 x 33 cm
Archives Otto Muehl/ MFGA Stiftung

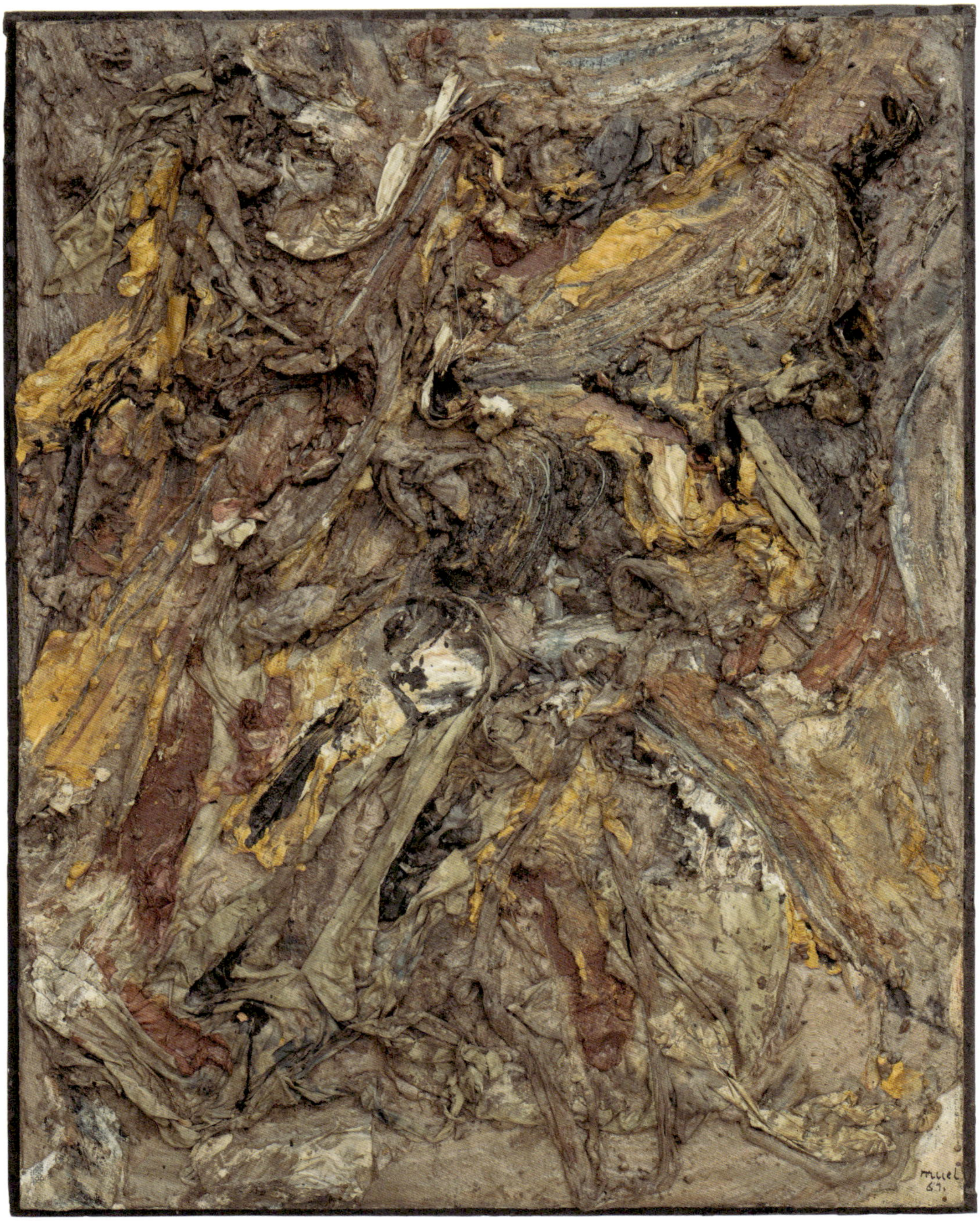

Fig. 122
Otto Muehl
Untitled, 1961
Various materials on hard fibreboard
82,4 x 66,5 cm
WAM – Wiener Aktionismus Museum, Vienna, Collection K.

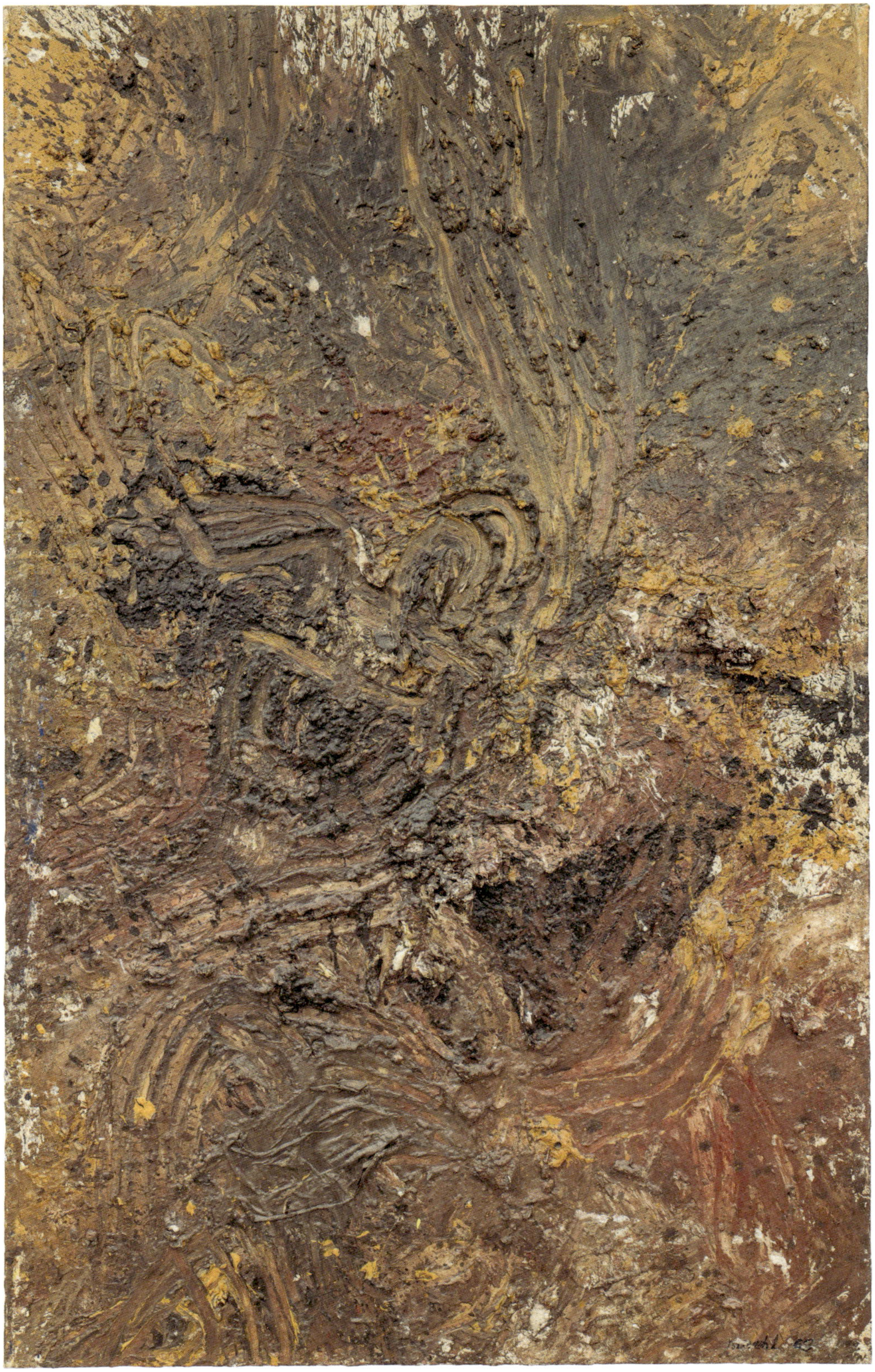

Fig. 123
Otto Muehl
Untitled, 1963
Fabric, earth, dispersion on canvas
220,5 x 141,5 cm
WAM – Wiener Aktionismus Museum, Vienna

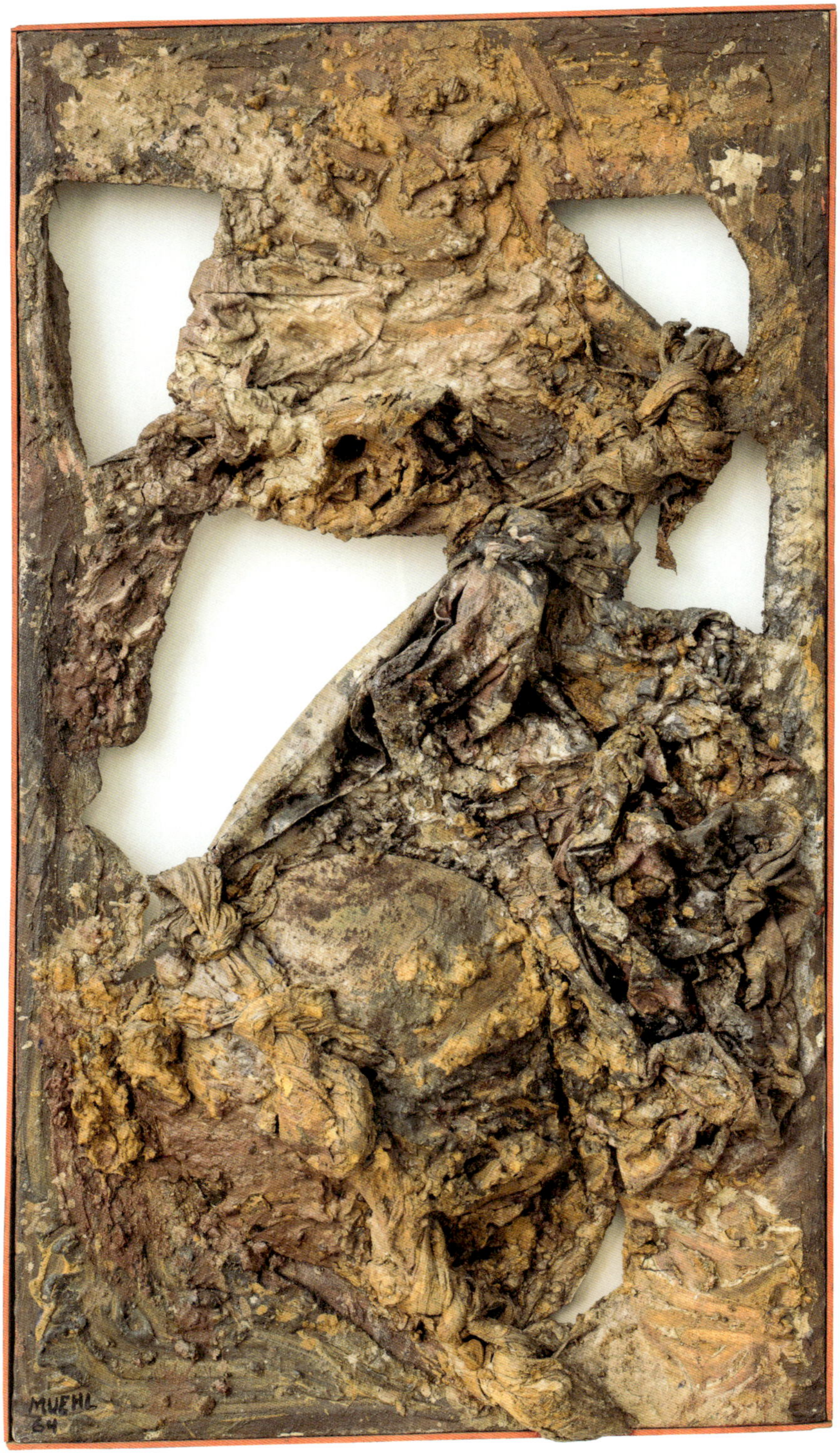

Fig. 124
Otto Muehl
Untitled, 1964
Sand, stones, cement, acrylic, mixed media on burlap
115 x 67 cm
WAM – Wiener Aktionismus Museum, Vienna, Collection K.

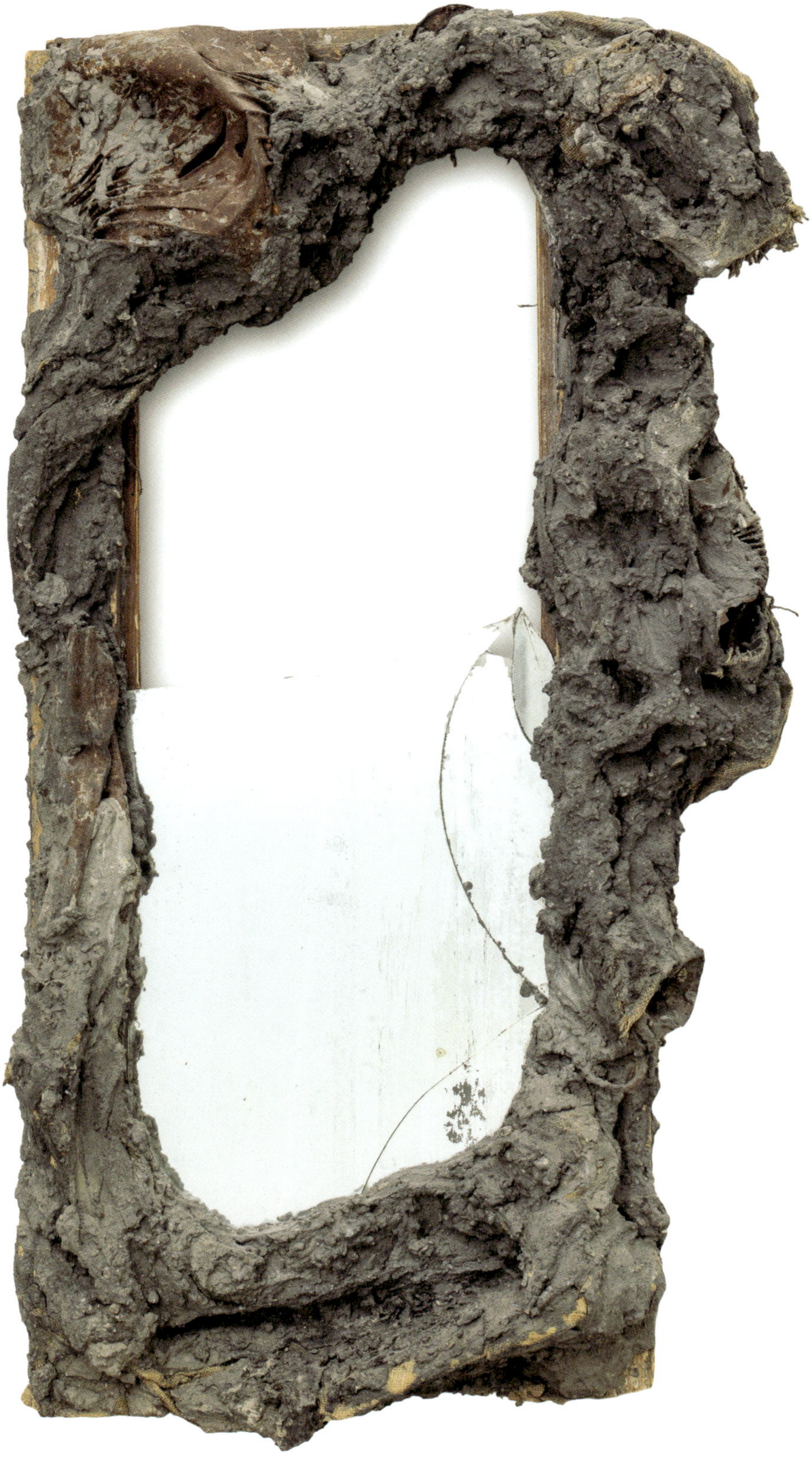

Fig. 125
Otto Muehl
Untitled, 1962
Mirror, burlap, various metal objects, cast with sand, stones and cement on wooden frame
113 x 66 x 22 cm
WAM – Wiener Aktionismus Museum, Vienna

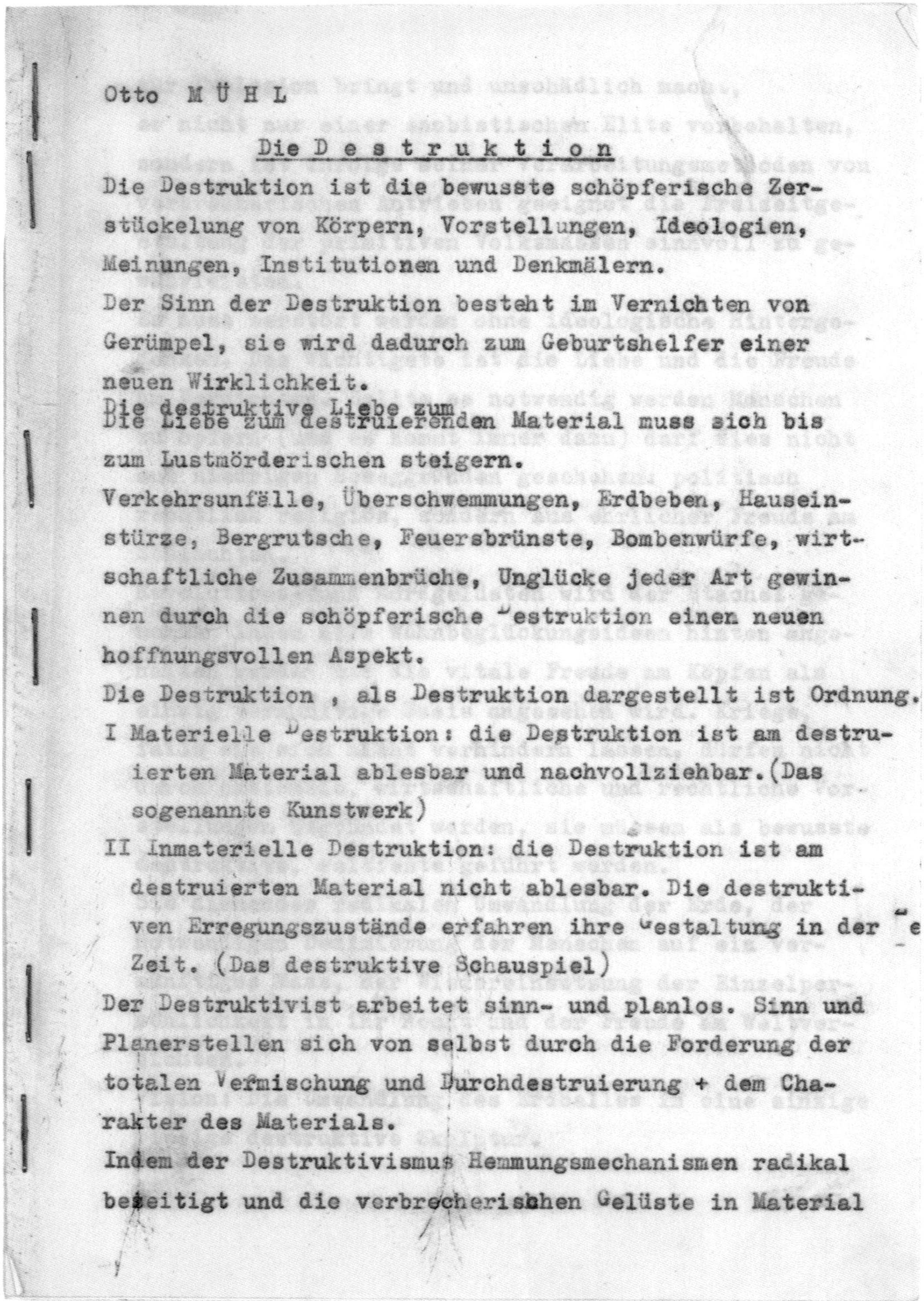

Otto M Ü H L

Die D e s t r u k t i o n

Die Destruktion ist die bewusste schöpferische Zerstückelung von Körpern, Vorstellungen, Ideologien, Meinungen, Institutionen und Denkmälern.

Der Sinn der Destruktion besteht im Vernichten von Gerümpel, sie wird dadurch zum Geburtshelfer einer neuen Wirklichkeit.

Die destruktive Liebe zum.

Die Liebe zum destruierenden Material muss sich bis zum Lustmörderischen steigern.

Verkehrsunfälle, Überschwemmungen, Erdbeben, Hauseinstürze, Bergrutsche, Feuersbrünste, Bombenwürfe, wirtschaftliche Zusammenbrüche, Unglücke jeder Art gewinnen durch die schöpferische Destruktion einen neuen hoffnungsvollen Aspekt.

Die Destruktion , als Destruktion dargestellt ist Ordnung.

I Materielle Destruktion: die Destruktion ist am destruierten Material ablesbar und nachvollziehbar. (Das sogenannte Kunstwerk)

II Inmaterielle Destruktion: die Destruktion ist am destruierten Material nicht ablesbar. Die destruktiven Erregungszustände erfahren ihre Gestaltung in der Zeit. (Das destruktive Schauspiel)

Der Destruktivist arbeitet sinn- und planlos. Sinn und Planerstellen sich von selbst durch die Forderung der totalen Vermischung und Durchdestruierung + dem Charakter des Materials.

Indem der Destruktivismus Hemmungsmechanismen radikal beseitigt und die verbrecherischhen Gelüste in Material

Fig. 126, 127
Otto Muehl
Die Destruktion (The Destruction), 1962
Typescript, stapled
21 x 14,8 cm
mumok – Museum moderner Kunst Stiftung Ludwig Wien

zur Explosion bringt und unschädlich mach.,
er nicht nur einer snobistischen Elite vorbehalten, sondern ist infolge seiner Verarbeitungsmethoden von verbrecherischen Antrieben geeignet die Freizeitgestaltung der primitiven Volksmassen sinnvoll zu gewährleisten.

Es muss zerstört werden ohne ideologische Hintergedanken. Das Wichtigste ist die Liebe und die Freude am Vernichten. Sollte es notwendig werden Menschen zu opfern (und es kommt immer dazu) darf dies nicht aus niedrigen Beweggründen geschehen: politisch rechtlich religiös, sondern aus ehrlicher Freude am Schlachten.

Revolutions- und Mordgelüsten wird der Stachel genommen indem alle Wahnbeglückungsideen hinten angehalten werden und die vitale Freude am Köpfen als einzig vernünftige Basis angesehen wird. Kriege, falls sie sich nicht verhindern lassen, dürfen nicht durch nationale, wirtschaftliche und rechtliche Vorstellungen begründet werden, sie müssen als bewusste destruktive, weltfeste geführt werden.

Sie dienender radikalen Umwandlung der Erde, der Notwendigen Dezimierung der Menschen auf ein vernünftiges Mass, der Wiedereinsetzung der Einzelpersönlichkeit in ihr Recht und der Freude am Weltvernichten.

Vision: Die Umwandlung des Erdballes in eine einzige riesige destruktive Skulptur.

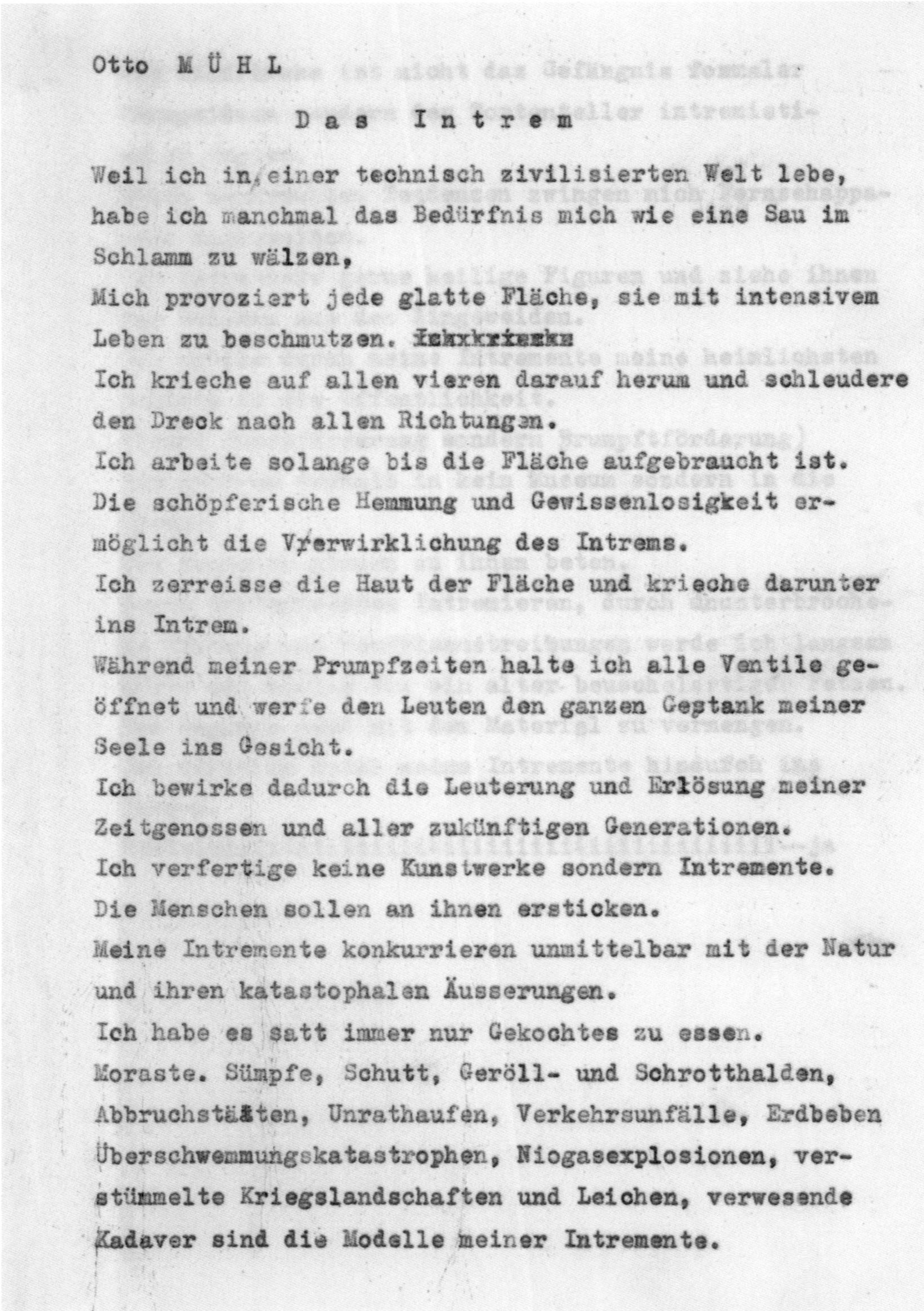

Otto M Ü H L

D a s   I n t r e m

Weil ich in einer technisch zivilisierten Welt lebe,
habe ich manchmal das Bedürfnis mich wie eine Sau im
Schlamm zu wälzen,
Mich provoziert jede glatte Fläche, sie mit intensivem
Leben zu beschmutzen. ~~Ichxkriechx~~
Ich krieche auf allen vieren darauf herum und schleudere
den Dreck nach allen Richtungen.
Ich arbeite solange bis die Fläche aufgebraucht ist.
Die schöpferische Hemmung und Gewissenlosigkeit er-
möglicht die Vrerwirklichung des Intrems.
Ich zerreisse die Haut der Fläche und krieche darunter
ins Intrem.
Während meiner Prumpfzeiten halte ich alle Ventile ge-
öffnet und werfe den Leuten den ganzen Gestank meiner
Seele ins Gesicht.
Ich bewirke dadurch die Leuterung und Erlösung meiner
Zeitgenossen und aller zukünftigen Generationen.
Ich verfertige keine Kunstwerke sondern Intremente.
Die Menschen sollen an ihnen ersticken.
Meine Intremente konkurrieren unmittelbar mit der Natur
und ihren katastophalen Äusserungen.
Ich habe es satt immer nur Gekochtes zu essen.
Moraste. Sümpfe, Schutt, Geröll- und Schrotthalden,
Abbruchstäaten, Unrathaufen, Verkehrsunfälle, Erdbeben
Überschwemmungskatastrophen, Niogasexplosionen, ver-
stümmelte Kriegslandschaften und Leichen, verwesende
Kadaver sind die Modelle meiner Intremente.

Fig. 128, 129
Otto Muehl
Das Intrem (The Intrem), 1962
Typescript, stapled
21 x 14,8 cm
mumok – Museum moderner Kunst Stiftung Ludwig Wien

Die Bildfläche ist nicht das Gefängnis fommaler Zwangsideen sondern der Tortenteller intremistischer Orgien.

Meine senkrechten Tendenzen zwingen mich Fernsehapparate auszuweiden.

Ich intremiere gerne heilige Figuren und ziehe ihnen den Schleim aus den Eingeweiden.

Ich spülle durch meine Intremente meine heimlichsten Gelüste in die Öffentlichkeit.

(Nicht Kunstförderung sondern Brumpftförderung)

Sie gehören deshalb in kein Museum sondern in die Kirche.

Die Menschen müssen zu ihnen beten.

Durch fortwährendes Intremieren, durch ununterbrochene Exzesse und Teufelsaustreibungen werde ich langsam mürbe und heilig wie ein alter beuschelartiger Fetzen.

Ich beginne mich mit dem Material zu vermengen.

Ich schleime durch meine Intremente hindurch ins Intrem.

Halleluiiiiiiiiiiiiiiiiiiiiiiiiiiiiiiiiiiiii--ja

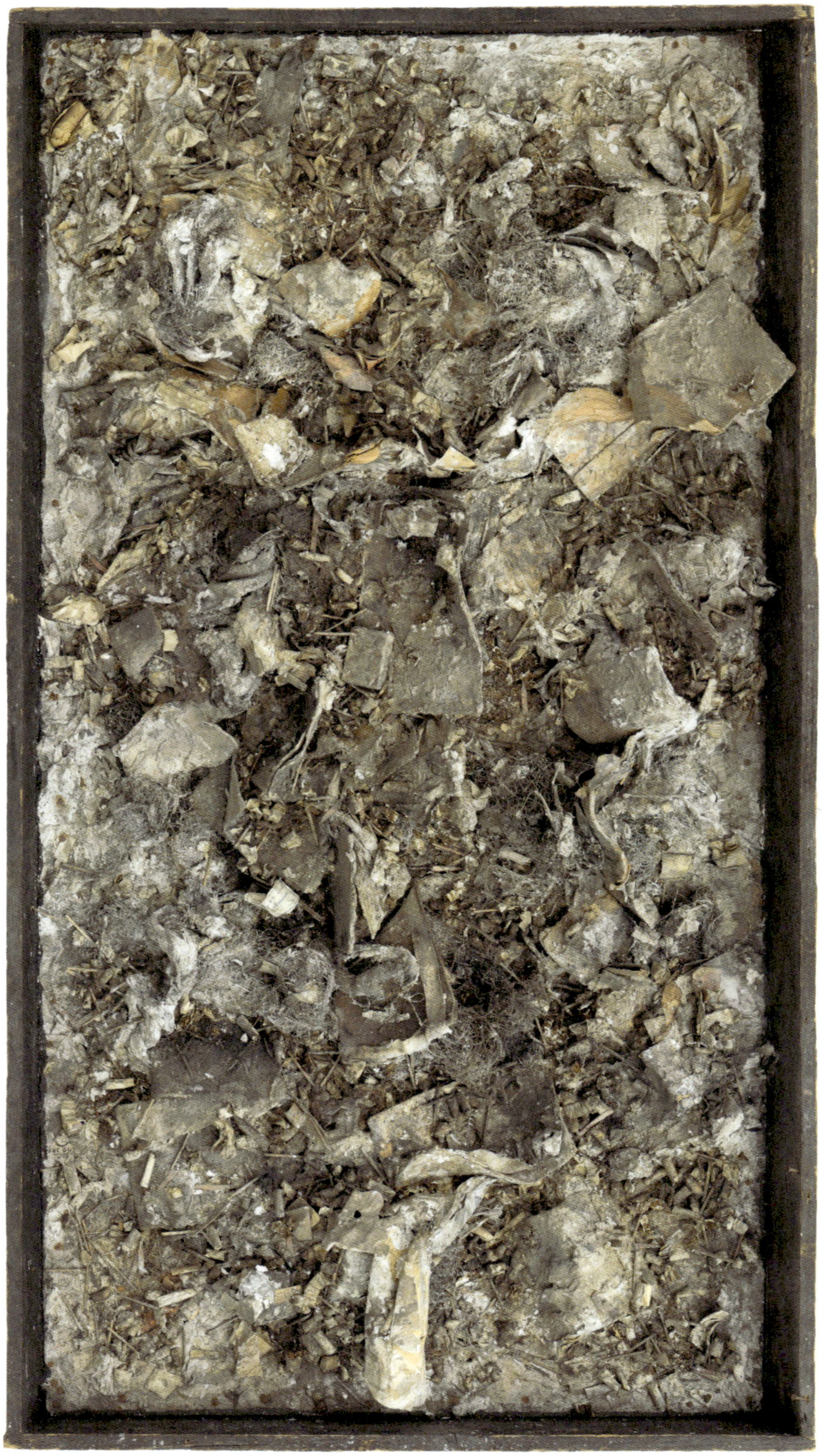

Fig. 130
Otto Muehl
Untitled, 1963
Burned materials in wooden box
72 x 132 x 16 cm
WAM – Wiener Aktionismus Museum, Vienna

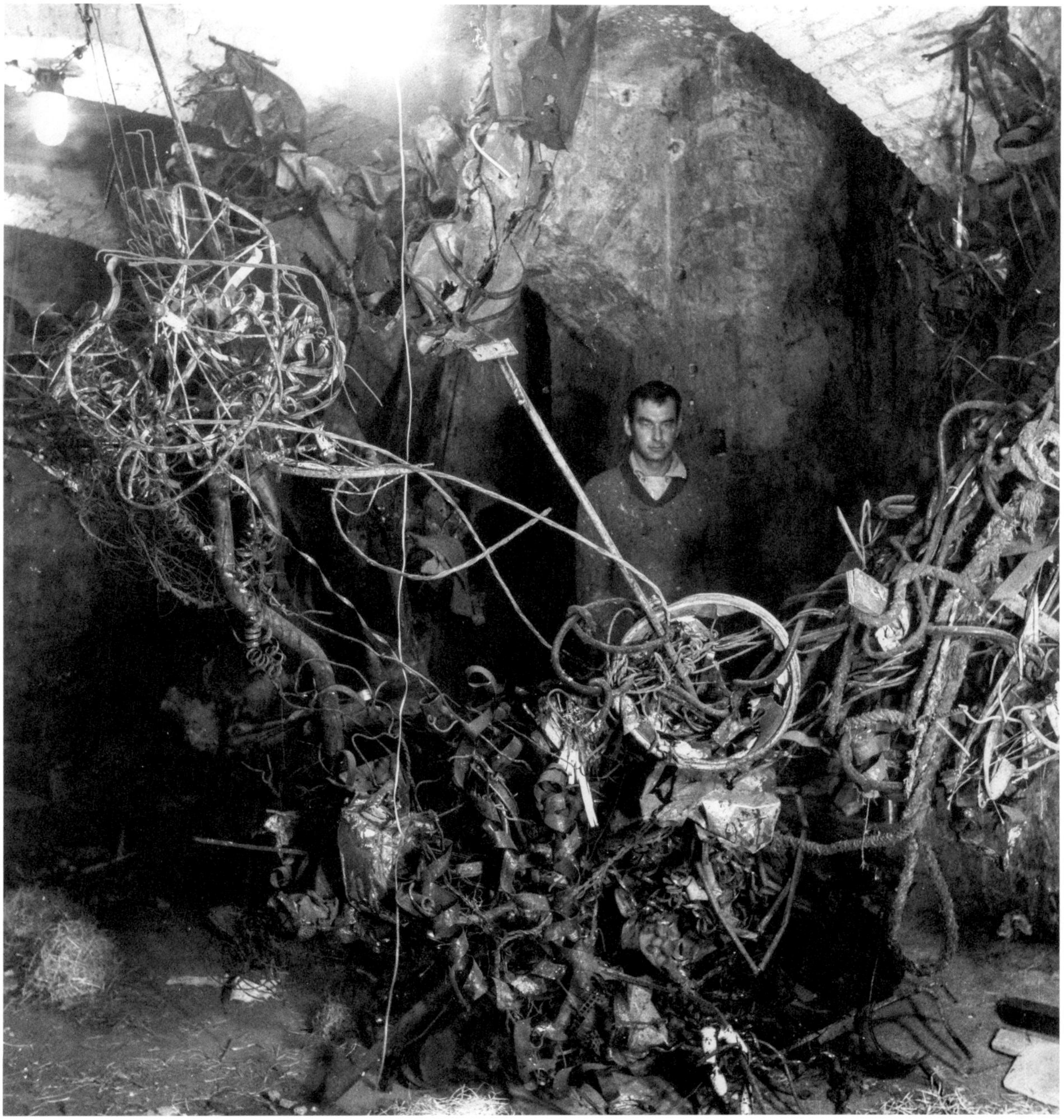

Fig. 131
Otto Muehl
Junk Sculpture, June 1962
(Created during the working retreat *Die Blutorgel* [The Blood Organ]
in Muehl's studio, Perinetgasse 1, 1200 Wien)
B/W photograph
photo: Adolf Frohner

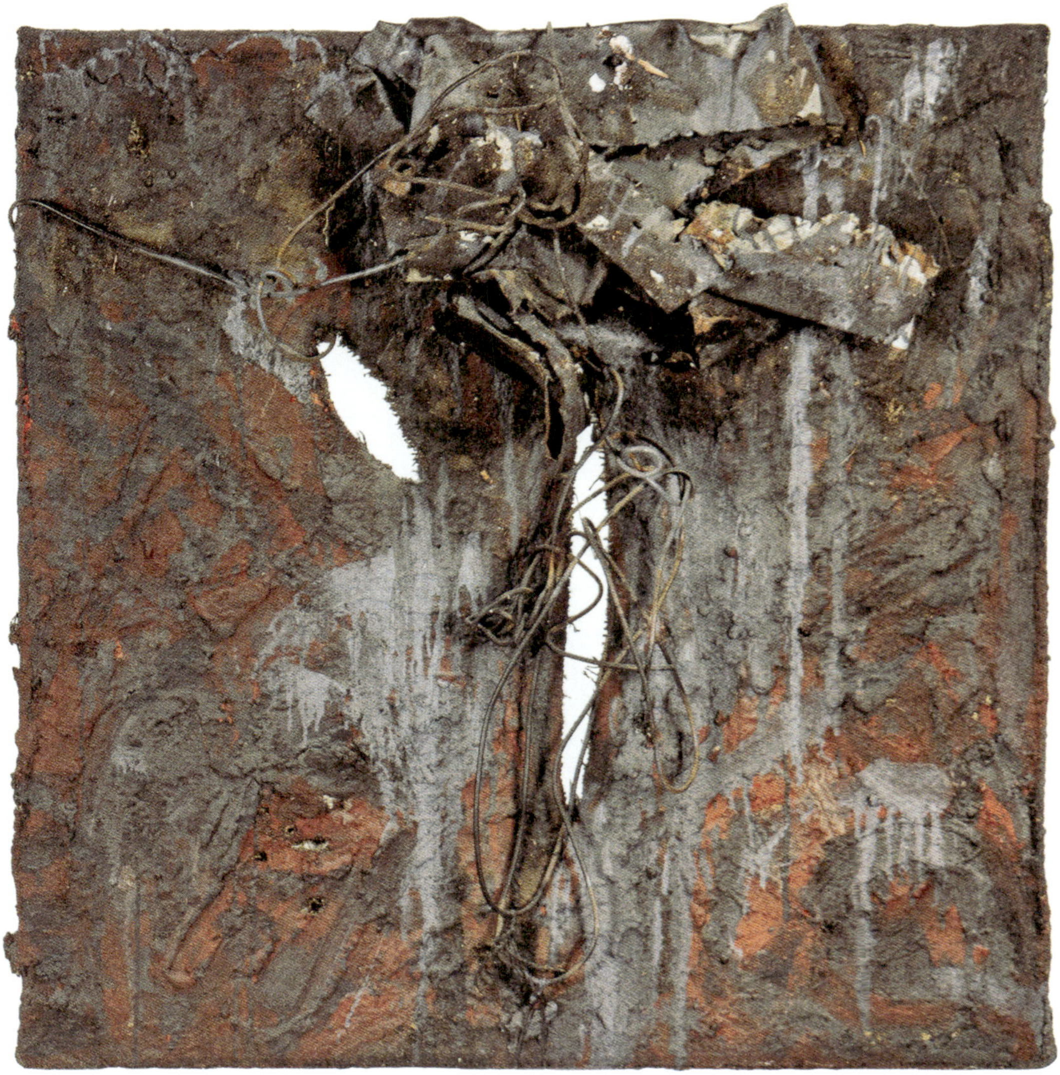

Fig. 132
Adolf Frohner
Untitled, 1963
Iron wire, iron sheet, pigment, oil paint, burlap, wood
96 x 96 x 3 cm
Collection P.

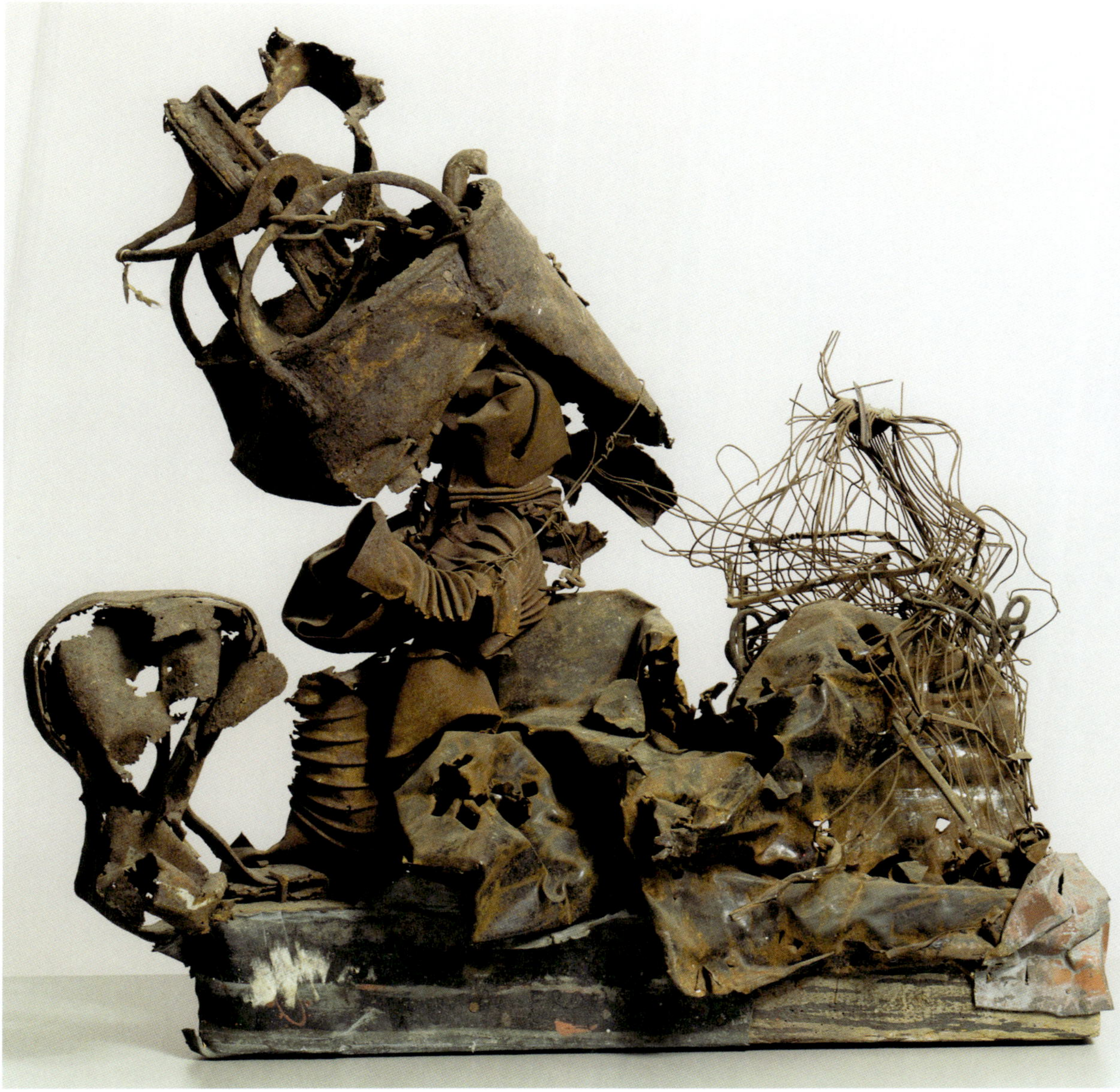

Fig. 133
Adolf Frohner
Junk Sculpture, 1962
Iron and sheet metal
76 x 80 x 40 cm
Private Collection

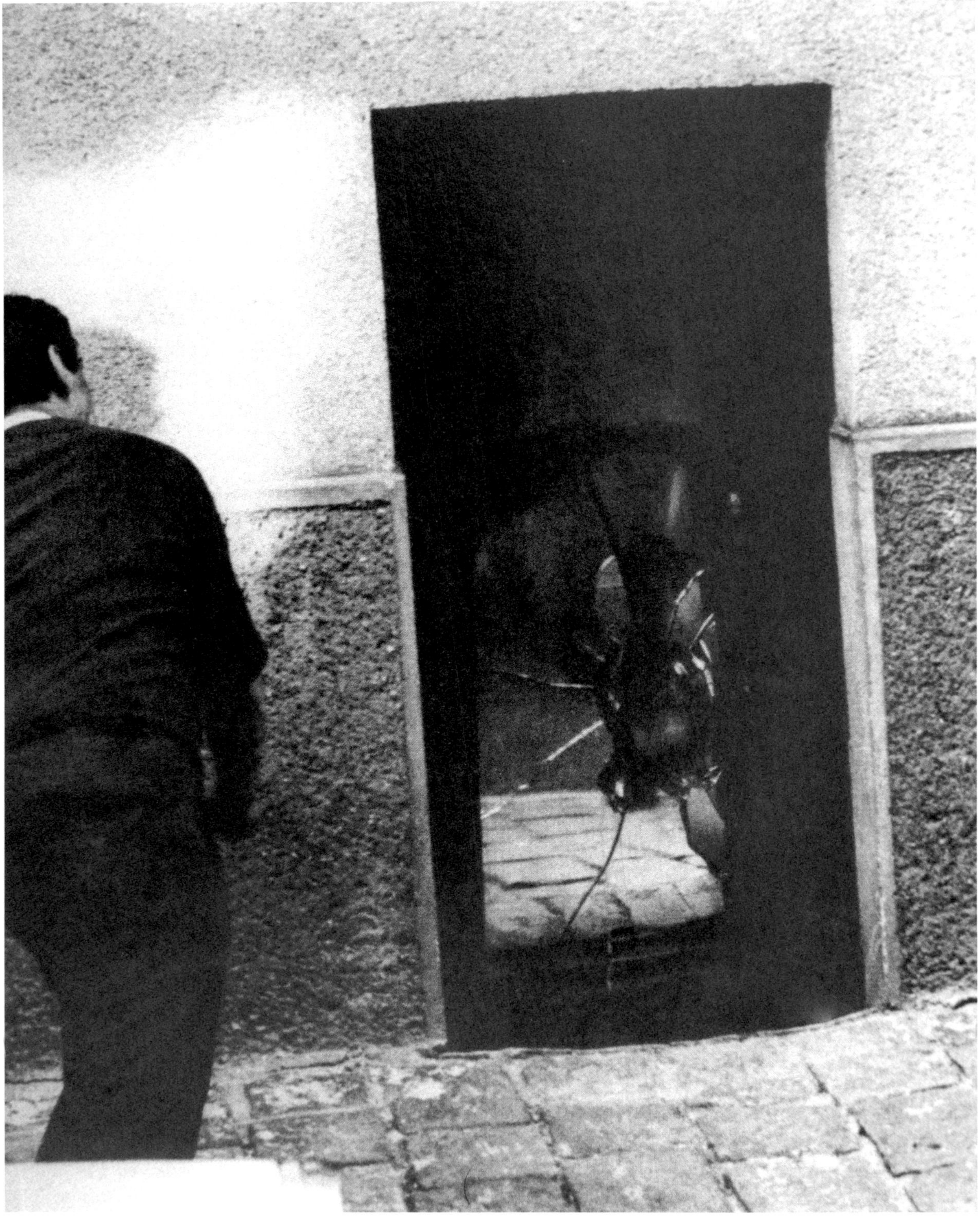

Fig. 134
Otto Muehl
Smashing a mirror in front of his studio, Perinetgasse 1, 1200 Vienna
Prelude to the *Fest des Psychophysischen Naturalismus* (Festival of Psycho-Physical Naturalism), 28 June 1963

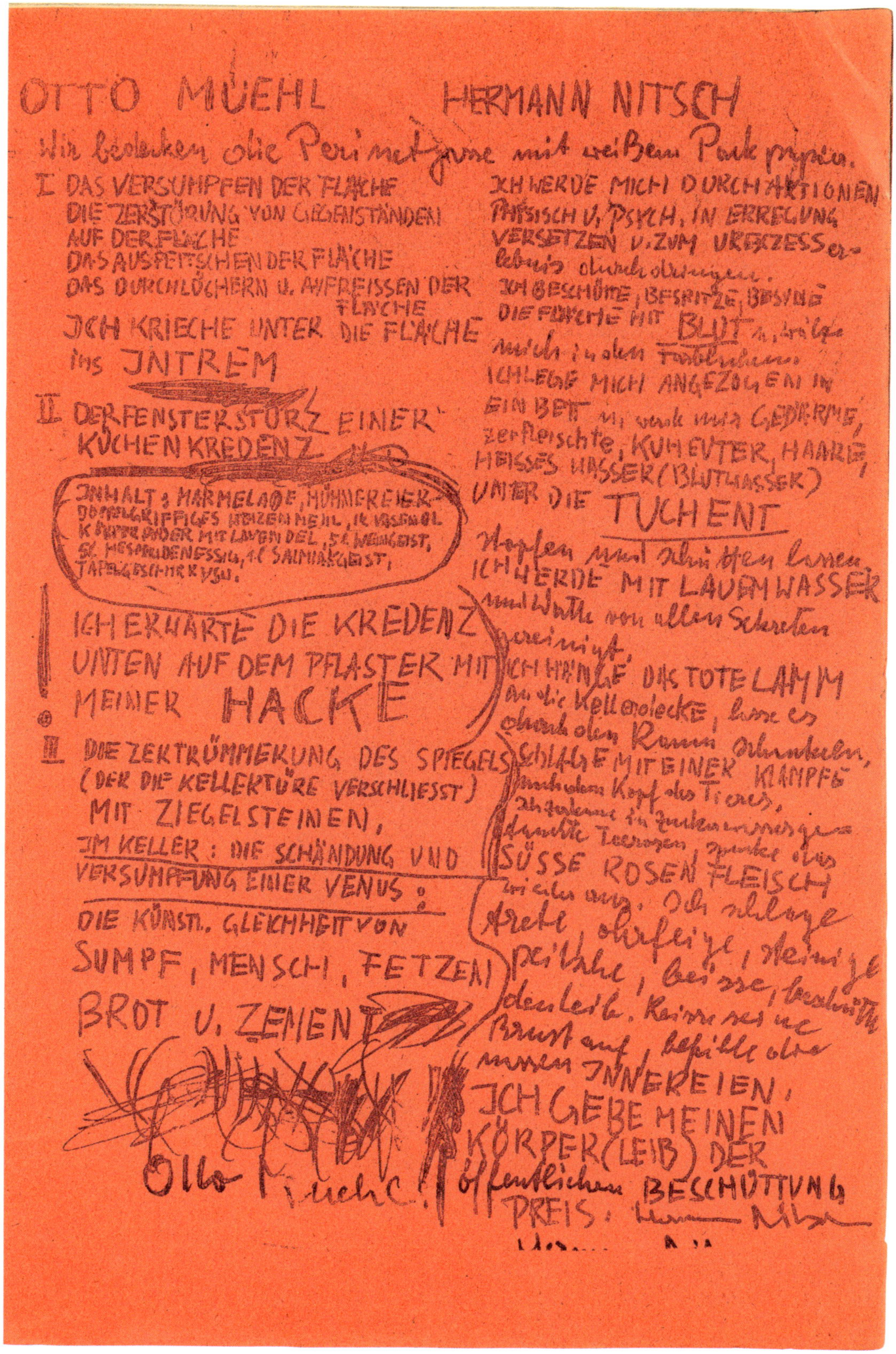

Fig. 135
Otto Muehl, Hermann Nitsch
Programme for *Fest des psychophysischem Naturalismus* (Festival of Psycho-Physical Naturalism), 1963
Matrix print (graphic design together with Günter Brus)
29,7 x 21 cm
mumok – Museum moderner Kunst Stiftung Ludwig Wien

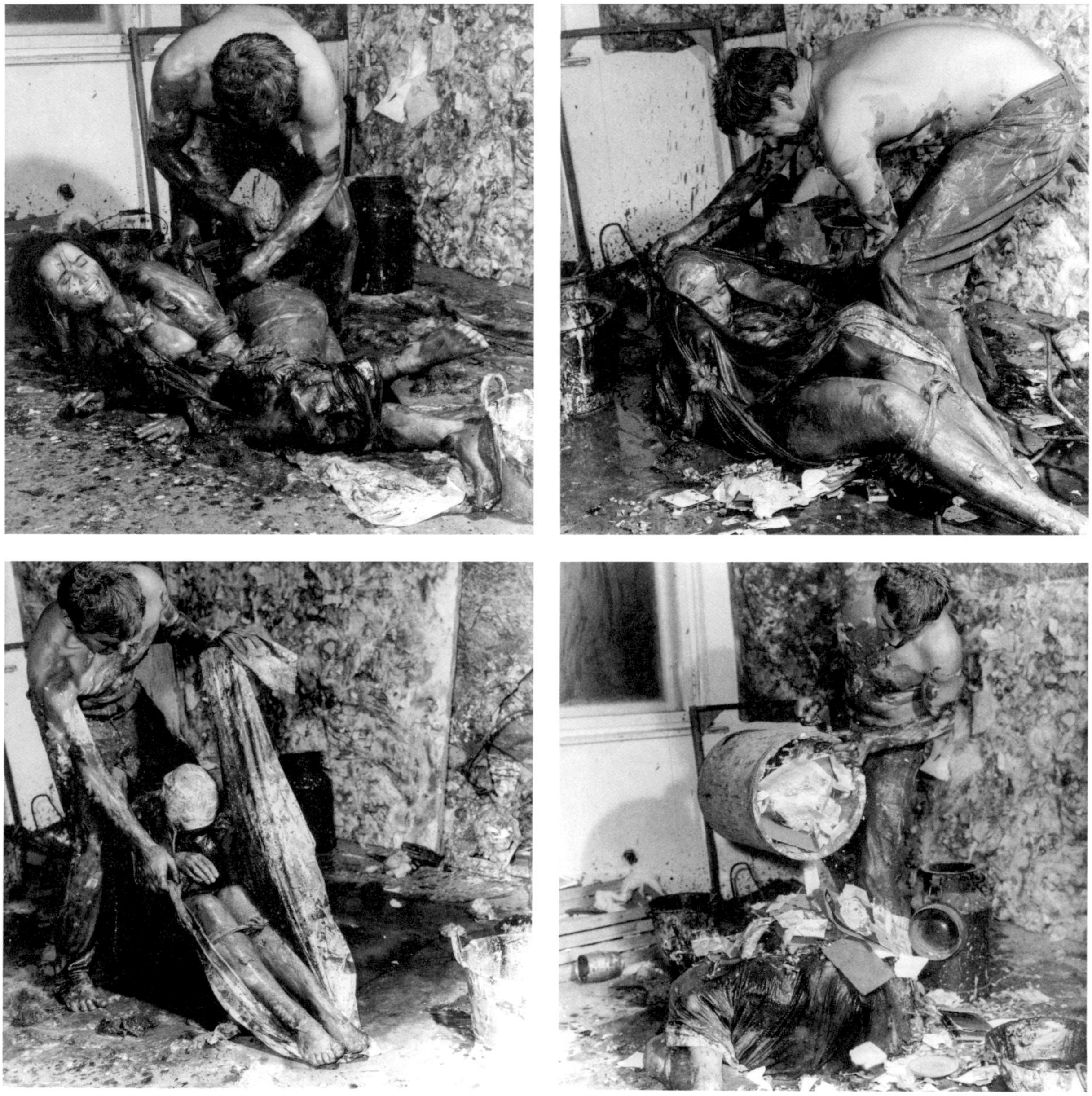

Fig. 136, 137, 138, 139
Otto Muehl
Materialaktion Nr. 1, Versumpfung eines weiblichen Körpers – Versumpfung einer Venus
(Material Action No. 1, Enmiring of a Female Body–Enmiring of a Venus), 1963
Muehl's apartment, Obere Augartenstraße 14 a/20, 1020 Vienna
B/W photographs
photo: Ludwig Hoffenreich
with: „Babsi“

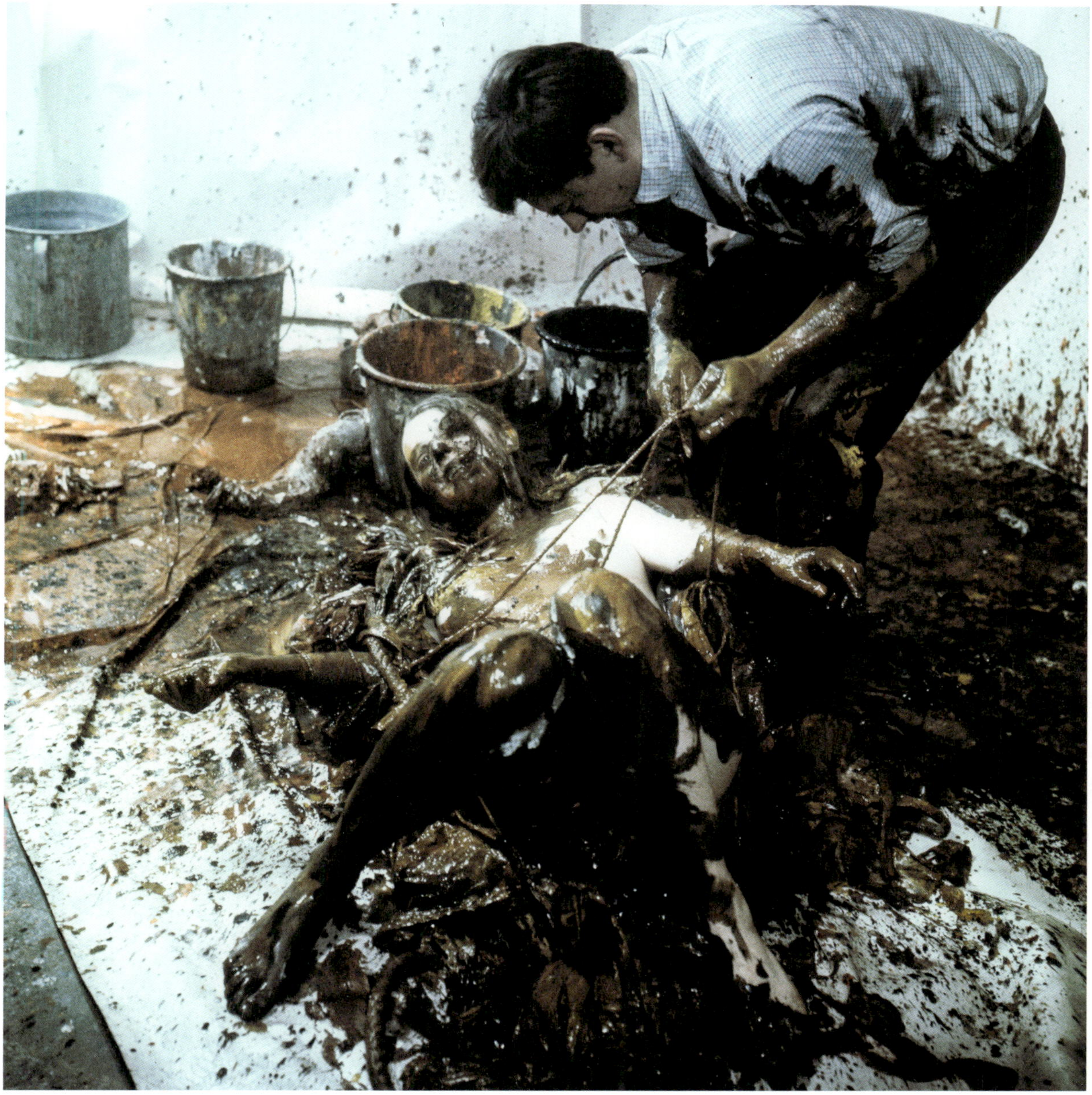

Fig. 140
Otto Muehl
Materialaktion Nr. 3, Klarsichtpackung – Versumpfung in einer Truhe – Panierung eines weiblichen Gesäßes – Wälzen im Schlamm (Material Action No. 3, Cling Film Wrapping–Enmiring in a Chest–Breadcrumbing a Female Body–Rolling in Mud), 26 February 1964
Muehl's apartment, Obere Augartenstraße 14 a/20, 1020 Vienna
Colour photograph
photo: Ludwig Hoffenreich
with: Ziemi Schieb

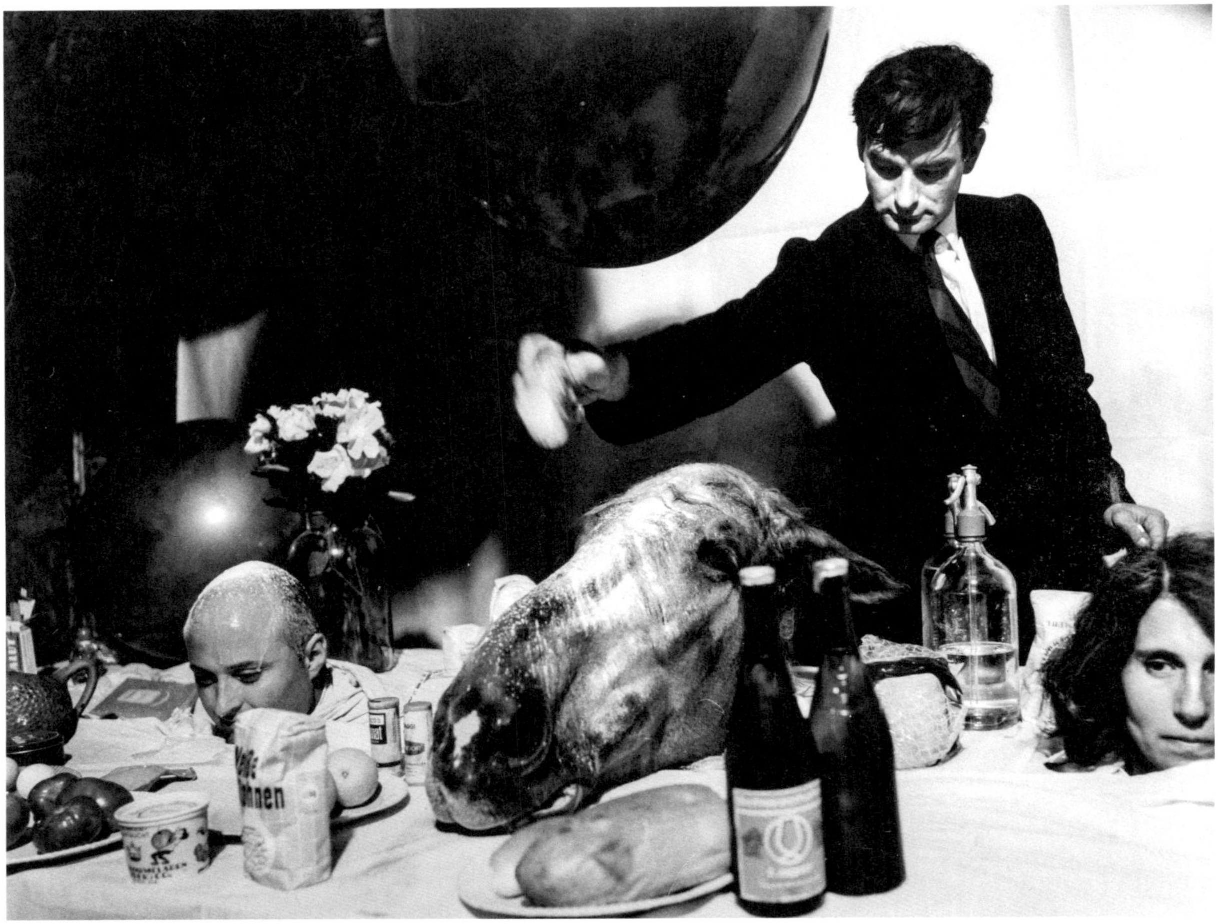

Fig. 141
Otto Muehl
Materialaktion Nr. 10, Stillleben – Aktion mit einem weiblichen, einem männlichen und einem Pferdekopf
(Material Action No. 10, Still Live–Action with a Female, a Male and a Horse's Head), 11 June 1964
Muehl's studio, Perinetgasse 1, 1200 Vienna
B/W photograph
Photo: Khasaq (Siegfried Klein)

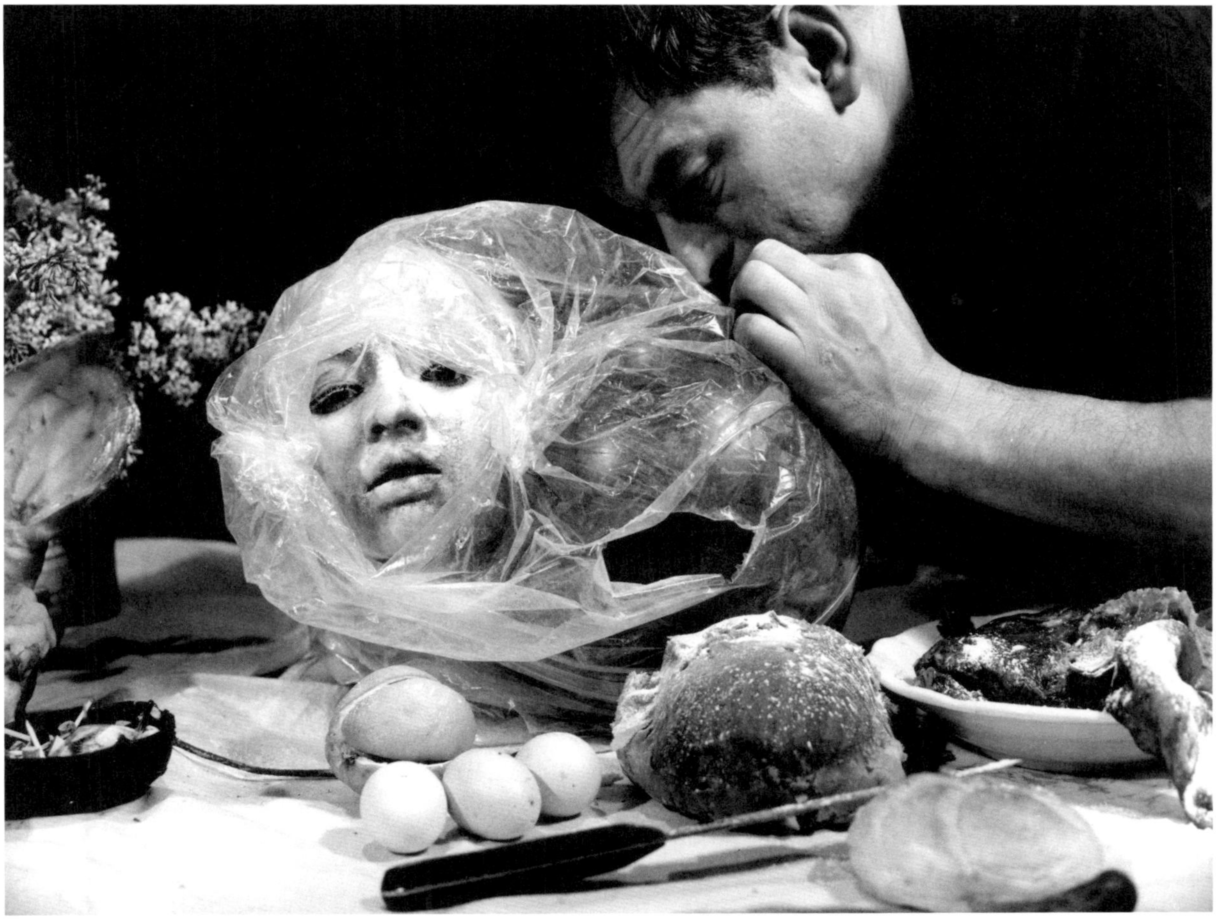

Fig. 142
Otto Muehl
Materialaktion Nr. 8, Stillleben – Aktion mit einem weiblichen Kopf und einem Schweinekopf
(Material Action No. 8, Still Life–Action with a Female Head and a Pig's Head), June 1964
Muehl's apartment, Obere Augartenstraße 14 a/20, 1020 Vienna
B/W photograph
photo: Ludwig Hoffenreich
with: Friedl Muehl

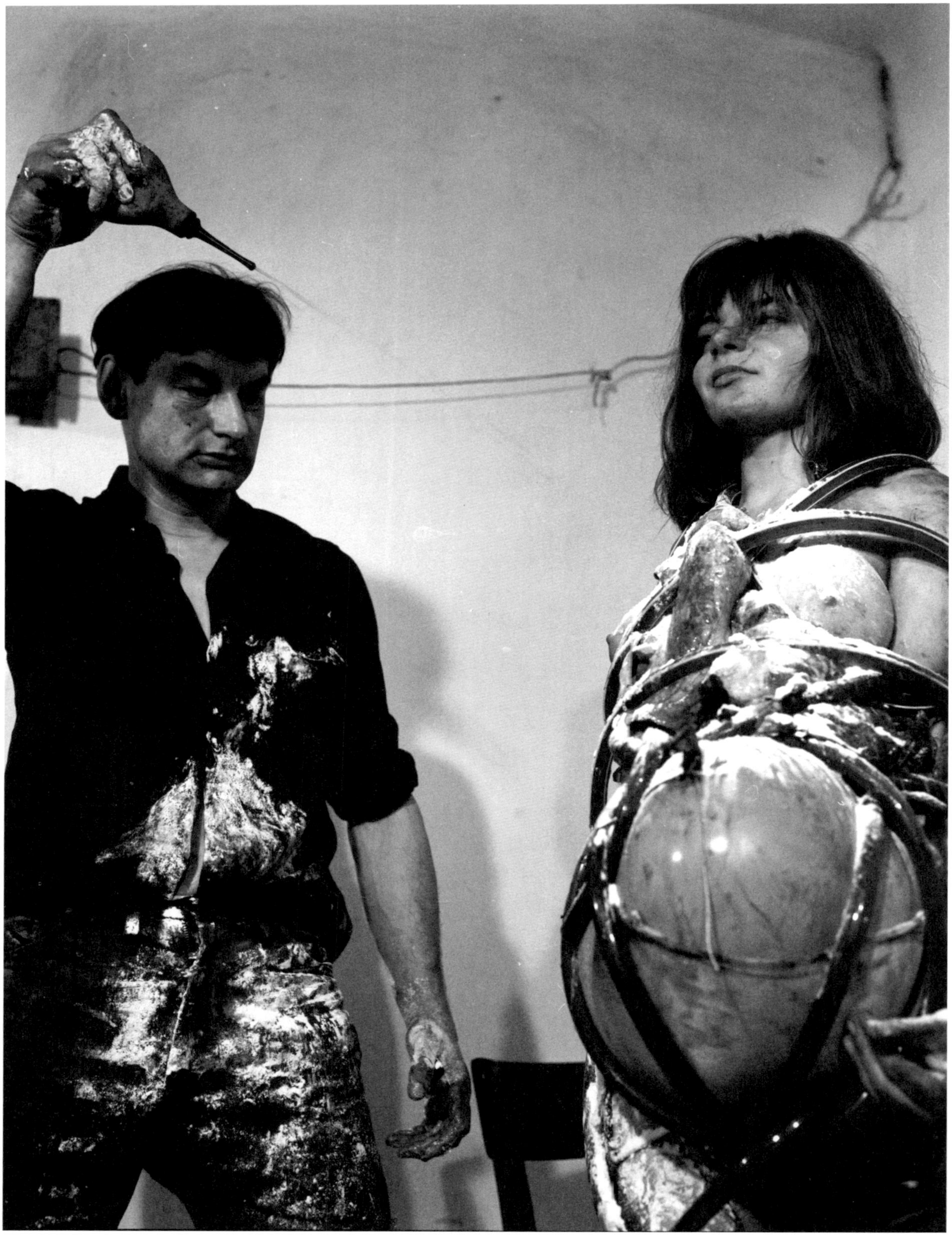

Fig. 143
Otto Muehl
Materialaktion Nr. 7, Nabelschnur – Darstellung einer Geburt
(Material Action No. 7, Umbilical Cord–Portrayal of a Birth), 16 May 1964
Muehl's apartment, Obere Augartenstraße 14 a/20, 1020 Vienna
B/W photograph
photo: Ludwig Hoffenreich
with: Gertrude Eder

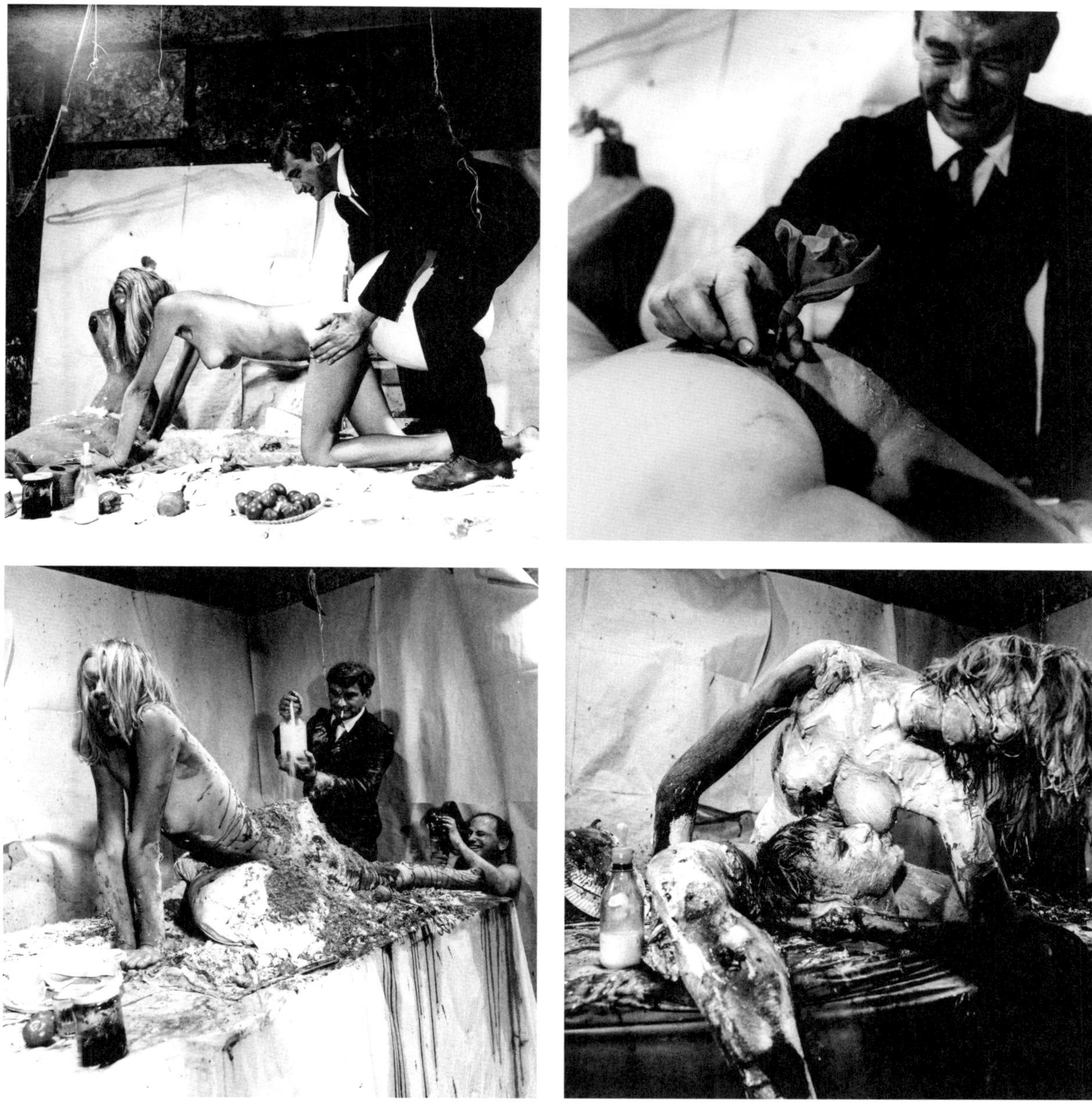

Fig. 144, 145, 146, 147
Otto Muehl
Materialaktion Nr. 11, Mama und Papa (Material Action No. 11, Mama and Papa), 4 August 1964
Muehl's studio, Perinetgasse 1, 1200 Vienna
B/W photographs
photo: Ludwig Hoffenreich
with: Ulla Holzbauer

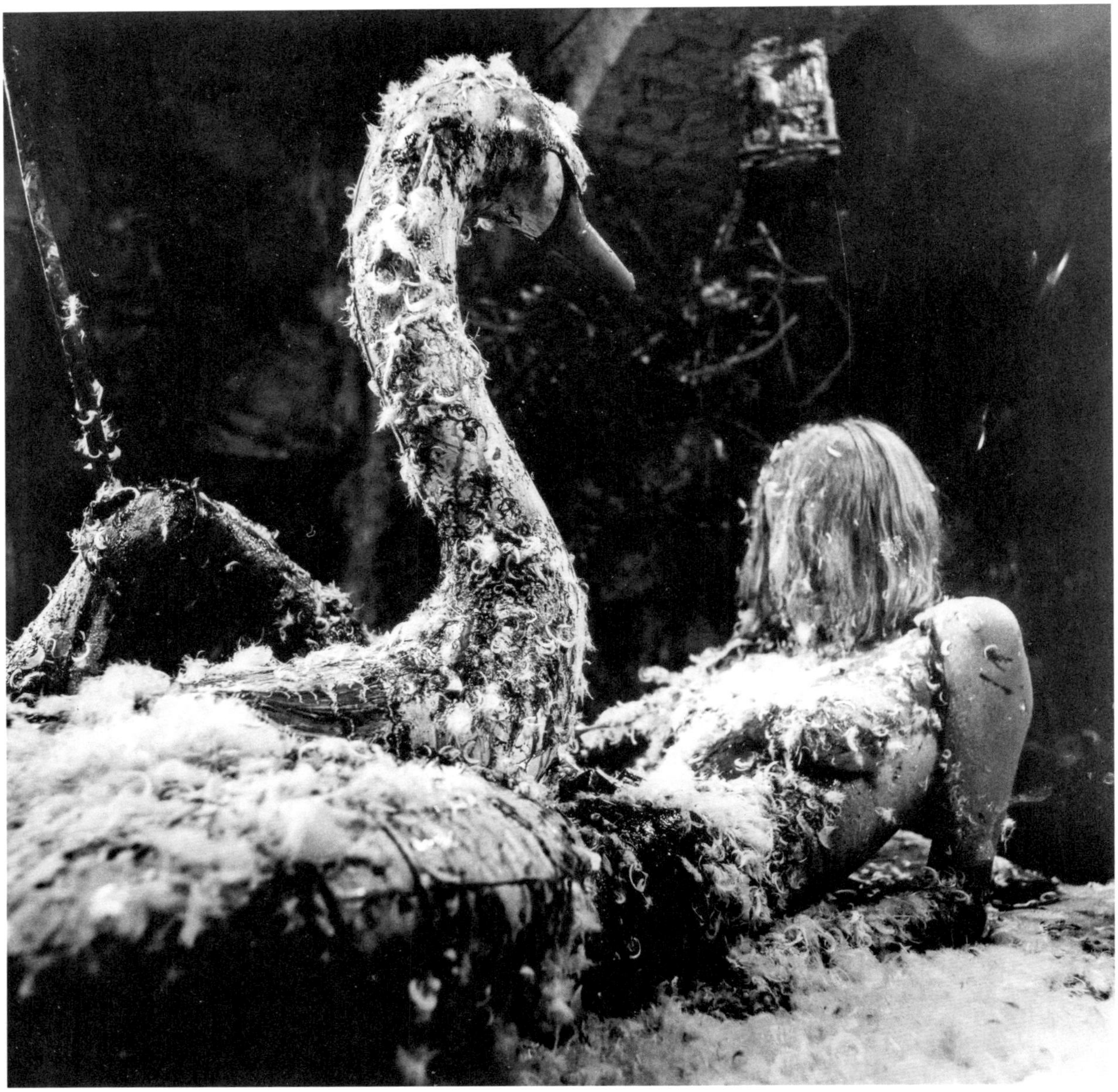

Fig. 148
Otto Muehl
Materialaktion Nr. 12, Leda mit dem Schwan (Material Action No. 12, Leda with the Swan), 20 August 1964
Muehl's studio, Perinetgasse 1, 1200 Vienna
B/W photograph
photo: Ludwig Hoffenreich
with: Ulla Holzbauer

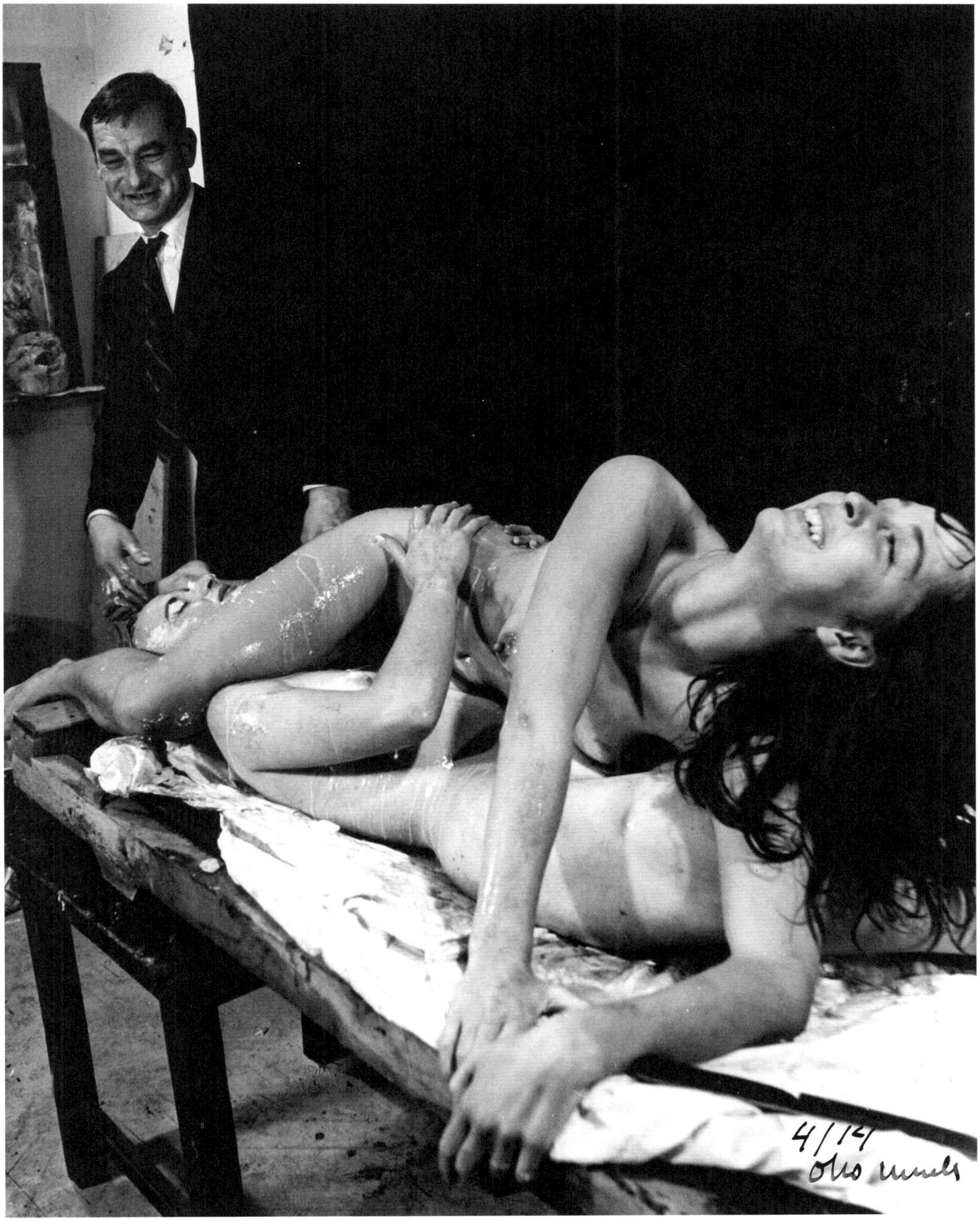

Fig. 149
Otto Muehl
Materialaktion Nr. 14, Cosinus Alpha (Material Action No. 14, Cosinus Alpha), November 1964
Muehl's apartment, Obere Augartenstraße 14 a/20, 1020 Vienna
B/W photograph
photo: Ludwig Hoffenreich
with: Friedl Muehl, Henny Petri

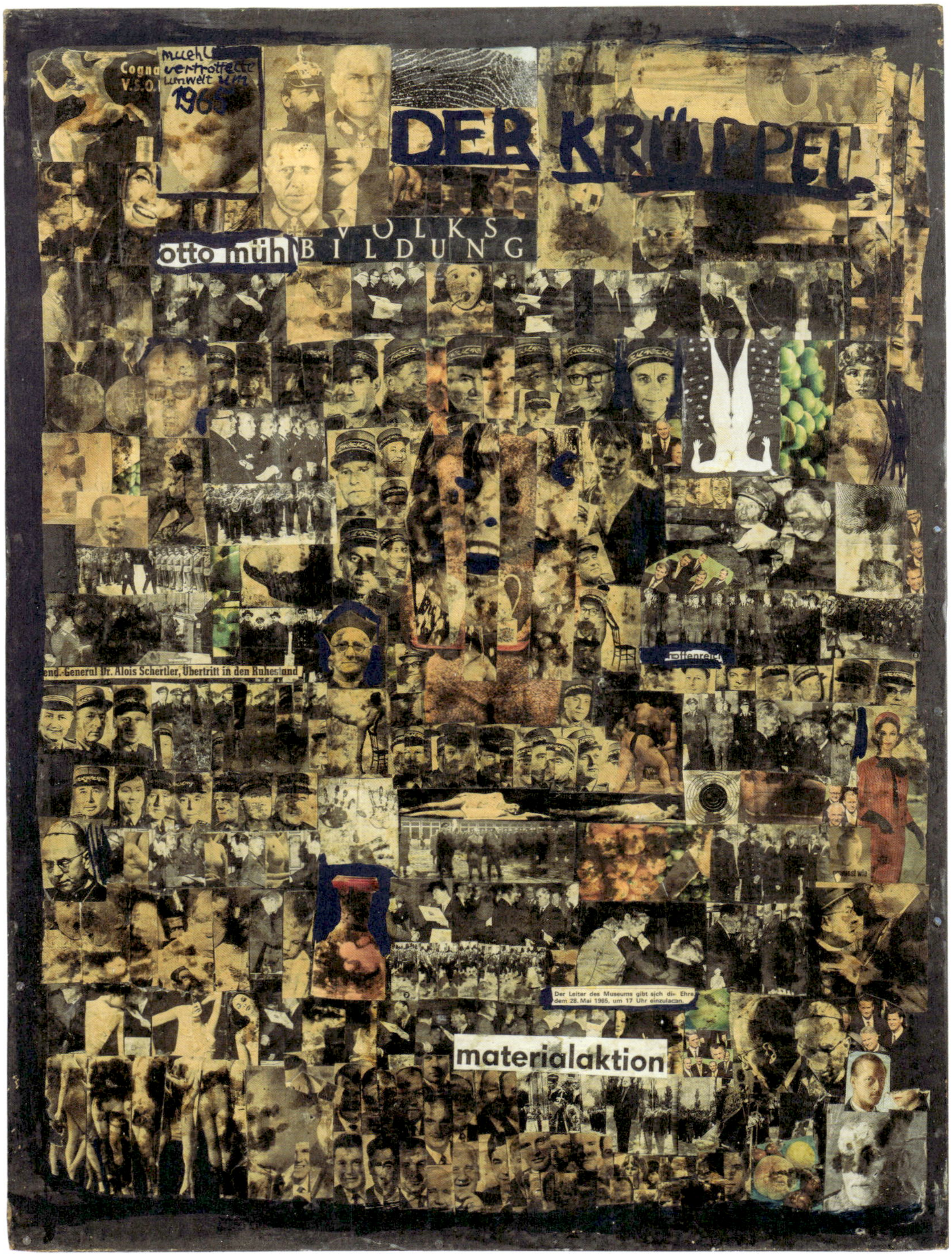

Fig. 150
Otto Muehl
Vertrottelte Umwelt (Idiotized Environment), around 1965
Clippings, dispersion on wood
84 x 64 cm
WAM – Wiener Aktionismus Museum, Vienna

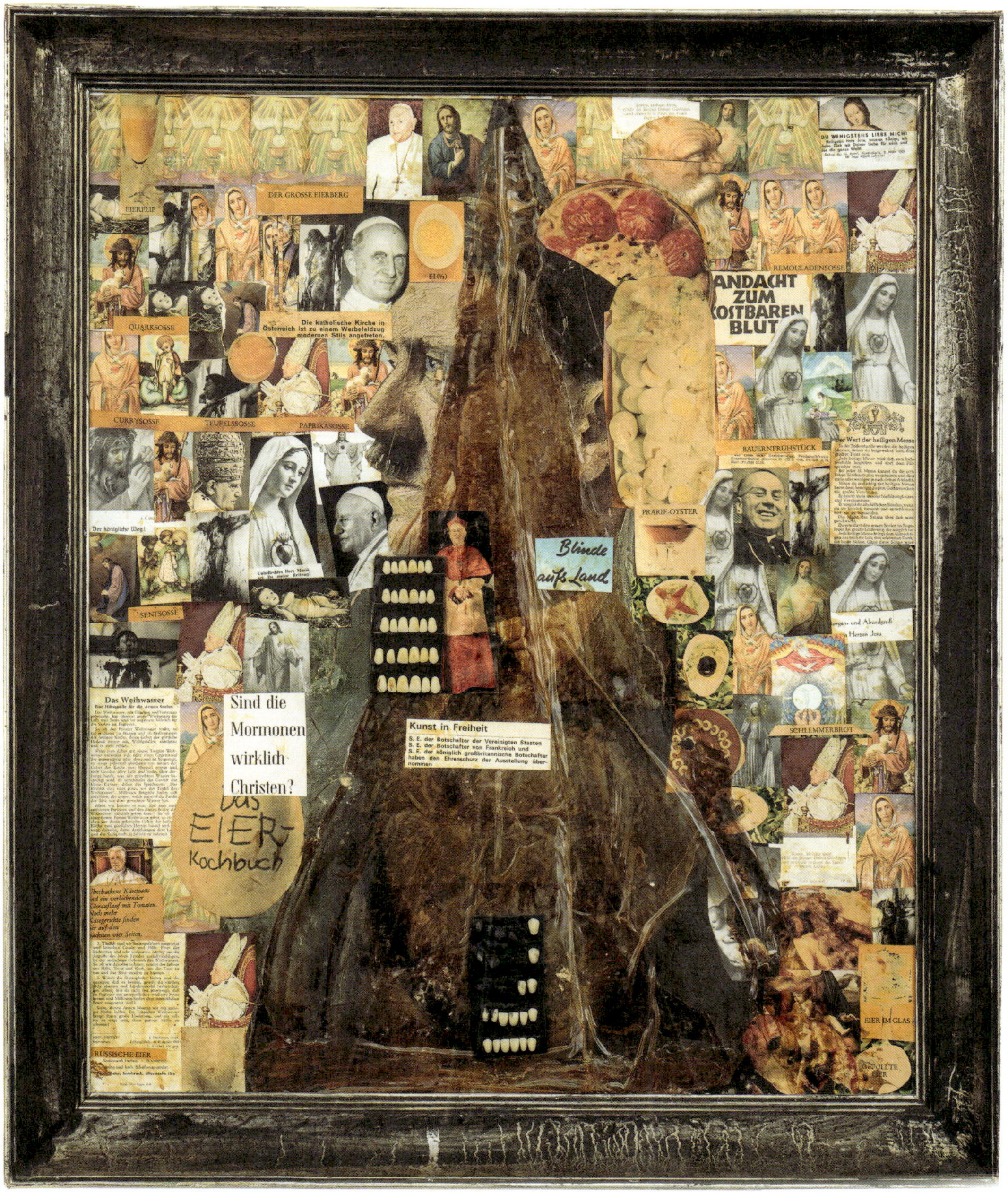

Fig. 151
Otto Muehl
Andacht zum kostbaren Blut (Devotion to the Precious Blood), 1966
Clippings, replacement teeth, dispersion on wood
82 x 70 cm
WAM – Wiener Aktionismus Museum, Vienna, Collection K.

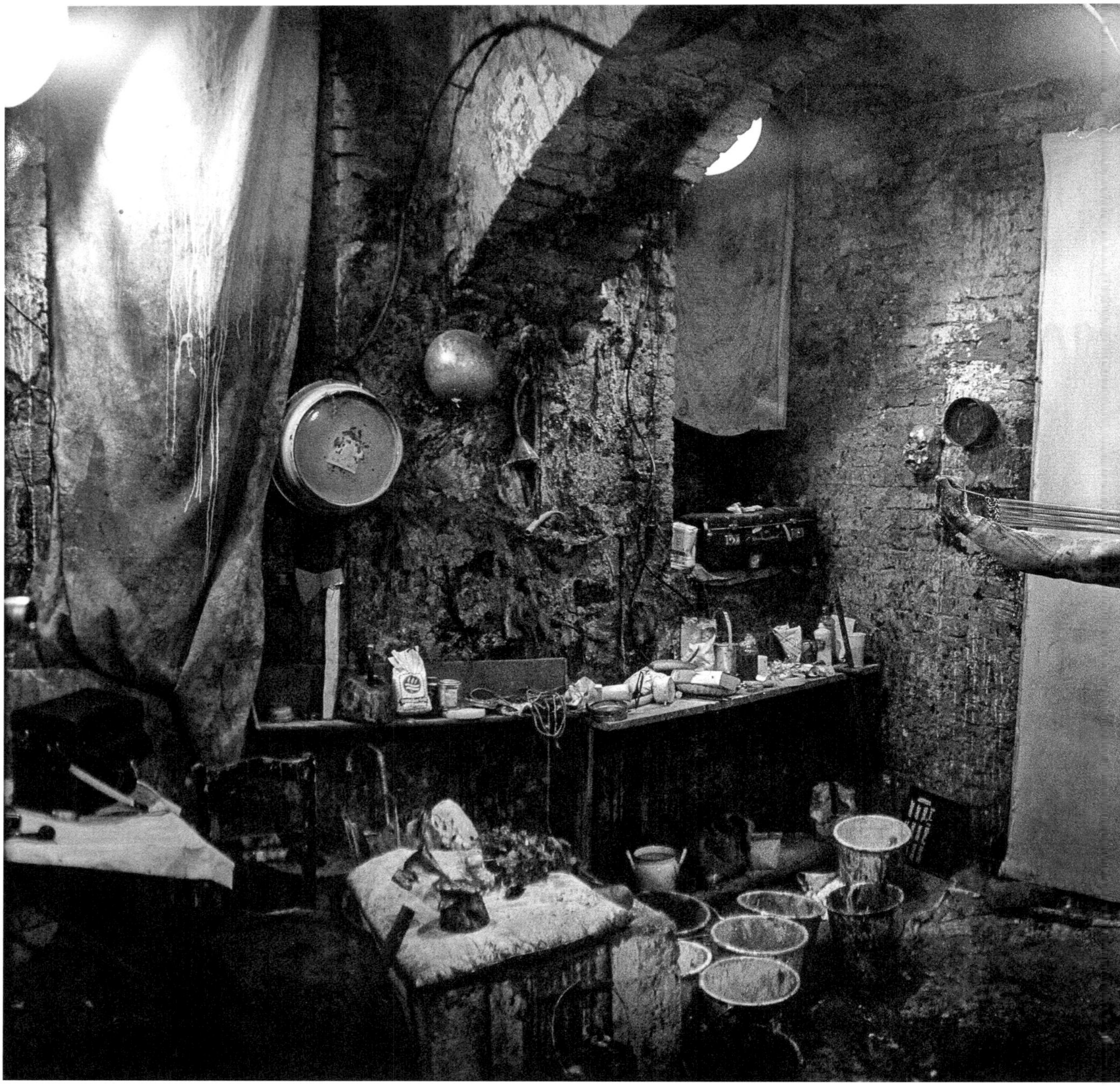

Fig. 152
Otto Muehl
Materialaktion Nr. 19, Bodybuilding (Material Action No. 19, Bodybuilding), 21 May 1965
Muehl's studio, Perinetgasse 1, 1200 Vienna
B/W photograph
photo: Marc Adrian

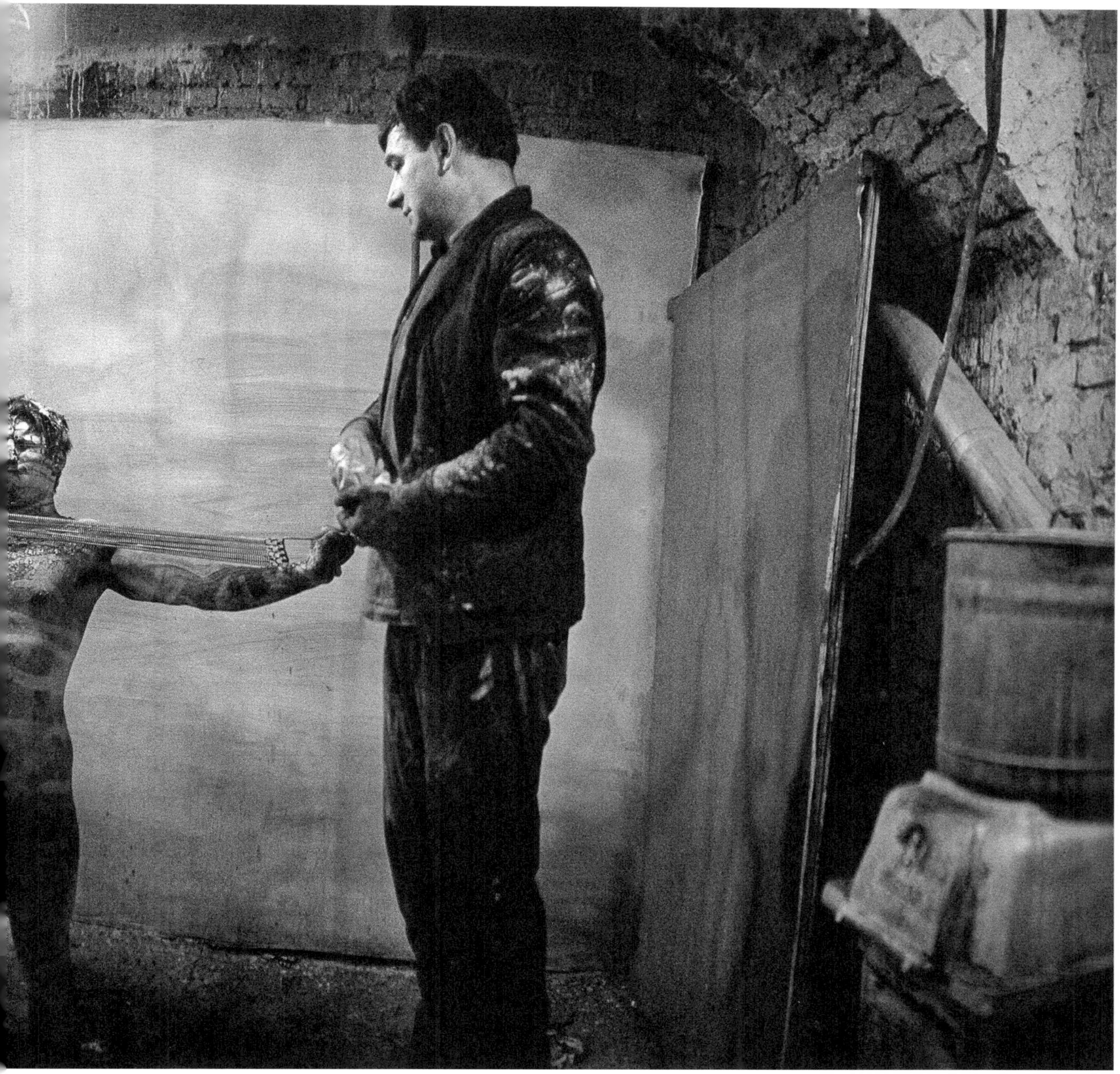

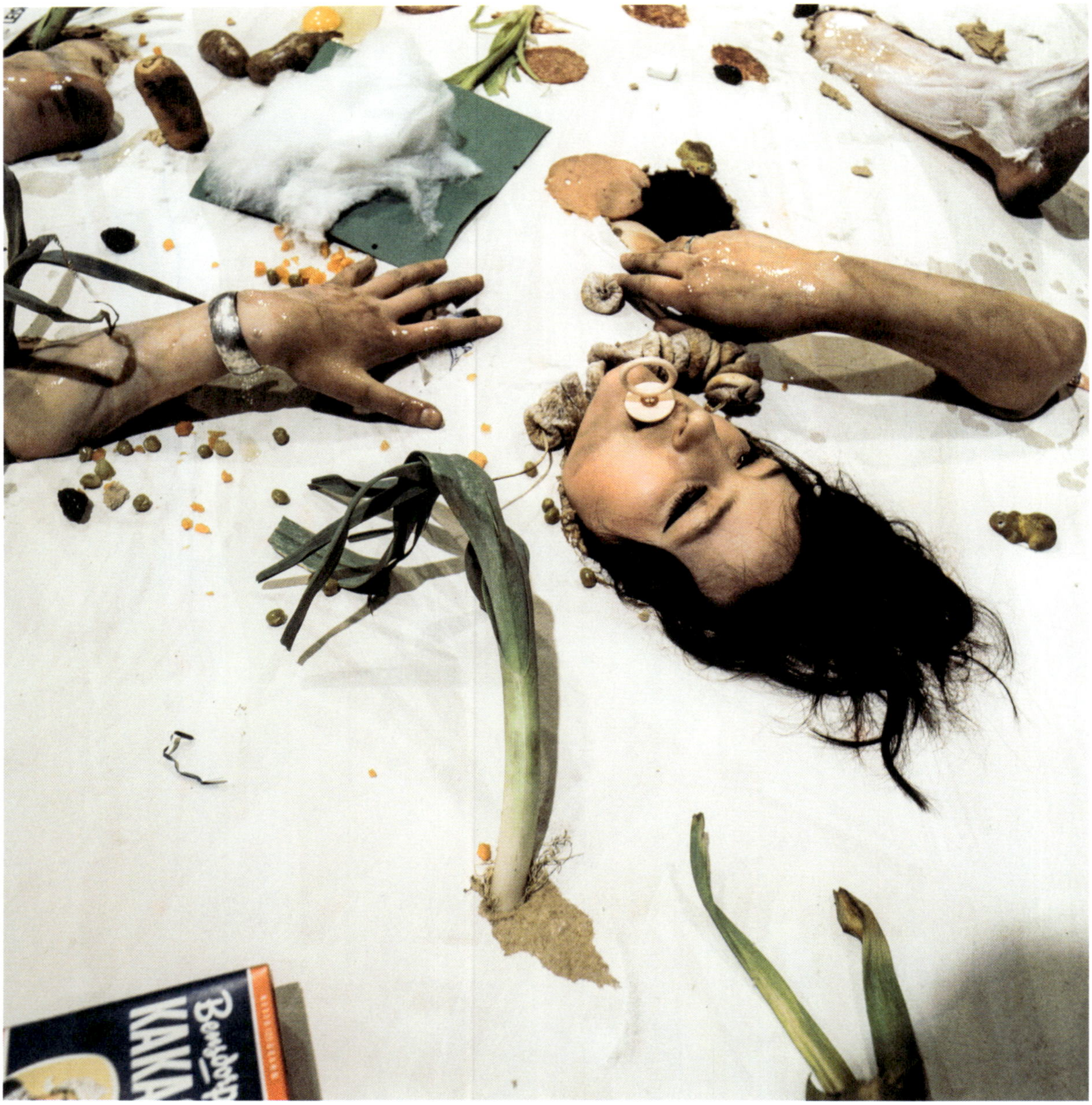

Fig. 153
Otto Muehl
Materialaktion Nr. 26, Nahrungsmitteltest (Material Action No. 26, Food Test), February/March 1966
Muehl's studio, Perinetgasse 1, 1200 Vienna
Colour photograph
photo: Ludwig Hoffenreich
with: Anna Brus, Ziemi Schieb

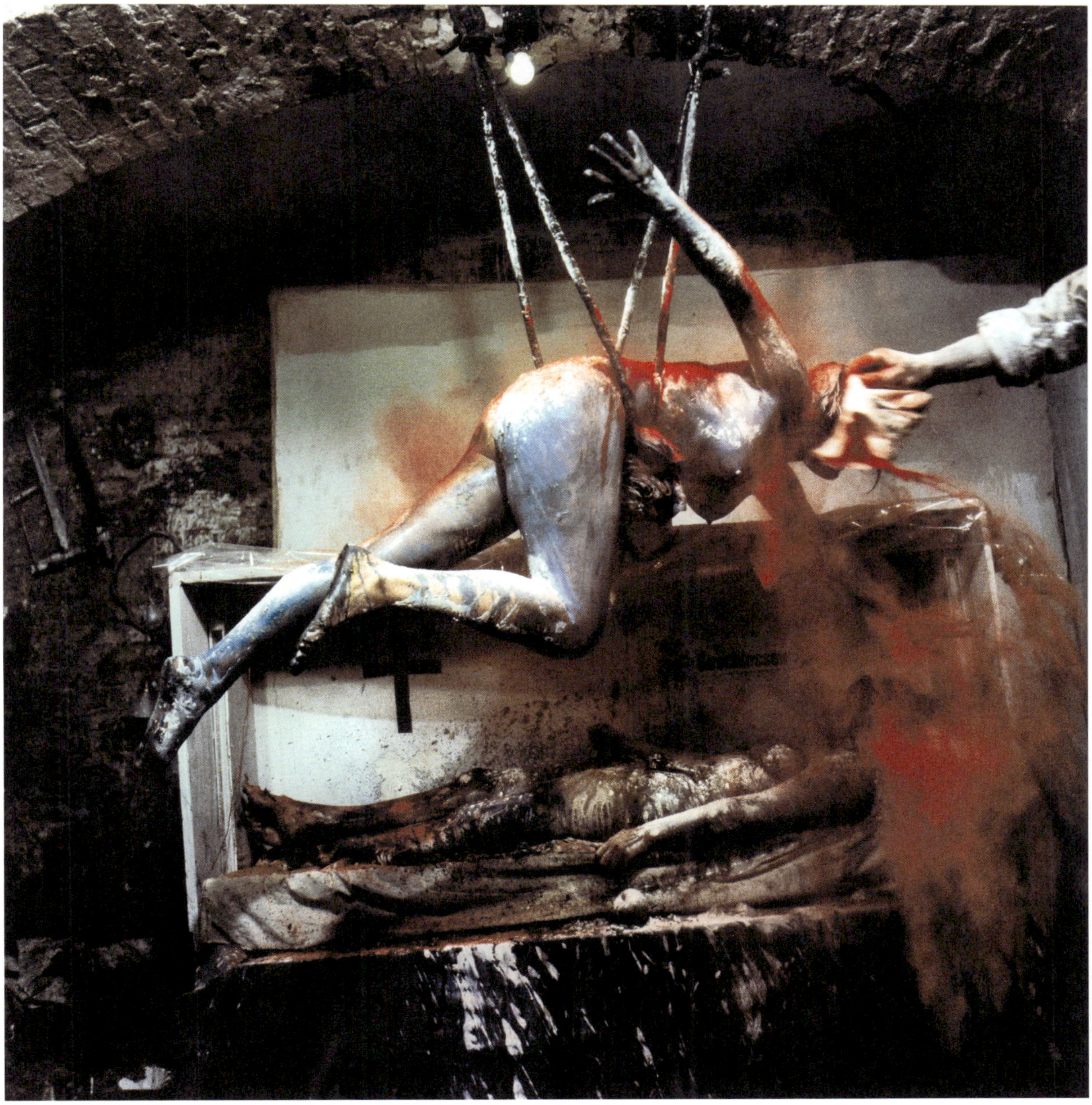

Fig. 154
Otto Muehl
Materialaktion Nr. 27, St. Anna (Material Action No. 27, St. Anna), March 1966
Muehl's studio, Perinetgasse 1, 1200 Vienna
Colour photograph
photo: Ludwig Hoffenreich
with: Anna Brus, Ziemi Schieb

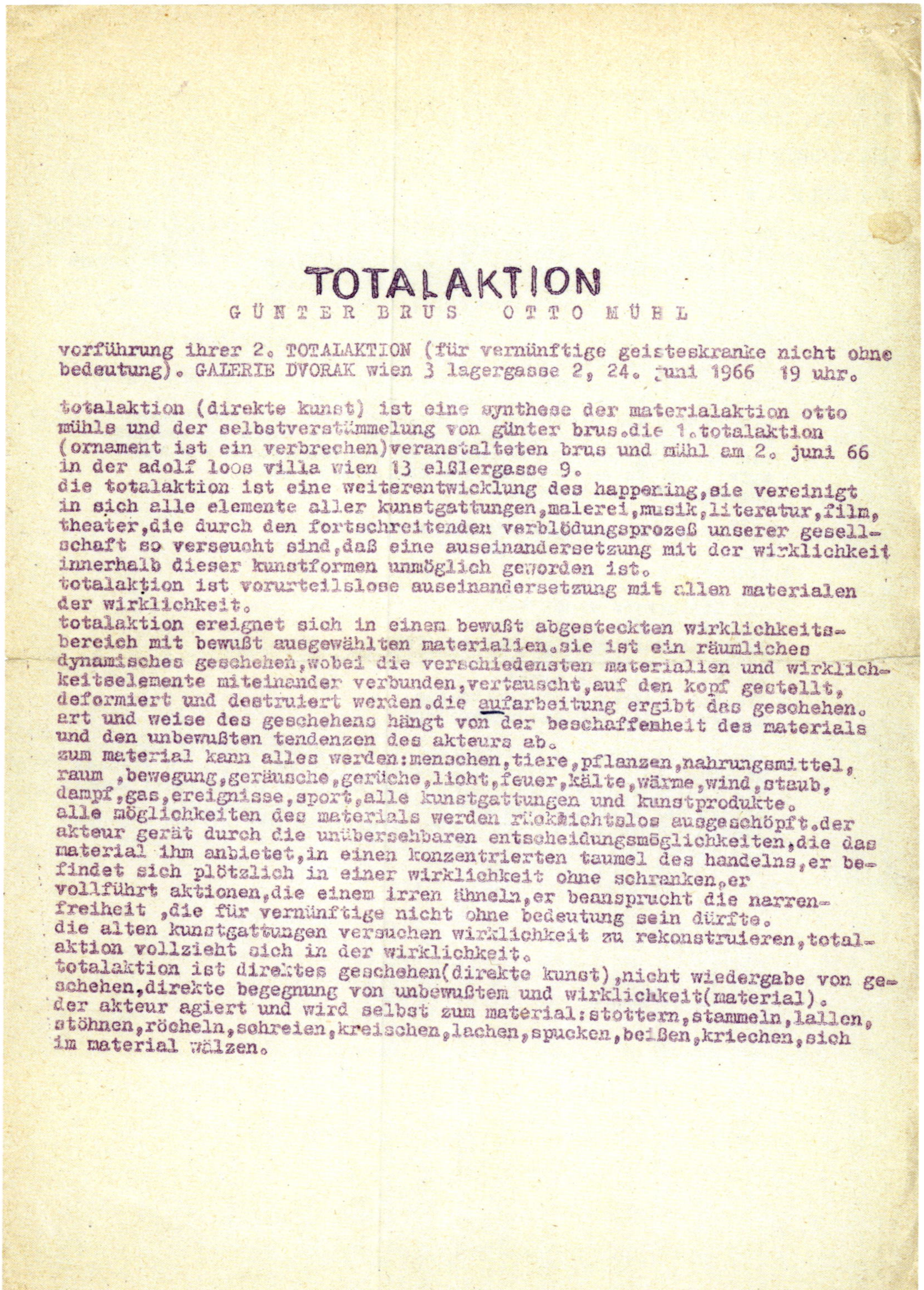

TOTALAKTION

G Ü N T E R B R U S   O T T O M Ü H L

vorführung ihrer 2. TOTALAKTION (für vernünftige geisteskranke nicht ohne
bedeutung). GALERIE DVORAK wien 3 lagergasse 2, 24. juni 1966 19 uhr.

totalaktion (direkte kunst) ist eine synthese der materialaktion otto
mühls und der selbstverstümmelung von günter brus.die 1.totalaktion
(ornament ist ein verbrechen)veranstalteten brus und mühl am 2. juni 66
in der adolf loos villa wien 13 elßlergasse 9.
die totalaktion ist eine weiterentwicklung des happening,sie vereinigt
in sich alle elemente aller kunstgattungen,malerei,musik,literatur,film,
theater,die durch den fortschreitenden verblödungsprozeß unserer gesell-
schaft so verseucht sind,daß eine auseinandersetzung mit der wirklichkeit
innerhalb dieser kunstformen unmöglich geworden ist.
totalaktion ist vorurteilslose auseinandersetzung mit allen materialen
der wirklichkeit.
totalaktion ereignet sich in einem bewußt abgesteckten wirklichkeits-
bereich mit bewußt ausgewählten materialien.sie ist ein räumliches
dynamisches geschehen,wobei die verschiedensten materialien und wirklich-
keitselemente miteinander verbunden,vertauscht,auf den kopf gestellt,
deformiert und destruiert werden.die aufarbeitung ergibt das geschehen.
art und weise des geschehens hängt von der beschaffenheit des materials
und den unbewußten tendenzen des akteurs ab.
zum material kann alles werden:menschen,tiere,pflanzen,nahrungsmittel,
raum ,bewegung,geräusche,gerüche,licht,feuer,kälte,wärme,wind,staub,
dampf,gas,ereignisse,sport,alle kunstgattungen und kunstprodukte.
alle möglichkeiten des materials werden rücksichtslos ausgeschöpft.der
akteur gerät durch die unübersehbaren entscheidungsmöglichkeiten,die das
material ihm anbietet,in einen konzentrierten taumel des handelns,er be-
findet sich plötzlich in einer wirklichkeit ohne schranken,er
vollführt aktionen,die einem irren ähneln,er beansprucht die narren-
freiheit ,die für vernünftige nicht ohne bedeutung sein dürfte.
die alten kunstgattungen versuchen wirklichkeit zu rekonstruieren,total-
aktion vollzieht sich in der wirklichkeit.
totalaktion ist direktes geschehen(direkte kunst),nicht wiedergabe von ge-
schehen,direkte begegnung von unbewußtem und wirklichkeit(material).
der akteur agiert und wird selbst zum material:stottern,stammeln,lallen,
stöhnen,röcheln,schreien,kreischen,lachen,spucken,beißen,kriechen,sich
im material wälzen.

Fig. 155
Günter Brus, Otto Muehl
Flyer *Totalaktion* (Total Action), Invitation to *2. Totalaktion (für vernünftige geisteskranke nicht ohne bedeutung)* (2nd Total Action [not without meaning for rational lunatics]),
Galerie Dvorak, Lagergasse 2, 1030 Vienna, 24 June 1966
Matrix print
29,7 x 21 cm
mumok – Museum moderner Kunst Stiftung Ludwig Wien

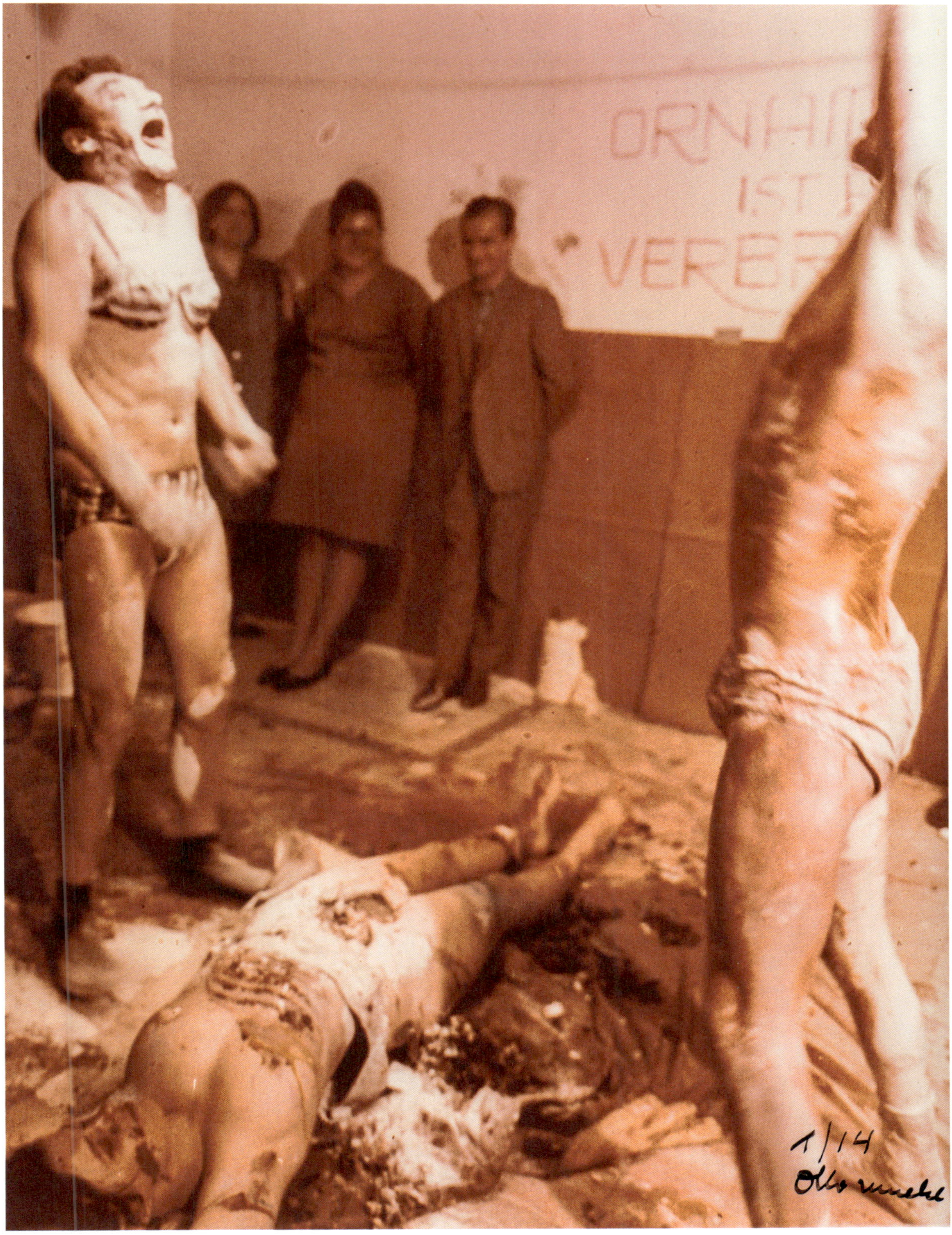

Fig. 156
Günter Brus, Otto Muehl
1. Totalaktion, Ornament ist ein Verbrechen (1st Total Action, Ornament is a Crime), 2 June 1966
House Heller (Architect: Adolf Loos), Elßlergasse 9, 1130 Vienna
Colour photograph
photo: Ludwig Hoffenreich
with: Ziemi Schieb

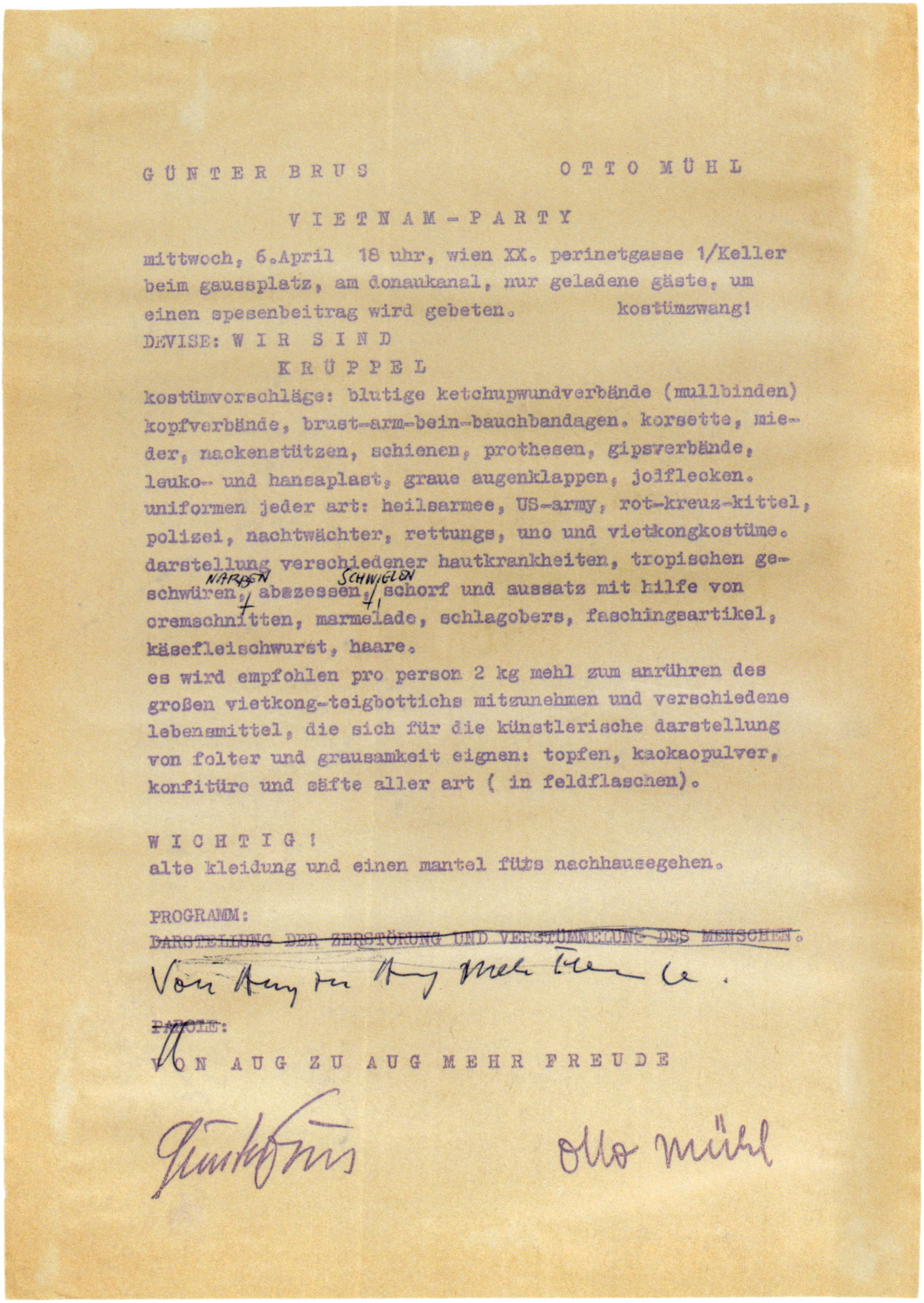

G Ü N T E R B R U S O T T O M Ü H L

V I E T N A M - P A R T Y

mittwoch, 6.April 18 uhr, wien XX. perinetgasse 1/Keller beim gaussplatz, am donaukanal, nur geladene gäste, um einen spesenbeitrag wird gebeten. kostümzwang!

DEVISE: W I R S I N D
K R Ü P P E L

kostümvorschläge: blutige ketchupwundverbände (mullbinden) kopfverbände, brust-arm-bein-bauchbandagen. korsette, mieder, nackenstützen, schienen, prothesen, gipsverbände, leuko- und hansaplast, graue augenklappen, jodflecken. uniformen jeder art: heilsarmee, US-army, rot-kreuz-kittel, polizei, nachtwächter, rettungs, uno und vietkongkostüme. darstellung verschiedener hautkrankheiten, tropischen geschwüren, NARBEN, abszessen, SCHWIELEN, schorf und aussatz mit hilfe von cremschnitten, marmelade, schlagobers, faschingsartikel, käsefleischwurst, haare.

es wird empfohlen pro person 2 kg mehl zum anrühren des großen vietkong-teigbottichs mitzunehmen und verschiedene lebensmittel, die sich für die künstlerische darstellung von folter und grausamkeit eignen: topfen, kakaopulver, konfitüre und säfte aller art (in feldflaschen).

W I C H T I G !
alte kleidung und einen mantel fürs nachhausegehen.

PROGRAMM:
~~DARSTELLUNG DER ZERSTÖRUNG UND VERSTÜMMELUNG DES MENSCHEN.~~
Von Aug zu Aug mehr Freude.

~~PAROLE~~:
~~V~~U O N A U G Z U A U G M E H R F R E U D E

Günter Brus Otto Mühl

Fig. 157
Günter Brus, Otto Muehl
First invitation to the action *Vietnamparty* for 6 April 1966
(The action actually took place on 4 July 1966 at Muehl's studio Perinetgasse 1, 1200 Vienna.)
Matrix print
WAM – Wiener Aktionismus Museum, Vienna, Collection K.

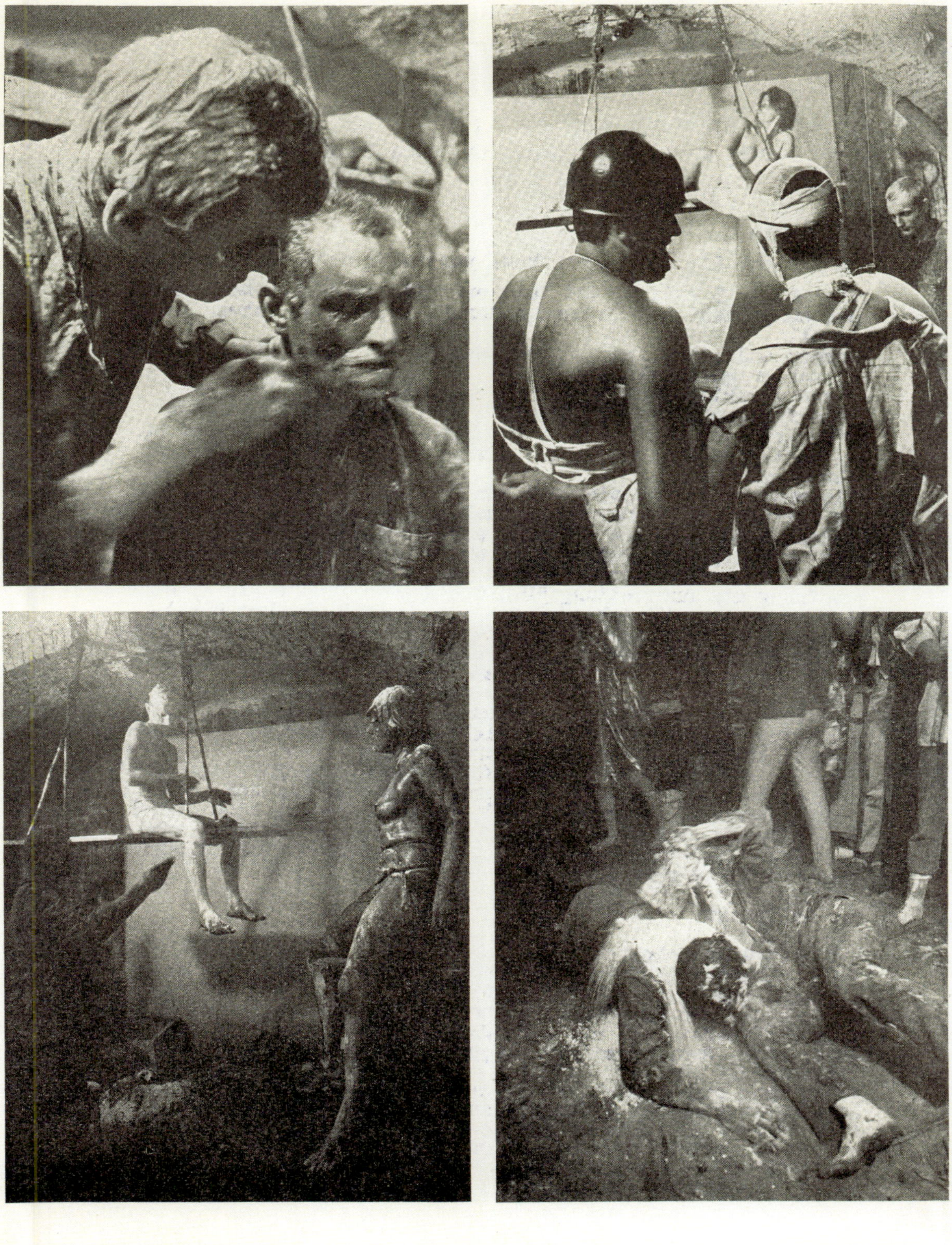

Schnappschüsse von der Vietnam-Party

Fig. 158
Schnappschüsse von der Vietnamparty (Snapshots from the Vietnamparty)
Newspaper report about the *Vietnamparty* on 4 July 1966 at Muehl's studio Perinetgasse 1, 1200 Vienna
Offset print
WAM – Wiener Aktionismus Museum, Vienna, Collection K.

D I A S

DESTRUCTION IN ART SYMPOSIUM - LONDON SEPTEMBER 1966

Activities by members of the Institute of Direct Art, Vienna

Symposium - Africa Centre

Teilnahme an der Dokumentationsausstellung. Brus, Mühl, Nitsch waren vertreten mit Fotos, Manifesten und theoretischen Texten.

Symposium - Africa Centre, 1o.9.66

Peter Weibel: Lecture - Direct Art
Otto Mühl: "Translation - Action for two Voices"
Günter Brus: "Head-Destruction"
Hermann Nitsch: Lecture, Discussion - O.M. Theatre

Symposium - Africa Centre, 11.9.66

Kurt Kren: 13 Films, 16 mm

Conway Hall, 12.9.66

Concert by Brus and Mühl: "Breath - Exercises"

St Brides Institute, 13.9.66

Brus and Mühl present Direct Art: "Ten Rounds for Cassius Clay"

Africa Centre, 15.9.66

Films by Kren, Nitsch, Mühl, Brus

Slides by Mühl, Nitsch, Brus

Simultanious - Action by Günter Brus, Otto Mühl, Hermann Nitsch, Peter Weibel, Al Hansen (Usa)

St Brides Institute, 16.9.66

Hermann Nitsch: Action O.M. Theatre (5.Abreaktionsspiel)

Fig. 159
Programme of the Austrian contributions to the *Destuction in Art Symposium* London, September 1966
Matrix print
29,7 x 21 cm
mumok – Museum moderner Kunst Stiftung Ludwig Wien

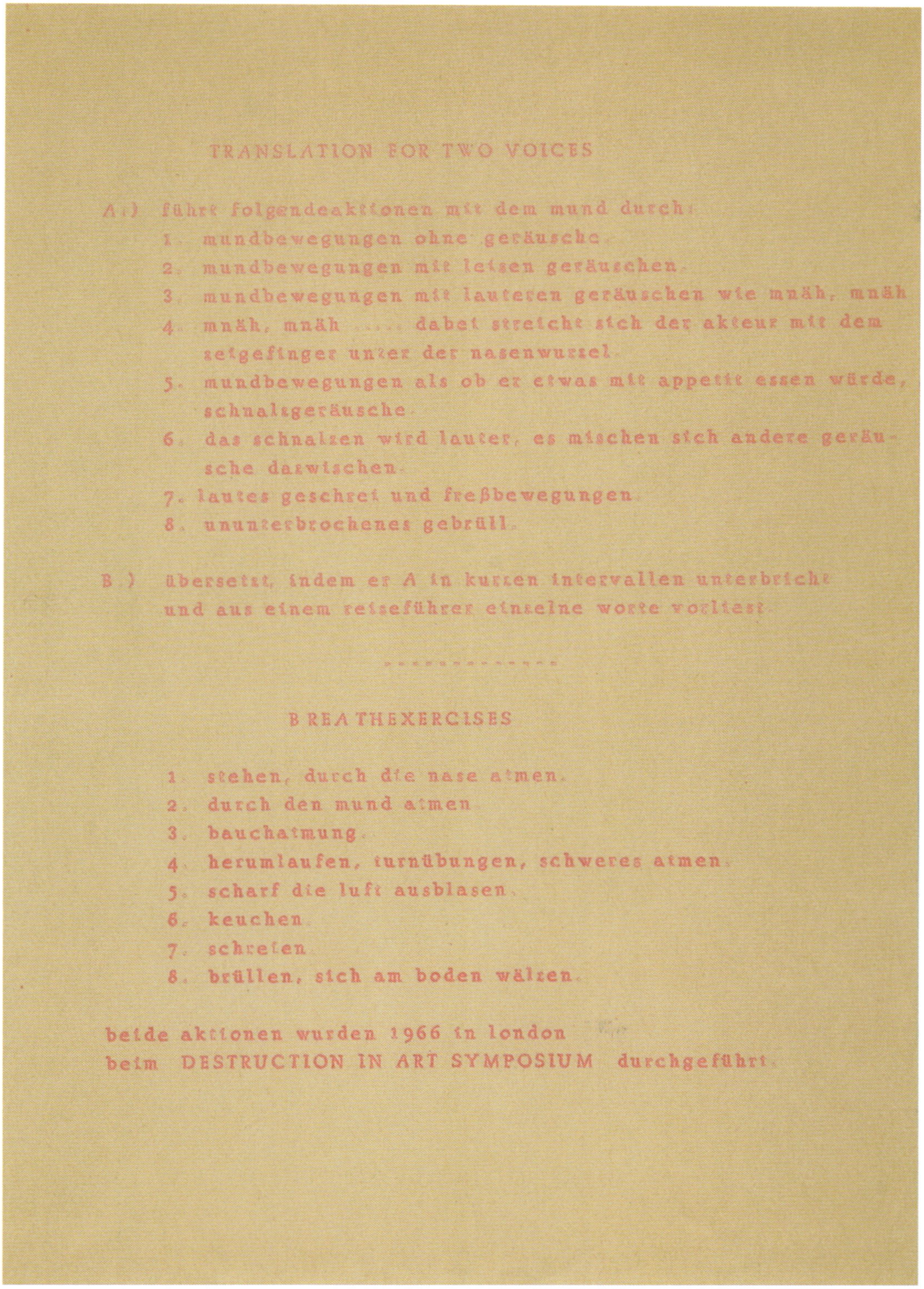

TRANSLATION FOR TWO VOICES

A.) führt folgendeaktionen mit dem mund durch:
1. mundbewegungen ohne geräusche.
2. mundbewegungen mit leisen geräuschen.
3. mundbewegungen mit lauteren geräuschen wie mnäh, mnäh
4. mnäh, mnäh ..... dabei streicht sich der akteur mit dem zeigefinger unter der nasenwurzel.
5. mundbewegungen als ob er etwas mit appetit essen würde, schnalzgeräusche.
6. das schnalzen wird lauter, es mischen sich andere geräusche dazwischen.
7. lautes geschrei und freßbewegungen.
8. ununterbrochenes gebrüll.

B.) übersetzt, indem er A in kurzen intervallen unterbricht und aus einem reiseführer einzelne worte vorliest.

\- - - - - - - - - - - - -

BREATHEXERCISES

1. stehen, durch die nase atmen.
2. durch den mund atmen.
3. bauchatmung.
4. herumlaufen, turnübungen, schweres atmen.
5. scharf die luft ausblasen.
6. keuchen.
7. schreien.
8. brüllen, sich am boden wälzen.

beide aktionen wurden 1966 in london
beim DESTRUCTION IN ART SYMPOSIUM durchgeführt.

Fig. 160
Günter Brus, Otto Muehl
Programme for the actions *Translation for Two Voices* and *Breath Exercises*, at the *Destruction in Art Symposium* London, 10 September 1966
Matrix print
29,7 x 21 cm
mumok – Museum moderner Kunst Stiftung Ludwig Wien

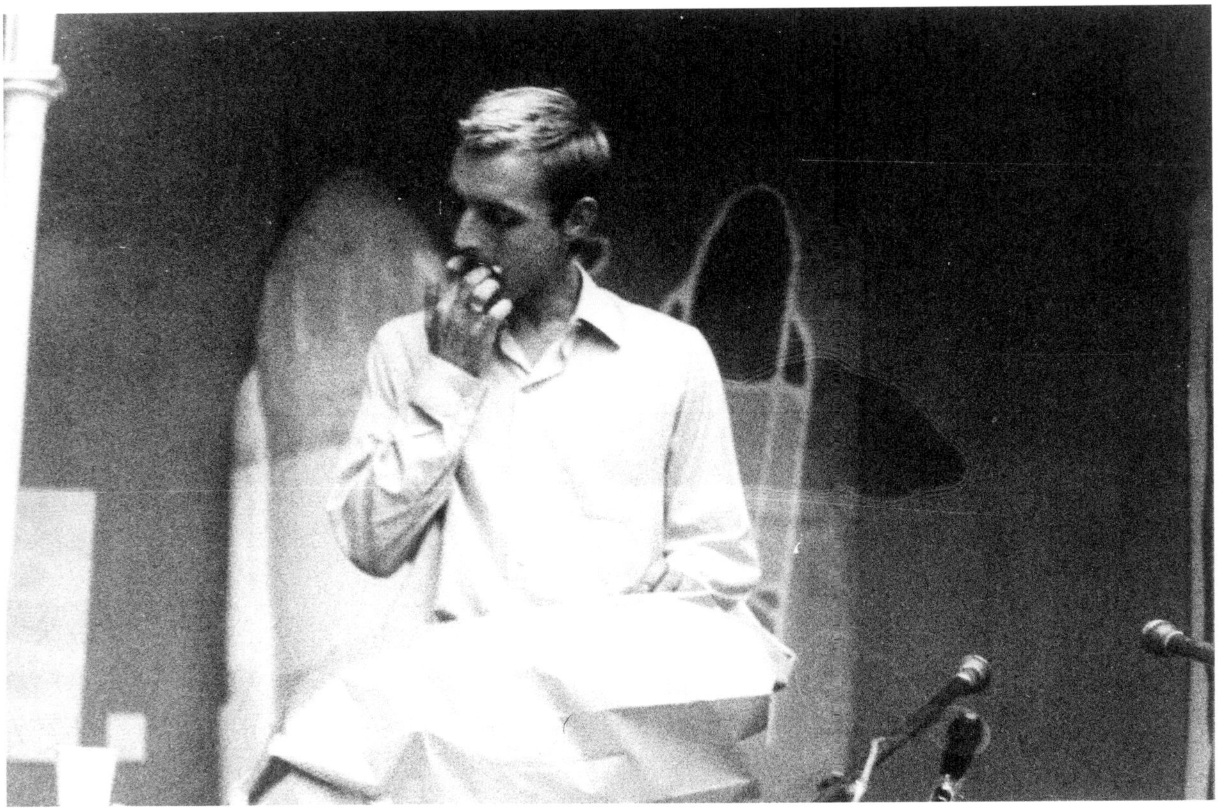

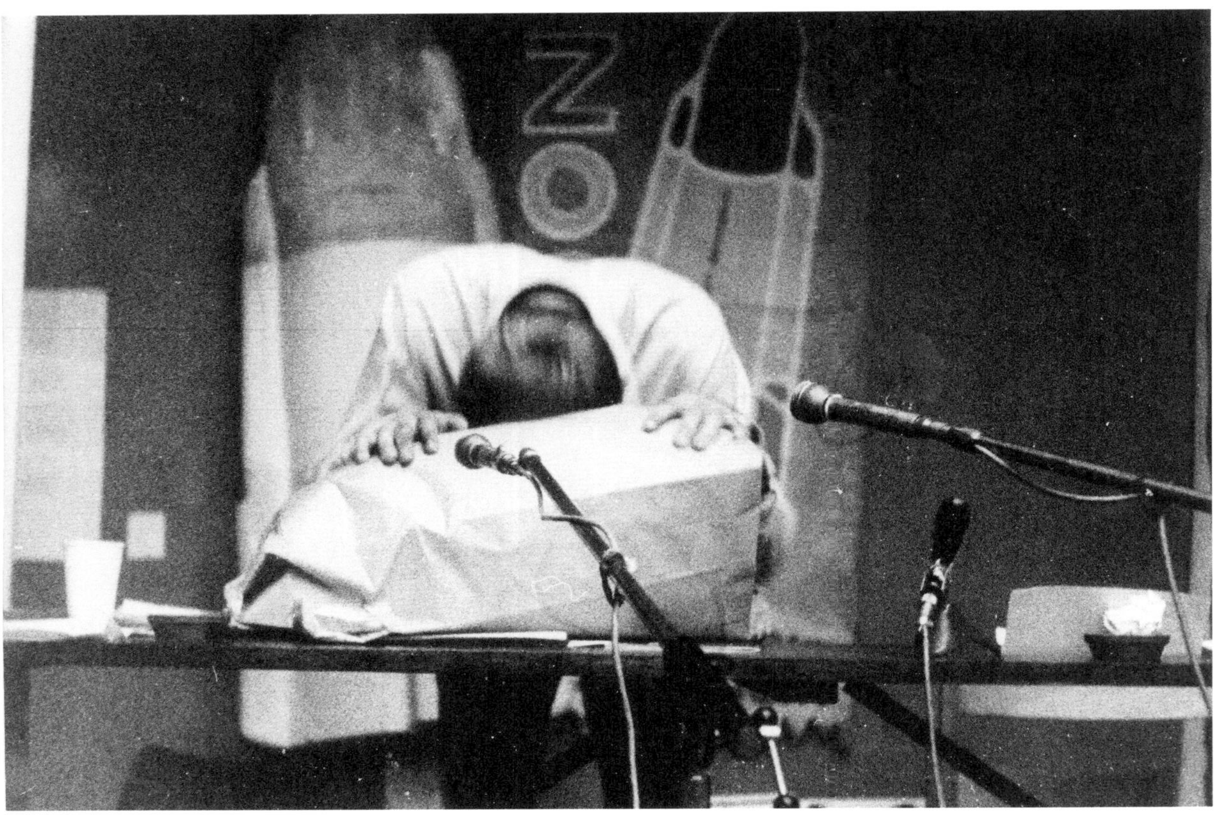

Fig. 161, 162
Günter Brus
Head Destruktion, 10 September 1966 at the *Destruction in Art Symposium*
Africa Centre, 38 King Street, London WC2
photo: Hanns Sohm

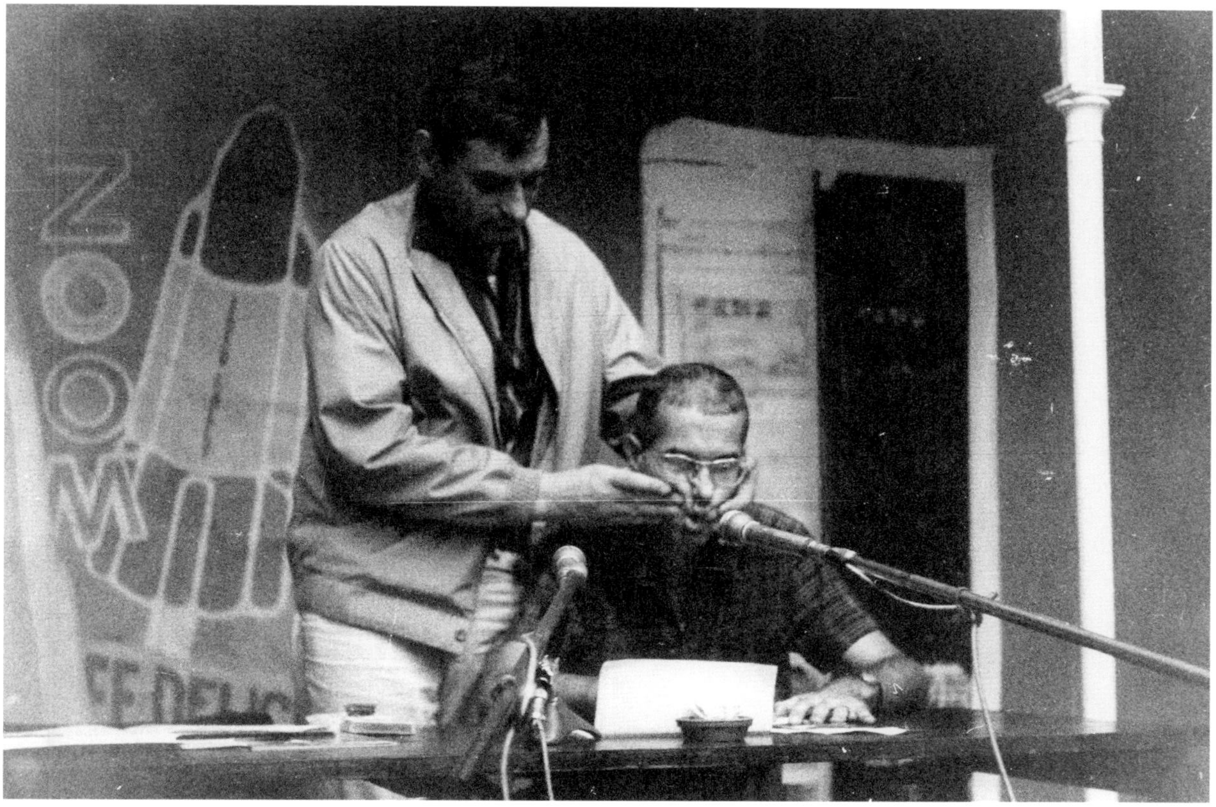

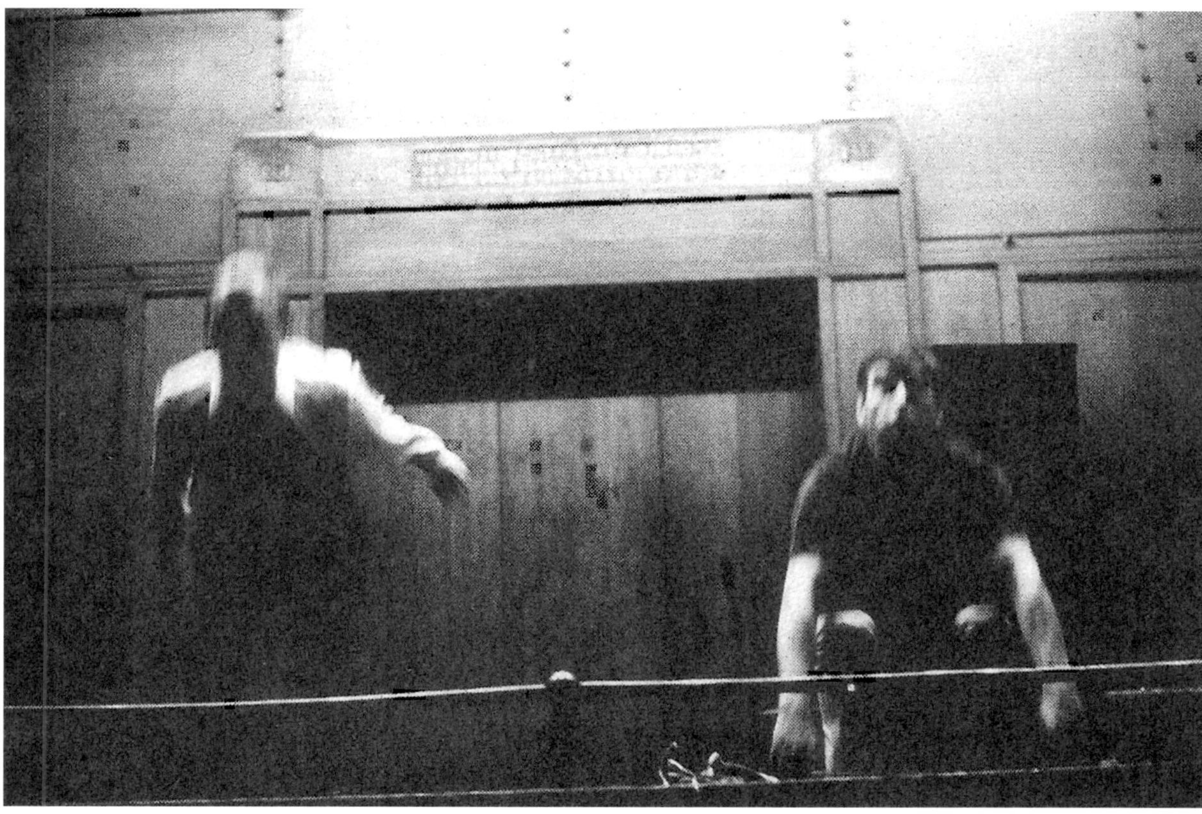

Fig. 163
Otto Muehl
Translation – Action for Two Voices,
10 September 1966 at the *Destruction in Art Symposium*
Africa Centre, 38 King Street, London WC2
B/W photograph
photo: Hanns Sohm

Ab. 164
Günter Brus, Otto Muehl,
Breath Exercises, 12 September 1966
at the *Destruction in Art Symposium*
Conway Hall, 25 Red Lion Square, London WC1
B/W photograph
photo: Hanns Sohm

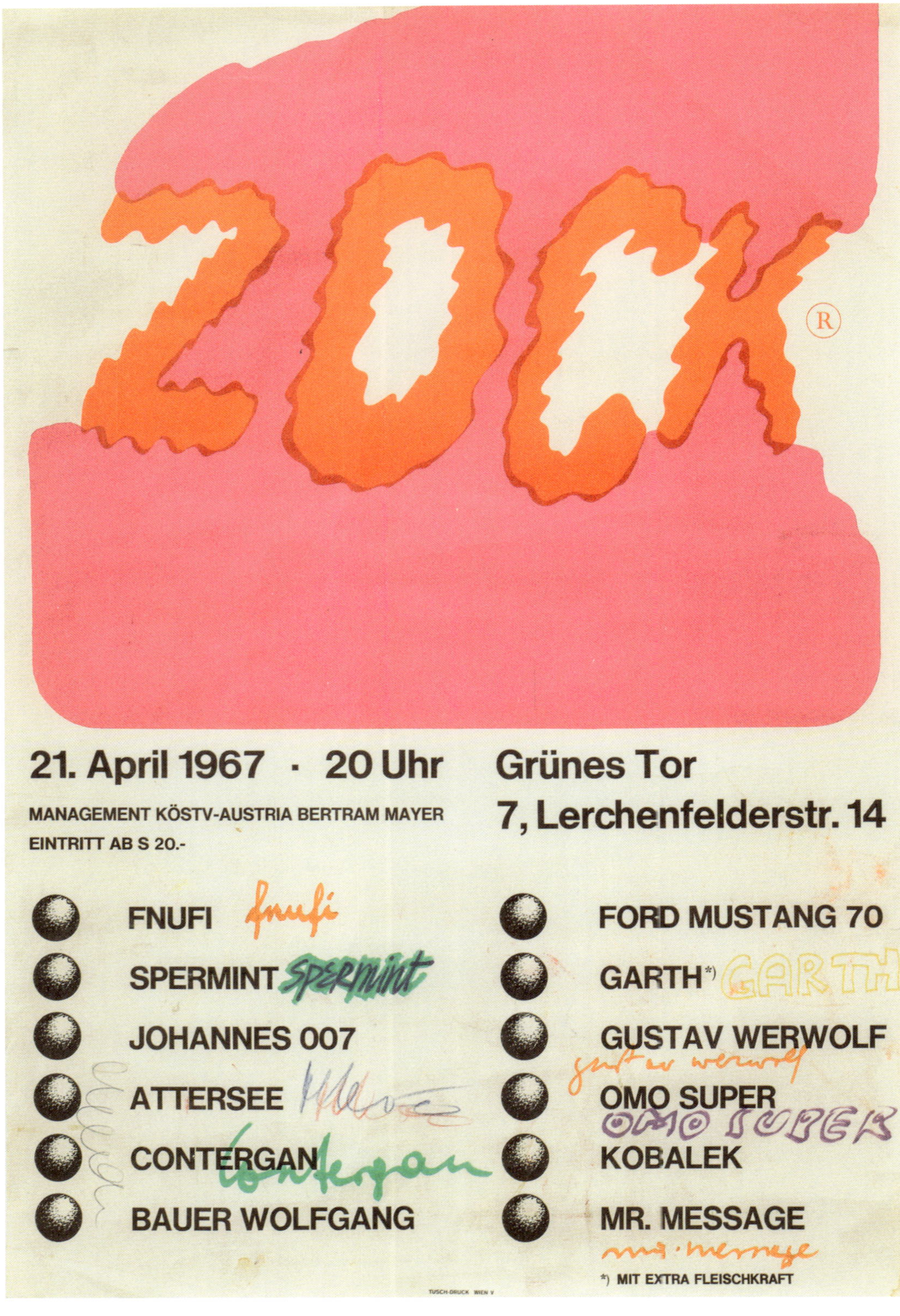

F ig. 165
Walter Pichler
Poster for the *Zock Fest* (Zock Festival), 1967
Silkscreen, felt pen on paper
58 x 41 cm

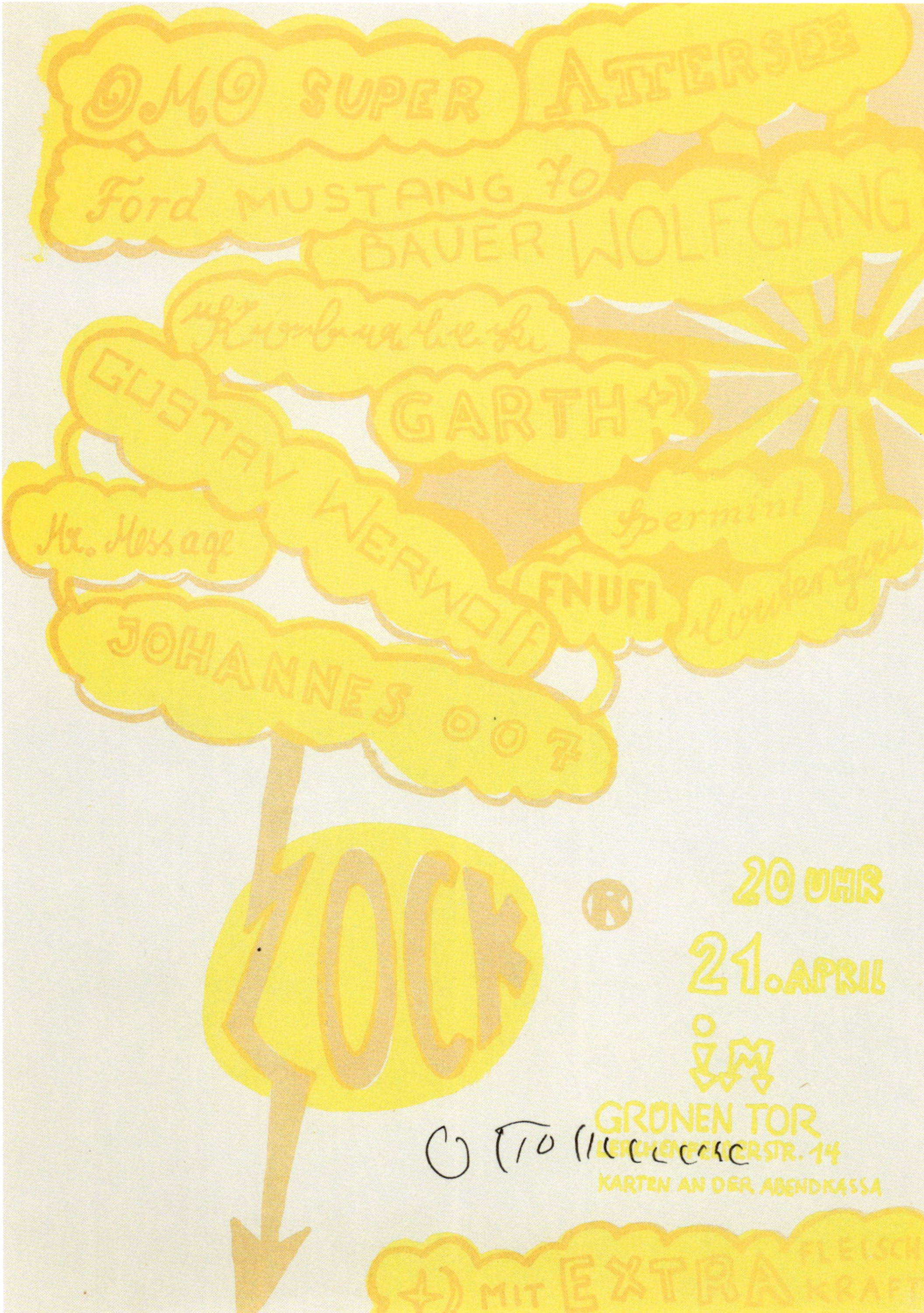

Fig. 166
Announcement of the *Zock Fest* (Zock Festival), 1967
Print on paper
29,6 x 20,9 cm

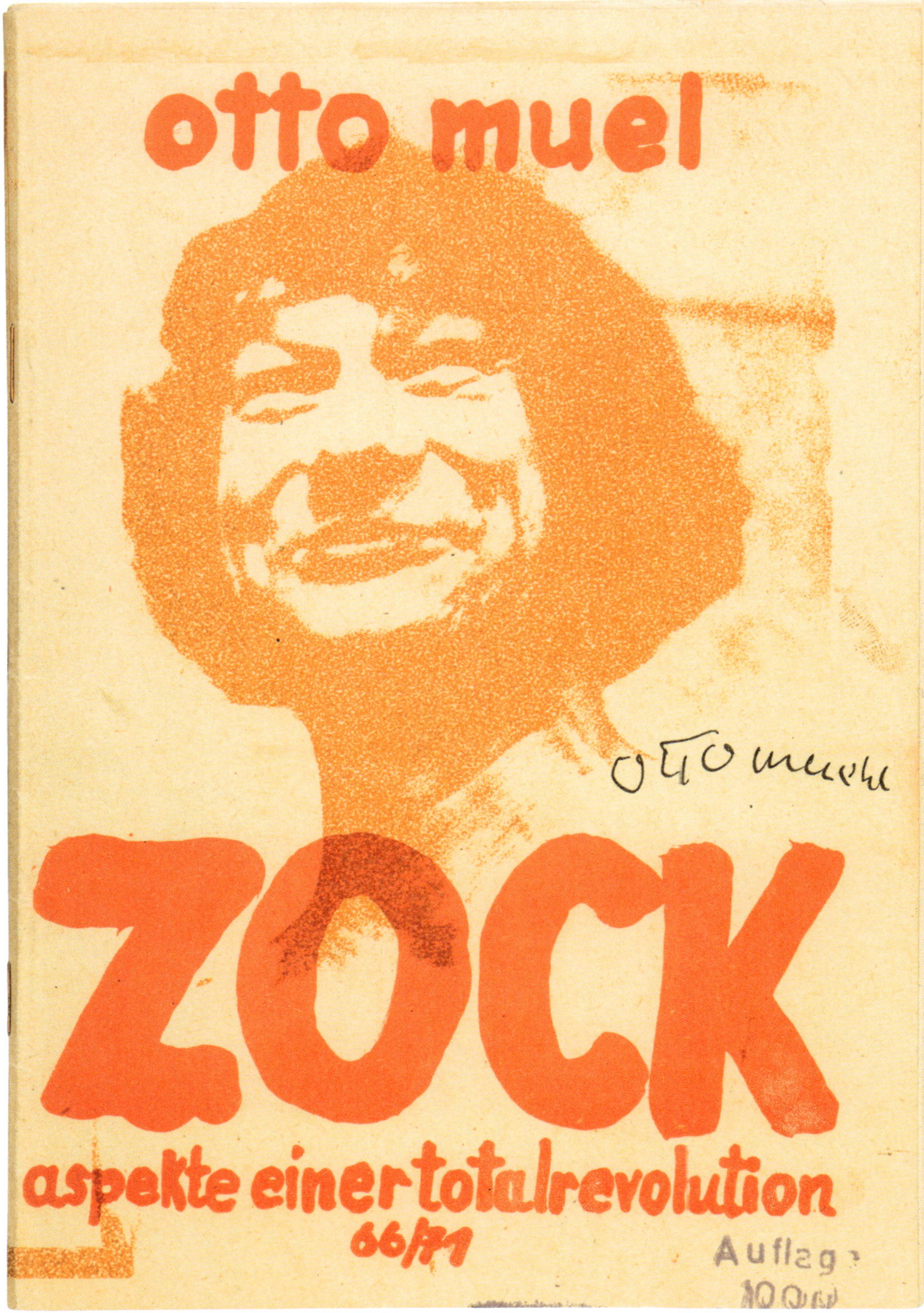

Fig. 167, 168
Otto Muehl
Zock Booklets, 1967–71
Self-publishing

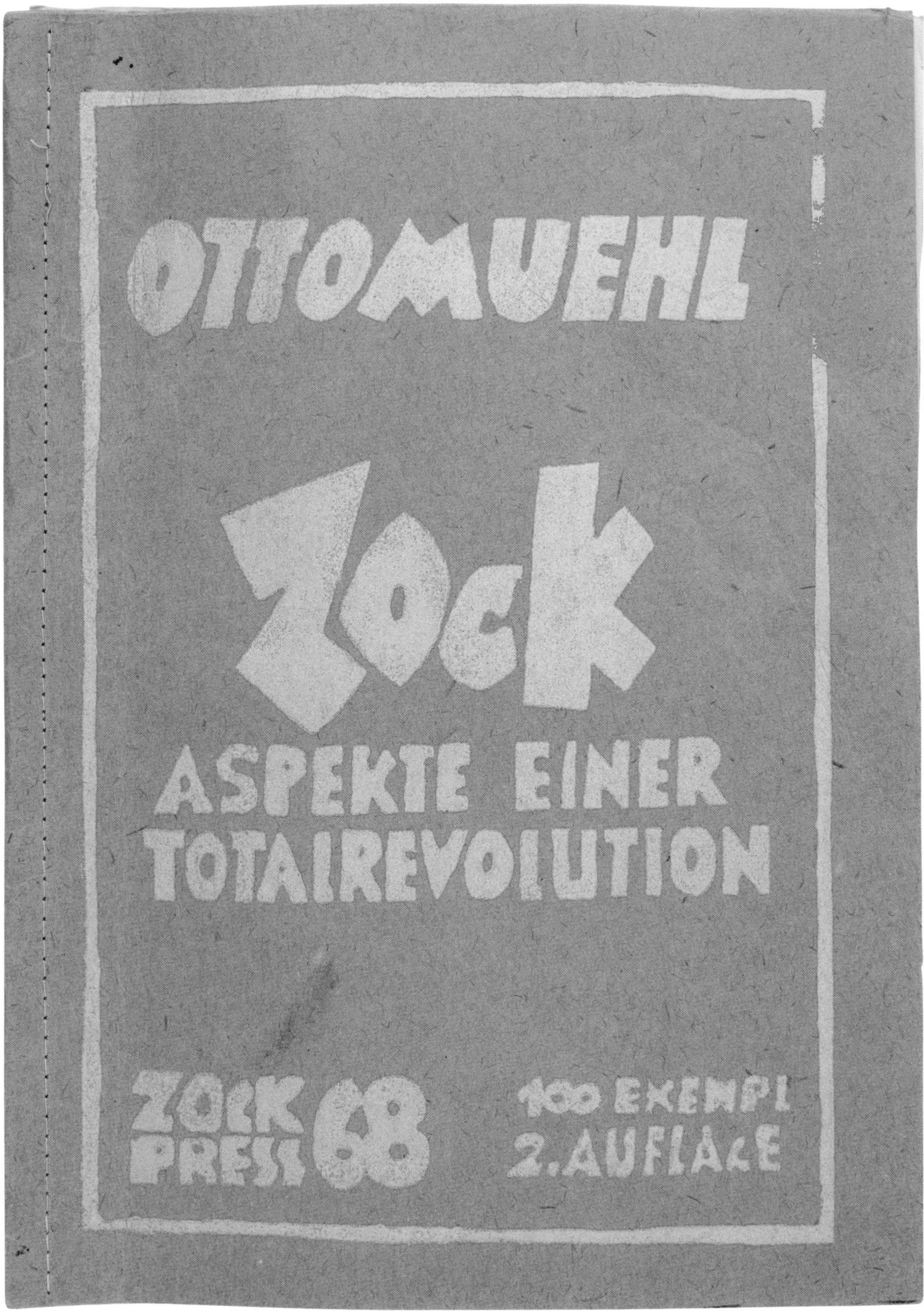
OTTOMUEHL
ZOCK
ASPEKTE EINER
TOTALREVOLUTION
ZOCK PRESS 68
100 EXEMPL
2. AUFLAGE

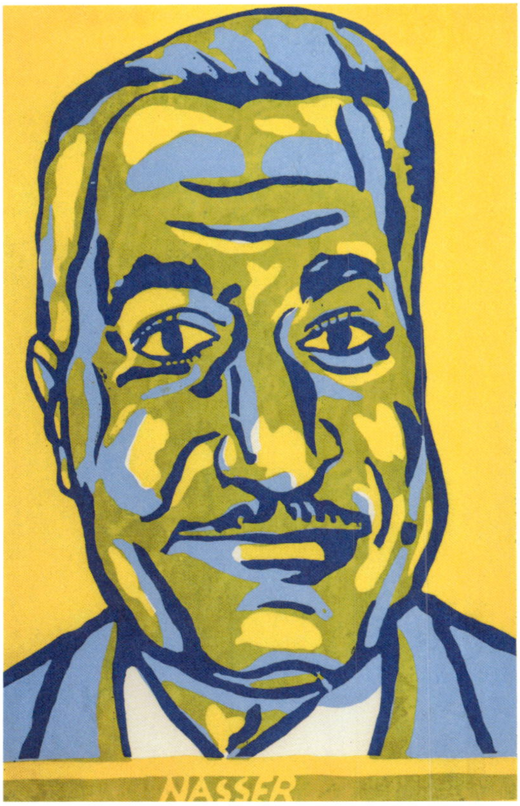

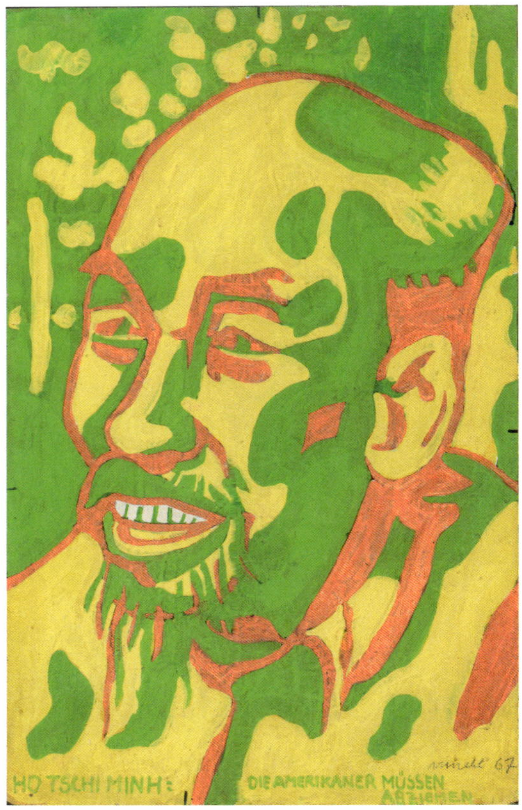

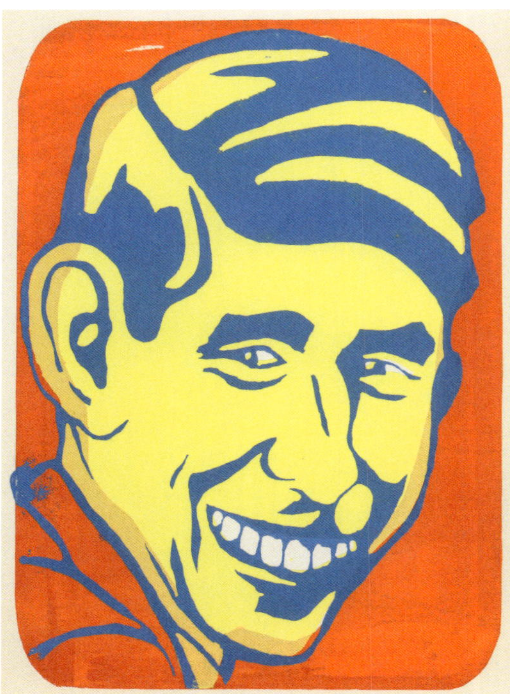

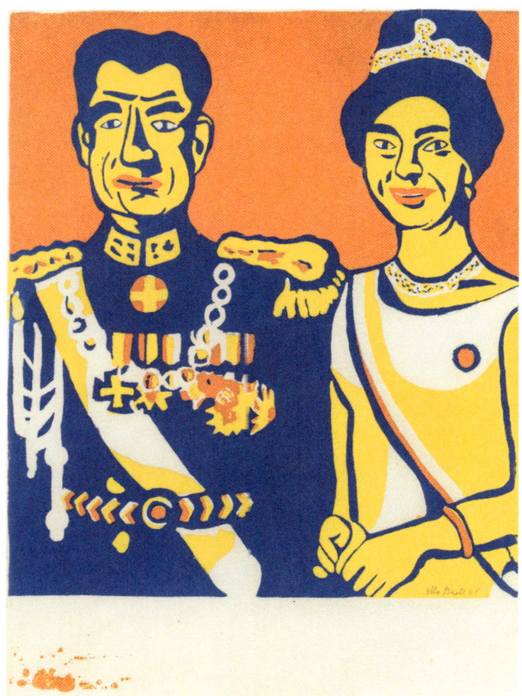

Fig. 169
Otto Muehl
Nasser, 1967
Silkscreen on paper
75 x 45 cm
WAM –
Wiener Aktionismus
Museum, Vienna

Fig. 170
Otto Muehl
Ho Tschi Minh, 1967
Oil on wood
60 x 45 cm
WAM –
Wiener Aktionismus
Museum, Vienna

Fig. 171
Otto Muehl
Prinz Charles, 1967
Silkscreen on paper
60 x 46 cm
WAM –
Wiener Aktionismus
Museum, Vienna

Fig. 172
Otto Muehl
Schah Reza Pahlavi and Farah Diba, 1967
Silkscreen on paper
77 x 68 cm
WAM –
Wiener Aktionismus
Museum, Vienna

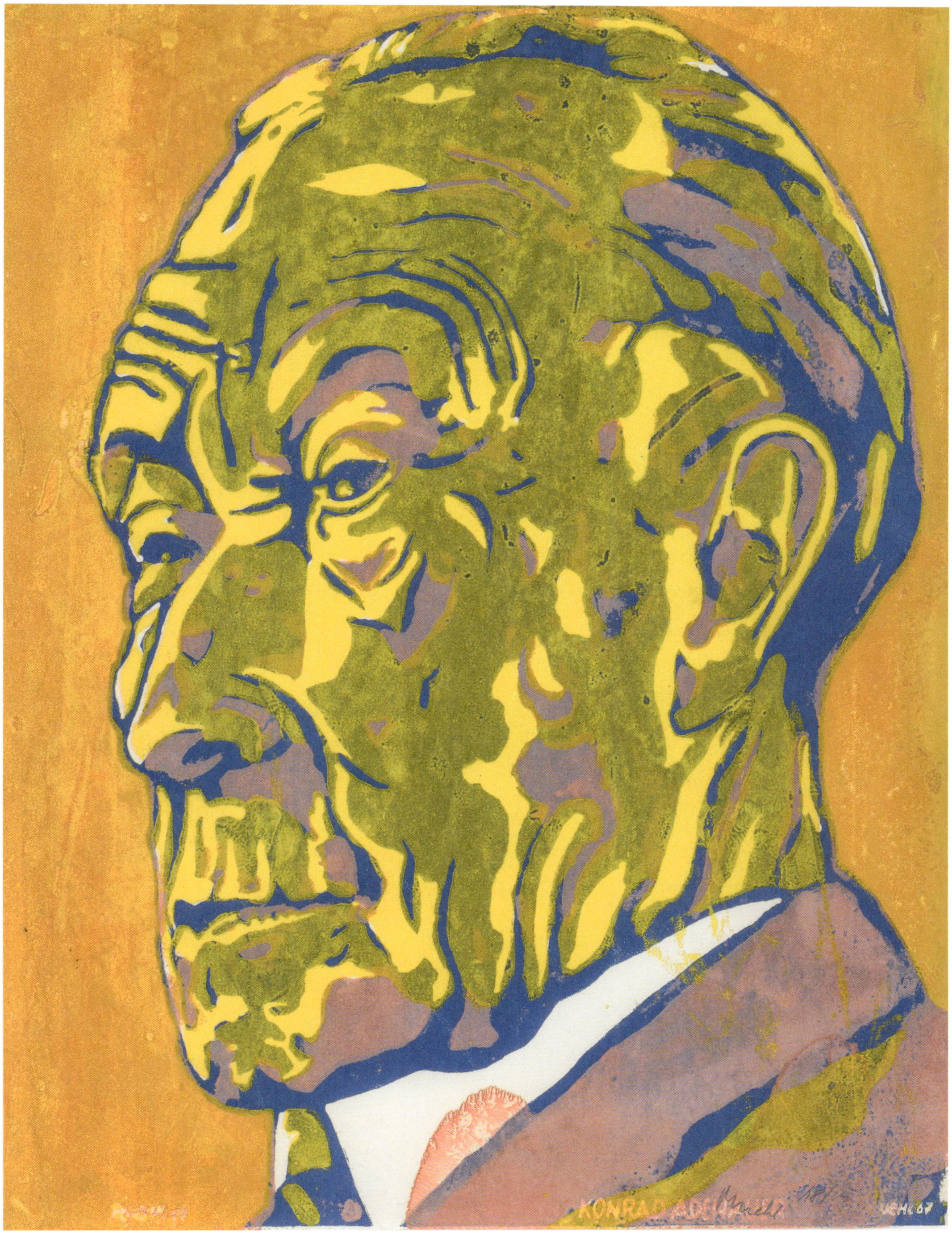

Fig. 173
Otto Muehl
Konrad Adenauer, 1967
Silkscreen on paper
90 x 70 cm
WAM – Wiener Aktionismus Museum, Vienna

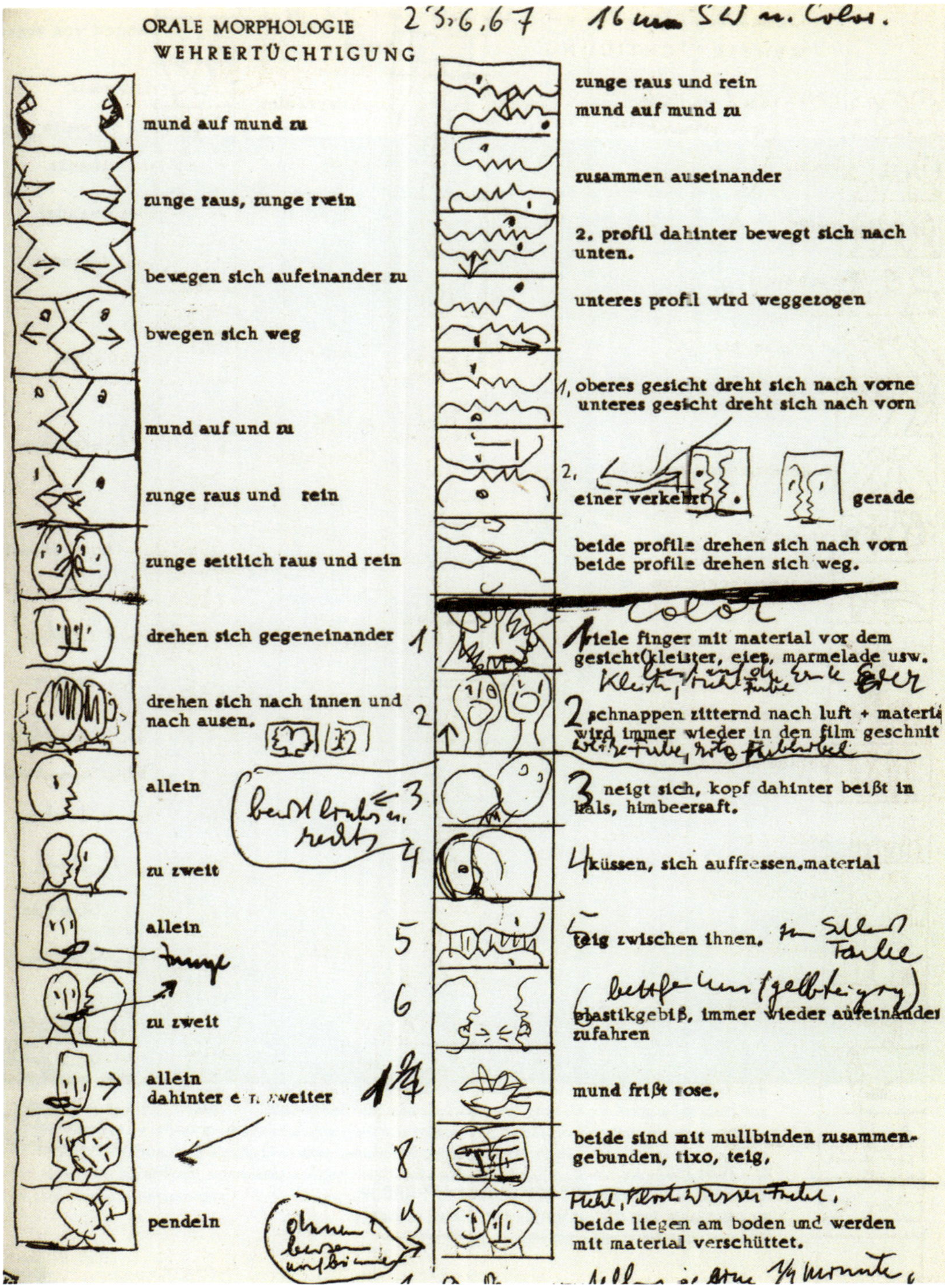

Fig. 174
Otto Muehl
Orale Morphologie (Oral Morphology), score for the film *Wehrertüchtigung* (Military Training), 23 June 1967
printed in *Mama und Papa* (Mama and Papa), Frankfurt/M. (Kohlkunstverlag), 1969

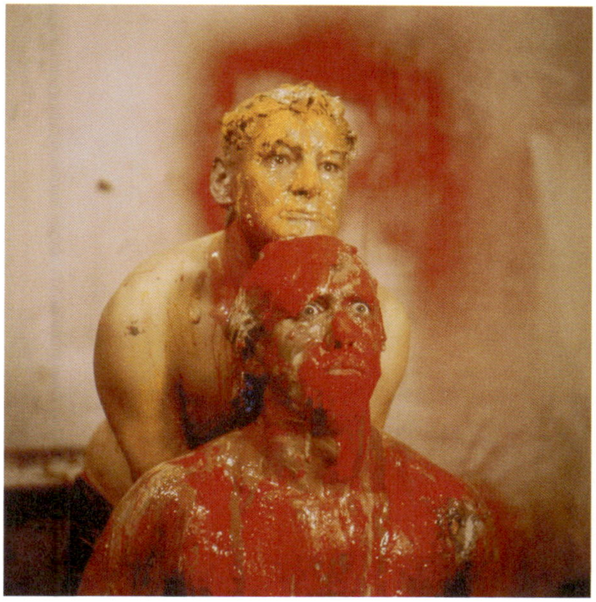

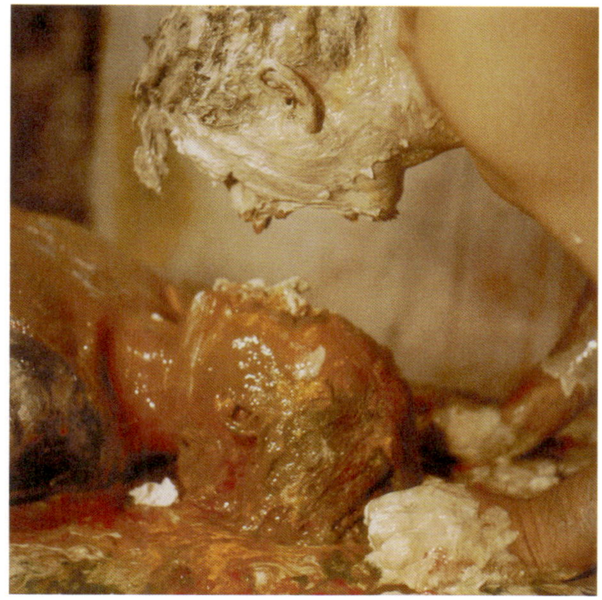

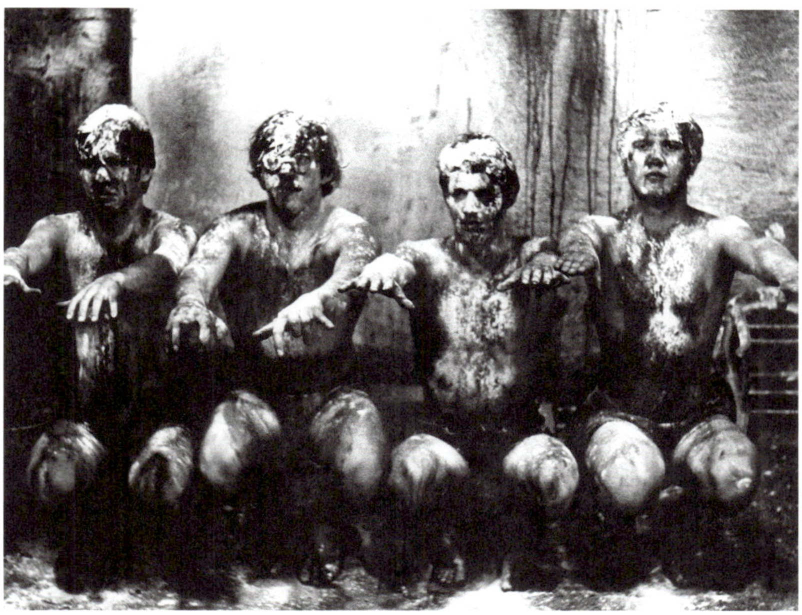

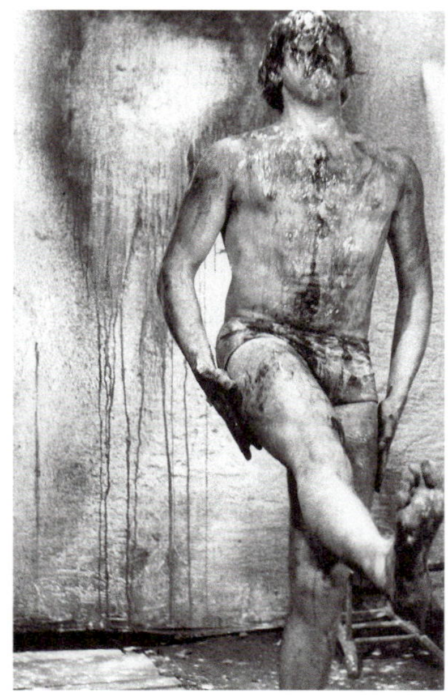

Fig. 175, 176, 177, 178
Otto Muehl
Wehrertüchtigung (Military Training), 23 June 1967
Muehl's studio, Perinetgasse 1, 1200 Vienna
Colour photographs, b/w photographs
photo: Ludwig Hoffenreich
with: Direct Art Group (Otmar Bauer, Walter Michael Pühringer, Herbert Stumpfl, Kurt Zein)

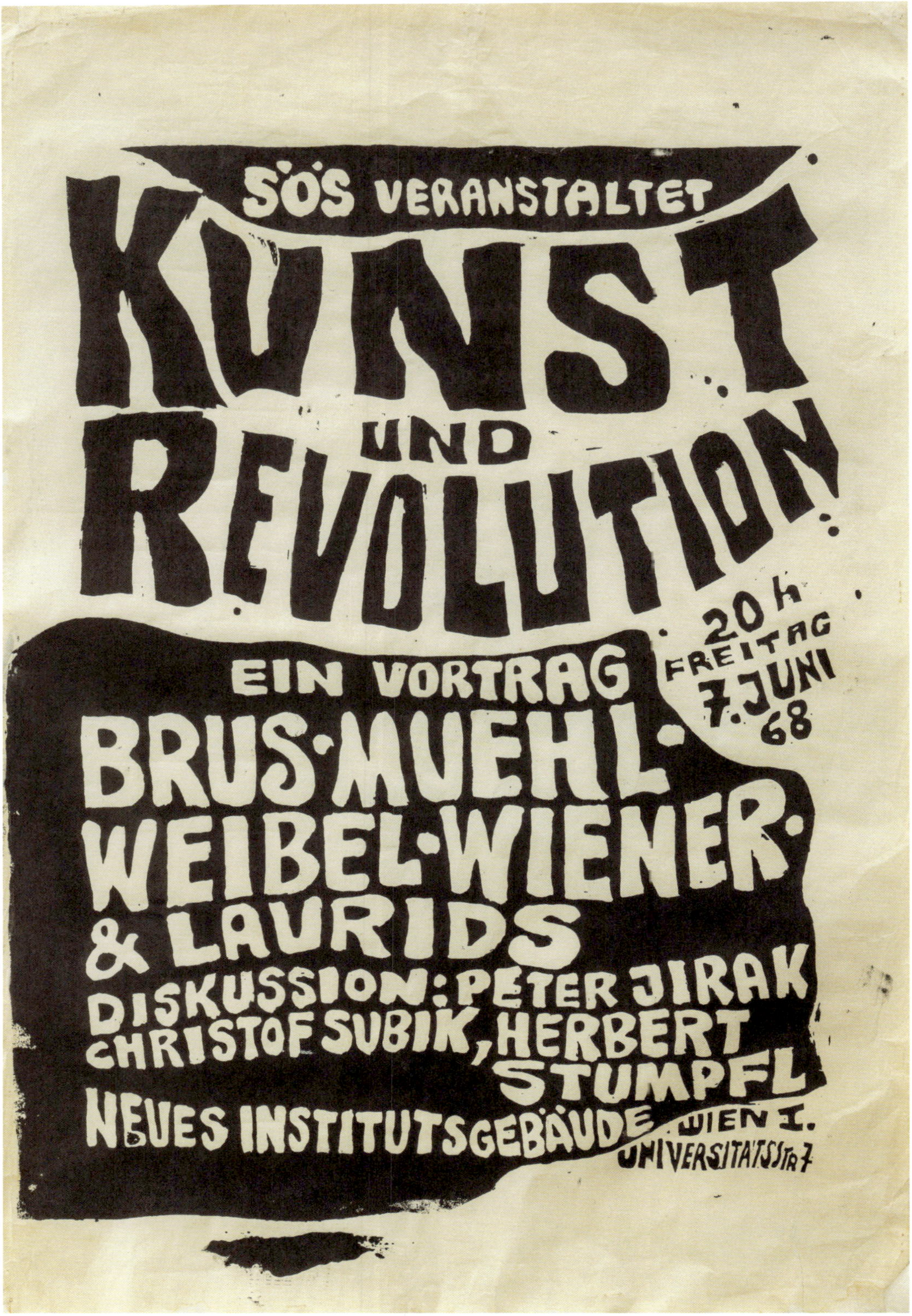

Fig. 179
Günter Brus
Poster for the event *Kunst und Revolution* (Art and Revolution),
one of three colour versions, 1968
Silkscreen on paper
100 x 70 cm
WAM – Wiener Aktionismus Museum, Vienn, Collection K.

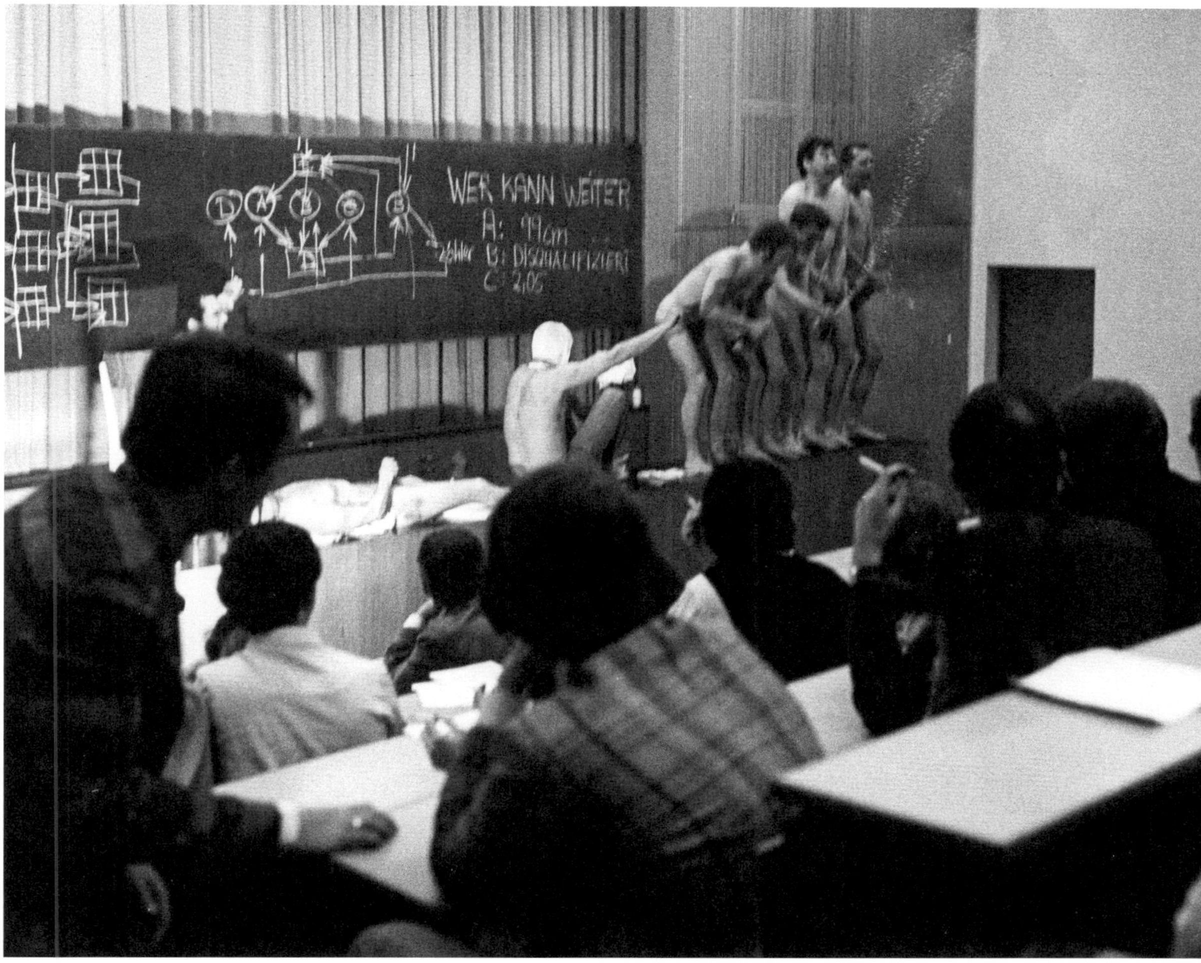

Fig. 180
Günter Brus, Otto Muehl, Peter Weibel, Oswald Wiener and others
Kunst und Revolution (Art and Revolution), 7 June 1968
Universiy of Vienna, Lecture Hall 1 of the Neue Institutsgebäude, Universitätsstraße 7, 1010 Vienna
B/W photograph
photo: Khasaq (Siegfried Klein)
with: Direct Art Group (Otmar Bauer, Dieter Haupt, Herbert Stumpfl, Anastas [Josef Kainz], Franz Kaltenbäck, MalteOlschewski [Laurids])

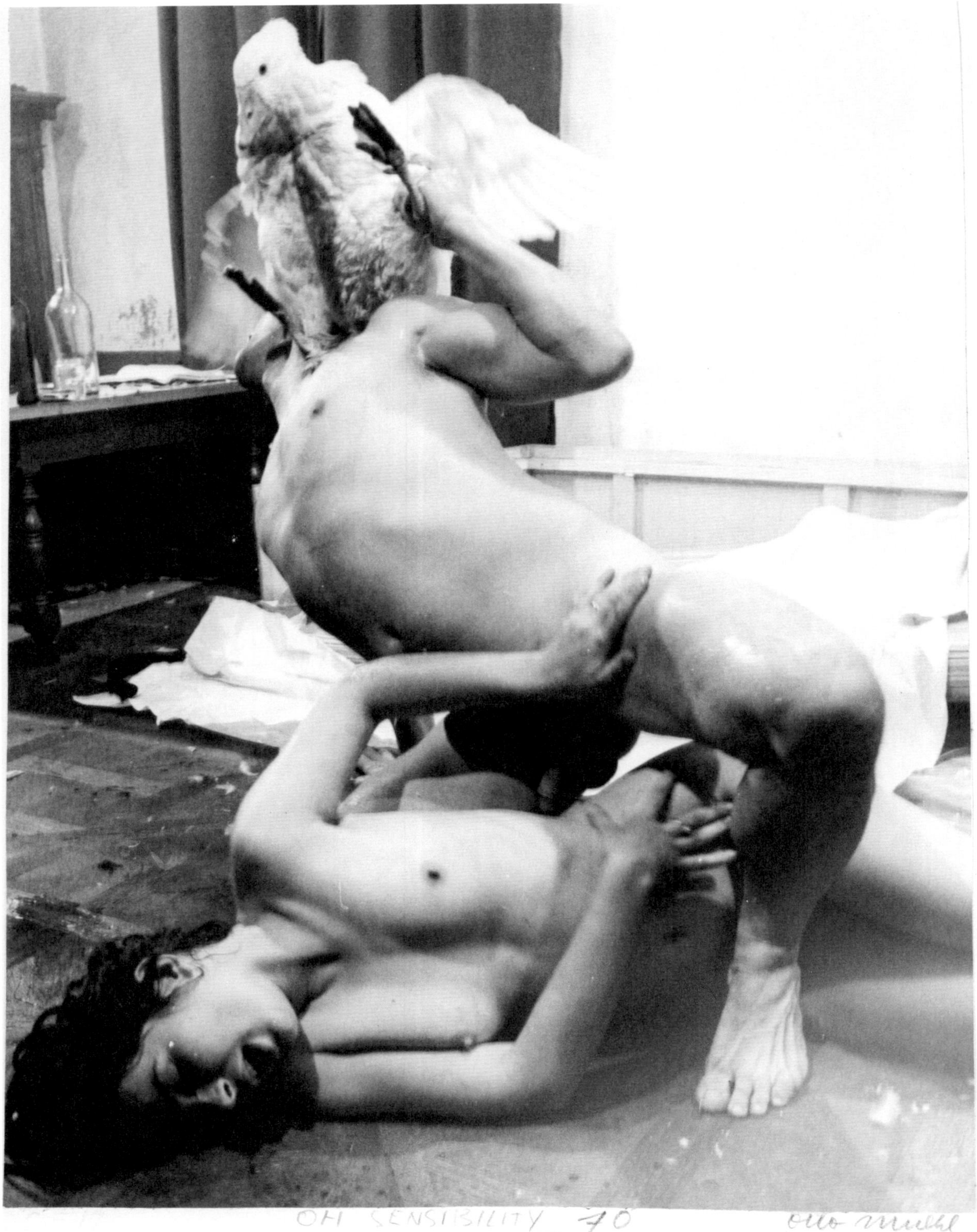

Fig. 181
Otto Muehl
Oh Sensibility, summer 1970
Muehl's apartment, Praterstraße 32/2/12, 1020 Vienna
B/W photograph
photo: Ludwig Hoffenreich

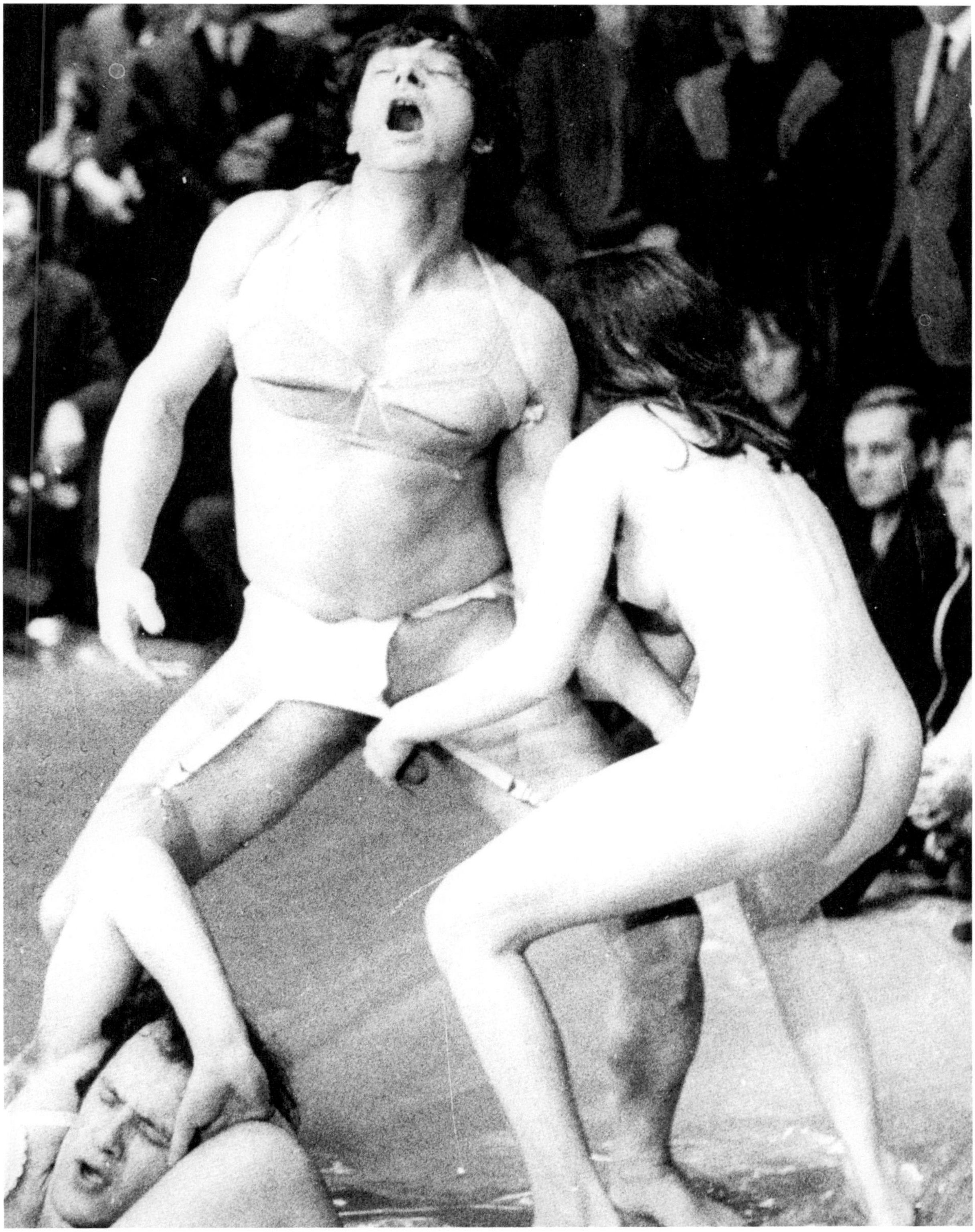

Fig. 182
Otto Muehl
Manopsychotisches Ballett 1 (Mano-Psychotic Ballet 1), 8 November 1970
Kölnischer Kunstverein (exhibition *Happening & Fluxus*)
B/W photograph
photo: Thomas Hesterberg

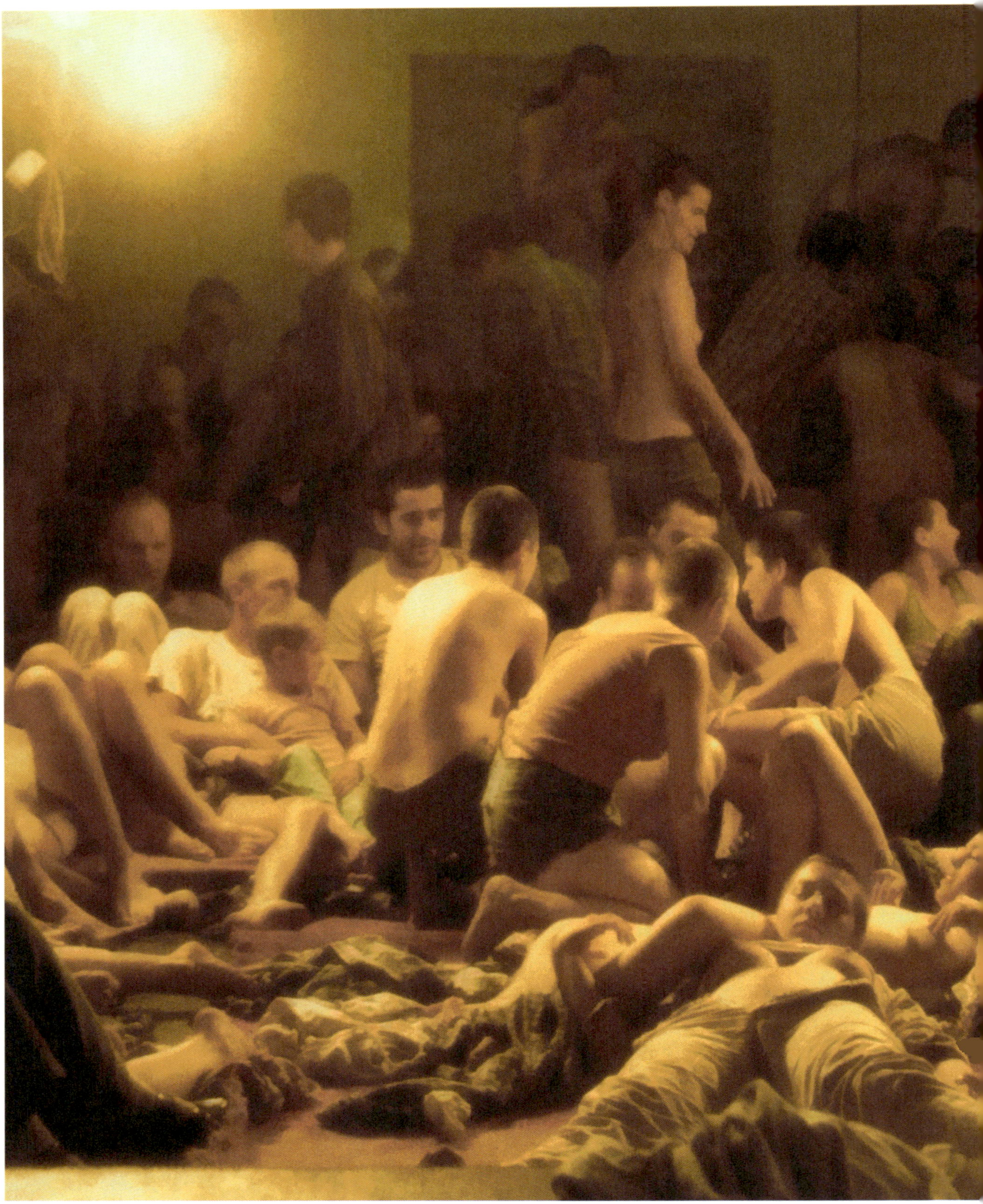

Fig. 183
Theo Altenberg
Danach. Nach den Selbstdarstellungen (Afterwards. After the Self-Presentations), 1976
Colour photograph, print on Kodak photographic paper
79 x 108cm
Edition 2001, 1/6
Private Collection

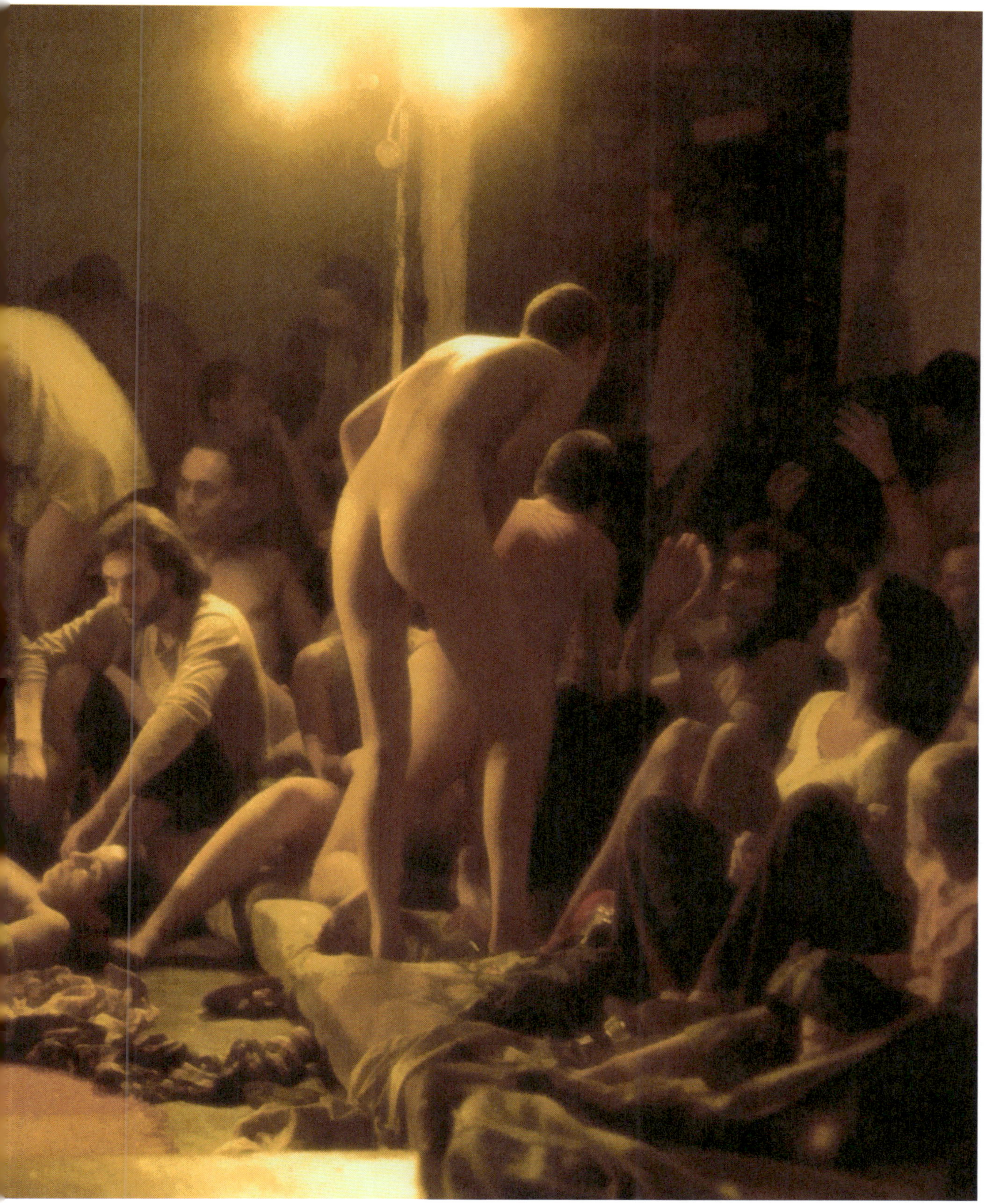

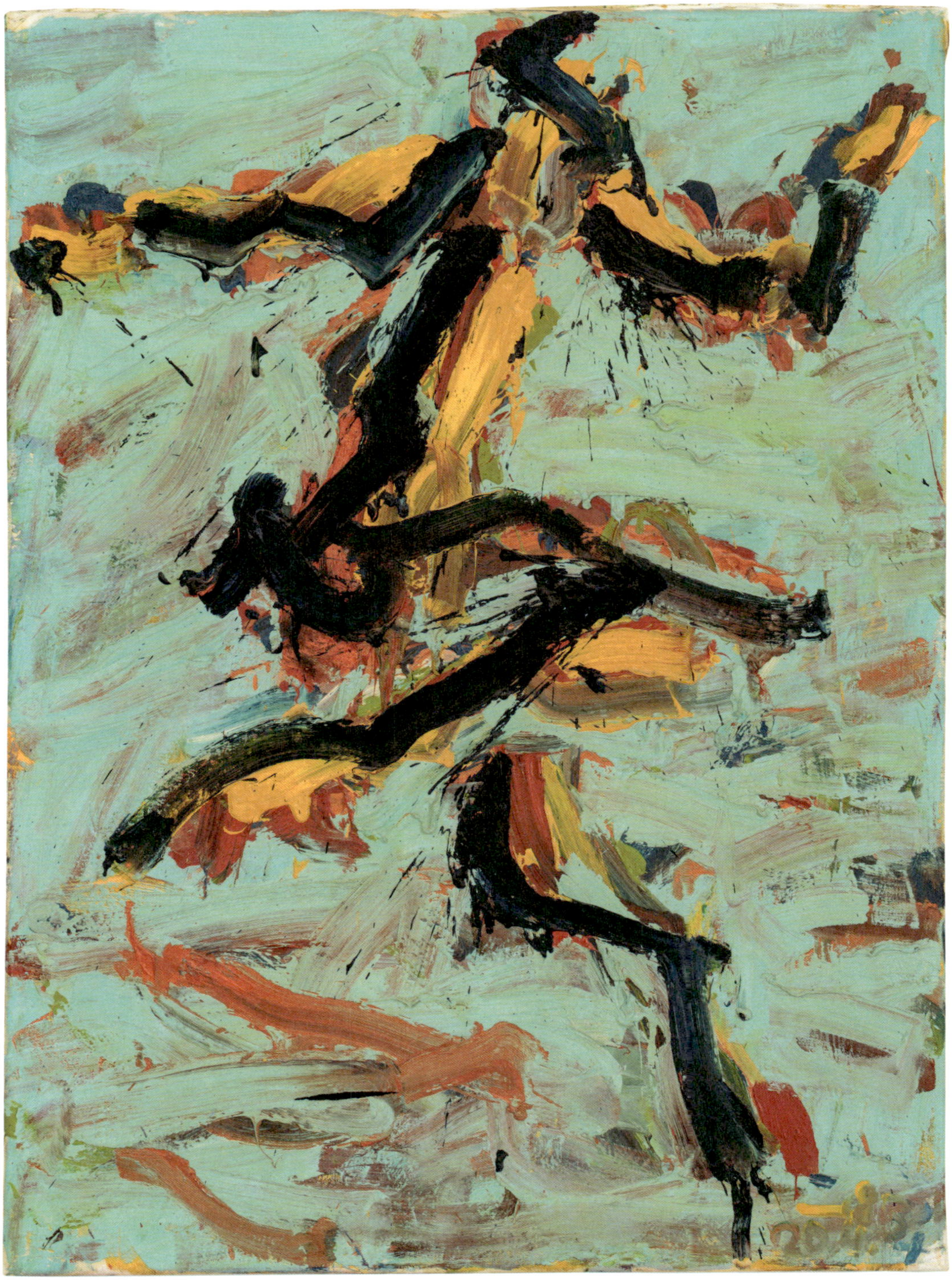

Fig. 184
Otto Muehl
Untitled, 1983
Oil on canvas
120 x 90 cm
WAM – Wiener Aktionismus Museum, Vienna

Fig. 185
Otto Muehl
Untitled, 1988
Oil, sand on hard fibreboard
85 x 100 cm
WAM – Wiener Aktionismus Museum, Vienna

Rudolf Schwarzkogler

From the very beginning, Schwarzkogler's work is characterised by a cool, calculating, precise approach which contrasts with the more expressive, highly body-motoric ones of Brus, Muehl, and Nitsch.

Even a figurine, composed of geometric shapes (around 1961/62, Fig. 186) from his earliest period, is placed strictly axially into the picture and the unnaturally artificial alignment of its head and hands is defined by a geometric order. Blue and white, which would later play a central role in the artist's work, are already the dominant colours. A comparable precision and mannerism determine the dandyish poses that Schwarzkogler adopted around the same time when he made himself available as a model for a photo series by Wilfried Klanjsek-Bratke, a classmate at the Graphische Lehr- und Versuchsanstalt. They show the ambiguous image of an artist who, on the one hand, playfully and dreamily holds a flower in his hands and, on the other hand, focuses directly on the viewers or looks past them with a cool and emotionally distant gaze. (Fig. 1, 187)

Panel Paintings, Object Paintings, Actions

The few surviving panel paintings, created before Schwarzkogler's actions, are stylistically disparate and show influences that are very different from those in the early works of his Actionist colleagues. Although he also made some gesturally abstract pain-tings, the majority of the pictures refer to much calmer and more conceptual international positions which were current at the time. All of these emphasise the substantiality and presence of the materials used, which links them to Schwarzkogler's intentions: a pasty white picture with six dots pressed into the surface within an oval (Fig. 188) is clearly reminiscent of Lucio Fontana's *Conzetti spaziali* (Spatial Concepts), which he made from the late 1940s onwards, by actually piercing his canvases in the form of dots in order to break the painterly illusionism and thereby include "real" space. A mono-chrome blue picture (Fig. 191), in turn, clearly speaks of the great admiration that Schwarzkogler had for Yves Klein. In his *Monochromes bleus* (Blue Monochromes), Klein worked with pure pigment which he applied to the canvas using a special process without any binding agent. On the one hand, this was intended to emphasise the material qualities of the paint, but on the other, the large powdery blue areas were intended to evoke experiences that go beyond the substantial existence of the picture. In his own monochrome blue painting Schwarzkogler, however, presents the materiality of the colour without any claim to transcendence. He used bound pigment and in the upper part of the painting, starting from the left edge,

18
See: Eva Badura-Triska, Hubert Klocker, *Rudolf Schwarzkogler. Leben und Werk*, Klagenfurt (Ritter Verlag), 1992, p. 40/41.

19
Here, Schwarzkogler follows Nitsch's Table Actions, the first of which he participated in as an actor (7 January 1965). (Fig. 20)

he worked a piece of string into the surface, on which the colour accumulated and then ran down like a drip painting, leaving correspondingly pasty traces. In another painting, *Untitled*, made around 1962/63 (Fig. 190), he has marked out a blue square using a string, while the rest of the surface is covered in a patchwork like manner with roughly cut or torn yellow-painted pieces of paper of various shapes and sizes. Not least because of the colour used, this is reminiscent of Klein's gold leaf works, the so-called *Monogolds*, but also of Piero Manzoni's *Achromes*, structured from pieces of canvas glued on top of each other, which he regards as manifestations of pure being.

Schwarzkogler left the picture plane as early as 1962 when he painted over a white-primed wooden crucifix, carved by himself, in blue. (Fig. 189) This work was created shortly after Nitsch had carried out his *1st Action*, in which he stood in front of a white wall, as if crucified, and had Muehl pour blood on him. (Fig. 12) Schwarzkogler and Nitsch, who met at the Graphische Lehr- und Versuchsanstalt, were closely connected, both artistically and as friends. Nitsch reported that Schwarzkogler hung this crucifix in his apartment above a copy of his 1962 manifesto *Die Blutorgel* (The Blood Organ), whose content the two discussed intensively.[18]

The blue painting of this white-primed crucifix already refers to Schwarzkogler's *1. Aktion, Hochzeit* (1st Action, Wedding), which he realised three years later, on 6 February 1965 in the apartment of his fellow student Heinz Cibulka in front of a small audience of friends. It was still strongly painterly in its approach and he also explicitly describes it as a *Malaktion* (Painting Action, Fig. 194–198, 228). In the opening sequence, Schwarzkogler stood like a priest or shaman behind a table on which objects and substances were laid out–including organic objects such as dead fish or plants.[19] He manipulated them in a way that was intended to enhance their sensory experience–for example he poured paint and other substances over them or crumbled earth. Inevitably, their potential, albeit unnamed, connotations also came into play –such as the fact that fish, for example, can be read as symbols of Christ. In another scene, a cloth stretched between the ceiling and the floor–ultimately a white canvas–was cut open and through the resulting slit, in a sort of symbolic wedding, a "bride" dressed in white–as a piece of physical reality–was lifted into the action space and showered with paint.

Schwarzkogler transcended the picture plane further in a series of works in which he mounted objects–again in a strictly geometric arrangement –on white-primed square chipboard panels, including aggressive objects such as razor blades, but also bread.

Four pieces of this kind are solely documented by photographs (Fig. 192) and only a single one survived. This (Fig. 193) consists of two square chipboard panels which are mounted in such a way inside a wooden frame that a gap between them is created, which opens up a view of the wall or the room behind it. In this way, Schwarzkogler also broke up the closed picture plane. The remaining surfaces serve as areas to deploy a language of concrete objects: while there is a black-painted strip separated by a string at the upper edge of the picture, near the lower edge there is a white-painted bottle cork, in which a razor blade is vertically embedded. This can be read as an erect penis that has been injured and understood as a symbol of male castration anxiety. It is no coincidence that Schwarzkogler entitled this work *Sigmund Freud Bild* (Sigmund Freud Picture).[20]

It is no longer possible to determine whether these object collages were created before or after Schwarzkogler's *1st Action*. In terms of form and content, there are fewer parallels to his *1st* than to his *2nd*, *3rd* and *4th Actions* (Fig. 199 – 208) which took place in the summer and December of 1965 and were of a completely different nature.[21] They belong to the type of Staged Photography which Brus was the first to practice in December 1964 with his *2nd Action* (Fig. 60–68) and which Schwarzkogler–also with his *2nd Action* (spring 1965)–took up shortly afterwards and developed his own content and imagery within this framework. All of these actions, which took place without an audience, solely for the purpose of being captured photographically (and in the case of the *4th Action* also filmically[22]), were recorded exclusively in black and white. Similar to his object collages, Schwarzkogler here arranged objects–as well as human and animal bodies–against neutral white backgrounds in a way that suggests associations and symbolic interpretations. In terms of content, there are parallels to Brus' Self-Painting and self-injury actions in that he brought terrifying objects into contact with bodies and thus staged emblems of existential exposure and vulnerability. Similar to Nitsch, he thereby also addressed Freudian topoi, such as–by means of blindfolds or bandaged penises–the fear of castration or blinding related to the theme of Oedipus.

While Brus mainly operated with destructively aggressive and terrifying instruments such as hoes, saws or hammers, Schwarzkogler's objects predominantly aimed at healing, such as syringes, knives, scissors, gauze bandages, plasters, medicine bottles, and tubes.

The artist had inherited this medical equipment from his father, who was a doctor and had taken his own life before Stalingrad after losing both legs. As metaphors of an ideal state of purity–and thus of recovery and counterpoints to the motifs of injury–

20
Such an interpretation is not only supported by statements from Schwarzkogler's partner Edith Adam (in her working sessions with Eva Badura-Triska and Hubert Klocker 1990–1992), but it is also obvious in view of the generally Freudian-influenced content of Vienna Actionism and particularly with regard to the iconography of Hermann Nitsch, who explicitly addressed the topic of castration in his writings.

21
On the issue of dating these actions, see Badura-Triska, Klocker, Vienna *Actionism* (see note 11), p. 362, note 19.

22
This action was filmed by Günter Brus. See in this book p. 252, note 7.

Schwarzkogler introduced two elementary abstract geometric bodies into this imagery: two different white spheres–a ball of cloth tied together with a string and a balloon covered with gauze bandages–as well as a black square (a black glass plate).

Schwarzkogler's *6th* and last individual *Action* (Fig. 209, 210)[23], carried out in the spring of 1966, differs structurally from his *2nd*, *3rd*, and *4th Actions* in several respects. Once more it was designed exclusively for the camera, but unlike the previous ones, it took place in a situation marked much more clearly three-dimensionally by several spatial edges. The artist, completely bandaged in white and thus depersonalised, now acted himself, but not in a way that aimed at frontal, static images, but showing phases of movement. He actively enacted operations aiming at elementary experiences, such as the perception of light and warmth, handling dead chickens or the white ball and the black mirror as forms of relating oneself to a space.

23
Schwarzkoglers *5th Action* is subdivided into 5a, 5b, and 5c, which were actually three individual actions, that constitute a category of their own, as they were all collaborations with Nitsch.

24
Loose pages from booklet II, verso, in: Badura-Triska, Klocker, *Rudolf Schwarzkogler* (see note. 18), Fig. 179.

Late Conceptual Work

In terms of content, this already leads to the conceptual drawings and texts that Schwarzkogler created after his last individual action and until his premature death. With these, he took a very specific, independent path within Vienna Actionism. He designed situations in which no longer one actor, but everyone should encounter intense sensual experiences on their own bodies. In doing so, he conceived a fundamentally different role for the recipients than was usually the case in Vienna Actionism, and thus already pointed to developments in international art of the 1970s, in which numerous experiential spaces were created.

In drawings and texts, he designed "conscious situations", which he called "constellations of being"[24] and in which elementary sensory perceptions are offered in a form that is "formally clarified = purified" (Fig. 212) through the artist's selection and compilation. These appeal to all the senses and encompass a broad spectrum of expressions of life and bodily functions.

A large proportion of these drawings and texts are designs for environmental situations, as places for registering selected sensory impressions, (Fig. 213–220) including the consumption of food, the perception of smells, the experience of warmth or cold ("outbreak of sweat"), but also certain materials and surfaces ("brook", "aluminum", "strip of grass") and much more. In some of them, the artist prescribed very precise, specific body postures for the recipients, sometimes with an almost geometrically exact alignment. These are predominantly tense, often physically uncomfortable positions, which are intended to guarantee the most intense experience precisely through the required control and concentration.

In addition, Schwarzkogler designed sequences of actions as "chains of experience" (Fig. 212), which can also run over longer periods of time and apart from perception processes require the conscious performance of elementary life functions. He designed meal sequences, planned washing and bathing, and demanded conscious breathing, sweating, inhalation, or certain sleeping times. He also prescribed walks, looking at the landscape, observing the stars, and actions and behaviours such as: "letting hair and beard grow [...], not looking into any wells, not out of any windows, staying awake, sleeping in a glass house on the bare ground until it rains." (Fig. 220)

In keeping with his concern to convey the most unadulterated elementary experiences possible, free from any ballast of civilisation, Schwarzkogler spoke of "art as a purgatory of the senses" or an "aesthetic panorama" as the "GERM CELL OF A NEW ART OF REGENERATED CAPACITY FOR EXPERIENCE", as well as of an "EFFECTIVE GESAMTKUNSTWERK." (Fig. 212)

Beyond the communication of intensive perceptions, all of this is about achieving states of physical and mental purity and health, which should be achieved through reduction and liberation from everything unnecessary. In this regard, Schwarzkogler also spoke of the "art of painting as art of healing". (Fig. 212) In fact, his instructions sometimes sound like medical prescriptions or rules for health cures and are partly based on concrete methods such as those of Sebastian Kneipp's water cures. In their call for a conscious, controlled approach to physical experiences, they correspond to religious, especially Eastern ideals of life, whose physical and spiritual practices the artist partly appropriated. In a broader sense, Schwarzkogler was thus pursuing a core concern of Vienna Actionism, namely the purification and healing of society as the basis for a new beginning after the catastrophe of World War II.

In the last two years before his premature death, the artist himself underwent excessive fasting without medical supervision which put a great deal of strain onto him both physically and mentally. He withdrew more and more and finally in his drawings and texts questioned the possibility of experiencing and grasping a binding, authentic reality by addressing the boundaries between reality, illusion, vision, and fantasy. He also considered whether and how a differently constructed body would change our perception of reality.

On 20 June 1969, Schwarzkogler died after falling out of the window of his apartment. It will remain forever unclear whether it was an intentional suicide or whether, in a hallucinatory way, he thought – perhaps inspired by Yves *Klein's Leap into the Void* – that he could fly.

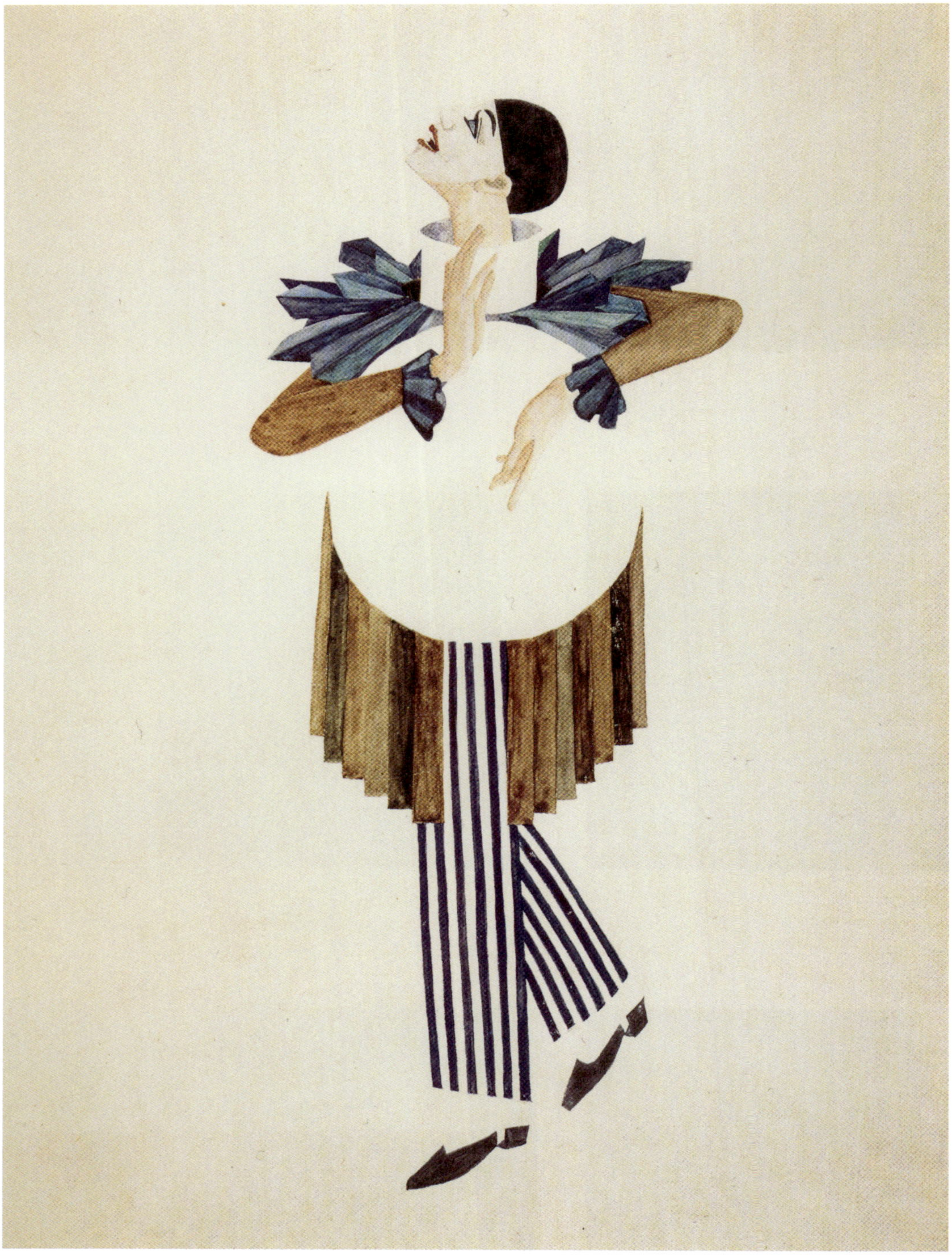

Fig. 186
Rudolf Schwarzkogler
Untitled (figurine), around 1961/1962
Watercolour on cardboard
23,9 x 18 cm
Private Collection

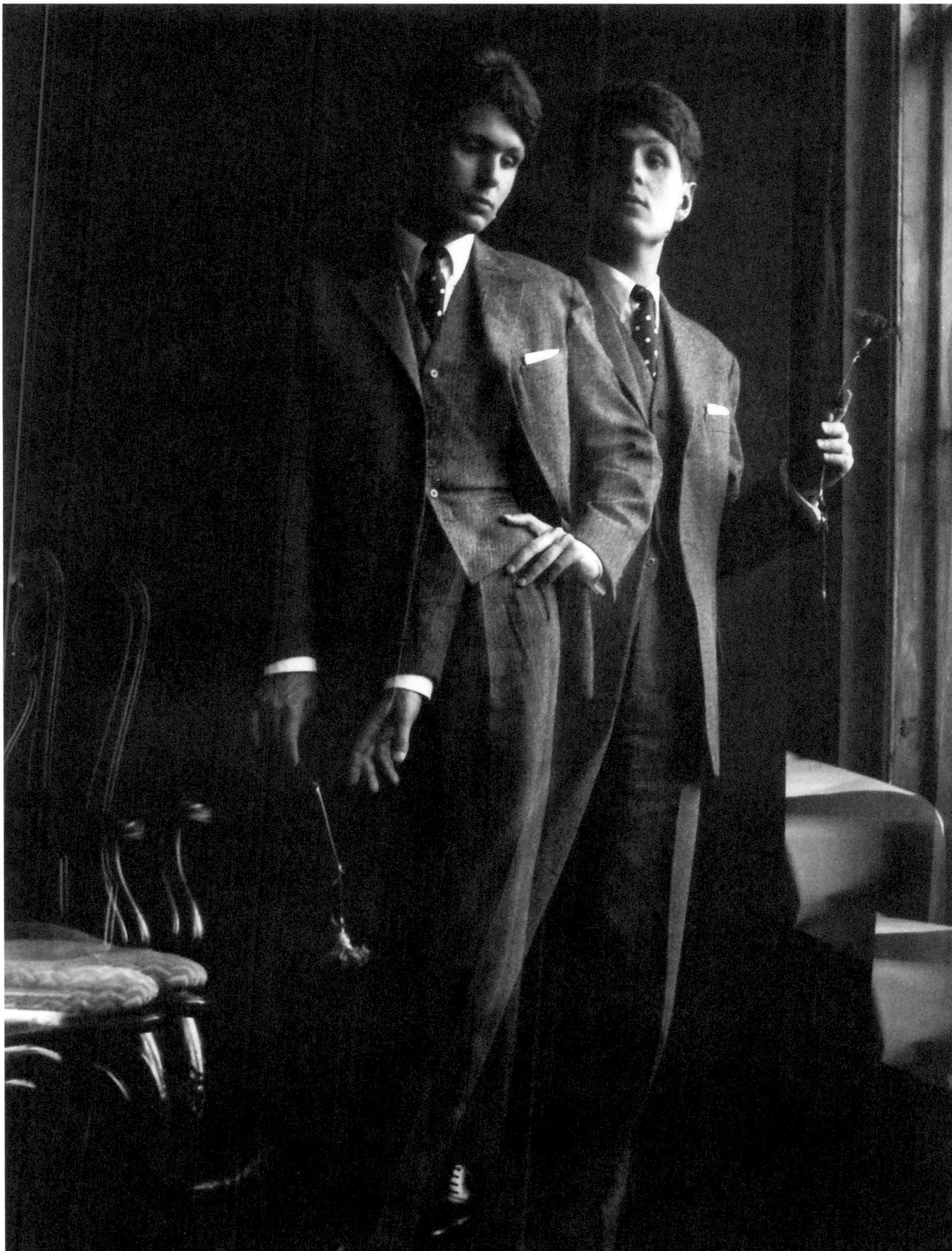

Fig. 187
Wilfried Klanjsek-Bratke
From a series of photographs with Rudolf Schwarzkogler, 1961/1962
B/W photograph
mumok – Museum moderner Kunst Stiftung Ludwig Wien

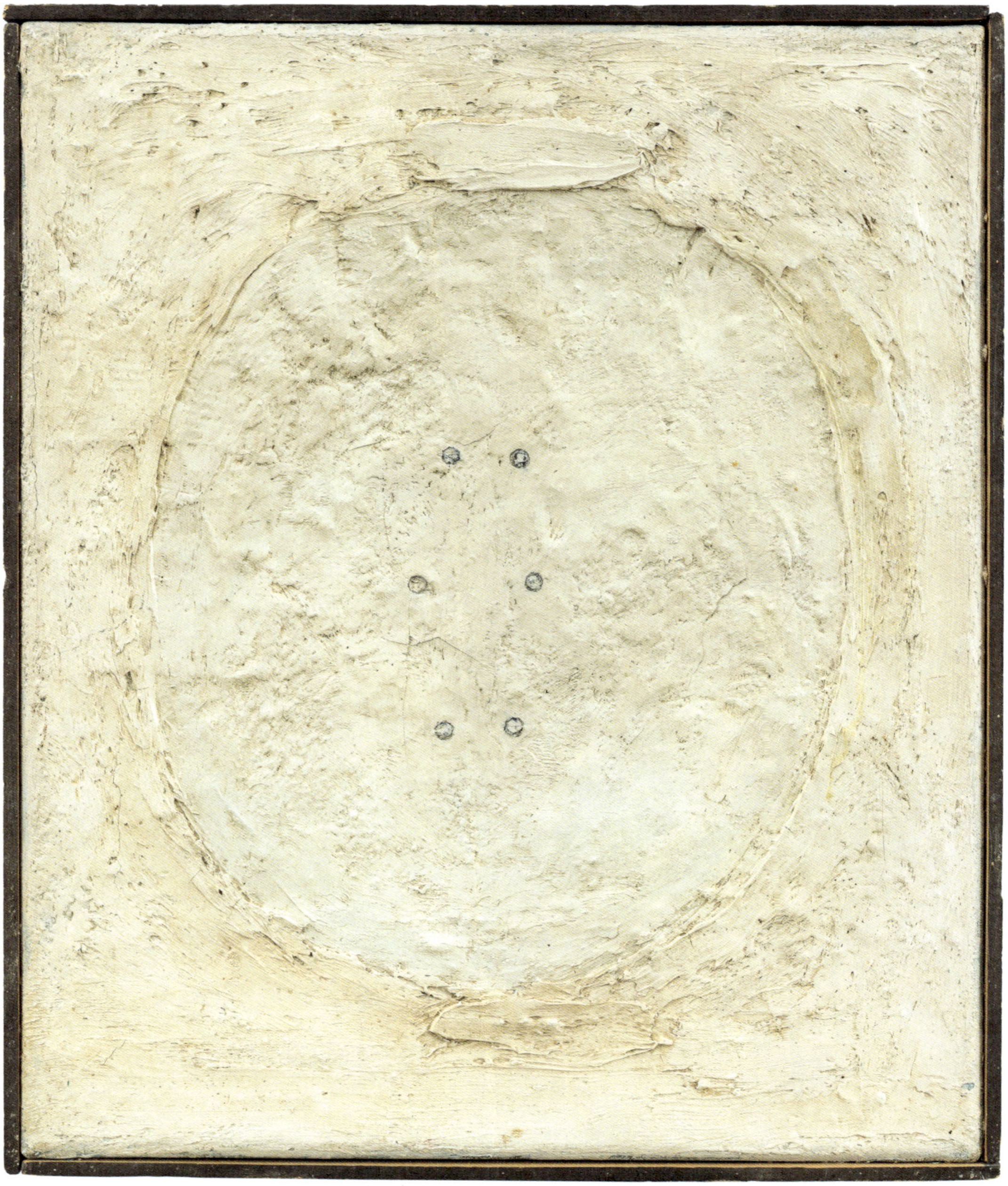

Fig. 188
Rudolf Schwarzkogler
Untitled, around 1961/1962
Oil, pencil on canvas
36 x 31 cm
WAM – Wiener Aktionismus Museum, Vienna, Collection K.

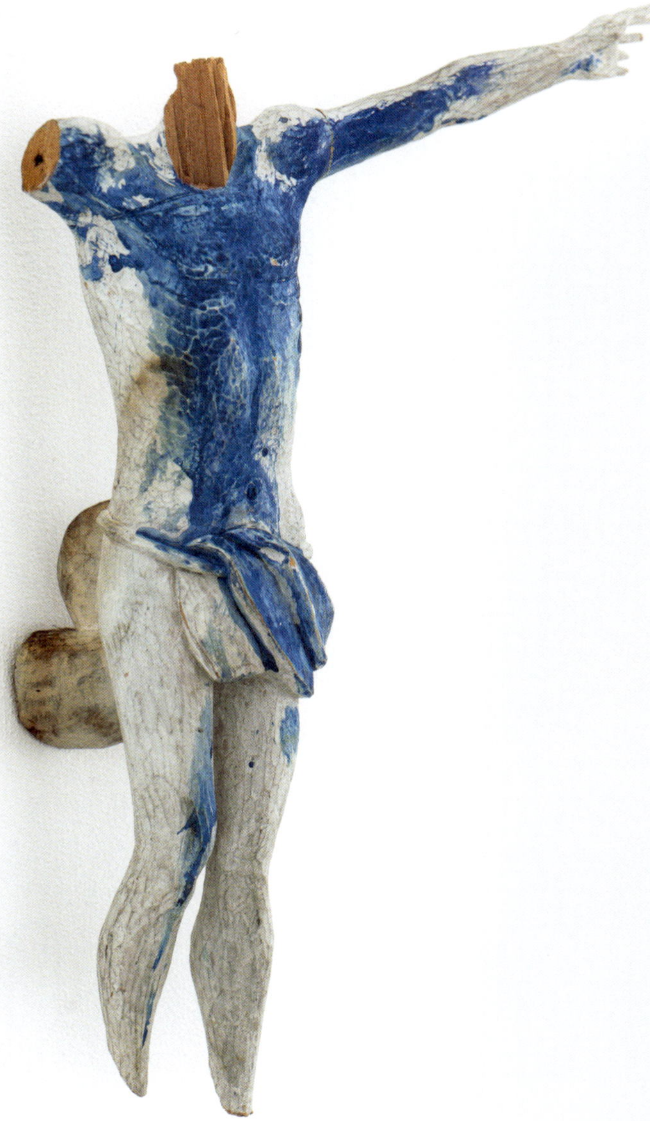

Fig. 189
Rudolf Schwarzkogler
Untitled, Crucified, around 1962
Ink and oil crayon on wood
23,3 x 17,4 x 6 cm
WAM – Wiener Aktionismus Museum, Vienna, Collection K.

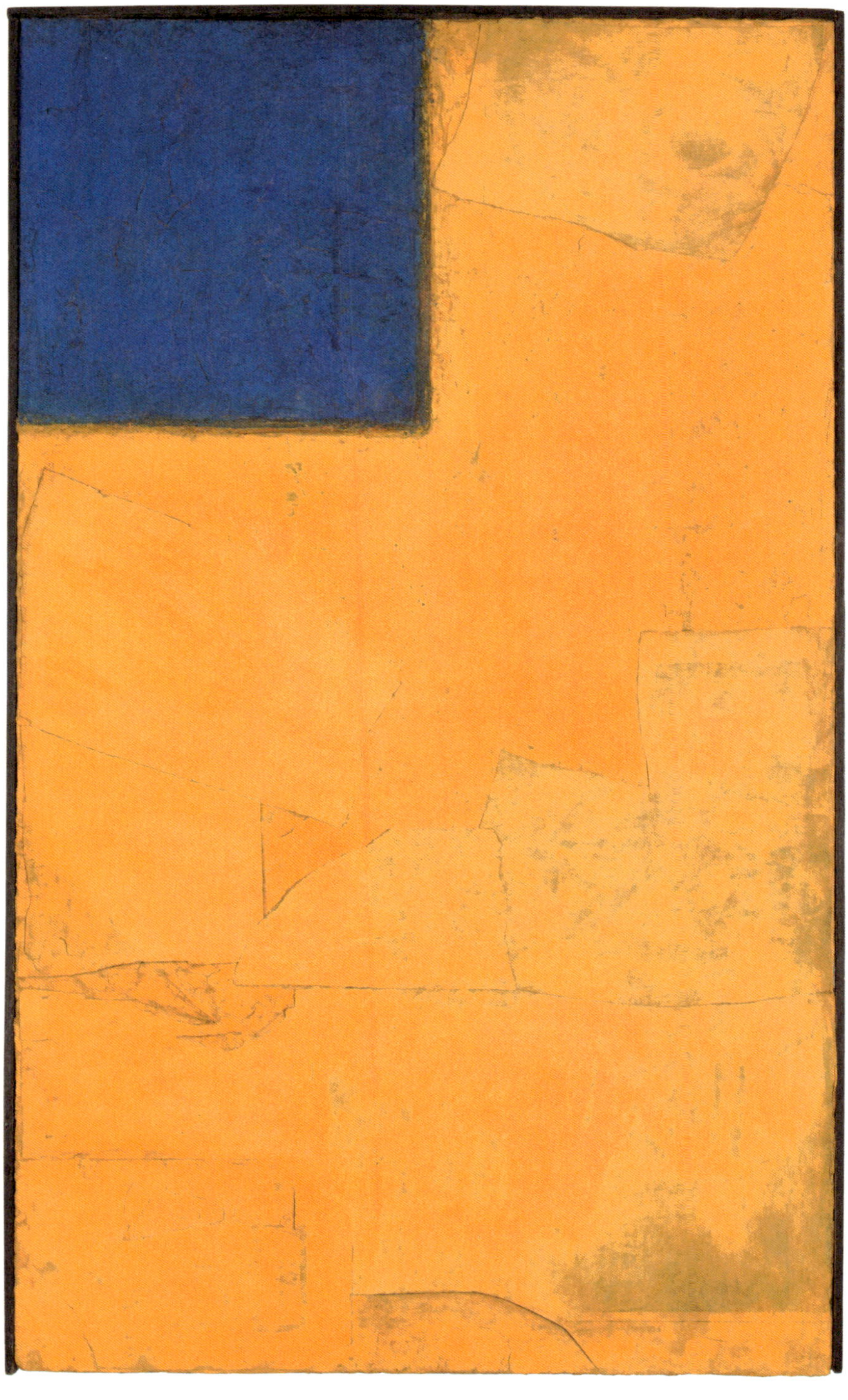

Fig. 190
Rudolf Schwarzkogler
Untitled, around 1962/1963
Acrylic, plaster and pieces of paper on wood
77 x 46 x 4,8 cm
mumok – Museum moderner Kunst Stiftung Ludwig Wien,
on loan from the Österreichische Ludwig-Stiftung

Fig. 191
Rudolf Schwarzkogler
Untitled, around 1962/1963
Acrylic, string on burlap
120,5 x 100 cm
mumok – Museum moderner Kunst Stiftung Ludwig Wien,
on loan from the Österreichische Ludwig-Stiftung

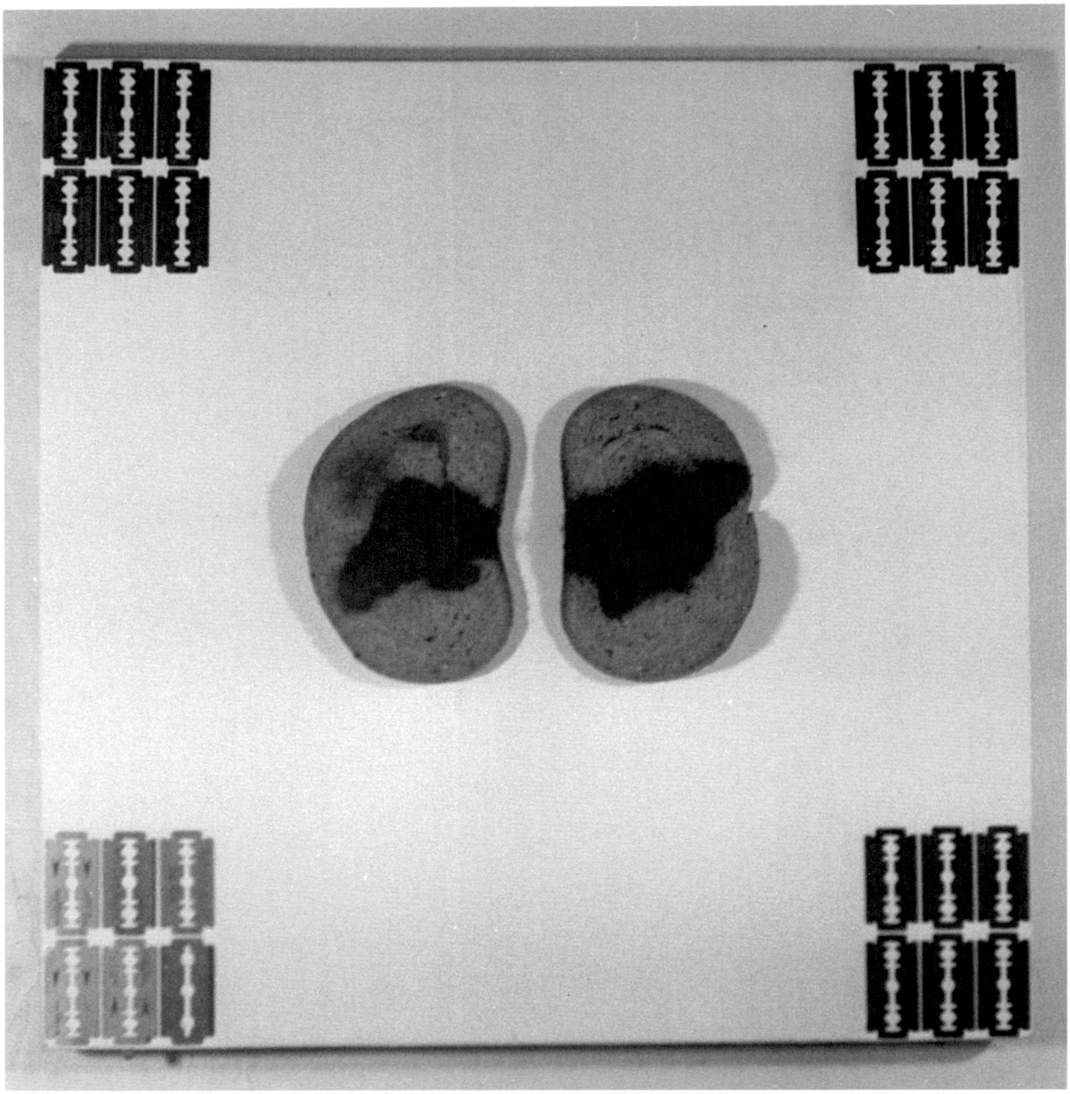

Fig. 192
Rudolf Schwarzkogler
Untitled, object collage, around 1965/1966
Razor blades and bread on wood
destroyed

Fig. 193
Rudolf Schwarzkogler
Ohne Titel, *Sigmund Freud Bild* (Sigmund Freud Picture), around 1965
Varnish, string, cork, razor blade, fibreboard, wood
107,5 x 53,2 cm
mumok – Museum moderner Kunst Stiftung Ludwig Wien,
on loan from the Österreichische Ludwig-Stiftung

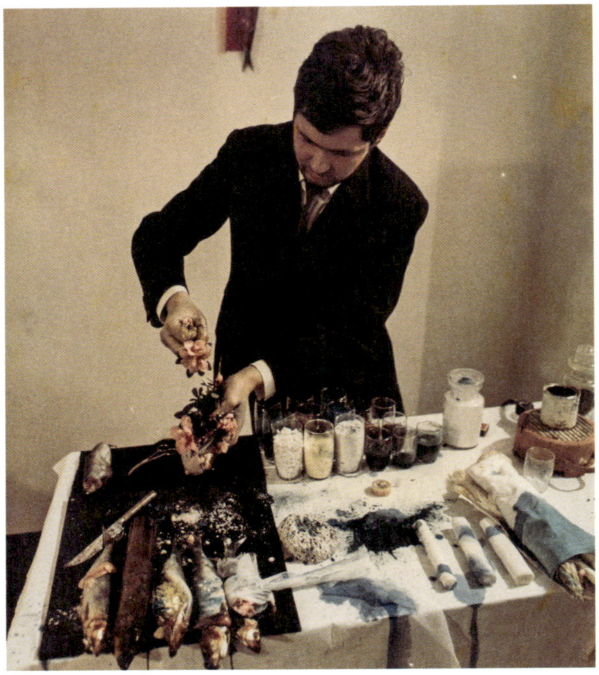

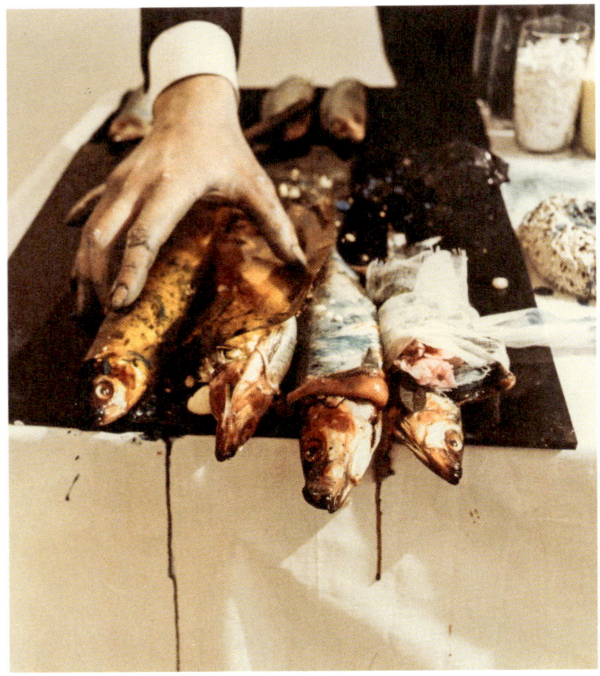

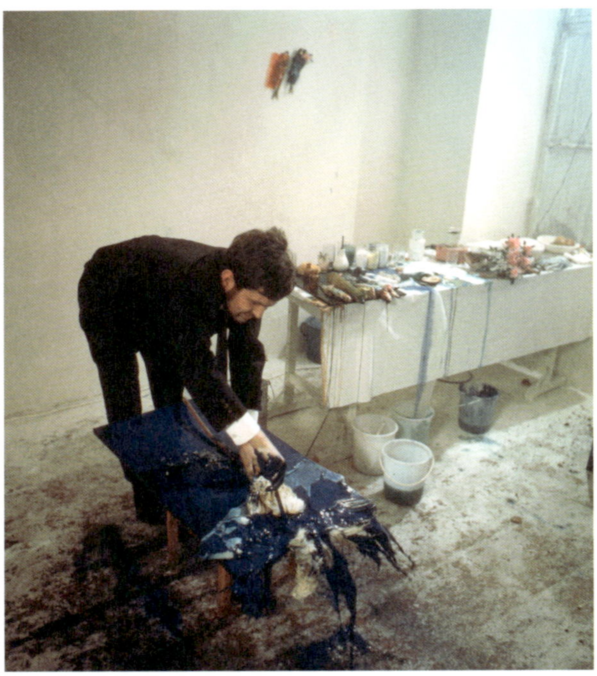

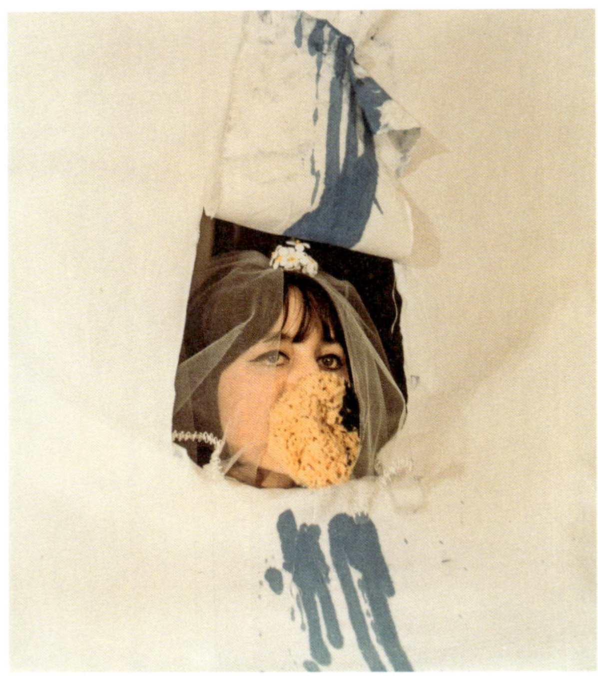

Fig. 194, 195, 196, 197, 198
Rudolf Schwarzkogler
1. Aktion, Hochzeit (1st Action, Wedding), 6 February 1965
Heinz and Franziska Cibulka's apartment, Kaiserstraße 16, 1070 Vienna
Colour photographs
photo: Walter Kindler
with: Anna Brus, Heinz Cibulka

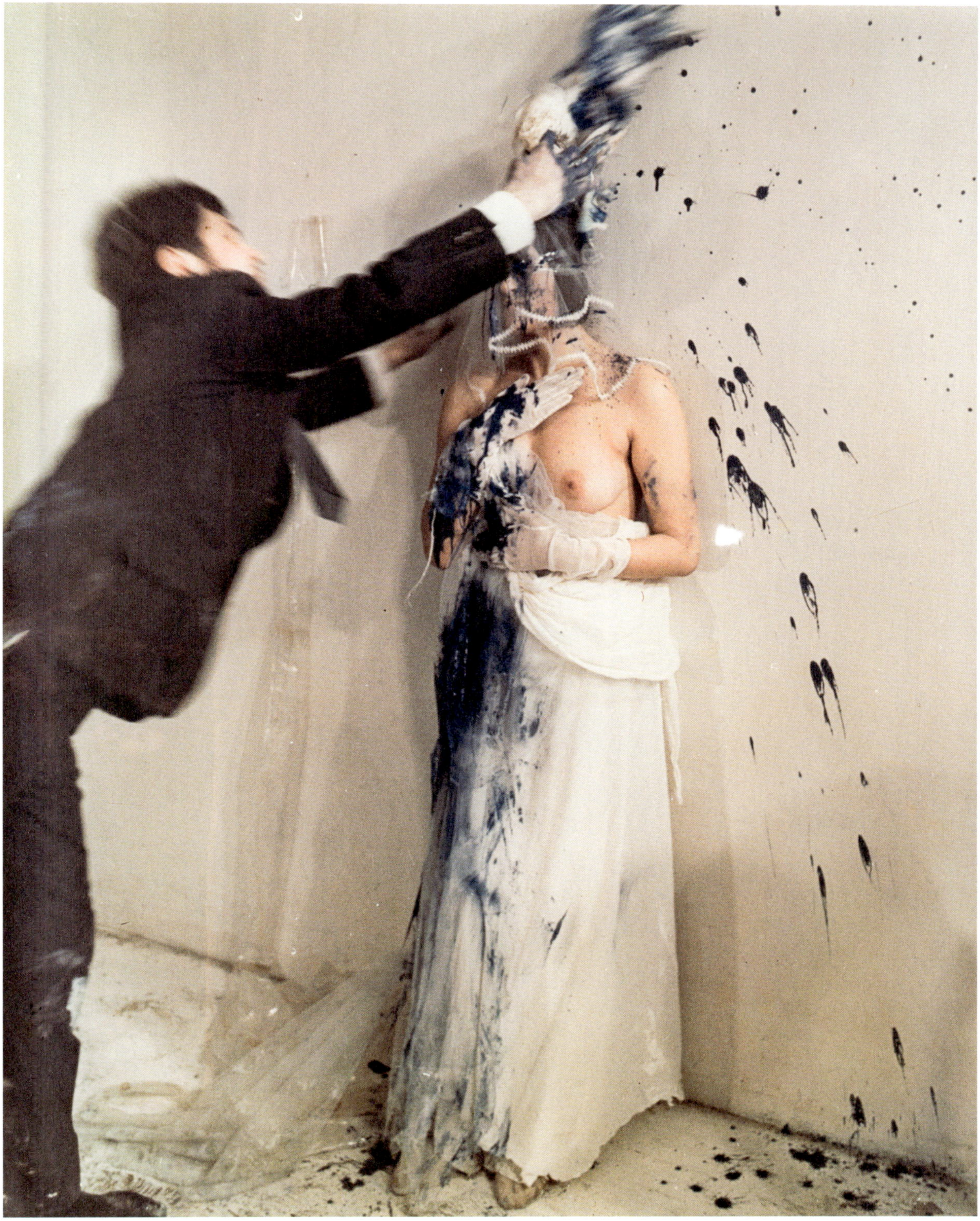

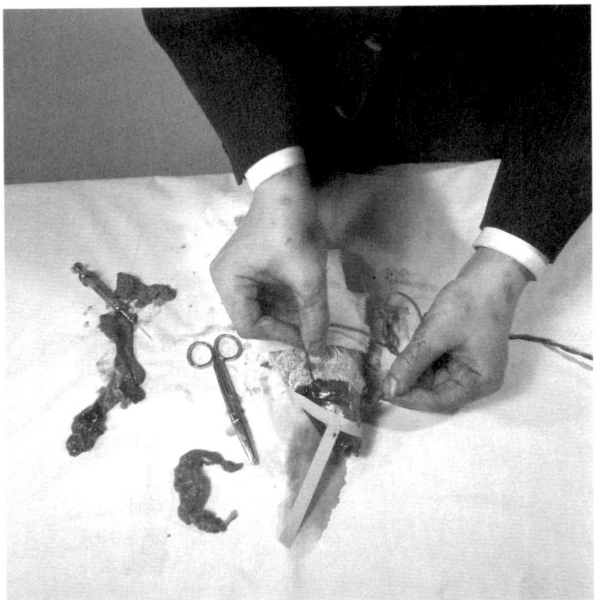

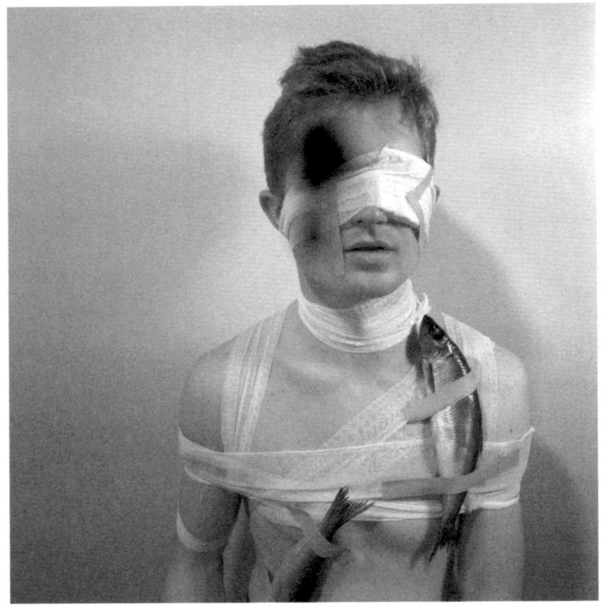

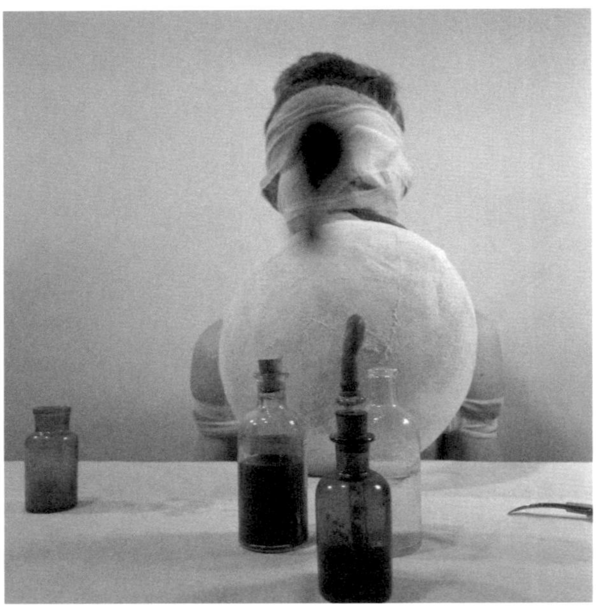

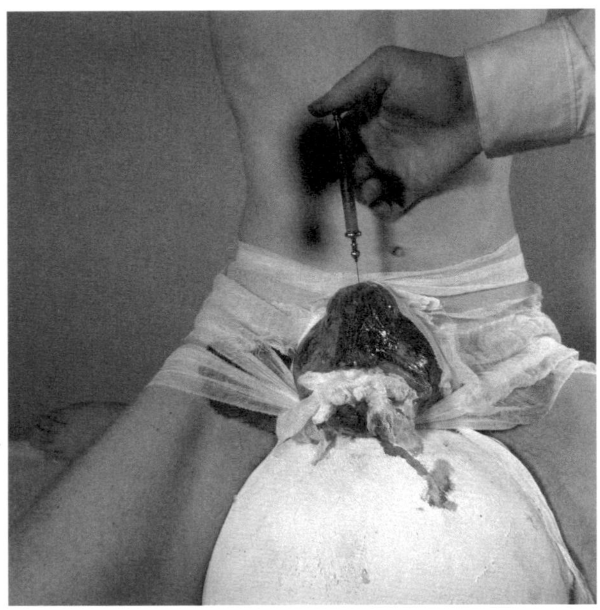

Fig. 199, 200, 201, 202, 203
Rudolf Schwarzkogler
2nd Action, summer 1965
Heinz and Franziska Cibulka's apartment, Kaiserstraße 16, 1070 Vienna
B/W photographs
photo: Ludwig Hoffenreich
with: Heinz Cibulka

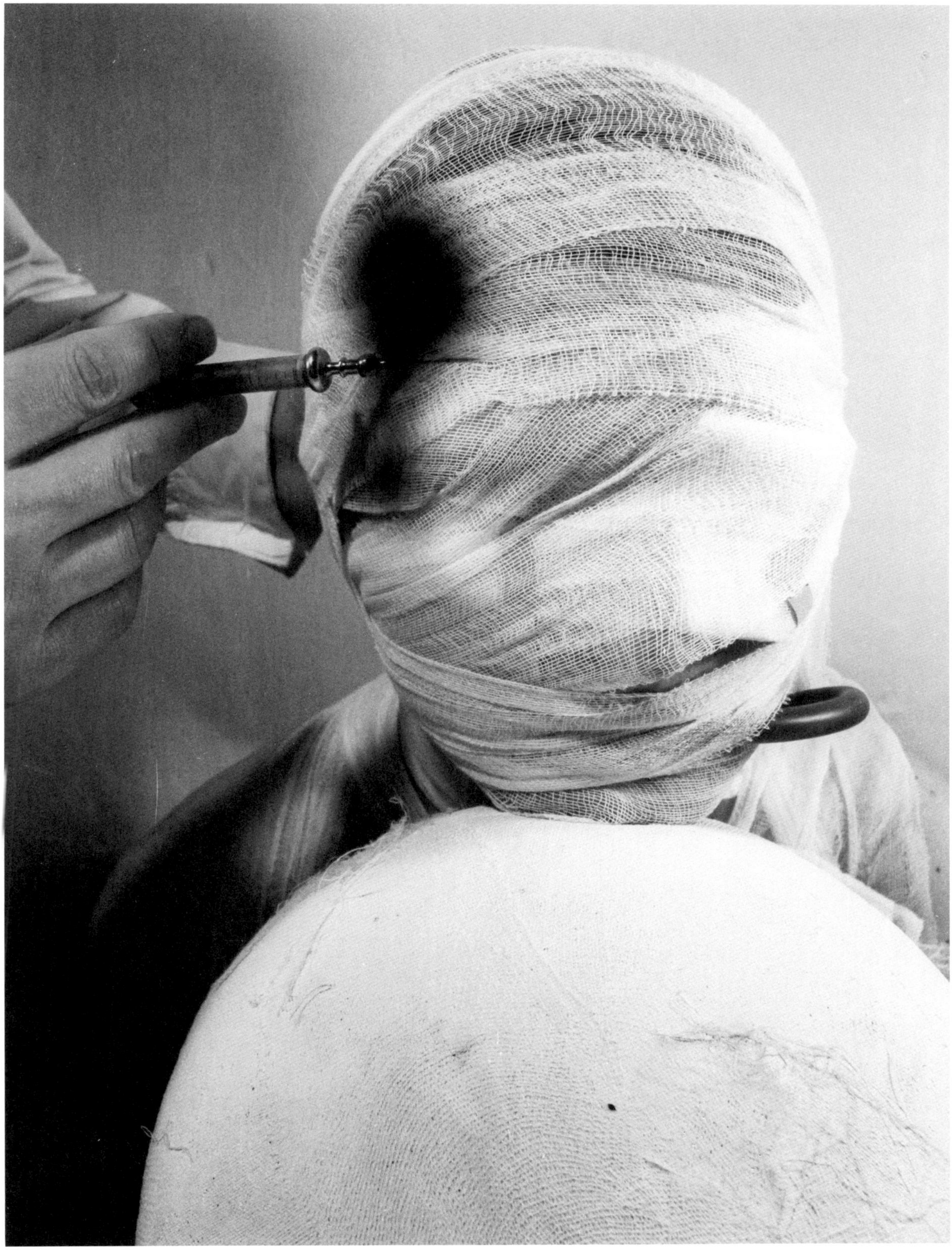

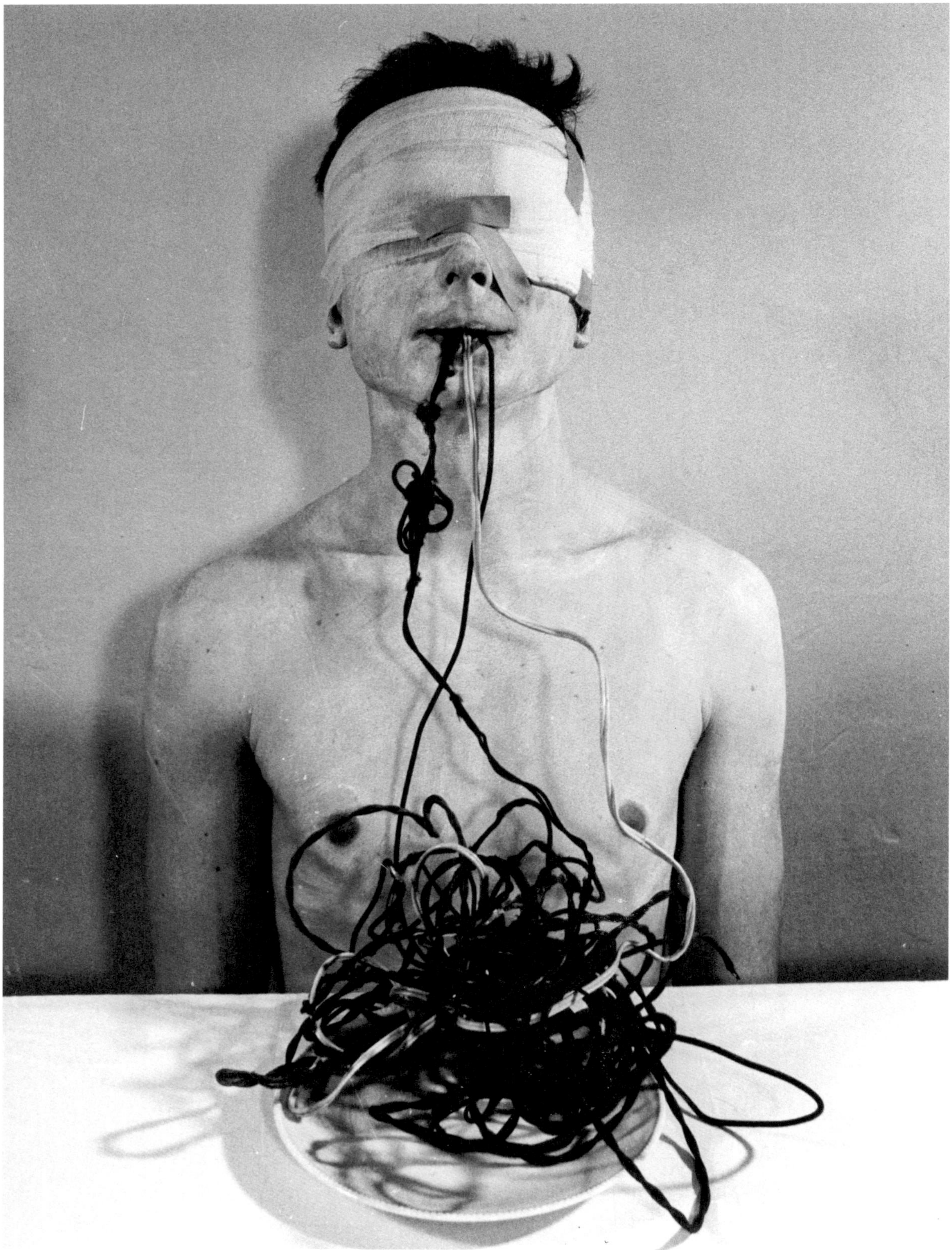

Fig. 204, 205
Rudolf Schwarzkogler
3rd Action, summer 1965
Heinz and Franziska Cibulka's apartment, Kaiserstraße 16, 1070 Vienna
B/W photographs
photo: Ludwig Hoffenreich
with: Heinz Cibulka

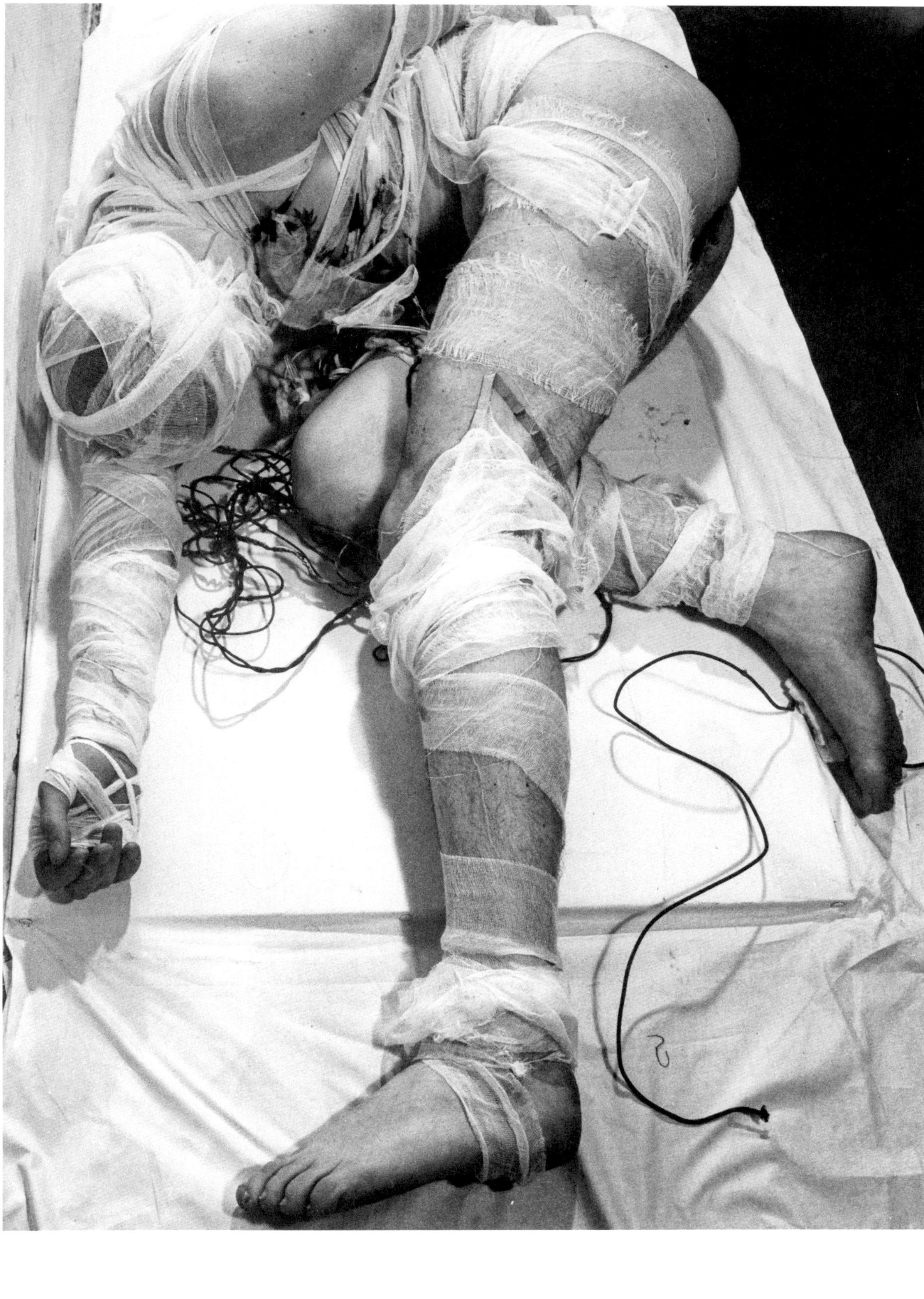

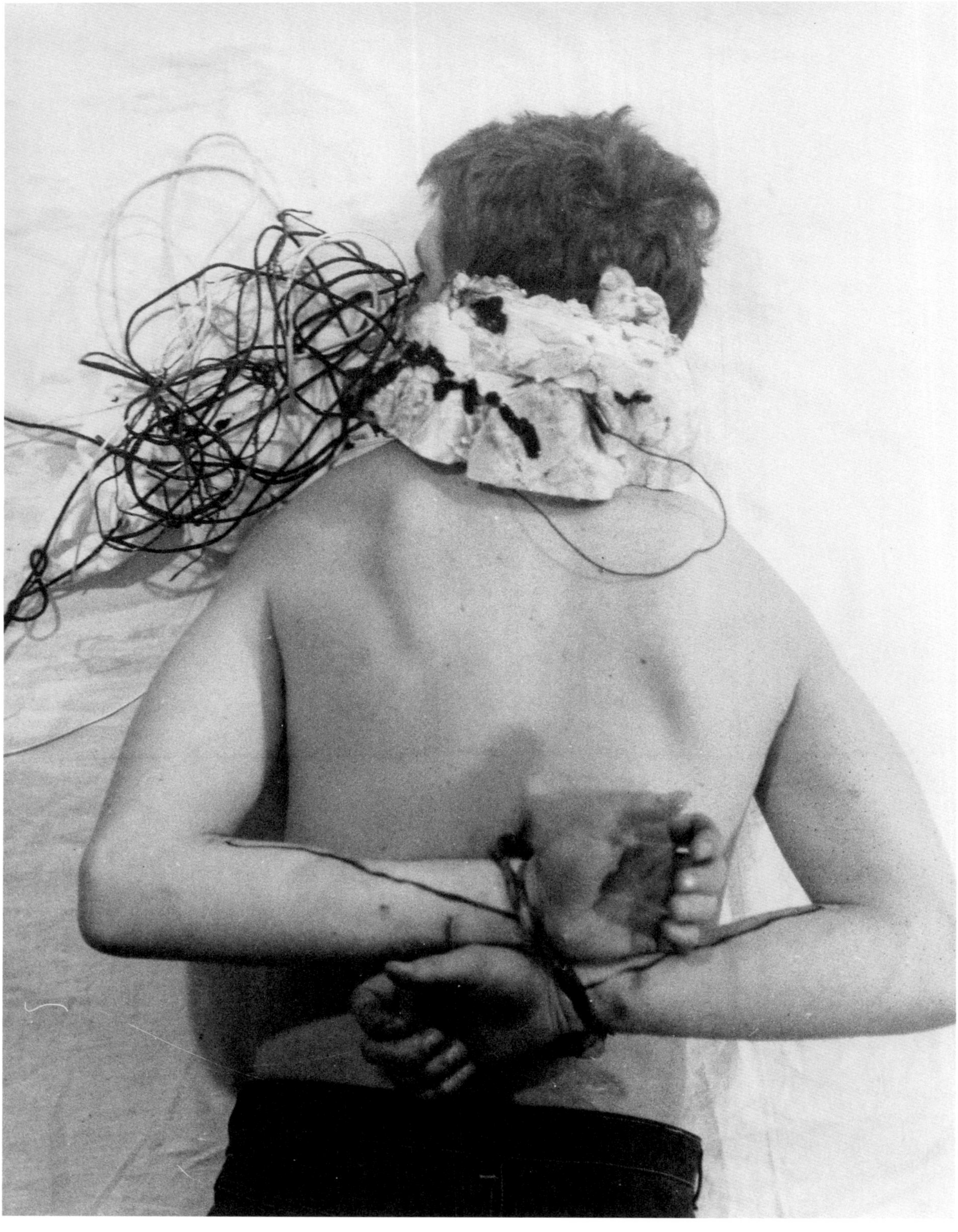

Fig. 206, 207, 208
Rudolf Schwarzkogler
4th Action, 18 December 1965
Heinz and Franziska Cibulka's apartment, Kaiserstraße 16, 1070 Vienna
B/W photographs
photo: Franziska Cibulka
with: Heinz Cibulka

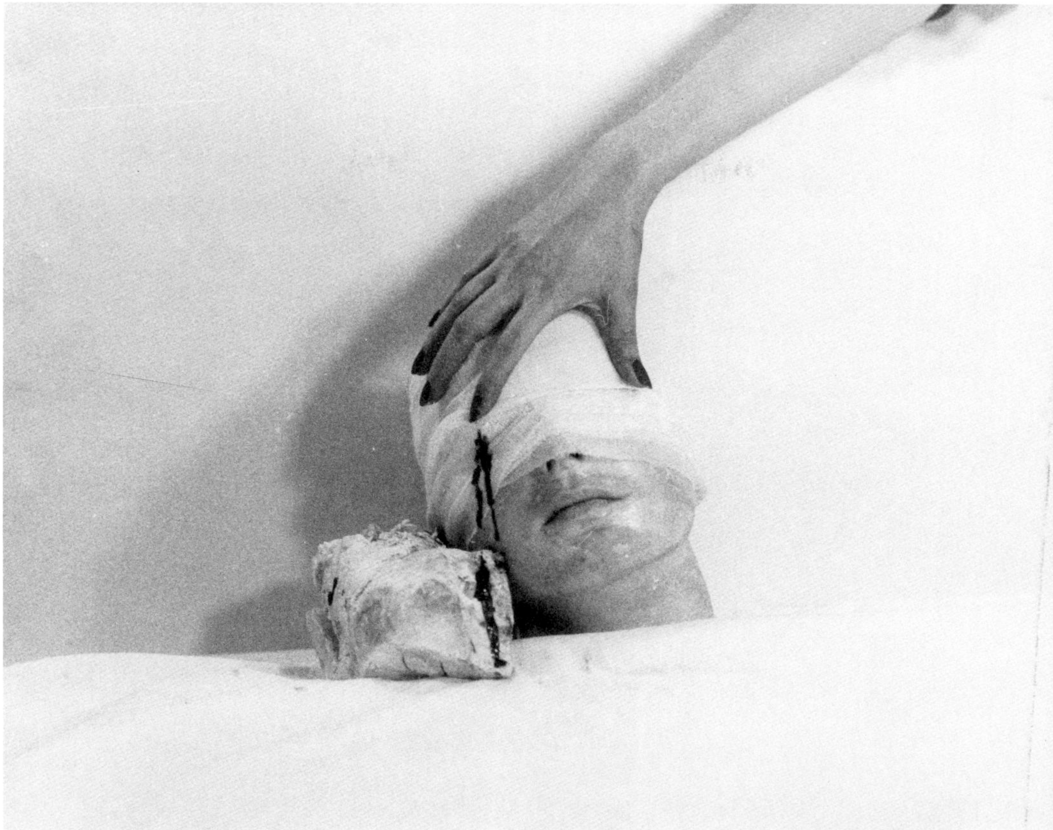

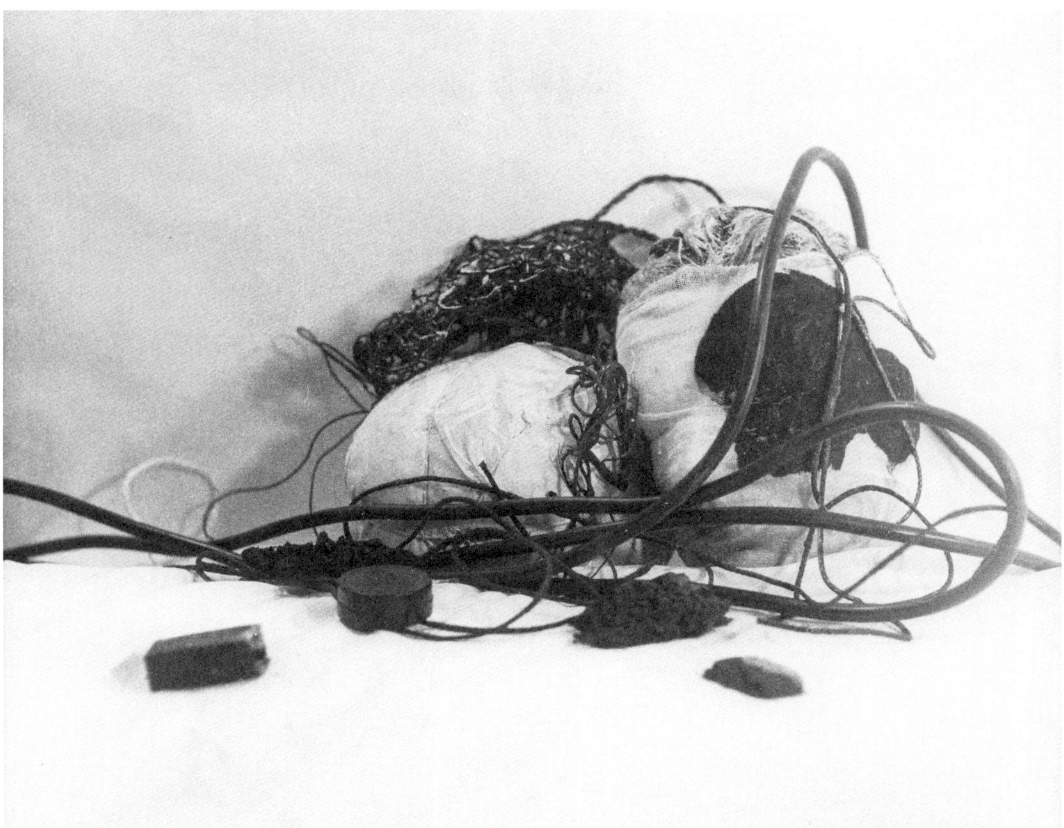

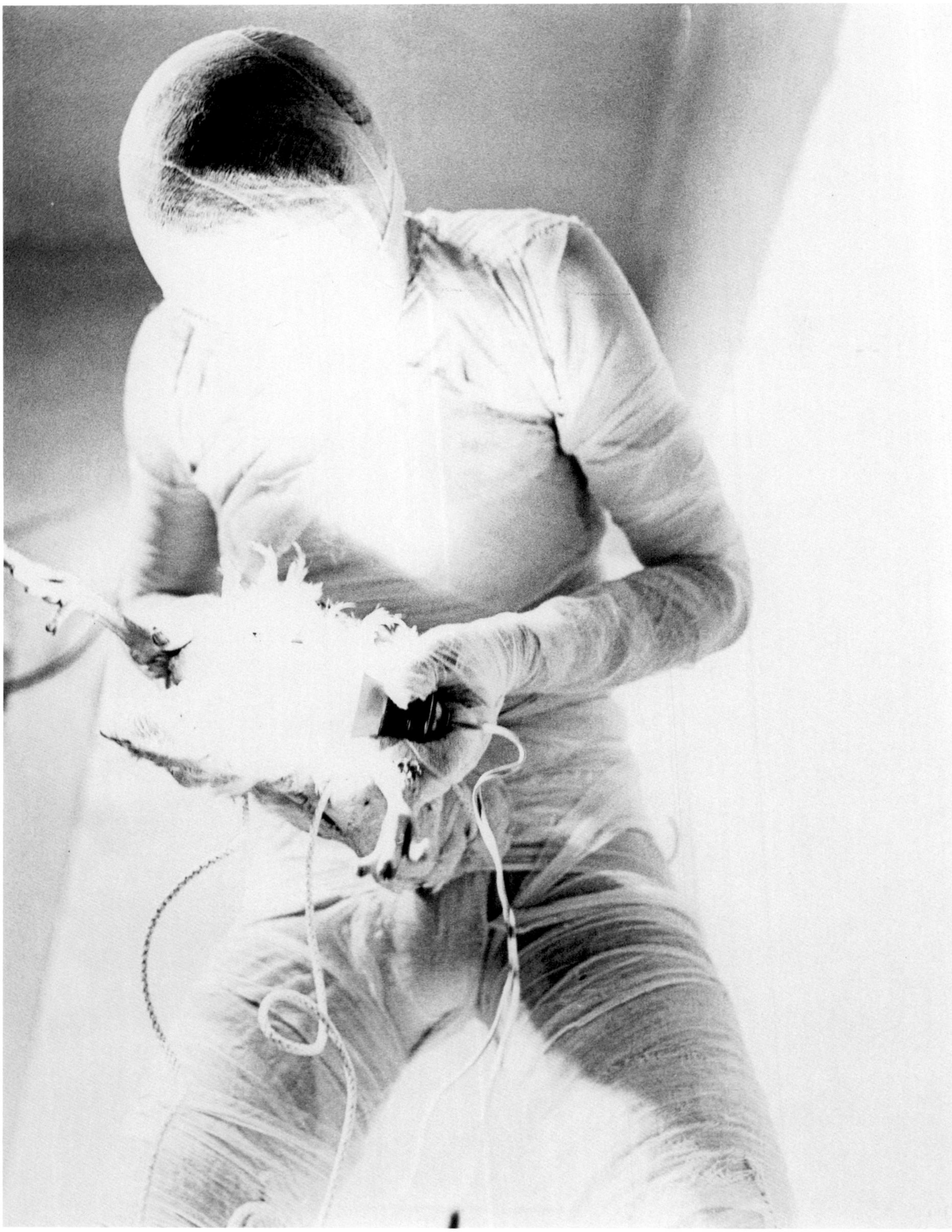

Fig. 209, 210
Rudolf Schwarzkogler
6th Action, spring 1966
Schwarzkogler's apartment, Werdertorgasse 17/3/11, 1010 Vienna
B/W photographs
photo: Michael Epp

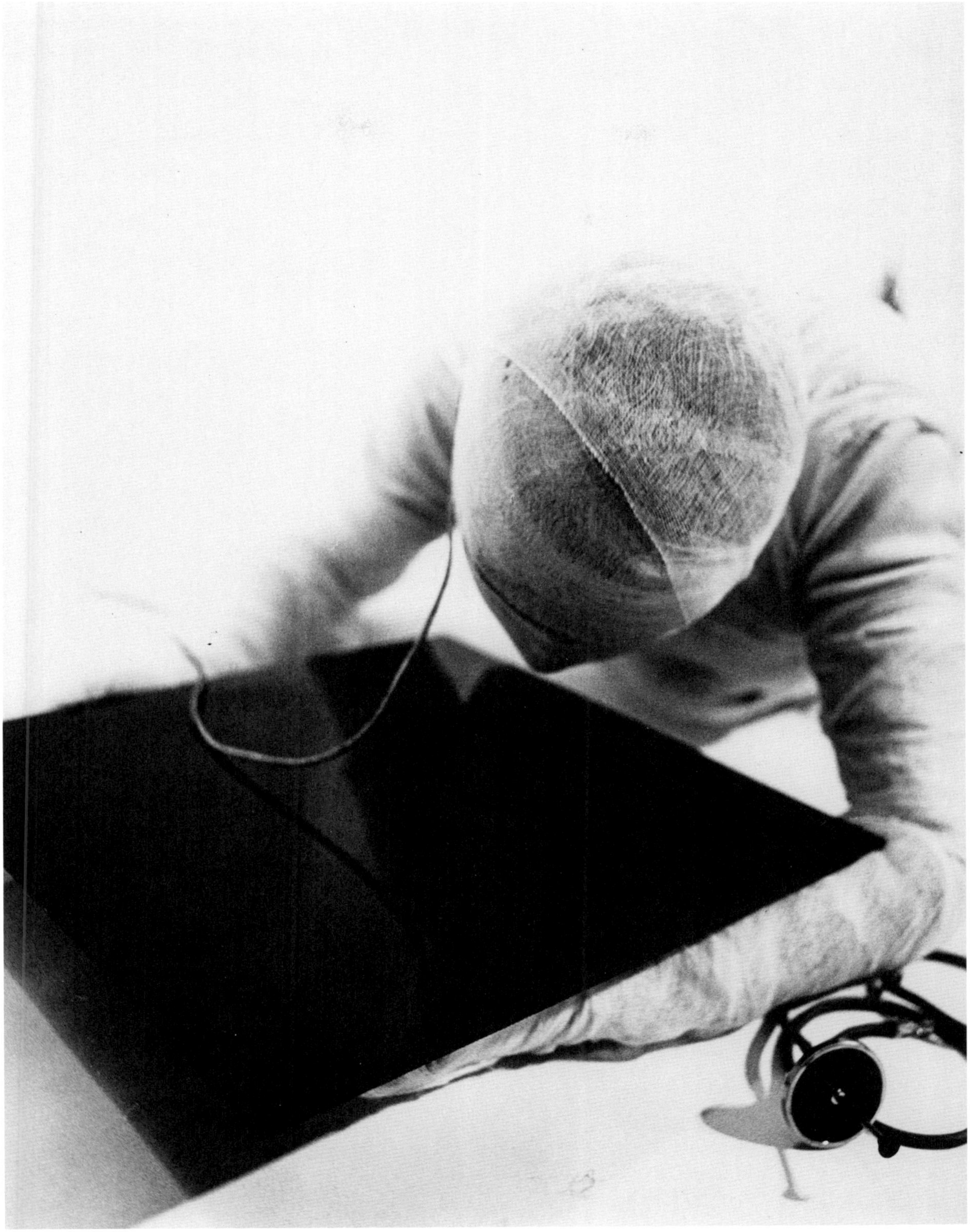

manifest PANORAMA""II!

malerei als verbrechen

Fig. 211
Rudolf Schwarzkogler
Text 5, *manifest PANORAMA ""II!*, between 1966 and 1968
Typescript on paper
29,7 x 21 cm
mumok – Museum moderner Kunst Stiftung Ludwig Wien,
on loan from the Österreichische Ludwig-Stiftung

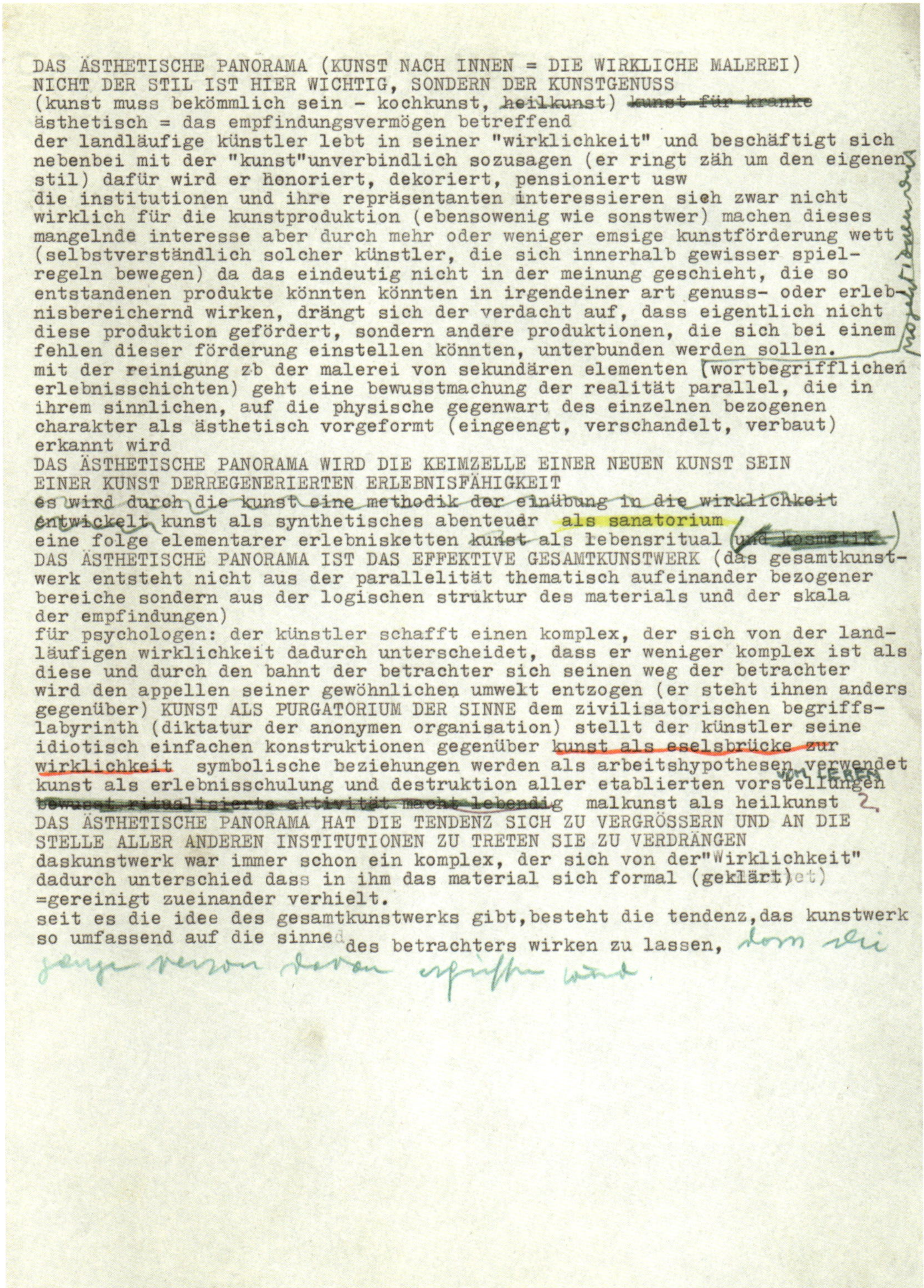

DAS ÄSTHETISCHE PANORAMA (KUNST NACH INNEN = DIE WIRKLICHE MALEREI)
NICHT DER STIL IST HIER WICHTIG, SONDERN DER KUNSTGENUSS
(kunst muss bekömmlich sein - kochkunst, ~~heilkunst~~) ~~kunst für kranke~~
ästhetisch = das empfindungsvermögen betreffend
der landläufige künstler lebt in seiner "wirklichkeit" und beschäftigt sich nebenbei mit der "kunst"unverbindlich sozusagen (er ringt zäh um den eigenen stil) dafür wird er honoriert, dekoriert, pensioniert usw
die institutionen und ihre repräsentanten interessieren sich zwar nicht wirklich für die kunstproduktion (ebensowenig wie sonstwer) machen dieses mangelnde interesse aber durch mehr oder weniger emsige kunstförderung wett (selbstverständlich solcher künstler, die sich innerhalb gewisser spielregeln bewegen) da das eindeutig nicht in der meinung geschieht, die so entstandenen produkte könnten könnten in irgendeiner art genuss- oder erlebnisbereichernd wirken, drängt sich der verdacht auf, dass eigentlich nicht diese produktion gefördert, sondern andere produktionen, die sich bei einem fehlen dieser förderung einstellen könnten, unterbunden werden sollen.
mit der reinigung z.b der malerei von sekundären elementen (wortbegrifflichen erlebnisschichten) geht eine bewusstmachung der realität parallel, die in ihrem sinnlichen, auf die physische gegenwart des einzelnen bezogenen charakter als ästhetisch vorgeformt (eingeengt, verschandelt, verbaut) erkannt wird
DAS ÄSTHETISCHE PANORAMA WIRD DIE KEIMZELLE EINER NEUEN KUNST SEIN
EINER KUNST DERREGENERIERTEN ERLEBNISFÄHIGKEIT
~~es wird durch die kunst eine methodik der einübung in die wirklichkeit entwickelt~~ kunst als synthetisches abenteuer als sanatorium
eine folge elementarer erlebnisketten ~~kunst~~ als lebensritual ~~und kosmetik~~
DAS ÄSTHETISCHE PANORAMA IST DAS EFFEKTIVE GESAMTKUNSTWERK (das gesamtkunstwerk entsteht nicht aus der parallelität thematisch aufeinander bezogener bereiche sondern aus der logischen struktur des materials und der skala der empfindungen)
für psychologen: der künstler schafft einen komplex, der sich von der landläufigen wirklichkeit dadurch unterscheidet, dass er weniger komplex ist als diese und durch den bahnt der betrachter sich seinen weg der betrachter wird den appellen seiner gewöhnlichen umwelt entzogen (er steht ihnen anders gegenüber) KUNST ALS PURGATORIUM DER SINNE dem zivilisatorischen begriffslabyrinth (diktatur der anonymen organisation) stellt der künstler seine idiotisch einfachen konstruktionen gegenüber kunst als eselsbrücke zur wirklichkeit symbolische beziehungen werden als arbeitshypothesen verwendet kunst als erlebnisschulung und destruktion aller etablierten vorstellungen VOM LEBEN
~~bewusst ritualisierte aktivität macht lebendig~~ malkunst als heilkunst 2.
DAS ÄSTHETISCHE PANORAMA HAT DIE TENDENZ SICH ZU VERGRÖSSERN UND AN DIE STELLE ALLER ANDEREN INSTITUTIONEN ZU TRETEN SIE ZU VERDRÄNGEN
daskunstwerk war immer schon ein komplex, der sich von der"Wirklichkeit" dadurch unterschied dass in ihm das material sich formal (geklärt)
=gereinigt zueinander verhielt.
seit es die idee des gesamtkunstwerks gibt,besteht die tendenz,das kunstwerk so umfassend auf die sinne des betrachters wirken zu lassen, dass die ganze person davon ergriffen wird.

Fig. 212
Rudolf Schwarzkogler
Text 3, *DAS ÄSTHETISCHE PANORAMA* (THE AESTHETIC PANORAMA), around 1967/1968
Typescript, ballpoint pen, felt pen, coloured pencil on paper
29,7 x 21 cm
mumok – Museum moderner Kunst Stiftung Ludwig Wien,
on loan from the Österreichische Ludwig-Stiftung

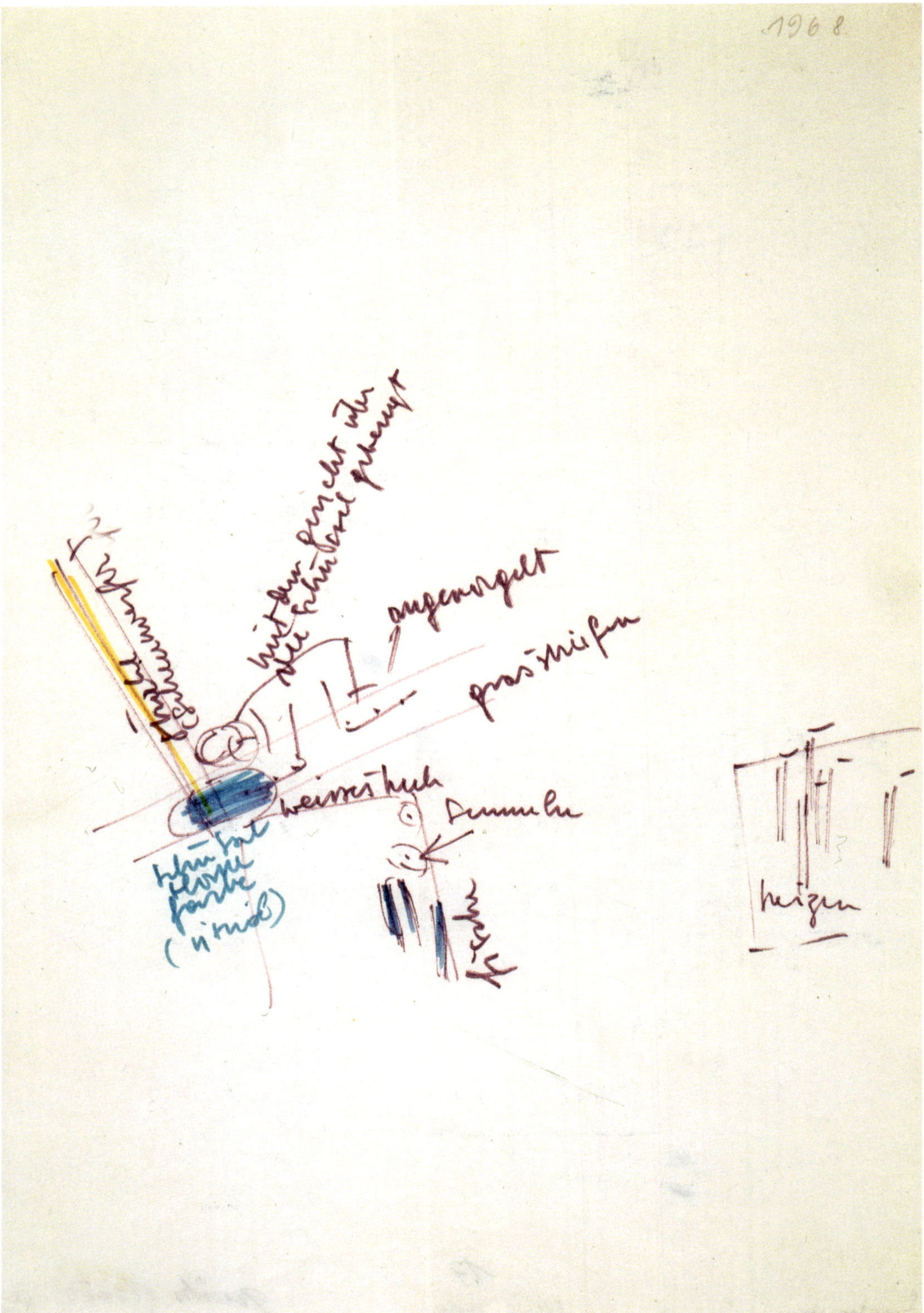

Fig. 213
Rudolf Schwarzkogler
Drawing 17, 1968
Felt pen on paper
29,7 x 21 cm
mumok – Museum moderner Kunst Stiftung Ludwig Wien,
on loan from the Österreichische Ludwig-Stiftung

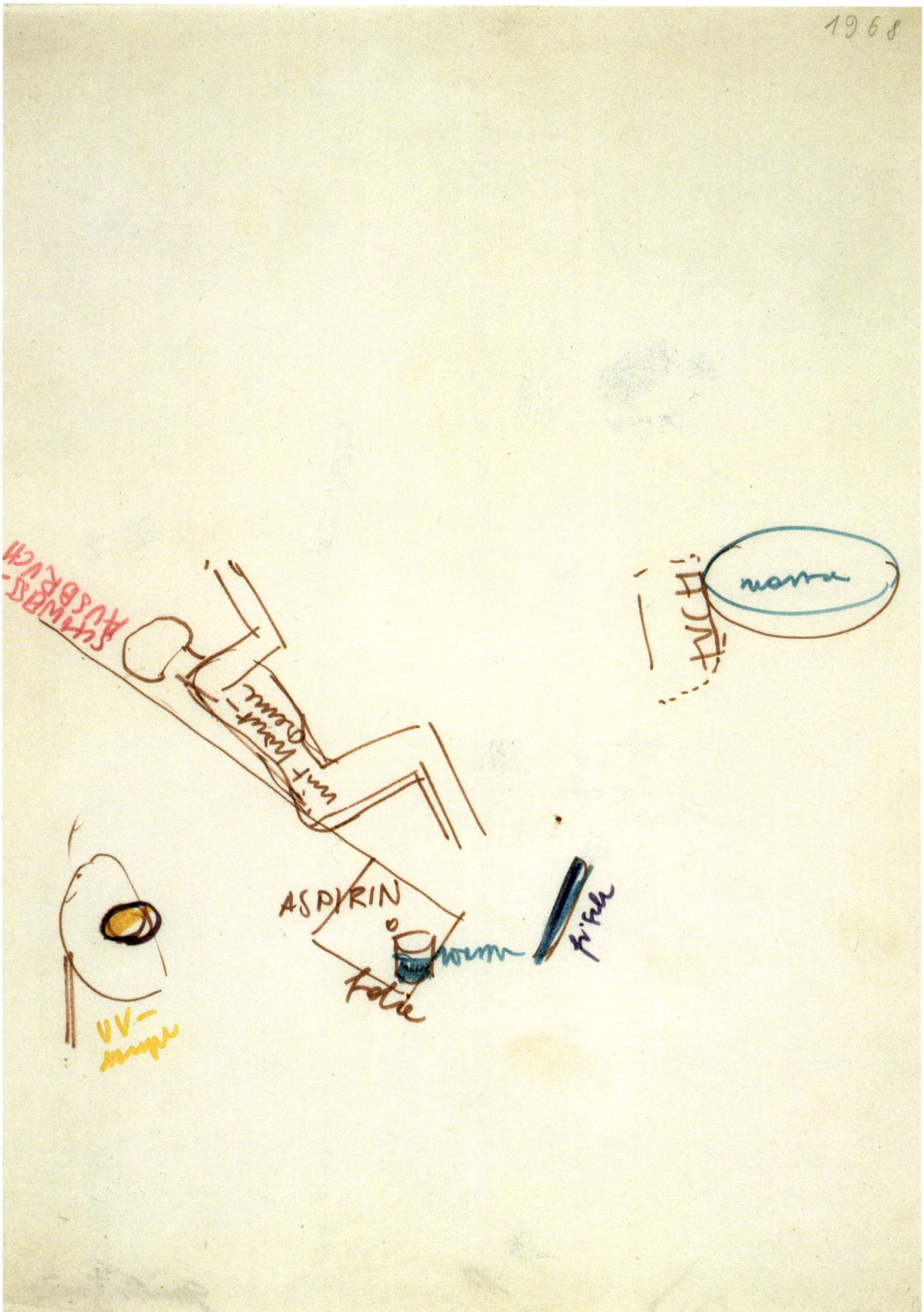

Fig. 214
Rudolf Schwarzkogler
Drawing 18, 1968
Felt pen on paper
29,7 x 21 cm
mumok – Museum moderner Kunst Stiftung Ludwig Wien,
on loan from the Österreichische Ludwig-Stiftung

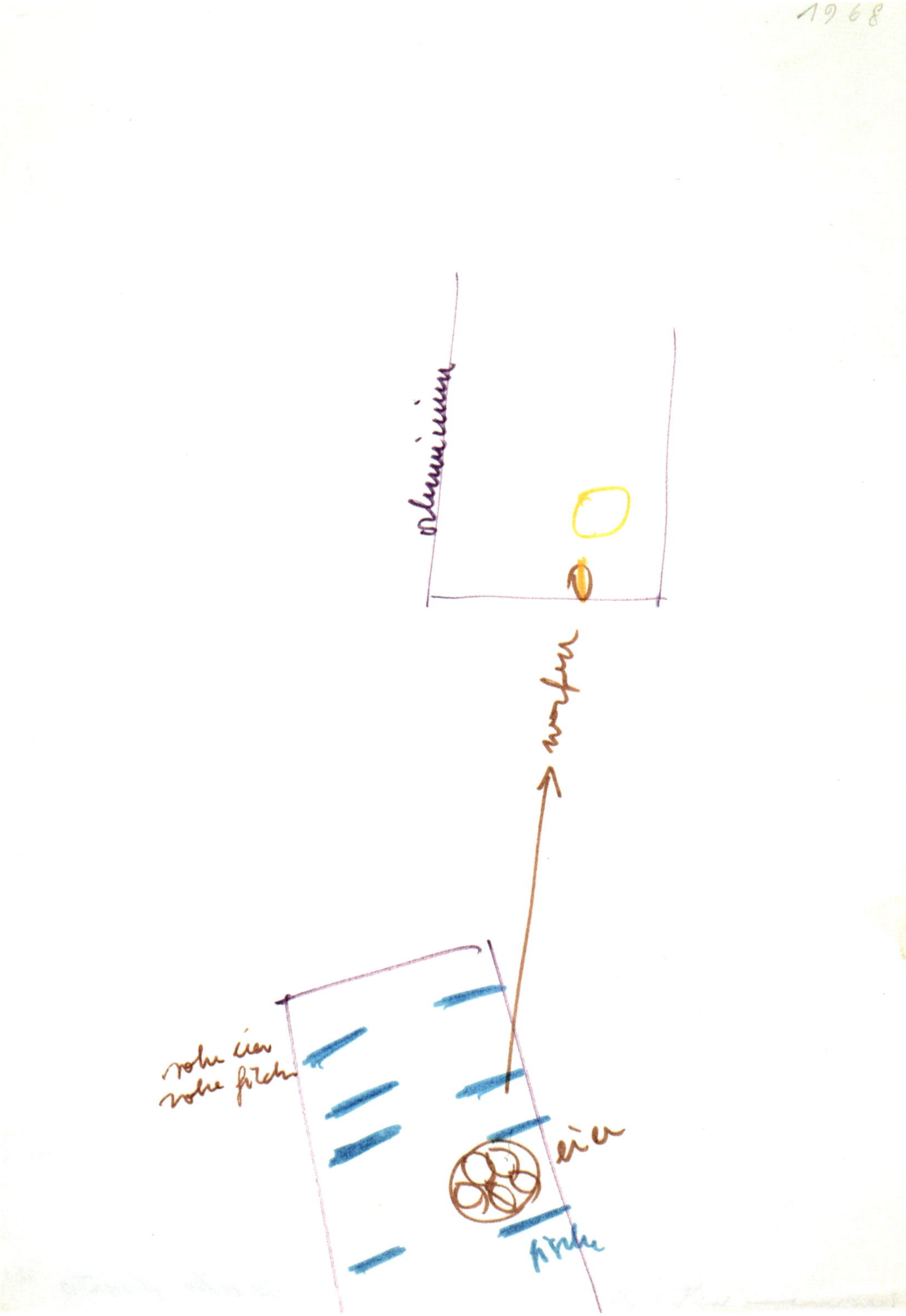

Fig. 215
Rudolf Schwarzkogler
Drawing 21, 1968
Felt pen on paper
29,7 x 21 cm
mumok – Museum moderner Kunst Stiftung Ludwig Wien,
on loan from the Österreichische Ludwig-Stiftung

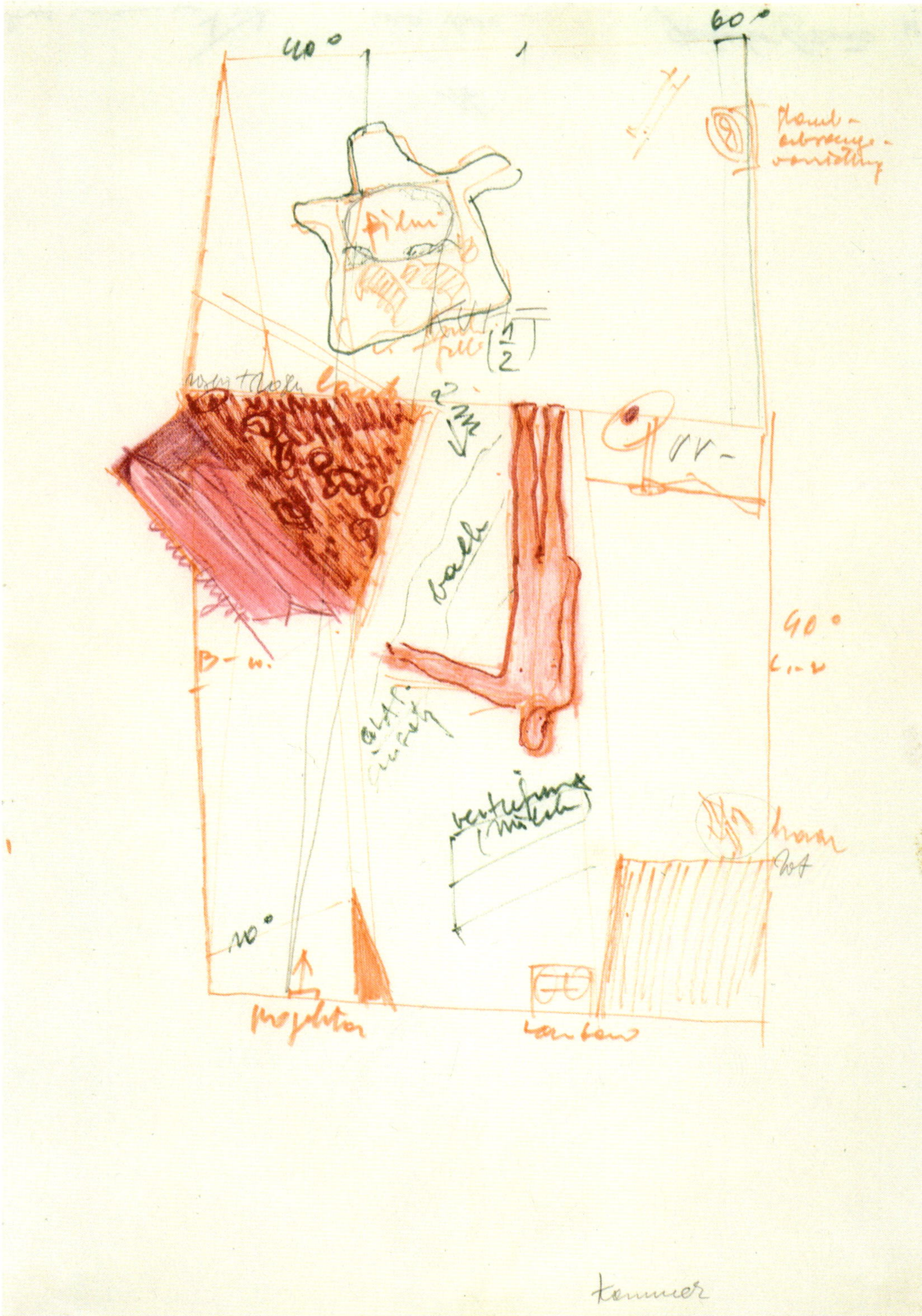

Fig. 216
Rudolf Schwarzkogler
Drawing 16, *kammer* (chamber), 1968
Felt pen on paper
29,7 x 21 cm
mumok – Museum moderner Kunst Stiftung Ludwig Wien,
on loan from the Österreichische Ludwig-Stiftung

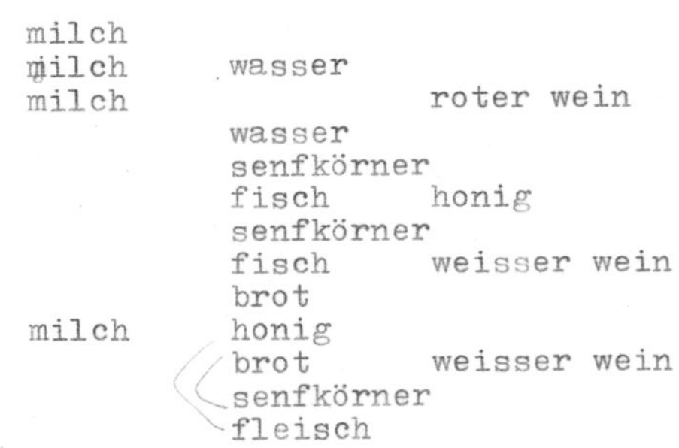

milch
milch wasser
milch roter wein
wasser
senfkörner
fisch honig
senfkörner
fisch weisser wein
brot
milch honig
brot weisser wein
senfkörner
fleisch

Fig. 217
Rudolf Schwarzkogler
Text 19, 1968
Typescript, pencil on paper
29,7 x 21 cm
mumok – Museum moderner Kunst Stiftung Ludwig Wien,
on loan from the Österreichische Ludwig-Stiftung

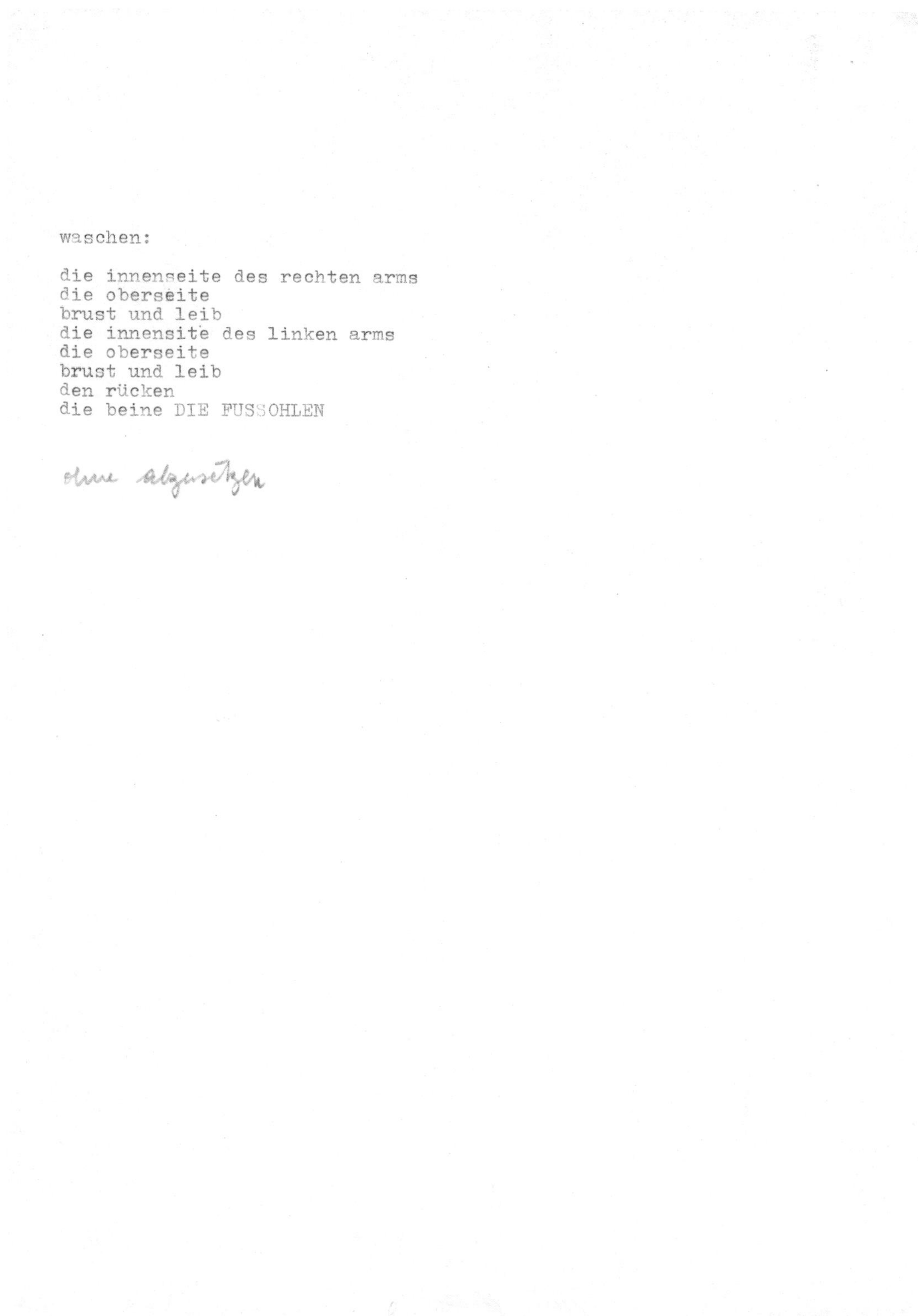

waschen:

die innenseite des rechten arms
die oberseite
brust und leib
die innensite des linken arms
die oberseite
brust und leib
den rücken
die beine DIE FUSSOHLEN

ohne abzusetzen

Fig. 218
Rudolf Schwarzkogler
Text 44, *waschen* (washing), 1968
Typescript, pencil on paper
29,7 x 21 cm
mumok – Museum moderner Kunst Stiftung Ludwig Wien,
on loan from the Österreichische Ludwig-Stiftung

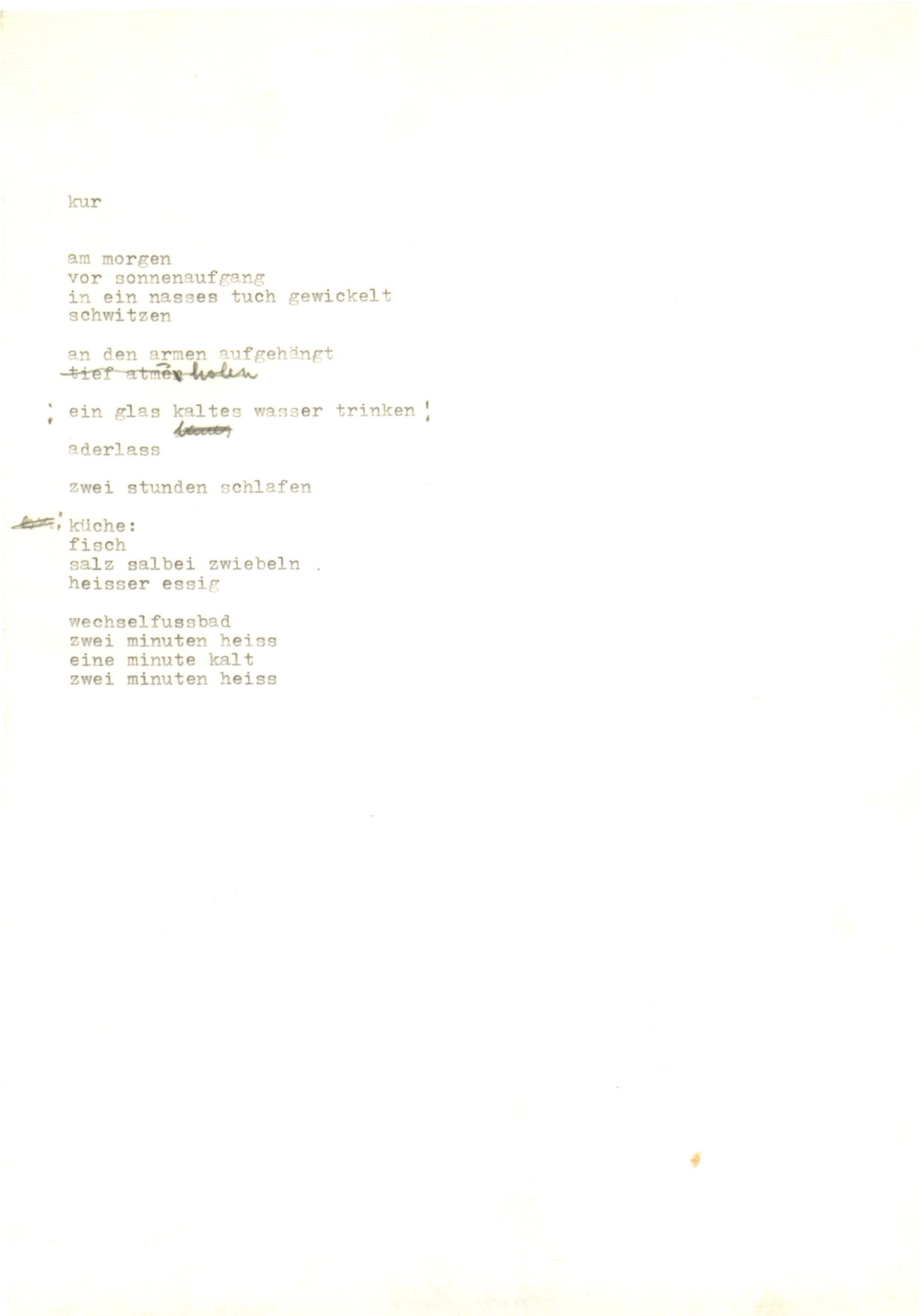

kur

am morgen
vor sonnenaufgang
in ein nasses tuch gewickelt
schwitzen

an den armen aufgehängt
~~tief atmen~~ holen

ein glas kaltes wasser trinken

aderlass

zwei stunden schlafen

küche:
fisch
salz salbei zwiebeln
heisser essig

wechselfussbad
zwei minuten heiss
eine minute kalt
zwei minuten heiss

Fig. 219
Rudolf Schwarzkogler
Text 54, *kur* (cure), 1968
Typescript, pencil on paper
29,7 x 21 cm
mumok – Museum moderner Kunst Stiftung Ludwig Wien,
on loan from the Österreichische Ludwig-Stiftung

haar und bart wachsen las sen
fasten und heisse dampfbäder
atem anhalten
nichts gesalzenes essen
in keinen brunnen aus keinem fenster schauen
wachen
in einem glashaus auf der blanken erde schlafen
bis es regnet

Fig. 220
Rudolf Schwarzkogler
Text 58, 1968
Typescript, pencil on paper
29,7 x 21 cm
mumok – Museum moderner Kunst Stiftung Ludwig Wien,
on loan from the Österreichische Ludwig-Stiftung

Eva Badura-Triska

PHOTOGRAPHY AND FILM IN VIENNA ACTIONISM

232–261

Naturally, photography and film are of great importance in Vienna Actionism as ephemeral actions can only be transmitted through these media. Yet, the artists had an ambivalent relationship to them. After all, they had set out to—as they put it—operate "directly" with concrete bodies, objects and substances in space and time, and thus to avoid the translation of this work into an artistic medium, especially into that of painting. Photo and film, as the only possible forms of preserving such works, however, inevitably bring a media layer back into play, which the artists had to accept; although compared to today's media discourse, they only reflected on it to a limited extent.

In principle, all four wanted photography and film to be utilised in the most neutral way possible. By this they meant that these should not develop a noticeable life of their own, but rather convey the concrete event of the action as authentically as possible. The basic counter argument to this is that no carrier medium can ever be made to disappear. But of course, the desire to withdraw these as much as possible is understandably in line with the concerns of these artists; and in fact, a large proportion of the photographs and films that were created during their actions highly correspond to this aim. Still, also within Vienna Actionism, the utmost neutrality of these media is not always achieved in practice—particularly not in film—even when the artists themselves were responsible for or controlled the use of the cameras.

Like so many things in this movement, the question what roles photography and film played is one that cannot be answered in general terms. Photography is here not equal to photography, as film is not equal to film. Once again, it is important to keep numerous differentiations in mind, and ultimately to view each photo and film individually and describe its specific status. It is, however, possible to list categories into which the individual works can be divided.

The term documentation often comes up—especially in connection with photography, but also with film—and of course is not wrong. Obviously, every photo or film documents a specific action. However, a gradual distinction must be made as to the extent to which the quality and intention of the documentary is in the foreground, as in many cases these static and moving images also have independent artistic values, which were generated by the Actionists as well as by the photographers and filmmakers.

Working Conditions and Guidelines Given to the Photographers and Filmmakers

Action does not equal action in Vienna Actionism and their different types also implied different forms of work and possibilities for the photographers and filmmakers. What was particularly important here is the question of whether actions were aimed at an audience present on site or not. Only a few events in Vienna Actionism were publicly accessible to a broad audience–such as the *Fest des Psychophysischen Naturalismus* (Festival of Psychophysical Naturalism, 1963, Fig. 134, 135), Günter Brus's *Wiener Spaziergang* (Vienna Walk, 1965, Fig. 73), the Zock-Fest (Zock-Festival, 1967, Fig. 165, 166), the *Direct Art Festival* (1967, Fig. 87–91) or the *Kunst und Revolution* (Art and Revolution) event (1968, Fig. 97, 98, 179, 180), as well as a series of actions that Günter Brus, Otto Muehl and Hermann Nitsch realised abroad after 1968. Significantly more actions took place in the studios and apartments of the artists or their friends. A number of them can be described as semi-public, in the sense that anyone who received the information–via invitations and/or word of mouth–could come, but in practice the circle of spectators was relatively limited. Both the public and semi-public actions were characterised by continuous–or largely continuous–course of events. When planning and realising these, the artists took no heed of the work of the photographers and filmmakers. They hardly gave them any instructions beforehand, but they also did not impose any restrictions on them. They were allowed to move freely on the site and choose their respective positions and thus viewing angles as they wished. This, however, meant that when several photographers and/or filmmakers were present, some of them would, time and again, be in the field of vision of their colleagues and be visible in their pictures. (Fig. 25, 26, 32, 73, 146) As the artists always designed their actions with the intention of creating strong pictorial aesthetic qualities from the outset, it was not difficult to find "good" images in these actions.

Another type of action was explicitly not designed for an audience, but was carried out solely with a view to making photographs and films–although every so often friends and acquaintances were present and watched here as well. Actions of this kind were de facto photo/film sessions, in which arrangements of bodies, objects and substances were composed, photographed and in some cases filmed–a procedure which in principle is analogous to the way painters compose things in order to depict them as still lifes. In such cases one speaks of Staged Photography–a genre whose earliest representatives include the Vienna Actionists, but was likewise practiced by numerous other action and performance artists.

Unlike in painting, here, progressive sequences of images were usually created within a setting–which meant that bodies and objects were repeatedly placed in different relations to each other, or objects and substances added or exchanged. This resulted in series of photographs that function either as individual images or as a part of sequences. In one such session, several settings could be created, which meant that several sequences could be developed and photographed. Within this type of action there was a variant to which Nitsch referred as change "on stage", meaning that certain operations (such as pouring liquids onto a body, or the change of objects) were carried out as continuous movements while photographs were being taken and/or filming was in operation.

In these sessions, the task of the photographers and filmmakers was more precisely defined and their creative freedom was very limited. They had to portray these arrangements as objectively as possible. The artists–unless they acted themselves, like Brus and, in some cases, Rudolf Schwarzkogler– occasionally even looked through the lens themselves to check that the images, which they had composed, corresponded to their intentions in the photos.

In December 1964, Brus was the first to realise an action of the Staged Photography type (Fig. 60–68) and in the period up to spring 1966 all four artists practised this form very intensively, turning to it less frequently afterwards. Schwarzkogler used it most often. With the exception of his *1. Aktion, Hochzeit* (1st Action, Wedding) in February 1965, all of his six actions belong to this type.

A hybrid form is constituted by the actions carried out without an audience, where a series of smaller staged scenes were photographed and/or filmed.[1]

1
An early example of this is Otto Muehl's Materialaktion Nr. 11, *Mama und Papa* (Material Action No. 11, Mama and Papa), 1964 (Fig. 144–147).

The Photographers

In the early phase of Vienna Actionism, the photographers were mainly friends and acquaintances of Brus, Muehl, Nitsch and Schwarzkogler, such as Peter Jurkowitsch, Kari Bauer, Hans Niederbacher, Franziska Cibulka, Michael Epp, Walter Kindler, Wilfried Klanjsek-Bratke, and Marc Adrian, but also the then already renowned Austrian photographer Franz Hubmann. In June 1962, at "the working retreat" *Die Blutorgel* (The Blood Organ) of Adolf Frohner, Muehl and Nitsch, Ludwig Hoffenreich (a retired newspaper editor known to Muehl) photographed for the first time. He would become the main photographer of Vienna Actionism. At Muehl's *Material Action No. 3* in February 1964 (Fig. 140), another important photographer, Siegfried Klein (about whom little is known) joined. When he took photos for the Actionists, he used the pseudonym Khasaq. In 1964/1965 he recorded actions by all four artists, during which he and Hoffenreich also repeatedly took photographs alongside each other. At Brus's *1. Aktion, Ana* (1st Action, Ana, 1964, Fig. 50–57) this led to arguments between the two, resulting in Hoffenreich's early departure. After a long break, Khasaq appeared once more in 1968–interestingly at the later scandalized event *Kunst und Revolution* (Art and Revolution, Fig. 97, 98, 179, 180) at the University of Vienna, although he only took a few images there. Hoffenreich as well as Khasaq had top-class cameras: the former used a Hasselblad and the latter a Linhof product.

Brus, Muehl, and Schwarzkogler also photographed their colleagues' actions on several occasions. Only Nitsch, who was generally more sceptical about photographic documentation, never did this with other artists, but did so in the case of his own Körperaktionen (Body Actions), at which his then-wife , Eva, took pictures, too. Even the filmmaker Kurt Kren photographed at two actions of Brus in 1967. (Fig. 84–86)

Hoffenreich only once accompanied the Actionists to a performance abroad, namely to Nitsch's *31. Aktion, Maria Empfängnis* (31st Action, Immaculate Conception, 1969, Fig. 36) in Munich. On the other occasions, the job was either carried out by artist friends who were traveling with them, or by local artists or other people brought in by the organisers.[2]

Very early on, press photographers were present at public actions and especially during larger public events–such as the actions by Nitsch and Brus in the Aktionsraum 1 (1970) in Munich (Fig. 106)–members of the audience took pictures.

Due to costs, black and white images were produced more often than coloured ones.

Which prints were available to the artists in the 1960s and what did they do with them?

In the 1960s, it was not possible for Brus, Muehl, Nitsch and Schwarzkogler to develop all images taken during their actions, for financial reasons. On the contrary, they could only afford a few prints. The photographers worked for them free of charge, and the agreement with Hoffenreich and Khasaq (Siegfried Klein) was that the artists paid for the photo material and then received contact sheets. From these they selected individual images, from which enlargements were made. Undoubtedly, they would have liked larger numbers developed, but in principle it was in their interest to have selections made from the abundance. Yes, even more, the artists also determined the crop of the photographic "raw material" and marked it on the contact sheets (Fig. 225, 226).[3] In this way, they drew attention to what was essential to them–often just single details–and also ensured that well-composed images were created. This approach offers particularly clear evidence of their pictorial thinking, and of the fact that their ephemeral actions should result in and be preserved as pictures. Schwarzkogler

2
In 1964, at Muehl's *Materialaktion Nr. 9* (Material Action No. 9) in Düsseldorf, the first action of Vienna Actionism abroad, it was Kari Bauer and Manfred Leve (photographer of numerous Fluxus events in Germany and a lawyer in everyday life). At the *Destruction in Art Symposium* in London (Fig. 33, 34, 159–164), it was the Stuttgart dentist and collector Hanns Sohm, who passionately followed and documented the avant-garde and counter-culture scene in the 1960s. The latter again photographed Muehl's and Nitsch's actions on the occasion of the exhibition *Happening und Fluxus* (Happening and Fluxus) at the Kölnischer Kunstverein in 1970, as well as other Nitsch actions, including his first *24-Stunden-Spiel* (24-Hour-Play) in 1975 (*50th Action*). The people who photographed Nitsch's actions abroad in the late 1960s and early 1970s included his second wife Beate, the photographer and historian of photography Ute Eskildsen, as well as Stefan Moses who was already well-known to a wider audience at that time for his photographs of people and life in Germany. The artists Jonas Mekas and Al Hansen, as well as the artist Shigeo Kuboto, later Nam June Paik's wife, and Peter Moore (a collector and prominent photographer of numerous Happenings, Fluxus activities as well as of the events at the Judson Dance Theater) were among those who took photographs at Nitsch's actions in New York. Ugo Molas, who rose to prominence as an artist photographer, worked for Muehl in Milan in 1969. Klaus Eschen, who photographed almost all of the extreme actions that Günter Brus carried out privately in Berlin and publicly in the Kunstraum 1 in Munich in 1969/1970, after his escape from Vienna, was the son of the Berlin photographer Fritz Eschen who initially worked as a photojournalist until he became a lawyer in 1967. As such, he was the co-founder of the Socialist Lawyers' Collective in Berlin, which existed from 1969 to 1979 and, amongst others, defended RAF members. Eschen later became a notary and a constitutional judge in Berlin. In the late 1960s, the photographer and filmmaker Lisl Ponger joined the circle of people around the Vienna Actionists and took photographs at Muehl's actions as well as at Hermann Nitsch's visits to a slaughterhouse.

3
Such determinations of crops were not only carried out immediately after the actions, but often also years later and, again and again, not only by the artists themselves but also by people close to them. After the death of Rudolf Schwarzkogler, this was–amongst others–done by his partner Edith Adam and artist friends, especially Günter Brus and Hermann Nitsch.

ummed up this point ofview most succinctly when he wrote: "the act of painting itself can be liberated from the compulsion of having the relics as its aim in that it is placed before the reproducing apparatus, which takes up the information."(Fig. 224) Thus, due to their preservation through the use of photography and film, the results of "direct" work with concrete bodies, objects and substances become artefacts again, which on a structural level are comparable to the classic panel painting, albeit with crucial differences: With action photography, one should rather speak of images, that differ from traditional paintings in that they can be handled with great flexibility. The artists did not choose just one crop but repeatedly selected different ones. They even had other people choosing them[4] and especially after the 1960s, the Actionists also used photographs without specifying any. Furthermore, there are no specifications as to the size in which these photos should be developed—this remains undefined until today. The decision is left to those who exhibit these pictures. During their lifetime and with the consent of the artists, the images were developed and shown both in very small and very large formats and they were even projected onto the wall as slides (sometimes quite large).

4 See note 3.

The Artists' Handling of the Photographs Available to them in the 1960s

The few photographic images that the Vienna Actionists had printed in the 1960s were used in a variety of ways, always emphasising their aesthetic qualities. Above all, the artists took them as materials for collages—and thus again for the creation of pictorial artefacts. In such works, Brus and Nitsch combined contact sheets amongst others with objects of the kind they utilised in their actions. In Brus's case, he for instance incorporated thumbtacks or razor blades (Fig. 229) and Nitsch took bandages or bloody cloths (Fig. 230). In one of his collages Muehl inscribed himself into art history by combining contact sheets of his actions with details from paintings by Matthias Grünewald, Dutch painters, or Pablo Picasso. (Fig. 231) Schwarzkogler, in turn, precisely organised a compilation of selected details from the photos of his first action in strictly mathematical proportions. (Fig. 228)

A particularly interesting (temporary) collage was a photo wall that Brus, Muehl and Nitsch put together at the *Destruction in Art Festival* in London, after they had been asked to bring pictures along. On a large wall in the event hall, they compiled images of different sizes, which showed various actions by all three of them. The largest of these had the maximum size of what was technically and financially possible for them at the time (Fig. 232).

Another use for photographs in Vienna Actionism were posters and invitation cards that announced their actions. Here, obviously, photographs of previous actions had to be taken. (Fig. 15, 16, 227) Only very rarely were action photographs shown in exhibitions in the 1960s. One example was a 1965 presentation of Brus's informal paintings in the Junge Generation gallery, at the opening of which the artist realised his action *Malerei–Selbstbemalung–Selbstverstümmelung* (Painting-Self-Painting-Self-Mutilation, Fig. 74, 227). Here, photos of previous actions hung in a row on the wall. Equally rare during this decade was the appearance of action-photographs in exhibition catalogues or magazines.[5]

5
See Eva Badura-Triska, Hubert Klocker (ed.), *Vienna Actionism. Art and Upheaval in 1960s' Vienna, Vienna* / Cologne (mumok, Museum moderner Kunst Stiftung Ludwig Wien / Verlag der Buchhandlung Walther König), 2012, p. 132.

How should the action photographs be handled today?

Anyone who exhibits these pictures today has a great amount of freedom in terms of their presentation; or to put it differently, people must decide for themselves. As already mentioned, the artists neither gave instructions regarding the size in which the images should be developed, nor whether certain crops determined by them or others should be selected or if the “raw material” should be shown. They also did not define which photos should be exhibited and which ones not. Furthermore, it is unclear how the pictures should be framed, either with a passe-partout or without, either with a background-paper or without, and which frames should be utilised. It is also not predetermined how they should be arranged on the wall. Should one hang each photo individually, in blocks or in rows? And at what distances from each other? Should an (often not easy) attempt be made to reconstruct the sequence within a respective action (which the artists themselves did not do), or should the subjects be related to one another according to (individual) aesthetic criteria and can several actions be even mixed together (like Nitsch often did)? And may the subjects be projected onto the wall as slides or slide sequences? All of this has already been done by the artists themselves, as well as by curators, and during their lifetime the artists never complained.

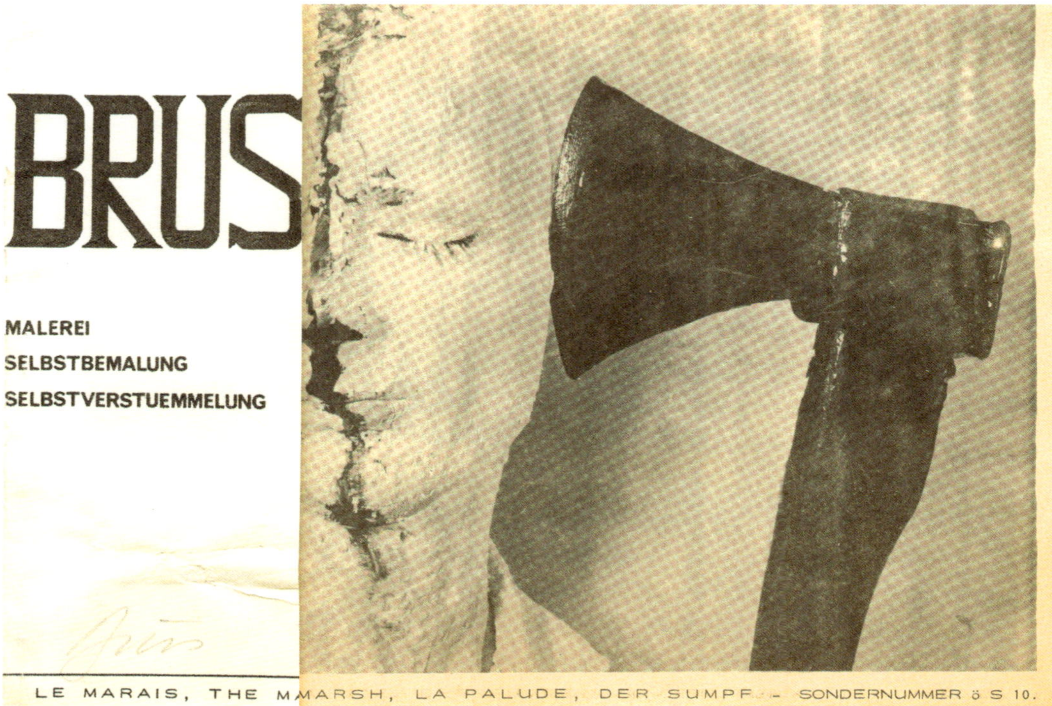

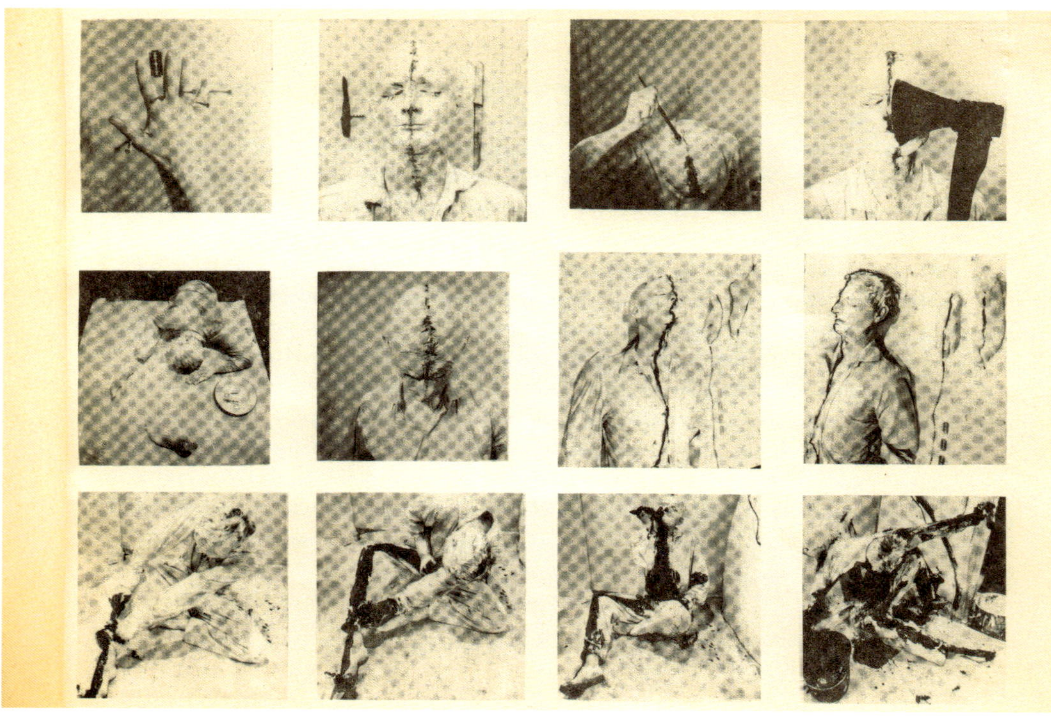

Fig. 221, 222, 223, 224
Title page and pages from the special issue of the magazine *Le Marais*, 1965
Print on paper
21 x 29,7 cm
WAM – Wiener Aktionismus Museum, Vienna, Collection K.

(Smart) der Länge nach auf. Ich schlage einen Drahtstift ins Ohr. Ich spalte meinen Kopf der Länge nach in zwei Hälften. Ich führe in meine Harnröhre Stacheldraht ein und versuche durch leichtes Drehen den Nerv zu reissen (Autozystoskopie). Ich beisse meine Pickel auf und sauge sie aus. Ich lasse alles fotografieren und besichtigen.

Günter Brus 1965

S E L B S T B E M A L U N G ist eine Weiterentwicklung der Malerei. Die Bildfläche hat ihre Funktion als alleiniger Ausdrucksträger verloren. Sie wurde zu ihrem Ursprung, zur Wand, zum Objekt, zum Lebewesen, zum menschlichen Körper zurückgeführt. Durch die Einbeziehung meines Körpers als Ausdrucksträger entsteht als Ergebnis ein Geschehen, dessen Ablauf die Kamera festhält und der Zuschauer miterleben kann. Der Raum, mein Körper und alle Objekte, die sich im Raume befinden, werden verwandelt. Alles wird weiss gestrichen, alles wird zur "Bildfläche": Büro, Museum, Rumpelkammer, Kaffeehaus, Maschinenhalle, Operationszimmer, Haftzelle, Toiletteanlage, Schlachthalle, Palmenhaus, Badezimmer, Amerikanische Küche, Senkgrube, Sauna, Fussballstadion, Sitzungssaal, Polizeistube, Krematorium, Zentralfriedhof, Seziersaal (auch Leichen können verwendet werden), leerer Raum usw.

S E L B S T B E M A L U N G = bewältigte S E L B S T V E R S T U E M M E L U N G
Sich selbst bemalen, strangulieren, zwicken und zwacken, in einem weissen Klosett sitzen und sich bis zum Blutsturz peinigen, ich habe nie genug Hackmesser, Haumesser, Schlachtmesser, Rasierklingen, Bratenmesser, Wimpernscheren, Stricknadeln, Kneipzangen, Jätekrallen, Halbmondmesser, Pickelreisser, Mitesserausquetscher, Geflügelscheren, Krebsscheren, Okuliermesser, Reisszirkel, Betäubungszangen, Stechzirkel, Graviernadeln, Schuhzwecken, Spitzstichel, Drahtstifte, Heftklammern, Stecheisen, Reissnägel, Schraubstöcke, Rasiermesser, Klauenreisser, Drillbohrer, Hautscheren, Teigradler, Drahtschlingen, Stacheldraht, Glassplitter, Schlachtschussapparate, Knochenraspeln, Garniernadeln, Fuchsschwänze, Stecknadeln, Sicherheitsnadeln und Messerchen, Federmesser, Hummerzangen, Schrottsägen, Zieselinstrumente, Keksausstecher, Stichsägen, Spitzhacken, Fingerschnittmesser, Klammern, Klemmen, Reishaken, Wiegemesser, Bienenstachel, Wespenstachel, Hornissenstachel, Ohrlöffel, Schlagbolzen usw. usw.

S E L B S T B E M A L U N G = unendlich ausgekostete S E L B S T E N T L E I B U N G

Günter Brus 1965

LE MARAIS bringt als erste Zeitschrift
Beiträge der WIENER AKTIONSGRUPPE
(Brus, Mühl, Nitsch, Schwarzkogler).

leib, fließt über und überspült die herabfallenden gedärme.

Nr0 schüttet (stark dunstendes) wasser in den aufgebrochenen leib des gekreuzigten knaben und über die am bett liegenden blutigen gedärme. Weiters spült und wäscht er mithilfe von watte und heißem wasser das blut aus der innenseite des aufgebrochenen leibes und spült und wäscht zusätzlich die eingeweide vom blut rein, indem er weiterhin aus einer schale heißes wasser darüberleert.

Nr1 schüttet lauen rotwein in den aufgebrochenen leib des gekreuzigten knaben und die am bett liegenden gedärme. Weiters spült und wäscht er mithilfe von watte, die er in lauen rotwein taucht, das restliche blut aus der innenseite des aufgebrochenen leibes.

Hermann Nitsch

entwurf P A N O R A M A I / malerei in bewegung — SCHWARZKOGLER

an die stelle der bildkonstruktion auf der fläche tritt die konstruktion der bedingten für den malakt als bestimmung des aktionsfeldes, des raums um den akteur, der realen vorgefundenen objekte der umwelt. der malakt selbst kann von dem zwang, die relikte zum ziel zu haben, befreit werden, indem er vor die reproduzierende apparatur gestellt wird, welche die information übernimmt. die zeit des malakts und die zeit der schaustellung werden eins. aus der bewegung und konfrontation der gewählten elemente entstehen variable montagen, aus deren umformung und aufeinanderfolge der zeitlich-dynamische ablauf der aktion. es wird die erweiterung bis zum totalen synästetischen akt möglich, der über alle sinne erlebt und von anderen mitvollzogen werden kann. als realer vorgang offenbart er seine form dem plastischen bild einer mehrfachen erfassung durch verschiedene apparaturen.

entwurf für eine vorführung — SCHWARZKOGLER

ich schnüre mit einem durchsichtigen nylonfaden zehn tote, weisse hühner zu einem ball zusammen und hänge sie mitten in einem frisch ausgekalkten raum. zehn mit gras gefüllte plasticsäcke stopfe ich in einen kinderwagen und breite darüber ein weisses tuch. ich tränke eine weisse herrenunterhose mit äther und lysoform, einer der zuschauer darf sie anziehen. nachdem ich ihm die augen mit mull verbunden habe, leere ich eine dose süsser kondensmilch auf das weisse tuch und er setzt sich darauf. er entleert die plastosäcke, ich fahre ihn unter die hühner, dann tunke ich die linke hand in büroleim und streiche damit sanft über das gefieder und seinen kopf. er beginnt wie ein hahn zu krähen, gleichzeitig hackt einer der zuschauer einen zwischen zwei resonanzkörper (blechdosen) gespannten draht auseinander, die hühner werden von mir mit heissem wasser, essig und süssem parfüm beschüttet und dann mit gelber staubfarbe bestäubt. der kinderwagen wird vom publikum durch anstossen herumgefahren, ich beschütte ihn mit einem kübel leimwasser und einem sack gelber farbe. wenn der kinderwagen unter den hühnern durchfährt, schreit das publikum dem mann darin kurz zu, und er versucht sie zu fassen. wenn er sie erreicht hat, schneide ich den nylonfaden durch.
alle verlassen den raum. der kinderwagen mit dem mann darin, der die hühner hält, wird von mir durch die strassen gefahren, das publikum folgt wie bei einer prozession.

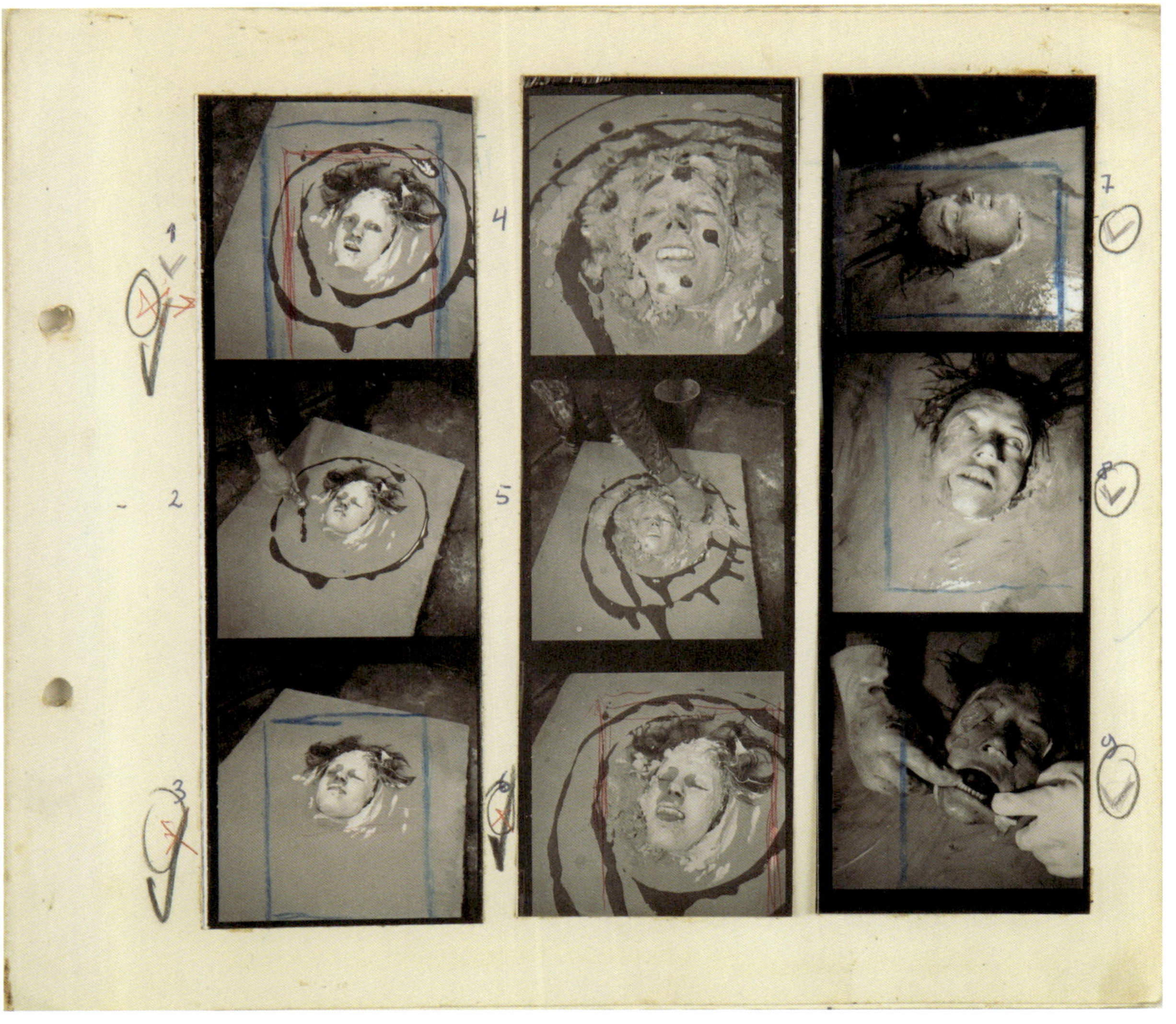

Fig. 225
Otto Muehl
Materialaction no. 18, Rumpsti Pumpsti (Crash Bang), 8 May 1965
Contact sheets on paper, ballpoint pen
21,5 x 25 cm
photo: Ludwig Hoffenreich
mumok – Museum moderner Kunst Stiftung Ludwig Wien

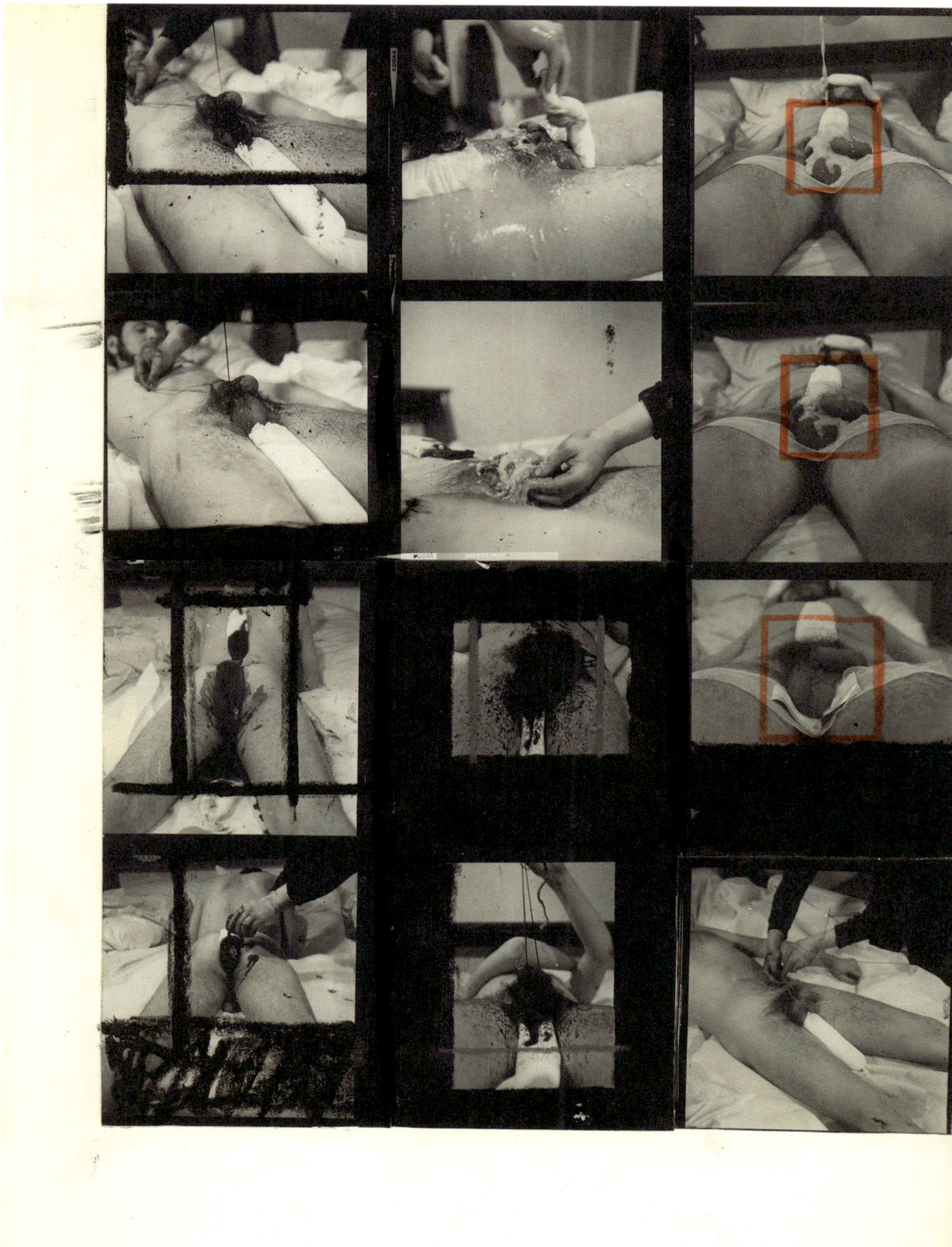

Fig. 226
Hermann Nitsch
8th Action, January 1965
Contact sheets on paper, ballpoint pen
29,7 x 21 cm
photo: Khasaq (Siegfried Klein)
mumok – Museum moderner Kunst Stiftung Ludwig Wien

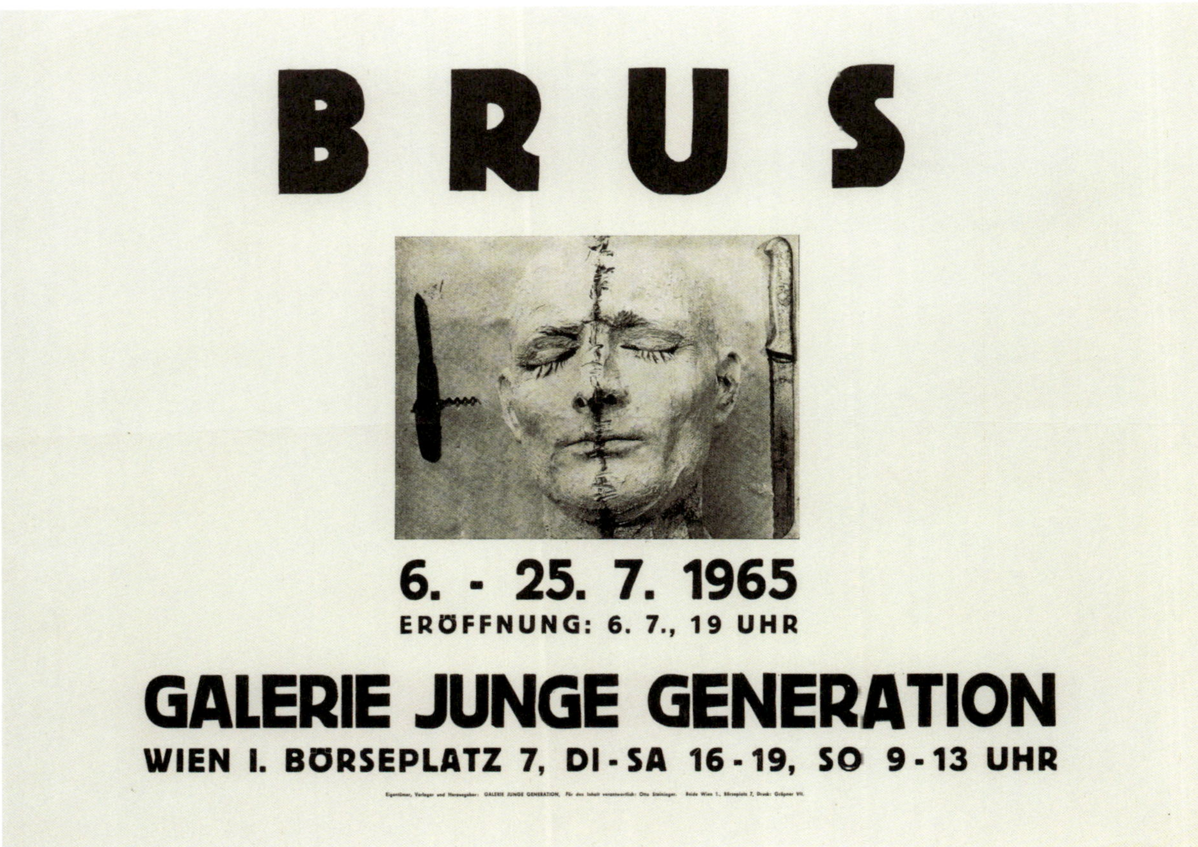

Fig. 227
Günter Brus
Poster for the exhibition by Günter Brus at the Galerie Junge Generation, 1965
Print on paper
43 x 60,5 cm
WAM – Wiener Aktionismus Museum, Vienna, Collection K.

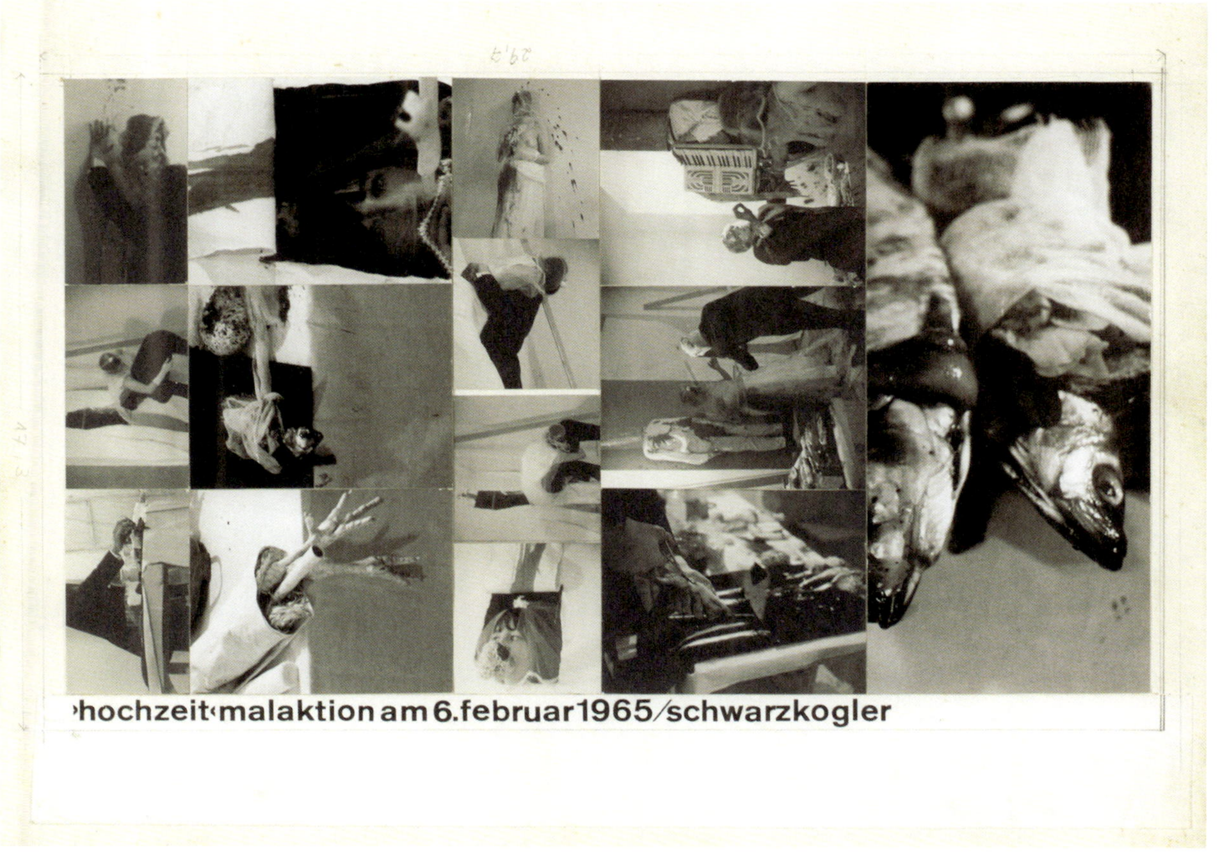

Fig. 228
Rudolf Schwarzkogler
Collage with photographs of the *1. Aktion, Hochzeit* (1st Action, Wedding), around 1965
Photographs, felt pen on cardboard
24 x 32 cm
mumok – Museum moderner Kunst Stiftung Ludwig Wien,
on loan from the Österreichische Ludwig-Stiftung

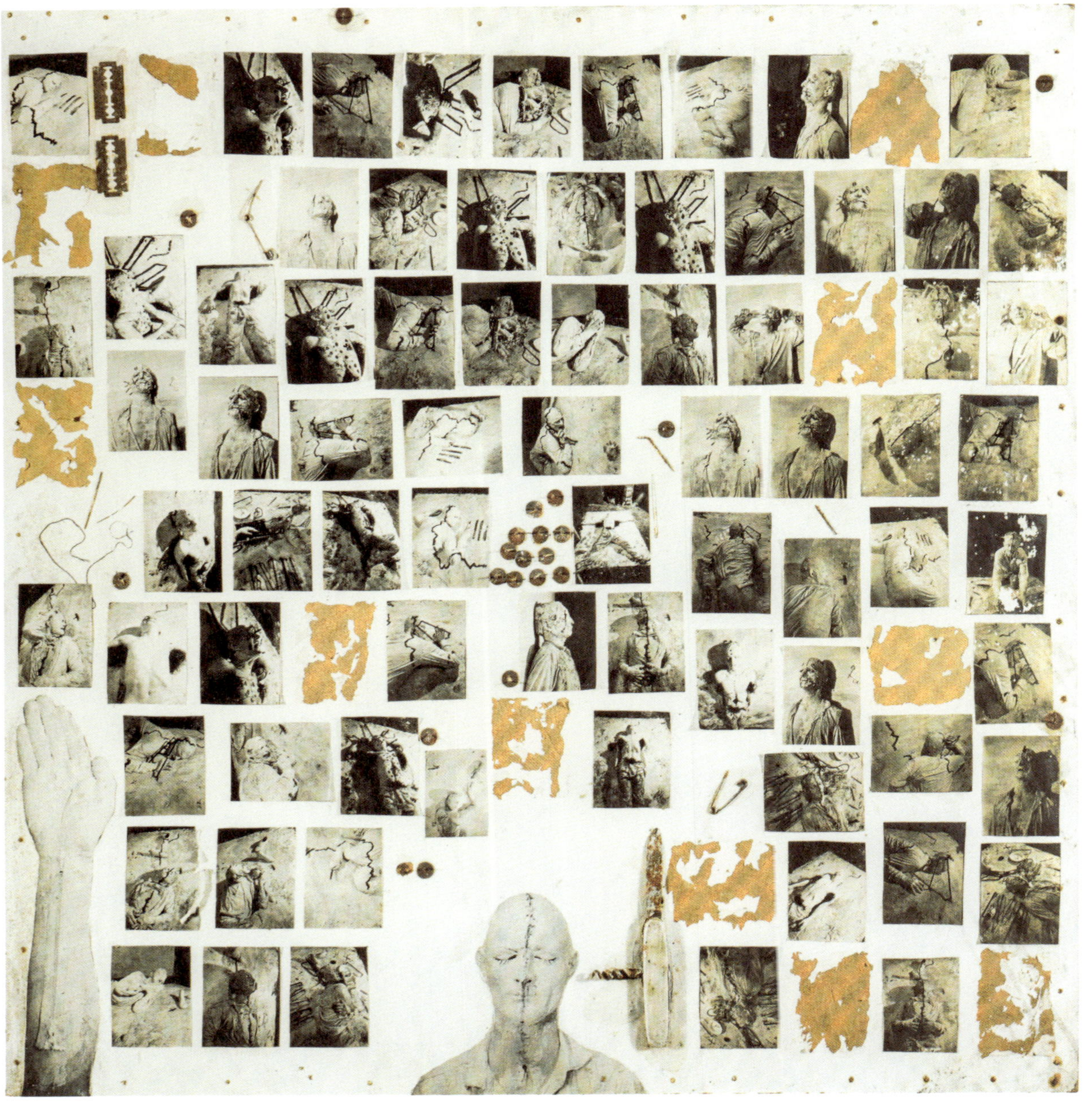

Fig. 229
Günter Brus
Untitled, 1965
Dispersion, photographs, various materials on fibreboard
77 x 77 cm
Scottish National Gallery of Modern Art, Edinburgh

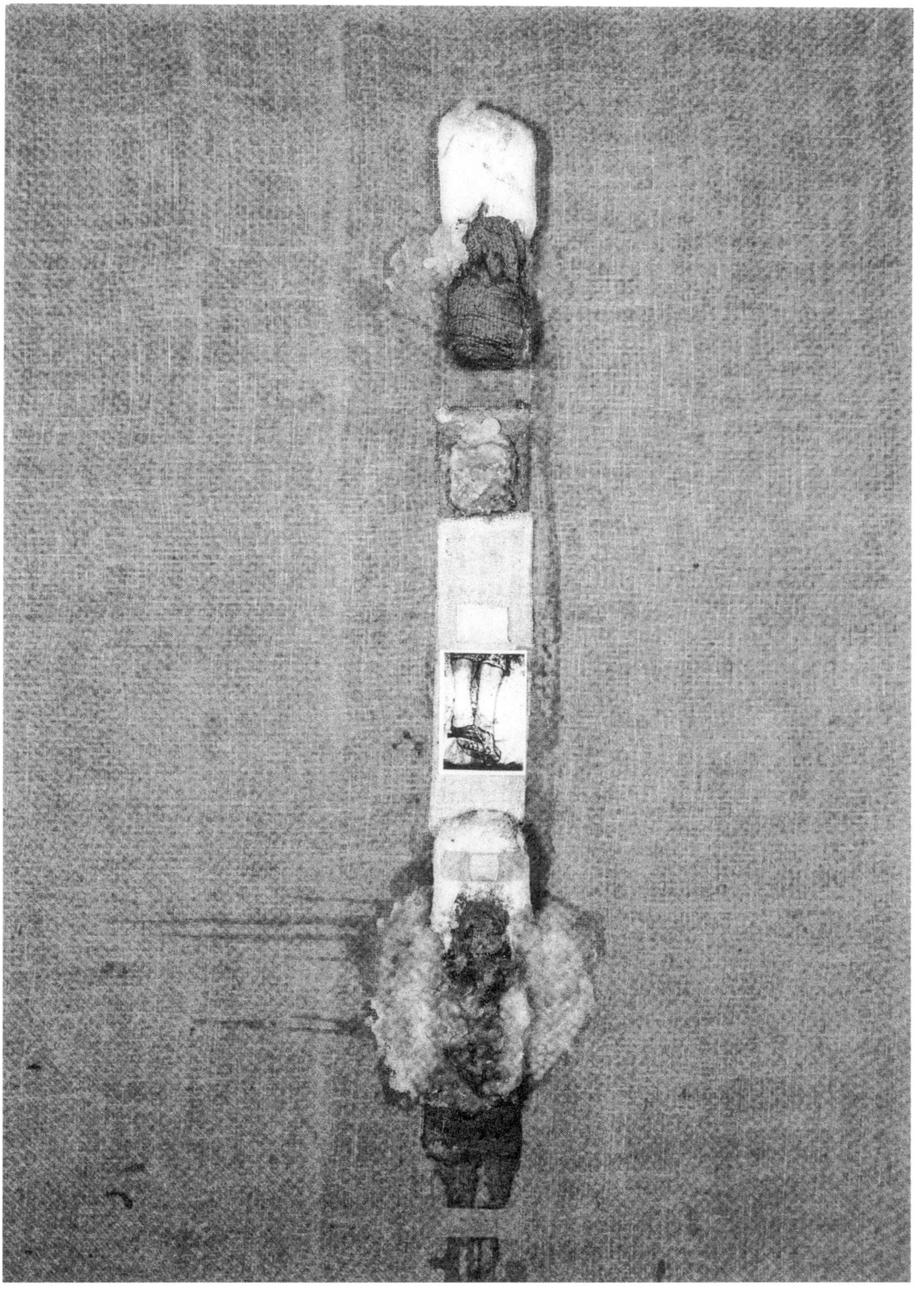

Fig. 230
Hermann Nitsch
Untitled, relict collage, 1964
Blood, chalk, wax, paper, photography, menstrual pad on burlap
105 x 84 cm
Collection Morra, Naples

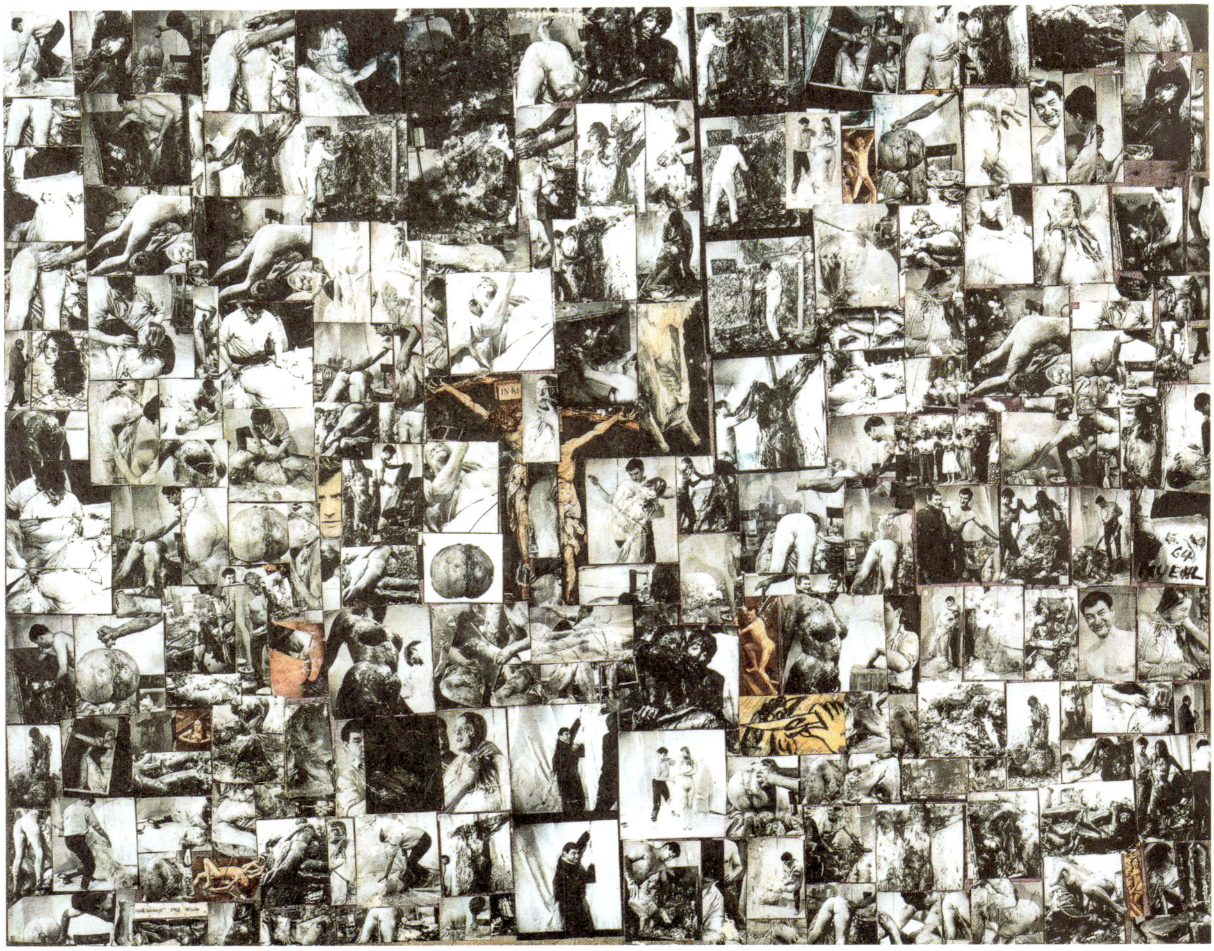

Fig. 231
Otto Muehl
Untitled, 1964
Photographs, magazine cuttings on wood
50 x 65 cm
mumok – Museum moderner Kunst Stiftung Ludwig Wien

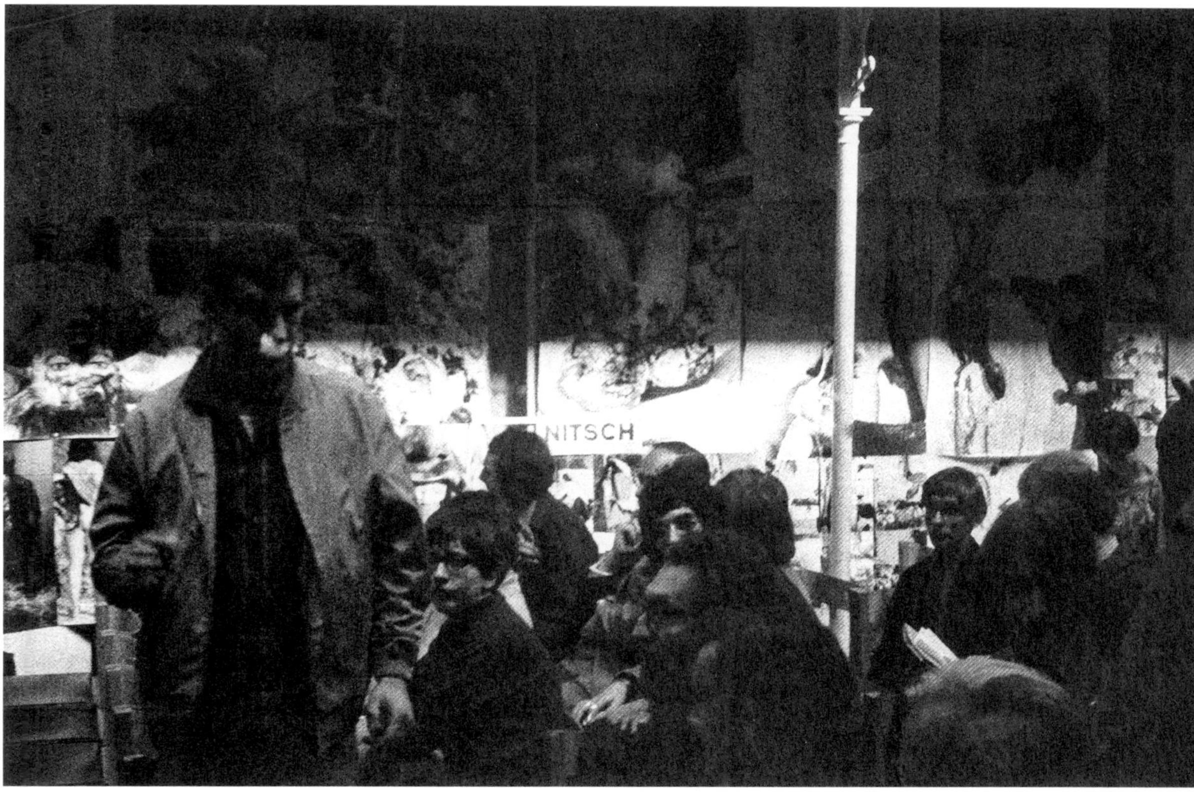

Fig. 232
Otto Muehl in front of the photo wall of the Vienna Actionists
at the *Destruction in Art Symposium* London, 1966
photo: Hanns Sohm

6
These comments on film in Vienna Actionism are based on the text by Gabriele Jutz, 'Vienna Actionism and Film', in: Badura-Triska, Klocker, *Vienna Actionism* (see note 5), pp. 136–157.

7
However, this film by Günter Brus is artistically very interesting, which is why it cannot be described as purely documentary.

8
12th, 15th, 17th, 18th, and 20th Actions. Nitsch himself used the expression Körperaktionen (Body Actions). See, among others, Hermann Nitsch, *Das Orgien Mysterien Theater. Die Partituren aller aufgeführten Aktionen* 1960–1979, vol. 1, Neapel, 1979, p. 118, 148, 228. The term Penisbespülungen (Penis Rinsings) was also used for some of these actions (Nitsch, *Das Orgien Mysterien Theater,* ibid., p. 94 and 97) and Bodygrammatik (Body Grammar) can be found in the literature, too.

Moving Images Between Documentary and Art Film[6]

The situation with film in Vienna Actionism is more complex than with photography, as more differentiations need to be pointed out. "Film is not equal to film" applies even more than "photography is not equal to photography". There are numerous different categories of film and in addition to that each artist had a different approach to this medium, which (like everything in this movement) also changed from the early 1960s to the early 1970s.

It should be emphasised that, as with photography, in film some actions were realised solely with a view to record them in this medium.

The Desire for "Purely Documentary" Films

The simplest category comprises the films whose sole aim was–or at least should be–to capture the sequences of actions. From the very beginning, all four artists had this wish, and as in photography, they first asked (artist) friends and acquaintances to take on this task. Already Nitsch's *1. Malaktion* (1st Painting Action, November 1960) was filmed (and interestingly not photographed) by a colleague from work. Three further ones were both photographed and filmed, but only the film of the *5th Painting Action* has been preserved. In Muehl's case, during his *Material Action No. 3* (in February 1964) an artist friend took moving pictures for the first time. Schwarzkogler also wanted to have his first action filmed, but this failed as the wrong material was bought. Brus here constitutes a special case, because already at his first action the high-profile avant-garde filmmaker Kurt Kren was at work, who did not pursue a documentary approach but had very special artistic intentions. (Fig. 233–238)

In addition, numerous amateur films were subsequently produced that were aesthetically unremarkable and, and, at times, even technically deficient, including some in which the artists themselves operated the equipment. For example, during Brus's *Wiener Spaziergang* (Vienna Walk, 1965, Fig. 73) Muehl and Schwarzkogler passed a super 8 camera to each other. Brus filmed Schwarzkogler's *4th Action* (1965, Fig. 206–208)[7] as well as Muehl's *Gehirnoperation* (Brain Operation, 1965) and *Astronaut* (1965). Schwarzkogler filmed Brus's *Starrkrampf* (Catalepsy, 1965), Muehl Brus's *Selbstverstümmelung* (Self-Mutilation, 1965) and *Transfusion* (1965, Fig. 77–81), as well as Nitsch's *9th Action* (1965, Fig. 21–23). Nitsch himself operated the camera for some of the Body Actions (Fig. 29) that were specifically staged to be photographed and filmed.[8]

Peter Weibel recorded several actions and Oswald Wiener filmed a few as well. Unfortunately not all of these films were preserved.

Parallel to this, in the mid-1960s, with Kurt Kren (from 1964) and Ernst Schmidt jr. (from 1965) two of the internationally most important avant-garde filmmakers of the time from today's perspective joined the circle of the Actionists. Here they identified visual material which fascinated them, and which they took as a basis for their own films. Their work, however, can most certainly not be described as documentary. On the part of the Actionists, this led to great dissatisfaction with the results and the decision to take on more responsibility for the filming of their actions themselves (with the help of cameramen[9]). Such was in particular the case with Muehl and Brus in the years 1967/68. This interest however soon expired and the subsequent films were once again subject to very conventional "purely documentary" modes, even when more and more professional people were operating the camera.[10]

The "neutral" documentary films also include the few recordings that television cameramen made for TV reports that were commissioned but never broadcast.[11]

Works by Avant-Garde Film Makers

The other extreme–the opposite of the amateur or conventional documentary films–were those by important experimental film makers. As the Vienna Actionists were at the forefront of the progressive art at their time it is not surprising that in the artistic fields where they collaborated with others, the leading figures of the avant-garde were willing to work with them, including in the realm of film. In Austria, these were Kurt Kren and Ernst Schmidt jr., who documented actions primarily in 1964 and 1965 as well as a few times afterwards. Aside from Nitsch's *9th Action*, which Kren filmed but the material is lost, the two only filmed actions by Brus and Muehl. This footage provided the basis for works which today are considered as masterpieces of the avant-garde cinema of the 1960s, but they do not document the course of the actions. For this reason, Brus and Muehl did not appreciate them and soon preferred that others do the job.

It would go too far here to describe the action-based films by Kren and Schmidt jr., or even analyse them, not least because, especially in Kren's case, these films cannot be treated uniformly as they cover a broad spectrum of cinematic possibilities and reflect the formal and content-related differences of the respective actions in very interesting ways.

Only a few examples should be highlighted here: In Brus's *1. Aktion, Ana* (1st Action, Ana, 1964), Kren reacted to its still very

9
Above all Helmut Kronberger and Peter C. Fluger.

10
In Austria these included Jörg Dobrovic, Hans Scheugl, Hermann Jauk as well as Günter Orban, Helmut Pold, and Reinhard Pyrker (from the film collective rosa-grün-blau/pink-green-blue) in Germany and Switzerland Merseburger (pseudonym for an unnamed person), Hans Peter Kochenrath, Ed and Irm Sommer, Werner Schulz, Jörg Siegerts, Peter (now Ludwig) Schönherr, Dieter Meier and Karl-Heinz Hein.

11
At the invitation of Wolfgang Kudrnofsky, Nitsch's *24th Action* and Muehl's *UN-Discussion* were recorded in 1967, but their broadcast was prohibited by the then television director Helmut Zilk. In 1968, Gerhard Zacharias filmed an action by Muehl in his apartment on Praterstrasse and in 1970 Peter Gorsen filmed Brus' *Psychodramulett* and Nitsch's *32nd Action* in Kunstraum 1 Munich for Hessischer Rundfunk. These recordings were not broadcast either.

painterly character with a very quick cut. (Fig. 233–238) He did this directly in the camera itself during the recording–a kind of Action Filming analogous to Brus's Action Painting. The result hopelessly overstrains the eyes of the viewers. On the other hand, Kren filmed Brus's action *Selbstverstümmelung* (Self-Mutilation) (1965) in an extremely slow manner, which enables a precise and close up view of the artist's actions with various instruments with which he, among other things, smears a slimy substance onto his body. (Fig. 239–244)

Schmidt jr.'s film of Muehl's action *Bodybuilding* (Fig. 245–250) is a collage that uses the recorded footage twice, namely both in the positive and the negative, and mounts white frames as well as material destroyed by the incidence of light in between. There is also a snatchy soundtrack that has nothing to do with the action, consisting of various music pieces and excerpts from radio interviews. Furthermore, this audio track is not assigned to the image sequences in a fixed order, but randomly matches with the image material in a different way with each copy.[12] Similar in approach to *Bodybuilding* is Schmidt jr.'s handling of his footage taken at the event, *Kunst und Revolution* (Fig. 251–256), that went down in history as a "scandal action". Here, his form of processing the material intends to defuse the radicality of the evening.[13]

Actions on Film, whose Form Was Determined by the Artists Themselves

Dissatisfied with the avant-garde films by Kren and Schmidt jr., which do not present the actions in the desired neutral manner and indeed do not make them comprehensible at all, Brus and Muehl took the filming insofar into their own hands as they entrusted people with it, who did not pursue their own artistic aims. Interestingly, this also led them to develop their own reflections on the medium and its use for transmitting their actions–albeit only during the short period from spring 1967 to spring 1968. They put down their ideas in manifesto-like texts in which they spoke of "Cinema Direct Art" (Fig. 257, 258) as part of their concept of Direct Art, the term they had coined for their work in 1966. It is surprising that the approaches proposed (especially by Muehl) are not that far off from those of avant-garde film of the 1960s: one possibility mentioned is filming long frontal shots from a fixed camera position which are not edited at all–a method that Andy Warhol practiced in the 1960s. As one of his own examples for this Muehl cites his film *Zock Exercises* (1967), shot by cameraman Helmut Kronberger. The second–diametrically opposite–method montages the recorded material. This requires precise, almost squad-wise pre-planning of

12
The reason for this is that Schmidt jr. did not use perforated tape.

13
The purely documentary recordings, which Reinhard Pyrker made that evening, appear to lack tension in comparison.

the action and film sequences and an intensive post-production on the editing table–which is not unlike the methodology used by Kren and Schmidt jr. Here Muehl cites the filming of his action *Wehrertüchtigung* (Military Training, 1967) (Fig. 174–178) as an example, as well as his own film *Grimuid* (1967, Fig. 259–260) which he realised independent of any action.

Brus's trilogy, *Pullover, Osmose, Einatmen und Ausatmen* (Pullover, Osmosis, Breathing In and Breathing Out, 1967, Fig. 261–264), which was conceived exclusively for the film camera, corresponds to Muehl's first method. In this touching work, the artist deals with the elementary life event of childbirth, on the occasion of the imminent arrival of his daughter.

Nitsch was the one who was most sceptical about the medium of film because its screenings correspond to the principles of the proscenium stage, which he wanted to abandon with his new understanding of theatre. Moreover, the engagement of all the senses–one of the most important concerns of his concept of a *Gesamtkunstwerk*–is not possible in film. But he did not want to forego the use of this medium either, although he emphasised, both with regard to photography and film, that his actions should be recorded "as simple as possible –without any antics".[14] That is why he filmed a number of his Body Actions from the mid-1960s himself[15], the results, however, which are now lost, were technically imperfect according to his own records.[16]

Nitsch only developed a different approach to moving images from 1984 onwards, when video became available. Unlike film, this new medium does not necessarily require dark rooms and transcends the proscenium stage format by allowing footage captured from various viewpoints to be presented simultaneously side by side, as is possible with photographs or panel paintings.

Actions Commissioned by Artist Filmmakers for their Own Works

A very special category is constituted by two *films d'auteur* by the German couple Hans-Christoph Stenzel and Ursula Stenzel-Quast who specially commissioned actions from the Viennese artists in order to integrate the images into their own work. In 1968, they asked both, Brus and Muehl, to carry out an action whose visual materials they then used in their film *Die Blumen des Bösen* (The Flowers of Evil), which in turn associatively alludes to Charles Baudelaire's poems.[17] In 1971, for their film, *Komm in meinen dunklen Garten – Ein Requiem* (Come to My Dark Garden–A Requiem), they even developed special actions together with Nitsch that were

14
Nitsch, *Das Orgien Mysterien Theater* (see note 8), pp. 17-18.

15
Not a single film of Nitsch's actions that is subject to avant-garde principles exists, although progressive filmmakers were also involved in his actions, such as Kurt Kren (*9th Action*), Stan Brakhage (*16th Action*) and Peter Kubelka (*31st Action, Immaculate Conception*). However, their footage is considered lost, apart from a few frames that Stan Brakhage incorporated into his film cycle Songs (1964–1969).

16
See Nitsch, *Das Orgien Mysterientheater* (see note 8), p. 118.

17
Baudelaire's poems were read by Gerhard Rühm, who has translated and partly rewritten some of them for this occasion.
In addition to the action for their Film *Die Blumen des Bösen* (The Flowers of Evil), the Stenzels filmed another thematically related action by Brus on the same day and in the same setting, which the artist titled *Strangulation*.

rather unusual for the latter. These were realised over several days in the castle of Collodi and in the vineyards near Vinci.

Filmic Works by the Vienna Actionists That Are Not Based on Actions

It is hardly known that the artists of Vienna Actionism also conceived and sometimes realised cinematic works independently of any actions.

The film *20.September*, created in 1967 as a collaboration between Brus and Kren, constitutes a mixed form, which combines actionist events with moments captured from everyday life. In the context of Brus's Body-Analytical Actions, it thematises defecation. The film begins with scenes taken with a hidden camera showing women who feel unobserved defecating, and ends with close-ups of Brus's own evacuation of the bowels.

While *20.September* still contains a small appearance of the artist, *Intelligenztest* (Intelligence Test, 1969), which was directed by Brus, is not connected to any of his actions. This film was unfortunately lost in 1993. According to the artist, the approximately ten-minute strip, in which Merseburger[18] operated the camera, aimed at the strongest taboo-breaking and shocking images, such as taking out a glass eye, which revealed a red eye socket, or urinating in a glass containing red roses and egg yolks.[19]

After his last action, Brus planned a film in which he wanted to deal with Vienna Actionism in a subjective way—a project for which there were (now lost) sketches, but which was never realised.[20]

Muehl's most important non-action based film is *Grimuid* (1967, Fig. 259, 260), also shot by Kronberger. It records the facial expressions of people from Muehl's circle of friends and acquaintances who look into the camera in a static position over a longer period of time—a concept that is reminiscent of Andy Warhol's *Screen Tests*.

At the beginning of the 1970s, Muehl created a film compilation in which he montaged many of the amateurish super 8 film recordings, shot during his actions up until 1966, together with external footage (such as scenes from Venice). Apparently, the strictly documentary material was too tensionless for him, and interestingly by collaging it, he resorted to the working methods of the avant-garde filmmakers Kren and Schmidt jr., which he had rejected at the time—albeit in a less aesthetically sophisticated manner. [21]

Schwarzkogler did not realise any autonomous films, but he had ideas for *films d'auteur* that went even further than those of his colleagues. The enthusiastic cineaste envisioned making larger films that would focus on historical figures. In his early days, he

18
See note 10.

19
Jutz, "Wiener Aktionismus und Film" (see note 6), p. 157, note 33.

20
Ibid.

21
Muehl even destroyed the unused remains.

thought about an absurdly surreal compilation of motifs from the Austrian Alps, in which the Styrian Archduke Johann would have played a key role. Towards the end of his life, he pursued the idea of making a film about the Bavarian King Ludwig II. He saw the latter as a kindred spirit, with whom he shared the desire for an artistically heightened, intensified perception of sensual reality and an aesthetisation of life in general.[22]

22
Among other things, Ludwig II. had a grotto built that could be illuminated in an intense blue, using electric light, to experience this colour–which was also so close to Schwarzkogler–in an intensified way. A sheet of paper exists of this project, showing sketches of five scenes. See Badura-Triska, Klocker, Vienna Actionism (see note 5), Fig. 168.

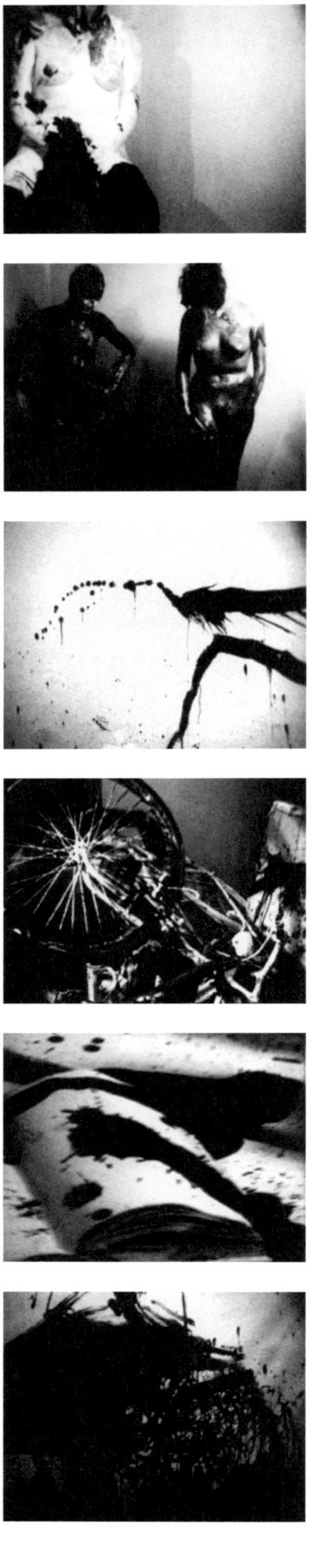

Fig. 233–238
Kurt Kren
8/64 Ana, 1964
16mm, b/w, silent
2 min 40 secs.

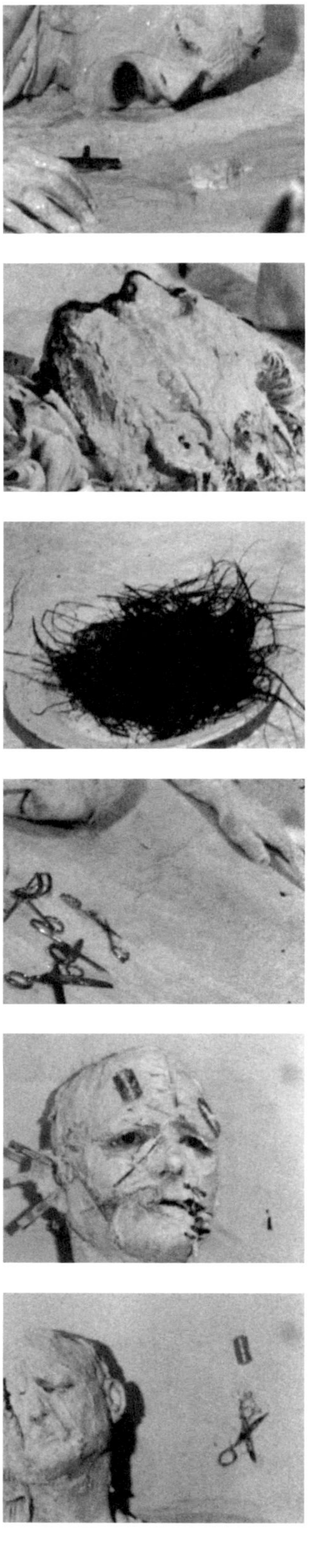

Fig. 239–244
Kurt Kren
10/65 Selbstverstümmelung
(Self-Mutilation), 1965
16mm, b/w, silent
5 min 19 secs.

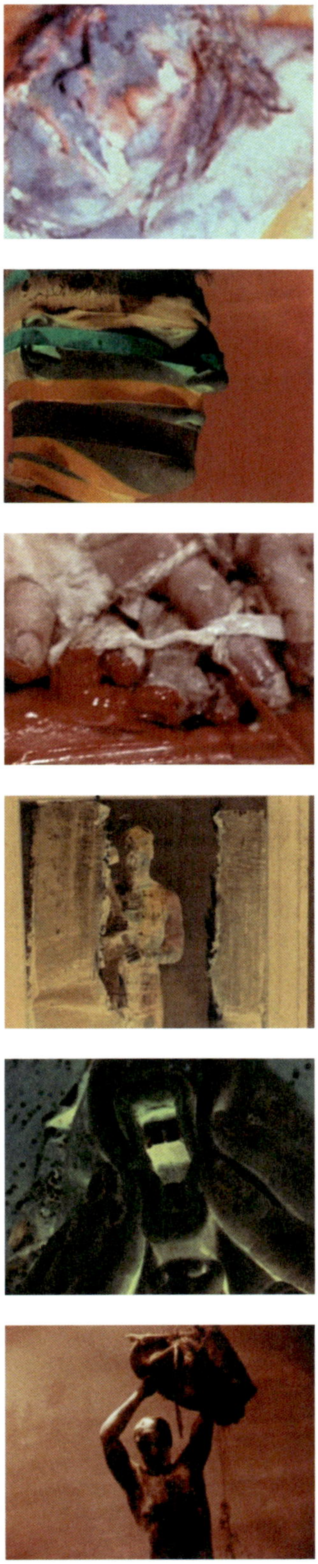

Fig. 245–250
Ernst Schmidt jr.
Bodybuilding, 1965/1966
16mm, colour, sound
9 min

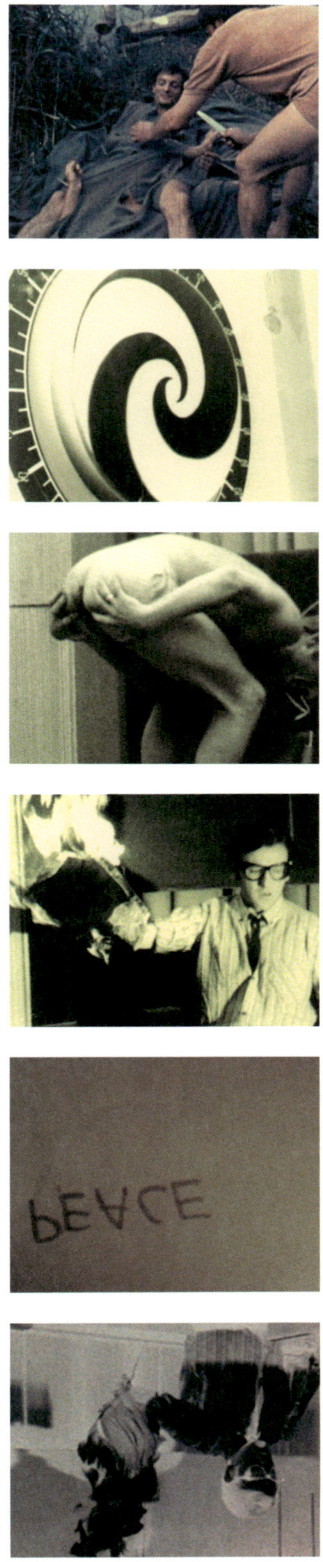

Fig. 251–256
Ernst Schmidt jr.
Kunst und Revolution
(Art and Revolution), 1968
16mm, colour, b/w, silent
2 min

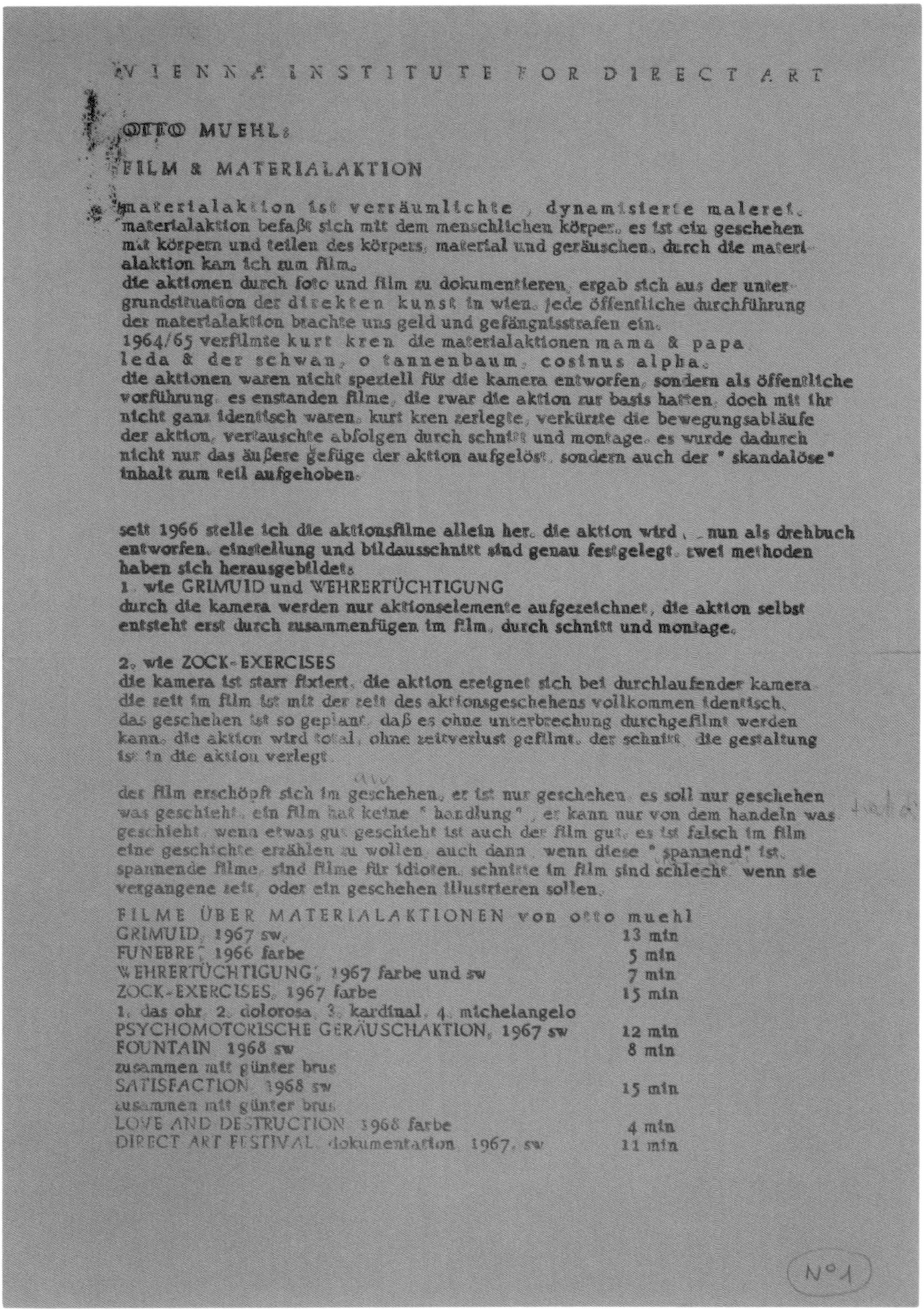

VIENNA INSTITUTE FOR DIRECT ART

OTTO MUEHL:

FILM & MATERIALAKTION

materialaktion ist verräumlichte , dynamisierte malerei. materialaktion befaßt sich mit dem menschlichen körper. es ist ein geschehen mit körpern und teilen des körpers, material und geräuschen. durch die materialaktion kam ich zum film.
die aktionen durch foto und film zu dokumentieren, ergab sich aus der untergrundsituation der direkten kunst in wien. jede öffentliche durchführung der materialaktion brachte uns geld und gefängnisstrafen ein.
1964/65 verfilmte kurt kren die materialaktionen mama & papa leda & der schwan, o tannenbaum, cosinus alpha.
die aktionen waren nicht speziell für die kamera entworfen, sondern als öffentliche vorführung. es enstanden filme, die zwar die aktion zur basis hatten, doch mit ihr nicht ganz identisch waren. kurt kren zerlegte, verkürzte die bewegungsabläufe der aktion, vertauschte abfolgen durch schnitt und montage. es wurde dadurch nicht nur das äußere gefüge der aktion aufgelöst, sondern auch der " skandalöse" inhalt zum teil aufgehoben.

seit 1966 stelle ich die aktionsfilme allein her. die aktion wird , nun als drehbuch entworfen. einstellung und bildausschnitt sind genau festgelegt. zwei methoden haben sich herausgebildet:
1. wie GRIMUID und WEHRERTÜCHTIGUNG
durch die kamera werden nur aktionselemente aufgezeichnet, die aktion selbst entsteht erst durch zusammenfügen im film, durch schnitt und montage.

2. wie ZOCK-EXERCISES
die kamera ist starr fixiert. die aktion ereignet sich bei durchlaufender kamera. die zeit im film ist mit der zeit des aktionsgeschehens vollkommen identisch. das geschehen ist so geplant, daß es ohne unterbrechung durchgefilmt werden kann. die aktion wird total, ohne zeitverlust gefilmt. der schnitt, die gestaltung ist in die aktion verlegt.

der film erschöpft sich im geschehen, er ist nur geschehen. es soll nur geschehen was geschieht. ein film hat keine " handlung" , er kann nur von dem handeln was geschieht. wenn etwas gut geschieht ist auch der film gut. es ist falsch im film eine geschichte erzählen zu wollen, auch dann , wenn diese " spannend" ist. spannende filme, sind filme für idioten. schnitte im film sind schlecht, wenn sie vergangene zeit, oder ein geschehen illustrieren sollen.

FILME ÜBER MATERIALAKTIONEN von otto muehl

GRIMUID, 1967 sw. — 13 min
FUNEBRE, 1966 farbe — 5 min
WEHRERTÜCHTIGUNG, 1967 farbe und sw — 7 min
ZOCK-EXERCISES, 1967 farbe — 15 min
1. das ohr, 2. dolorosa, 3. kardinal, 4. michelangelo
PSYCHOMOTORISCHE GERÄUSCHAKTION, 1967 sw — 12 min
FOUNTAIN, 1968 sw — 8 min
zusammen mit günter brus
SATISFACTION, 1968 sw — 15 min
zusammen mit günter brus
LOVE AND DESTRUCTION, 1968 farbe — 4 min
DIRECT ART FESTIVAL, dokumentation, 1967, sw — 11 min

N°1

Fig. 257
Otto Muehl
Flyer *Film und Materialaktion* (Film and Materialaction), 1968
Matrix print
29,7 x 21 cm
mumok – Museum moderner Kunst Stiftung Ludwig Wien

V I E N N A   D I R E C T   A R T

Günter Brus & Otto Muehl bringen im DIRECT ART FESTIVAL 1967 ihre bisher entwickelten Formen Direkter Kunst zur Darstellung.
Direkte Kunst unterscheidet sich deutlich vom happening amerikanisch-deutscher Prägung.
Wir glauben, daß das WIENER INSTITUT FÜR DIREKTE KUNST Aktionsformen hervorgebracht hat, wie sie sonst nirgends in der Welt existieren. Zu nennen sind:

1. Die PSYCHO-MOTORISCHE GERÄUSCHAKTION, die von B&M gemeinsam entwickelt wurde.
   Sie benützt den menschlichen Körper als bevorzugtes Ausdrucksmittel und aktiviert den Bewegungsmechanismus seiner Muskulatur und seiner Stimmbänder.
2. Die MATERIALAKTION, entwickelt von Otto Muehl.
   Die Behandlung nackter Körper mit Lebensmittel.
3. Das ORGIEN-MYSTERIEN-THEATER von Hermann NITSCH Nitsch. Es ist die Rückfuhrung des Theaters zu seinen Grund-Elementen
4. Die SELBSTVERSTÜMMELUNG von Günter Brus.
   Der eigene Körper als Aktions-Objekt (Selbst-Destruction)
5. Das CINEMA DIRECT ART
   Der Film als Konservierungsmittel von Direkter Kunst. Aktionen für den Film konstruiert.
   Muehl (8 Direct-Art-Filme, 16mm, Gesamt 45min)
   Brus (4 Direct-Art-Filme, 16mm, Gesamt 20 min)

Direkte Kunst und das happening entwickelte sich ausschließlich aus der Malerei. Später stießen auch Musiker dazu. Die Literaten konnten sich bis heute nicht von Wort und Text lösen.
Direkte Kunst lehnt jeden Versuch ab, Theaterstücke, Filme, Texte, Vernissagen oder Musikvorführungen, mit happening-artigen Einlagen aufzupolieren.
Direkte Kunst distanziert sich von jeder Art besoffener Party-Genialität.
Direkte Kunst distanziert sich von jeder Art Kunstausübung, die sich mit dem Herstellen von Bildern, Bildwerken, Skulpturen, Texten, Romanen, Filmen, Theaterstücken, Architektur-Schöpfungen, selbst mit noch so fortschrittlichen Materialien, und Musikpartituren allen Ernstes beschäftigt.

Fig. 258
Günter Brus, Otto Muehl
Flyer *Vienna Direct Art*, 1967
Matrix print
29,7 x 21 cm
mumok – Museum moderner Kunst Stiftung Ludwig Wien

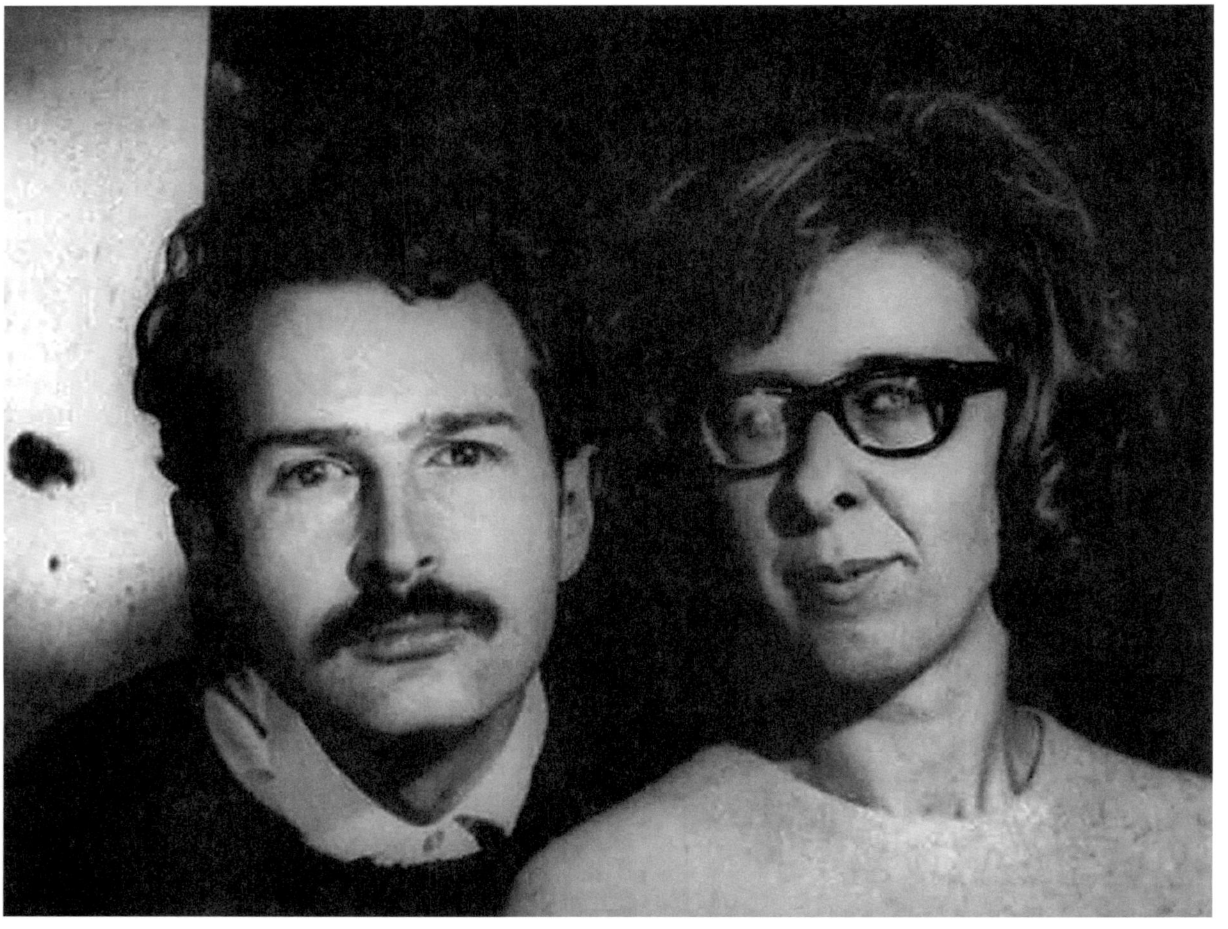

Fig. 259, 260
Otto Muehl
Grimuid, January till March 1967
16 mm, b/w, silent, 5 min, 23 secs.
Camera: Helmut Kronberger
with: Walter Ebner, Jörg Dobrovich, Erich Fischer, Britta Fleischmann, Dieter Haupt, Robert Klemmer, Otto Kobalek, Julius Mende, Hermann Nitsch, Peter Weibel, Oswald Wiener, Gottfried Schlemmer

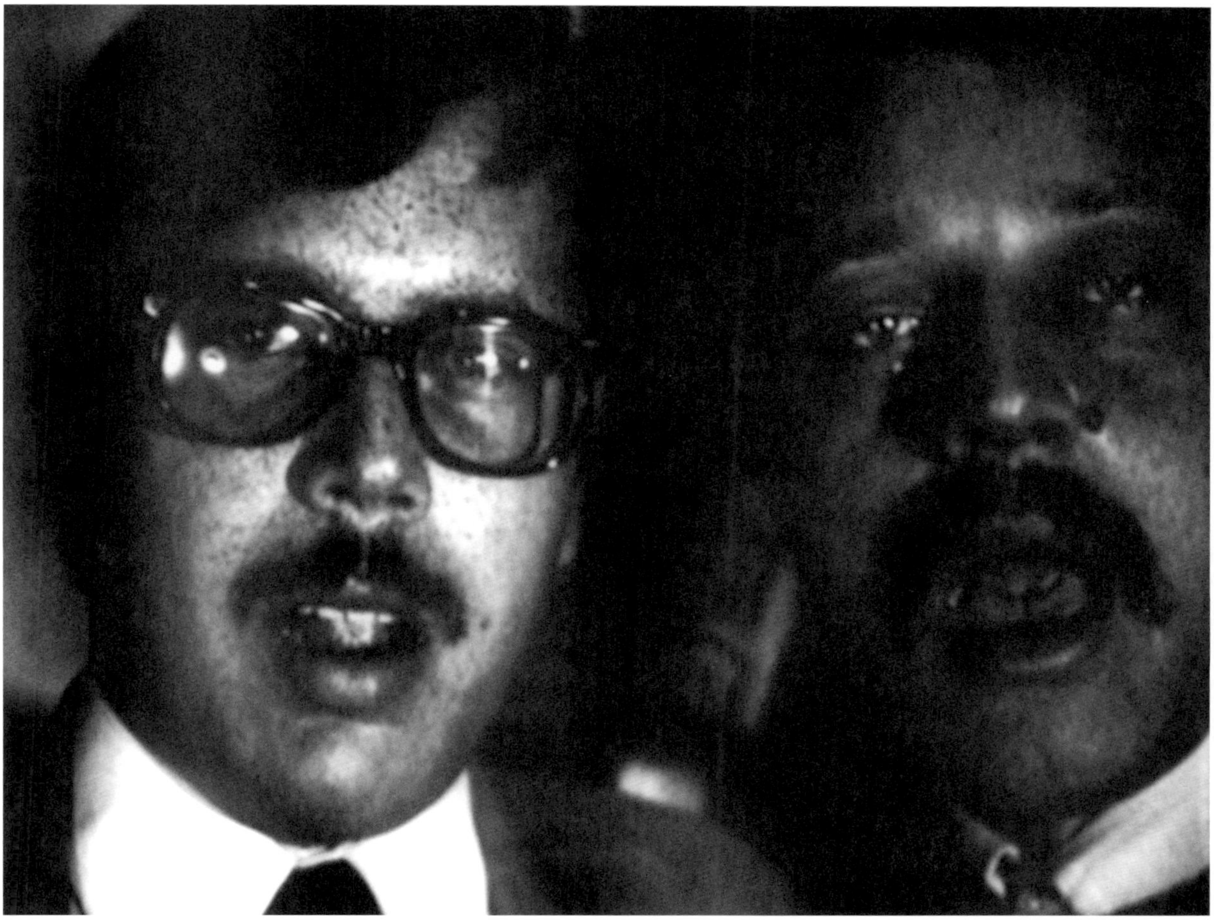

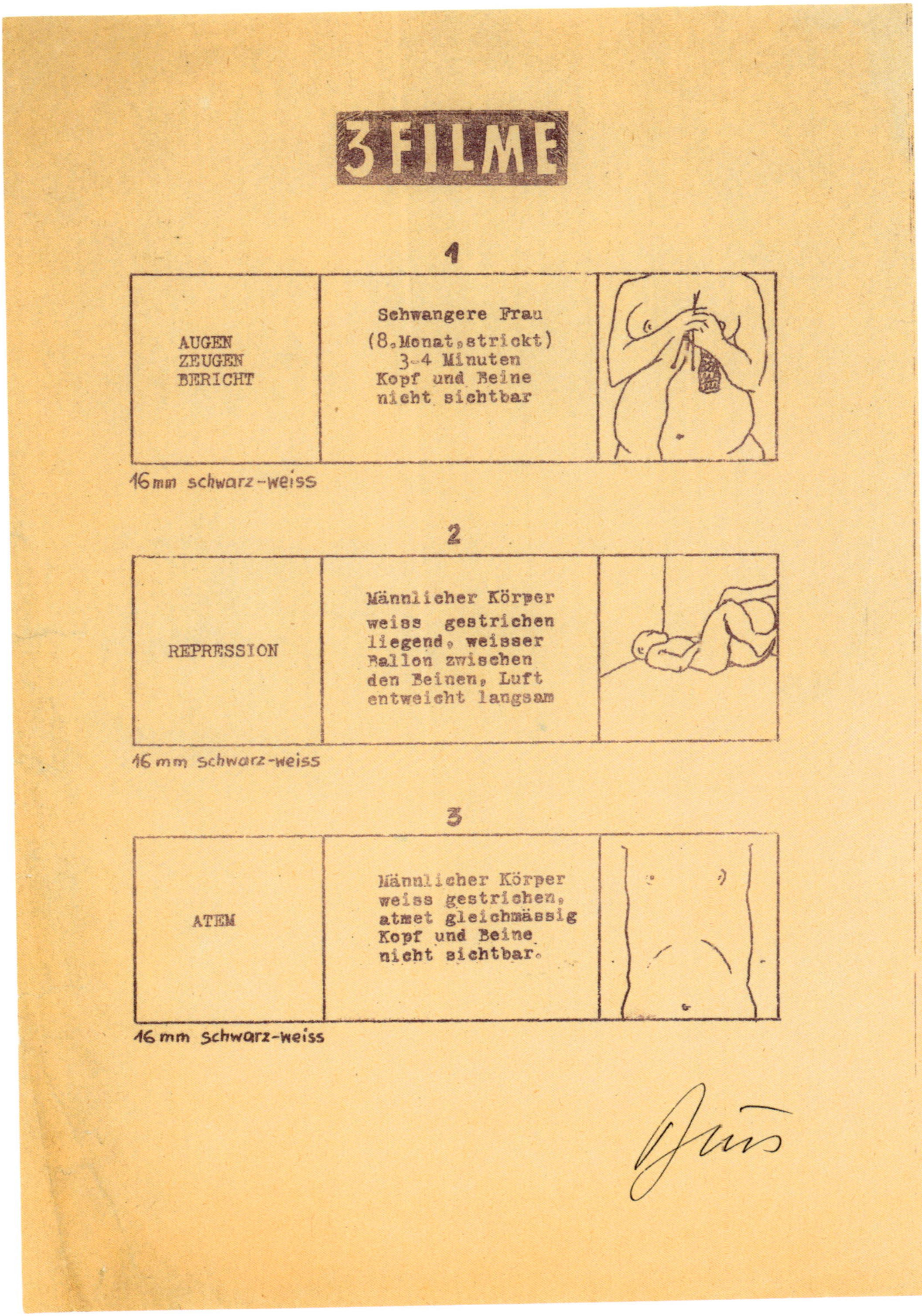

3 FILME

1

AUGEN ZEUGEN BERICHT	Schwangere Frau (8. Monat, strickt) 3-4 Minuten Kopf und Beine nicht sichtbar	

16 mm schwarz-weiss

2

REPRESSION	Männlicher Körper weiss gestrichen liegend, weisser Ballon zwischen den Beinen, Luft entweicht langsam	

16 mm schwarz-weiss

3

ATEM	Männlicher Körper weiss gestrichen, atmet gleichmässig Kopf und Beine nicht sichtbar.	

16 mm schwarz-weiss

Brus

Fig. 261
Günter Brus
Flyer *3 Filme* (3 Films), 1967
Matrix print
29,7 x 21 cm
WAM – Wiener Aktionismus Museum, Vienna, Collection K.

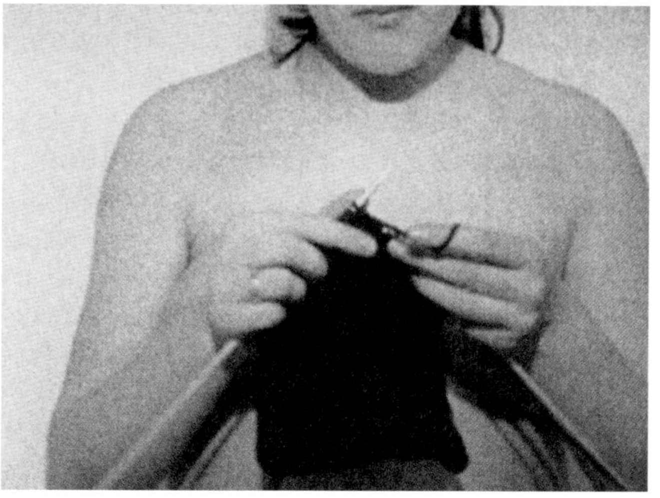

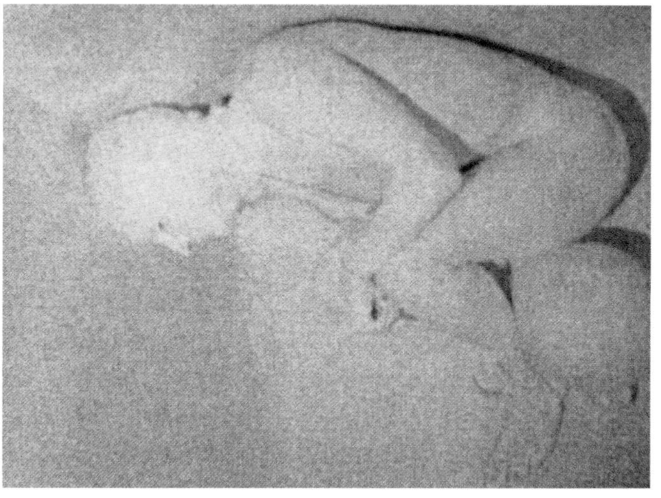

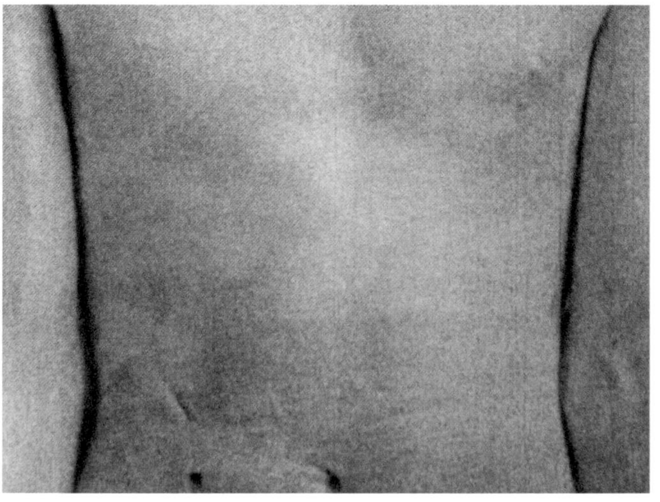

Fig. 262
Günter Brus
Pullover
February/March 1967
16 mm, b/w silent, 2 min, 4 secs.
Camera: Helmut Kronberger
with: Anna Brus

Fig. 263
Günter Brus
Osmose
February/March 1967
16 mm, b/w, silent,
2 min
Camera: Helmut Kronberger

Fig. 264
Günter Brus
Einatmen und Ausatmen
(Breathing In and Breathing Out)
February/March 1967
16 mm, b/w, silent,
2 min, 36 secs.
Camera: Helmut Kronberger

Lisa Moravec

THE ART OF PERFORMING: LOOKING BACK AT VIENNA ACTIONISM FROM THE PERSPECTIVE OF THE 2000S

The tension between art and society, which the Vienna Actionist digested through their actions in their studios, apartments and public places in the 1960s, increasingly functions within the neo-liberal culture industry in the twenty-first century. Since the early 2010s, artistic performances are regarded an integral part of the public and exhibition programs of cultural institutions. Visual artists, but also musicians and dancers explicitly produce performances for museums and galleries, which in turn simultaneously draw attention to the works and exhibitions on display. Today, the question of what makes such performances aesthetically interesting, or politically relevant, often takes a back seat. With the Vienna Actionists it was the other way around.

In the late 1960s, the institutionalised art scene was still very small in Vienna. The Museum des 20. Jahrhunderts—which had just opened in 1962, the very same year Hermann Nitsch's first action took place—paid no attention to such performative contemporary art practices. Even in the gallery scene, only few public spaces offered the four artists a forum to occasionally present their work. Günter Brus, Otto Muehl, Hermann Nitsch, and Rudolf Schwarzkogler developed their performative art practices under these circumstances: With their radical actions and daring display of human and animal bodies (often including blood), they reveal the limits and possibilities of artistic expression conveyed through the body and thereby pushed aesthetic boundaries. Today, their work does not only provide insights into the social disposition and artistic landscape in post-war Austria, but it also forms part of the historical foundation of what is today referred to as performance in English and German-speaking contexts.

The international (Western) establishment of performance in the twenty-first century reflects the increasing dissolution of specific artistic practices and disciplines. Since the middle of the twentieth-century, various neo-avantgardist, theoretical and artistic approaches have made artistic work tangible in space. The development of the performative and physical approach of the Vienna Actionists falls into this moment of time. But why are their works called *Aktionen*, and why are they themselves called Vienna Actionists?

Painting und Actionism

In retrospect, two dominant Western art movements in the post-war period can be identified as international points of reference for the Vienna Actionists. Two competing art critics in the US opened up a critical discourse about Abstract Expressionism. The formalist Clement Greenberg particularly supported Jackson Pollock, who made drip paintings by pouring or dripping paint onto the canvas lying on the floor. In contrast, the Marxist critic Harald Rosenberg understood the canvas as an "arena in which to act" and coined the term *Action Painting* to describe a politically motivated attitude amongst the artists that he supported.[1]

Parallel to this theoretical approach to painting, which considered the body as an active part, performative art movements started to emerge in the visual arts in the late 1950s. In North America, Great Britain and Germany, event-based art gave way to Happenings, Fluxus, Environments, Destruction in Art, Body Art, and Performance Art. These art forms broke with established and object-based concepts of art (drawing, painting, sculpture) and operated alongside media art (photography, film, video), which developed concurrently but at a slower pace. Instead of focusing on a traditionally produced "work of art", the artists who worked performatively with their bodies drew attention to the relation between embodiment and the social events happening around art events. Like abstract painting tested the boundaries of the medium of painting, such kinesthetic stagings of "art" (including those of the Vienna Actionists) addressed human ideals of freedom by exploring novel body-based possibilities for artistic expression.

The naturalised English terms of Happening or Body Art still manifest today that America increasingly developed into a cultural power centre in the 1950s and 1960s. The performative works of the Vienna Actionists, to which they themselves referred as *actions*, developed at the interface of these, back then new, performative art movements and Abstract Expressionism. They developed their actions through a critical examination of the novel possibilities of painting. Peter Weibel, an artist and writer working in the midst of Brus, Muehl, Nitsch, and Schwarzkogler, took up the term action in 1970, which all these artists had previously used in the 1960s, to describe their loose association as *Vienna Actionism*.[2]

The Four Vienna Actionists and Their Actions

The actions of the four men make visible the differences between the concrete socio-political situation and their artistic concerns. The legacy of the politicians who were in office during the Nazi era, the primacy of the Catholic Church, and the associated social problems were embodied in the artistic activities of the Actionists. Without any fear of loss or criticism, they questioned the political, aesthetic, and moral (especially in relation to sexual norms) values of the re-emerging bourgeois life after World War II in Austria with a powerful and psychologically charged urgency.

1
Harald Rosenberg, *The American Action Painters*, in: ARTnews, December 1952, p. 22–50.

2
Danièle Roussel, *Der Wiener Aktionismus und die Österreicher: Gespräche*, Klagenfurt (Ritte Verlag), 1995, p. 23 und 131. Also see weibel/export (ed.), *wien. bildkompendium wiener aktionismus und film*, Frankfurt am Main (Kohkunstverlag), 1970.

3
See in this book p. 145, note 15

Based on a physically mediated and socially situated questioning of the subject, the Vienna Actionists provocatively staged human and (parts of) animal bodies.

Muehl, about ten years older than the other three artists, called his early performative works *Materialaktionen* (Material Actions). He worked with his own body, as well as with those of women, other men, and animals. His performative works, such as his action *Scheißkerl* (Shithead, 1969), address sexual and other social taboos of the time from his male perspective. Muehl's rebellion against bourgeois norms in the 1960s later transformed into his artistically lived out form of utopia: in the AA-Commune (*Aktions-analytische Kommune*, Action-Analytical Commune)[3], or later also called AAO (*Aktionsanalytische Organisation*, Action-Analytical Organisation), his ideas about ways of living together degenerated, to such an extent, that he was convicted in court of several sexual incidents that occurred within this commune.

While interpersonal hierarchies and sexual impulses steered many of Muehl's actions, Nitsch created his own form of *Gesamtkunstwerk*. He started to conceptualise it theoretically in 1957 while still studying art. The strong emotions that his work with dead animals, bodily fluids and living human bodies evoked are typical of his aesthetic approach. Until his death in 2022, he staged theatrical performances of the *Orgien Mysterien Theater* (Theatre of Orgies and Mysteries), which expanded his early actions into a recurring and evolving narrative performed with larger groups as art rituals.

The performative practice of Brus emerged closely interwoven with the combination of art and life in Muehl's and Nitsch's actions. Although the critical examination of his own body was his focus, he also performed together with his wife Anna and on several occasions with other artists, amongst them Muehl. In an extreme and almost self-destructive way, he pushed the material means of his body, its functions and possible experiences to painful limits. While the skin initially functioned as a surface in Brus' practice to apply paint onto it, like a canvas, in the second half of the 1960s, it became a transformable interface that shows the connection between his inner emotional state and external actions. After his physically most extreme performance, *Zerreißprobe* (Stress Test, Fig. 106), he decided to stop performing actions in 1970.

Due to his early death, Schwarzkogler's artistic exploration of physically carried out actions in real space was even more short-lived than it was with Brus. Due to his shyness, his six actions always took place without a public audience. He performed his first ritual-like action, *Hochzeit* (Wedding, 1965, Fig. 194–198), in front of the other Actionists together with Anna Brus (as a bride), dead fish and various other, mostly organic materials. In the last years before his premature death, his practice became reduced to the development of concepts, focused on bodily perception. The artist died at the age of 28, after falling out of the window of his apartment; what caused this incident remains unclear until today.

The individual artistic approaches of the four Actionists were based on questioning the societal role of the artist. As Peter Weibel wrote about the works of Muehl and Brus in his essay, *On the Possibilities of Non-Affirmative Art*, "the artist, who is interested in freedom" dismantles societal ideologies "by denying it [art] the place of circulation" and regards artistic "material as a carrier of ideas".[4] The place of circulation that Weibel refers to here addresses the fact that the Actionists did not produce their work for a market. Since such performative works, unlike art objects, could not be sold, they could not be based on market prices; instead they were aesthetically oriented to the international trend to present performative works of art.

Although the Vienna Actionists focused primarily on developing their own work with human and animal bodies, they knew from a certain point onwards what was happening in international art scenes. Their participation in *Gustav Metzger's Destruction in Art Symposium* in London in 1966 brought them into direct contact with colleagues who also worked performatively Nitsch was also in contact with Jonas Mekas, Yoko Ono and Geoffrey Hendricks through his two trips to New York where he carried out his *27th Action* in 1968 in the courtyard of the now iconic Judson Church. When he and Brus travelled together to New York later, in 1974, they were able to consolidate their relationship with Al Hansen whom they had previously befriended together in London.[5]

Already in the late 1960s, the Vienna Actionists were considered controversial figures and met with rejection as they addressed social issues with their work. Although they operated in the aesthetic field of art, they–unlike other radical artists of subsequent generations–were faced with serious legislative counter reactions. The event *Kunst und Revolution* (Art and Revolution, Fig. 97, 98, 179, 180) led to the arrest and conviction of Brus and Muehl in 1968, and drastically changed the course of their biographies. It took several decades until they became culturally distinguished personalities.

4
Weibel, Peter, 'Von den Möglichkeiten einer Nicht-Affirmativen Kunst' (1965), *in: Kritik der Kunst, Kunst der Kritik: Es says& I say*, Wien/München (Jugend und Volk), 1973, pp. 34–49, here p. 38. Translation by the author.

5
See *Winterreise: From Asolo to New York and Vice Versa*, 1974, Verona (Archive F. Conz), 2007.

6
Conversation with
Florian Reither, 15 September 2023.

Actionist Positions in Art Since the 2000s

Similar to how the work of the Vienna Actionists already exposed a socially entrenched conservatism in Austria in the mid-twentieth-century, the exhibition of their work has become increasingly entangled with moral concerns since the 2010s. The cancel culture movement and the prevailing identity politics in the culture industry have reignited a regressive form of political correctness and social standardisation against which the Actionists already fought under the given circumstances in the 1960s. Despite the public's enduring affective reactions to the poignant aesthetics of the work of Brus, Muehl, Nitsch and Schwarzkogler, which they implemented with great urgency in the Austrian cultural landscape in the 1960s, the work of the Vienna Actionists continues to influence subsequent generations of artists.

Today, the formation of four men to the "artistic organism" Gelitin (originally Gelatin, founded in 1993) represents one of the most direct points of reference to the Vienna Actionists.[6] Critical of the oversaturated supply and overproduction of contemporary art, Gelitin's live performances, performative paintings and sculptural works embody a self-irony that intervenes in today's increasingly domesticated art world. Like the Vienna Actionists addressed social taboos, Gelitin is often confronted with commentaries about the provocative nature of their work as it is often so charged with satire that it humorously drags actions from everyday life into the realm of the absurd. Many of their performances are sexually connotated or arise in dialogue with the objects of other artists. For example, following an invitation of the British artist Sarah Lucas, Gelitin placed four living chickens into her exhibition NOB at the Vienna Secession in 2013.

The performances of the German artist Sophia Süßmilch (born 1983) are also influenced by the artistic legacy of the Vienna Actionists through her critical examination of it. In addition to her painting (in which she creates fantastic creatures and living environments on white canvas) and her forthright feminist criticism of men's patriarchal behaviour (which she propagates in virtual social media spaces), she often creates humorously staged actionist solo and group performances. These involve her own naked body, as well as those of other people, amongst them that of her mother. The intuition underlying her visual body performances reminds us that the actions of the Vienna Actionists were perceived as provocative precisely because the artists dared to put human body (parts) into action, regardless of preexisting artistic and accepted social norms. Süßmilch's approach to performance however differs

7
Conversation with Sophia Süßmilch, 13 September 2023.

8
Conversation with Xenia Lesniewski, 12 September 2023.

9
Conversation with Matthias Mollner, 15 August 2023.

from that of the Vienna Actionists, in the sense, that bodily performances function as a feminist means of expression in her practice.[7]

In a similar vein to the actionist performances of Sophia Süßmilch, the works of Xenia Lesniewski (born 1985) address themechanisms of consumer society in a playful manner. Her performative appearances, paintings, and installations explore these themes. A recurring focus of her work lies on the commodification and social representation of women. The connection between art and life in the works of the Vienna Actionists have, from an early age on, shaped Lesniewski's approach. Her fascination for Brus' actions motivated her to move to Vienna to study at the University of Applied Arts Vienna. Her interest in the self-destructive aesthetics of Brus' work is reflected in her preoccupation with different performative forms of image destruction which aims at, according to her, functioning both within, but also outside the value system of the art world.[8] Like Gelitin, Lesniewski also works in a collective. In 2014, she co-founded Club Fortuna, which now comprises of Nana Mandl, Verena Preininger, and Sarah Sternat.

In contrast to the two women and Gelitin, the Austrian Matthias Mollner (born 1984) creates performances and art objects that claim a high degree of autonomy.[9] His aesthetic approach aligns with that of the Vienna Actionists as he used his body as material and medium. In his performative works, Mollner also often integrates living animals (pigs and worms) and other organic materials (such as soil and plants). He has performed in a wide variety of urban spaces and cultural institutions, including Günther Domenig's deconstructive *Steinhaus*, in which he–similar to Brus in his actions–also often appeared (almost entirely) naked in front of an audience in the middle of the contorted architecture. The architectural spaces in which Mollner has presented his performances however neither define his approach, nor the themes that he takes up in them; instead, they productively inform his work and open up opportunities for him to further his aesthetic examination of the relationship between the human body and its socio-ecological environment.

Aesthetic Idiosyncrasy

Parallels can be drawn to the Vienna Actionists as the performances of these younger protagonists all address the role of art in society through their body-based critical engagement with it. The cultural self-reflexivity of their approaches and their direct engagements with the work of the Vienna Actionists enables us to identify similarities and differences between their work and that of Brus, Muehl, Nitsch and Schwarzkogler from the 1960s. As the performances of Gelitin, Süßmilch, Lesniewski, and Mollner similarly exhibit idiosyncratic aesthetic qualities, they do not directly play into the hands of the dominating neoliberal logic of the culture industry, in which performances are often merely programmed to function as another spectacular live event.

To get a clearer picture of what lies behind the inflationary term of performance within the visual arts today, it is helpful to remember the revolutionary aesthetics of the Vienna Actionists and the social context within which they showed their works. The authenticity, directness, and urgency of their actions continue to open up historical points of reference, until now, and spark the question of what makes "good" art. A critical examination of their already historical work, compared to the current situation of performative art, prompts reflections on how artists can actively perform in the culture industry today, without losing their bodily consciousness and giving up on their political stance; and this at a time when performative practices have already been domesticated as an interdisciplinarily operating category of art.

Eva Badura-Triska/Julia Moebus-Puck

ARTISTS' BIOGRAPHIES

Günter Brus

1938	Born in Ardning in Styria
1954 – 58	Studies at the Graz School of Applied Arts
1958	Move to Vienna. Enrolement at the Academy (today University) of Applied Arts, which he soon left again
1961	Military service
1964	1st Action *Ana*
1965	*Vienna Walk* action
1966	Participation in the *Destruction in Art Symposium* in London
1967	*Direct Art* Festival, Vienna (together with Otto Muehl)
1968	Participation in the event *Art and Revolution* in Lecture Hall 1 of the Vienna University, which led to a sentence of six months in prison
1969	Escape to Berlin
1970	Last action *Zerreißprobe* (Stress Test) at Aktionsraum 1 in Munich
1972	Participation in documenta 5
1979	Return to Graz, after his prison sentence was commuted to a fine
1996	Grand Austrian State Prize for Fine Arts
2004	Oskar Kokoschka Prize
2008	Foundation of the BRUSEUM in Graz
2023	Awarded the Ring of Honour of the City of Graz
2024	Dies in Graz

Otto Muehl

1925	Born in Grodnau in Burgenland
1944	Enlisted in the German army
1952	Completion of studies for a teaching degree in German and history begun in 1948 and start of art education studies at the Academy of Fine Arts Vienna
1954–63	Work as art therapist in a home for emotionally disturbed children
1960	First solo exhibition at the Junge Generation gallery, Vienna
1962	Working retreat *Die Blutorgel*, (The Blood Organ) Vienna (together with Adolf Frohner and Hermann Nitsch)
1963	*Fest des Psychphysischen* Naturalismus (Festival of Psychophysical Naturalism), Vienna (together with Hermann Nitsch)
1963	*1. Materialaktion Versumpfung eines weiblichen Körpers* - Versumpfung einer Venus (Material Action No. 1, Bogging Down a Female Body – Bogging Down a Venus)
1966	Participation in the *Destruction in Art Symposium* in London
1967	Participation in the *Zock-Fest* (Zock-Festival) in Vienna
1967	*Direct Art* Festival, Vienna (together with Günter Brus)
1968	Participation in the event *Kunst und Revolution* (Art and Revolution) in Lecture Hall 1 at the Vienna University, resulting in a two-month prison sentence
Around 1970	Founding of the Muehl commune in Vienna
1975	Relocation of the commune to Friedrichshof, Burgenland
1990	Dissolution of the commune at Friedrichshof
1991	Sentenced to seven years imprisonment for "having sexual intercourse with a minor, fornication with a minor, rape (in one case), abuse of authority, moral endangerment of persons under 16 years of age, giving false evidence in court and suppressing evidence"
1997	Released from prison, move to Moncarapacho, Portugal, where former communards had founded the Art-Life-Algarve commune
2013	Dies in Moncarapacho, Portugal

Hermann Nitsch

1938	Born in Vienna
1953 – 58	Studies at the Graphische Lehr- und Versuchsanstalt in Vienna
1957	First idea for the concept of his *Gesamtkunstwerk, the Orgien Mysterien Theater* (Theatre of Orgies and Mysteries)
1960	First Painting Actions at the Technische Museum in Vienna
1962	Working retreat *Die Blutorgel* (The Blood Organ), Vienna (together with Adolf Frohner and Otto Muehl)
1962	*1st Action* in Otto Muehls Wohnung, Wien
1963	*Fest des Psychphysischen Naturalismus* (Festival ofPsychophysical Naturalism), Vienna (together with Otto Muehl)
1966	Participation in the *Destruction in Art Symposium* in London
1967	Participation in the *Zock-Fest* (Zock-Festival) in Vienna
1968	First actions in New York
1971	Acquisition of Prinzendorf Castle, which became the centre of his Orgien Mysterien Theater
1972	Participation in documenta 5
1975	*24-Stunden Spiel* (24-Hour-Play) in Prinzendorf
1982	Participation in documenta 7
1984	*Drei-Tage-Spiel* (Three-Day-Play) in Prinzendorf
1988 – 01	Professorship at the Städelschule in Frankfurt
1998	*Sechs-Tage-Spiel* (Six-Day-Play) in Prinzendorf
2005	Grand Austrian State Prize for Fine Arts
2007	Opening of the nitsch museum, Mistelbach
2008	Opening of the museo nitsch, Naples
2022	Dies in Mistelbach

Rudolf Schwarzkogler

1940	Born in Vienna
1957 – 61	Studies at the Graphische Lehr- und Versuchsanstalt in Vienna
1963	Military service
1964	Participation as an actor in Otto Muehl's *Materialaktion Nr. 13, Luftballonkonzert* (Material Action No. 13, Balloon Concert)
1965	Actor in Hermann Nitsch's *7th* and *8th Actions*
1965	*1. Aktion, Hochzeit* (1st Action, Wedding), Vienna
1966	*6th* and last *Action*, Vienna
1966 – 69	Conceptual drawings and texts for the registration of selected sensory experiences
1969	Dies as a result of a fall from the window of his apartment in Vienna
1970	Exhibition of action photographs and concepts at the Galerie nächst St. Stephan, Vienna
1972	Participation in documenta 5

COLOPHON

Edited by
WAM Wiener Aktionismus Museum
Eva Badura-Triska
Julia Moebus-Puck

WAM Wiener Aktionismus Museum
Weihburggasse 26
A-1010 Vienna

T: +43 (0)1 35 35 07 0
www.wieneraktionismus.at

Translation and Copy-editing
Lisa Moravec, Judith Köhler

Art Direction
Jan Puck and Michael Menge

Graphic Design
Studio FRANZ

Typeface
Söhne Buch, Halbfett, Schmal Extrafett & NOE Display

Paper
Salzer ice white 130g/m²

Printing and Binding
Gerin Druck GmbH, Wolkersdorf

BUCH SYNERGIE .AT

ISBN: 978-3-96912-157-3
This publication is listed in both the Austrian and German National Bibliographies; detailed bibliographic information is available online at www.onb.ac.at and www.dnb.de.

Printed in Austria

WIENER AKTIONISMUS MUSEUM WAM

Image Rights
For the reproduced works by :
Otto Muehl, Hermann Nitsch and Alfons Schilling © Bildrecht, Vienna, 2025
Günter Brus © Estate of Günter Brus
Adolf Frohner © Frohner Stiftung Krems
Rudolf Schwarzkogler © Österreichische Ludwig-Stiftung

Photo Credits
© BRUSEUM (Estate of Günter Brus): Fig. 41, 42, 44, 48, 58–70, 74, 82, 83, 85–90, 112–119
© Glenstone Collection, Potomac, Maryland, Stefan Altenburger: Fig. 49
© Henning Wolters: Fig. 92–96
© Leopold Museum, Vienna: Fig. 133
© mumok – Museum moderner Kunst Stiftung Ludwig Wien: Fig. 1, 8, 9, 46, 126–129, 135, 142, 155, 159,160,174–178, 225, 226, 231, 233–260, 262
© mumok – Museum moderner Kunst Stiftung Ludwig Wien, loan from the Österreichische Ludwig-Stiftung: Fig. 187, 190–193, 199–220, 228
© Nitsch Foundation: Fig. 5, 12, 13, 19, 20, 35, 37–40, 60–68
© Staatsgalerie Stuttgart, Archive Sohm: Fig. 33, 34, 161–164, 232
© UMJ/N. Lackner: Fig. 100, 101
© WAM (kunst-dokumentation.com/Manuel Carreon Lopez): Fig. 2, 4, 10, 11, 14–18, 21–32, 36, 43, 45, 47, 50–57, 71, 75–81, 84, 91, 97–111, 120, 122–125, 130, 131, 136–141, 143–154, 156–158, 165–173, 179–182, 184, 185, 188, 189, 194–198, 221–224, 227, 261

Cover
Rudolf Schwarzkogler
4th Action, 1965
Photo: Franziska Cibulka

Sales and Marketing
DCV
sales@dcv-books.com
Published by DCV
www.dcv-books.com

DCV